Bar Kokhba

Bar Kokhba

The Jew Who Defied Hadrian and Challenged the Might of Rome

Lindsay Powell

Foreword by Dr Eric H. Cline

Pen & Sword
MILITARY

First published in Great Britain in 2021 by
Pen & Sword Military
An imprint of
Pen & Sword Books Ltd
Yorkshire – Philadelphia

ISBN 978 1 78383 185 2

Printed and bound in the UK by CPI Group (UK) Ltd,
Croydon, CR0 4YY.

Pen & Sword Books Limited incorporates the imprints of Atlas,
Archaeology, Aviation, Discovery, Family History, Fiction, History,
Maritime, Military, Military Classics, Politics, Select, Transport,
True Crime, Air World, Frontline Publishing, Leo Cooper, Remember
When, Seaforth Publishing, The Praetorian Press, Wharncliffe
Local History, Wharncliffe Transport, Wharncliffe True Crime
and White Owl.

For a complete list of Pen & Sword titles please contact

PEN & SWORD BOOKS LIMITED
47 Church Street, Barnsley, South Yorkshire, S70 2AS, England
E-mail: enquiries@pen-and-sword.co.uk
Website: www.pen-and-sword.co.uk

Or

PEN AND SWORD BOOKS
1950 Lawrence Rd, Havertown, PA 19083, USA
E-mail: Uspen-and-sword@casematepublishers.com
Website: www.penandswordbooks.com

For Mark

Partner and best friend, who has patiently accompanied me to more archaeological sites and museums than is reasonable to expect a non-historian to see in a lifetime.

תודה רבה

Contents

Foreword

In 1960, within the Cave of Letters located in the wadi known as Nahal Hever by the Dead Sea, the famous Israeli archaeologist Yigael Yadin found a dispatch written on wooden slates signed by 'Shim'on Ben Kosiba, President (or prince) over Israel.' There is an unconfirmed story that he subsequently took it to Yitzhak Ben-Zvi, who was president of Israel at the time, saluted, and said: 'Message from your predecessor, sir!'

Shim'on Ben Kosiba, better known by his nom de guerre 'Bar Kokhba' ('Son of the Star'), was the leader of the Second Jewish Revolt against Rome from 132–135 CE. Begun after the Roman emperor Hadrian visited the region in 129/130 CE and renamed Jerusalem as 'Aelia Capitolina', the revolt is most often referred to simply as the Bar Kokhba Rebellion. After initial success, and a period of several years, it failed in the end, utterly and totally. Bar Kokhba was killed at his stronghold of Betar (probably modern Battir, which has been excavated by archaeologists). The Jews were unable to throw the Romans out of Judaea and were themselves prohibited from visiting Jerusalem apart from one day each year. The Jewish diaspora subsequently began in earnest, destined to last nearly two thousand years, until 1948.

Bar Kokhba has been condemned by some academics as an irresponsible zealot who contributed to one of the three greatest defeats in Jewish history – the other two being the destruction of Jerusalem and the Temple by the Neo-Babylonians in 586 BCE and the Romans in 70 CE. And yet, in the 19th century, the fledgling Zionists, especially Max Nordau, Ze'ev Jabotinsky, and Theodor Herzl, all hailed and revered Bar Kokhba for his efforts, acclaiming him as "the last embodiment in world history of a battle-hardened and bellicose Jewry." And, in 1948, the newly minted Prime Minister of Israel, David Ben-Gurion, declared: 'The chain that was broken in the days of Shimon Bar Kokhba and Akiba ben Yosef was reinforced in our days, and the Israeli army is again ready for the battle in its own land.' Still today, Bar Kokhba is celebrated in song, known to most

Israeli schoolchildren as a national hero and warrior, despite the academic debates (see Cline (2004): 98, 134–35, with references).

There are a very limited number of people whose life, and death, still impact other centuries after they have shuffled off this mortal coil. There are fewer still who inspire entire movements, and migrations, such as the return to what is now modern Israel by the Zionists, after that same length of time. Are we to include Bar Kokhba in that short list as well? Most would argue yes; others would say no. But, even if yes, is it the man or is it the myth that inspires?

On the surface, Bar Kokhba would seem an unlikely member of such a group, but had his rebellion succeeded, things might have been different, especially since he was hailed as the messiah by his followers, most notably Rabbi Akiba. And, even though the revolution failed, memories of it have reverberated down through the years, especially of Rabbi Akiba being flayed alive by the Romans and uttering the last line of the Shema ('Hear, O Israel') with his final breath, eventually reaching the 19th century Zionists who remembered Bar Kokhba as the last Jewish hero who dared to fight against an oppressive enemy.

However, the real Bar Kokhba has remained an elusive figure, with little actually known about him or his life. Where did he come from and what was his background? Why was he the one who came to lead the uprising? Did he and his followers capture Jerusalem during their rebellion or was that simply a later story? Was he killed during the fighting in the last stand at Betar or was he captured and put to death by the Romans afterward?

In the well-written and accessible story told in the pages that follow, the inimitable Lindsay Powell follows this historical figure like a dogged detective on the trail of a fugitive, inviting us to accompany him through the twists and turns of a journey stretching from Hollywood and London to Jerusalem, Tel Aviv, En Gedi, Caesarea, and Herodium. We join him in exploring ancient sites and visiting knowledgeable museum curators. We read with him long lost letters discovered in dusty caves by archaeologists – missives sent and received by Bar Kokhba himself as well as more mundane records that make up a hidden archive once belonging to a woman named Babatha. And together we revisit the horrors of those who died in these caves during or after the revolt, unable to escape because the Roman soldiers had set up camps on the cliff tops directly above them, patiently waiting until those below died of starvation.

The contrast with the Roman emperor Hadrian, against whom Bar Kokhba was rebelling, and whom Powell explores in equally exquisite detail, is particularly striking. We learn of his passions and his foibles; his proclivity for travel and for construction throughout the empire; his love for a young man named Antinous; and both of their deaths, on either side of Bar Kokhba's own demise.

Let it be said that Powell's researches have resulted in an enthralling journey through history. It is a marvelous search for the man behind the myth, which is well worth reading. I hope that you enjoy it as much as I did.

Eric H. Cline
Washington DC
15 November 2020

Preface

Bar Kokhba is the search for the true story of the epic struggle between two strong-willed leaders over who would rule a piece of land. One was the cosmopolitan ruler of the vast Roman Empire, then at its zenith, who some regarded as semi-divine; the other was a military Jewish ruler in a district of a minor province who some believed to be the messiah. It is also the tale of the clash of two ancient cultures. One was the conqueror, seeking to maintain control of its hard-won dominion; the other was the conquered, seeking to break free and establish its independence. The ensuing war – fought between a highly-trained professional army on the one side and a highly-motivated citizen militia on the other – lasted a remarkable three and a half years, but there could only ever be one victor. The outcome of that David and Goliath conflict still reverberates down to our own time, even 1,900 years later.

The Roman called it Iudaea. The Jew called it Israel. The 'land flowing with milk and honey' (Deuteronomy 31:20), which some today call the 'Holy Land', has been a battleground for three millennia. Even when subjugated, the people of what was then known as Judea, now split between the State of Israel and Palestine (specifically The West Bank), have risen up time and time again to try to oust the occupying power. Among the many insurrections recorded during the Roman occupation was the 'First Jewish War' as it has come to be known. During this bloody rebellion, in 70 CE commander Titus Flavius and his legions destroyed the Second Temple in Jerusalem. They concluded their campaign three – or four – years later after successfully besieging the remaining rebels at Masada, but it was not the last time that the Jews attempted to oust the Romans from their holy land.

There was a '*Second* Jewish War'. Waged between 132 and 136 CE, it is less well-known than the first but, in the opinion of many – myself included – it was actually of greater consequence, both for the people of the heartland of Judea and for Judaism itself. Confusingly, the conflict is also called the 'Bar Kokhba War'. It is named after the man who roused his people to rebellion against the Romans, then led by Emperor Hadrian. So, who was this Bar Kokhba? How did the man who built the famous Wall in northern Britain respond to the challenger? Also how, in later ages, did this rebel with a cause become a hero for the Jews in the diaspora – indeed, a figure of hope for the foundation of a new Jewish homeland in modern times? As a historian and writer, these and more questions compelled me to follow the trail of evidence in search of the truth, and a good story. In the way Michael Wood went in search of King Arthur, this book describes my journey of discovery looking for Bar Kokhba.

I have been fascinated by the Bar Kokhba War for years. My interest in the subject was initially sparked when I read Yigael Yadin's book *Bar-Kokhba: The rediscovery of the legendary hero of the second Jewish Revolt against Rome* (1971). Then a member of the Ermine Street Guard, a registered charity, I wrote an article based on it for the Roman-period military re-enactment group's *Exercitus* magazine in 1987. My curiosity about that distant war and the people who fought it remained with me. When the British Museum held its spectacular *'Hadrian: Empire and Conflict'* exhibition in London in 2008, I was thrilled to see artefacts on display that I immediately recognized from Yadin's book.

I was exceptionally lucky that, as I embarked on this project in 2016, I learned that there were two temporary exhibitions going on in Israel. In Tel Aviv the Eretz Israel Museum was hosting 'Bar Kokhba: Historical Memory and the Myth of Heroism'. It covered the issues of the 'historical archaeological view' of the man, and 'the revival of Bar Kokhba as the archetype of Jewish heroism' in later times. In Jerusalem the Israel Museum was hosting 'Hadrian: An Emperor Cast in Bronze', which brought 'together, for the first time, the only three bronze portraits of the Roman emperor Hadrian to have survived from antiquity'. These two special events, together with visits to ancient sites in Israel and several newly-published academic books and papers that became available even as I was pursuing my enquiries, provided me with an unexpectedly rich vein of material.

Unlike the First Jewish War, which was described in great detail by Flavius Josephus, there was no equivalent historian who recorded the events of the Second Jewish War in a single continuous narrative. There *are* Roman sources to be sure. There is a passing remark by contemporary

Appian (in his *Syrian Wars*) and Pausanias (in his *Description of Greece*). There is a comment about it in a letter of Cornelius Fronto to the then Emperor Marcus Aurelius (*Letters, On the Parthian War*). Writing several decades after the war, Cassius Dio describes the uprising in his *Roman History*; it is preserved as an epitome – or a summarized form – by John Xiphilinus (Ioannis Xiphilinos), writing in the 1060s CE. There is a mention of it in the 'Life of Hadrian' by Aelius Spartianus – which may be a pen-name – in the so-called *Historia Augusta* (*HA* for short), believed to have been written in the fourth century.

To these 'pagan' sources can be added the early Christian writer Eusebius of Caesarea, who quotes Justin Martyr (Justinus Martyr) – a direct contemporary of Bar Kokhba – in his *Church History;* helpfully, he also gives us brief accounts of events for each year of the conflict in his *Chronicle*. There are also the writings of Paulus Orosius, Jerome (Eusebius Sophronius Hieronymus), Epiphanius of Salamis and John Malalas (Ioannis Malalas), who each add details to the story.

Unfamiliar to me were the Jewish sources of the 'Mishnah and Talmud Period', covering the years 70–640 CE, the time that elapsed between the independence of the Jewish People and their exile when Judaea was part of the Roman and Byzantine (Eastern Roman) Empires. In the canon of rabbinic literature, which interpret the *Torah* (the Hebrew Bible, being the first five books of the Old Testament), these are the *Midrash* ('interpretation'), *Talmud* ('teaching') and *Mishnah* ('repetition'). The *Midrash Halakha* deals with law and religious practice (Hebrew: *halakha*, literally 'the way to walk'), while the *Midrash Aggadah* interprets biblical narrative and explores tales and lore (*aggadah*) for its moral principles, the non-legalistic questions of ethics or theology, or creates homilies and parables based on the text. There are also two versions of the *Talmud*: one from Babylonia (*Talmud Bavli*); and another composed in Judea, from Jerusalem or Palestine (*Talmud Yerushalmi*). The Jerusalem version is shorter in length than the Babylonian and traditionally considered the less authoritative of the two *Talmudim*; however, dating to c. 400 CE it is closer to the events of the Bar Kokhba War and its actors. *Mishnah* is the first written collection of the Jewish oral traditions known as the 'Oral *Torah*'.

Neither the *Midrashim* nor *Talmudim* nor *Mishnah* are factual histories; they are primarily religious texts. As interpretations by rabbis and sages about how *Torah* can be applied to life, they reveal not only details of the conditions of daily life in cities, towns and villages, but also the range of political thought and messianic hope circulating at the time of the ancient war and in its aftermath. They may begin with a kernel of truth about a real event to explain a passage in the Hebrew Bible. Through them we learn something about the Jewish people's expectations and experiences of the *Melekh Moshiakh*, 'the King-Messiah', as one rabbi allegedly declared the protagonist. (Indeed, the working title for this book was *King Messiah's War: Hadrian, Bar Kokhba, and the Battle for Israel.*)

Archaeology has uncovered contemporary coins, even arms and armour – some of it Roman and repurposed by the Jewish rebels for their own use. In the 1950s and 1960s Yigael Yadin and his team found fragments of letters in caves in the valleys close by the Dead Sea. Amazingly, some were written – or at least dictated to a scribe – by the Jewish warlord himself! These important documents found in caves at Wadi Murabba'at are identified by the prefix *Mur*, and those in the so-called 'Cave of Letters' (properly 'Cave 5/6') in the Nahal Hever Valley with the prefix *P.Yadin*. As finds go these truly are 'sensational' and, compared to the over-use of the claim in virtually all press releases routinely issued today about archaeological discoveries, they *really did* 'rewrite the history books'. New translations of this correspondence between the rebel commander-in-chief and his deputies reveal how he conducted his war. Such details are normally denied to historians of other ancient world campaigns. The letters also reveal the *real name* of the Jewish warlord. How and why he received his *nom de guerre* Bar Kokhba, with its messianic connotations, is an important theme explored in my book.

The original written sources from antiquity, referenced in this book, are variously written in Aramaic, Greek, Hebrew, Latin and Syriac. Sometimes the meaning is obscure and one modern scholar's translation can be challenged by another. Often the texts are badly damaged or are no more than fragments where whole words are missing, in which case experts try their best to fill in these *lacunae* using their skill and judgement. To this material, archaeology, epigraphy, numismatics, papyrology, philology, military and religious studies can provide valuable insights, but these are also subject to interpretation and reinterpretation. New discoveries and theories can – and often do – overturn accepted ideas. Fully recognizing the challenges posed by the research material, this book represents my best attempt to build a coherent narrative of the events of 132–136 CE and

I readily accept that it cannot be the last word on the Bar Kokhba War and the man responsible.

Several different spellings of Hebrew names and places are possible in English. In translation the letters 'e' and 'i', 'k' and 'q', 'b' and 'f' or 'v', 's' and 'z' are interchangeable; for example, *shekel* and *sheqel*. For consistency, I have opted to spell the Jewish leader's moniker as Bar Kokhba (rather than Bar-Cochba, Bar Kochba or Bar Kokhva or Bar-Kosibah) where the 'kh' is pronounced 'ch' (as in the Scottish 'loch') and the 'ba' as in the French 'va'. I use Akiba in place of Akiva, Aquiba or Aquiva for the famous rabbi.

Where a city has a known, ancient name I prefer to use it since the modern name creates a false impression of the scale and feel of the place in antiquity. However, I use modern anglicized names for Athens (rather than Latin: Athenae; Greek: Athenai) and Rome (Roma). Recognizing that they were each very different places, where I use Jerusalem (rather than the Hebrew form Yerushalayim or Greek Hierosolyma) I refer to the Jewish city; for the imperial Roman city founded after 130 CE, however, I use the Latin name Aelia Capitolina (rather than Aelia Kapitolina as it appears on some coins). In respect of Judean places, for consistency I use Betar throughout (rather than Bettir, Beitar, Bethar, Betther, Bethther, Beththera, Biththira, Bithara or Bittîr) and Ein Gedi (rather than En-gedi or En Gedi). Where I refer to the Roman province, I use the form Province Iudaea or just Iudaea to distinguish it from the administrative district of Judea within it where the Bar Kokhba War was fought.

The Latin version is also used for Roman military officer ranks, arms, equipment and battle formations throughout since there is often no modern equivalent. For accuracy, I use the Latin spelling for the name Iulius rather than the anglicized Julius respectively.

Definitions of unfamiliar Jewish (Aramaic, Hebrew) and Roman (Latin, Greek) technical terms that I have used in the text are listed in the single Glossary at the end of the book.

The dating convention I use throughout is the 'Common (or Current) Era'. BCE – Before the Common Era – equates to BC ('Before Christ') and ends with 1 BCE. CE – Common Era – equates to AD ('Anno Domini') and begins with 1 CE (AD 1). No political correctness is intended; it is simply my choice as the author. There is, of course, no Year 0.

I began writing this book soon after my field research trip to England and Israel in June 2016. A number of work and life events interrupted my progress. Living at the time of the SARS-CoV-2 (aka COVID-19) pandemic in 2020 and having to comply with the executive order issued by the governor of the state of Texas to remain at home ('except to provide essential services or do essential things') presented me with the time and space to complete the book. The moment did something else I had not expected. Self-imposed isolation for days on end gave me an insight into how life may have been for people hiding in the caves across Judaea, staying out of sight from an ever-present enemy lurking outside; my survival, like theirs, depended on it. Writing about people of those days gave me a particular purpose in my own extraordinary times.

Adding to the upheaval, in the midst of the pandemic, there were the demonstrations against abuse of authority and systemic prejudice. From Minneapolis to Beirut, from Minsk to Hong Kong, people took to the streets to protest on behalf of those suffering injustices. In recent years there has also been a surge in anti-Semitism or anti-Judaism incidents in Europe, the Middle East and the USA, including horrible violent crimes with shootings at supermarkets and synagogues and stabbings at a *Hanukkah* party even while I wrote this book. Jews continue to be criticized and attacked just for wishing to remain a distinct social, cultural and religious group. The origin of anti-Semitism – the world's oldest conspiracy theory – is a theme indirectly addressed in this book.

The root of the word 'history' is the Greek *istoria* meaning 'inquiry' or 'learning through research'. Historian Dr Anita Shapira made this observation about Israel's first prime minister:

> Ben-Gurion believed the true historian was someone who 'investigates historical truth'. Yet he was quick to qualify that: 'I specifically say somebody who "investigates historical truth", not "knows historical truth". Because the true historian must have doubts about whether everything is known to him, yet he goes on investigating, wishing to establish what is true.'
>
> 'Ben-Gurion and the Bible: The Forging of an
> Historical Narrative?', *Middle Eastern Studies*,
> Vol. 33, No. 4, October 1997, 645–674.

'Investigating the historical truth' has been my 'North Star' in writing this book. To me, the job of a historian is to research, analyze and interpret events and the people who took part in them and to find the essential truth. I do so by critically studying a variety of evidence, historical documents and source materials; in this case there are no living survivors or witnesses to relate to me what they saw. I also interview subject matter experts and record their insights. Taking it all together, I then present as accurate and unbiased an account of my findings to the reader *sine ira et studio* (Tac., *Ann.* 1.1), and to point out where any ambiguity or doubt lies. My task as a writer, however, is to make the story compelling reading. In my telling no names have been changed. Out of respect for the dead I have told the story exactly as it occurred, or as far as it was possible for me to ascertain.

Si tibi terra levis. ת.נ.צ.ב.ה.

Lindsay Powell
Tisha B'Ab 2020
Austin, Texas

Acknowledgements

There are several people who deserve my thanks for helping me with this special project.

To my commissioning editor, Philip Sidnell at Pen and Sword Books, who responded enthusiastically to my proposal for this book and then showed great patience while waiting for the manuscript, I shall always be grateful. To the other hard-working members of the production team, Matt Jones and Paul Wilkinson at Pen and Sword and Mat Blurton of Mac Style, I offer my sincere thanks for turning my virtual files into lovely printed pages.

I feel deeply honoured that Dr Eric H. Cline agreed to write the foreword to *Bar Kokhba*. Eric is Professor of Classics and Anthropology in the Department of Classical and Near Eastern Languages and Civilizations at the George Washington University in the USA. He defines what it means to be a best-in-class expert in the archaeology and history of the ancient Near East. Eric has conducted dozens of field excavations in Israel and written numerous articles and several books, my personal favourite being *Jerusalem Besieged: From Ancient Canaan to Modern Israel* (2004). For his kindness, I offer my sincerest thanks.

One of the great joys of this project was conducting the field research, especially when it involved international travel. I am grateful to the many experts who kindly gave me their time. In London, Dr Thorsten Opper, Senior Curator of Greek and Roman Sculpture at the British Museum answered my questions about Hadrian, his life and times. In Jerusalem, Dr David (Dudi) Mevorah, Senior Curator of Hellenistic, Roman and Byzantine Archaeology, Israel Museum shared his insights about the war and its protagonists. In Tel Aviv, Sara Turel, Curator at Eretz Israel Museum, and Michal Bentovim, my informative guide, explained the influence of the Bar Kokhba story in the Jewish diaspora and in the state of Israel. Additionally, I would like to thank Milena Melfi, Assistant Curator of the Cast Gallery at the Ashmolean Museum, Oxford and Antonivs

Svbia, Priest of Antinous, in Hollywood, California, for sharing their insights on the relationship of Hadrian and Antinous. I would also like to acknowledge here the friendship and encouragement of my dear friends David and Roslyn Gutman in Atlanta, Georgia and Ovadia (Oved) Abed in Austin, Texas. Lastly, I record a special note of recognition to Asia Arutyunov in Petah Tikva, Israel who, during conversations on Facebook, alerted me to the Bar Kokhba exhibition in Tel Aviv, about which I would not otherwise have known: *Toda raba*!

This book tells the story of the conflict in both words and pictures. For helping me to illustrate this volume, I offer my thanks to the following: Dale Tatro of Classical Numismatics Group, Lancaster, Pennsylvania; Ira and Larry Goldberg of Ira & Larry Goldberg Coins & Collectibles, Los Angeles, California; Arturo Russo of Numismatica Ars Classica, London, UK and Zürich, Switzerland; Richard Beale of Roma Numismatics Limited, London, UK; Maxim Shick of Shick Coins, Askelon, Israel; and Carole Raddato of the *Following Hadrian* blog in Frankfurt am Main, Germany. I also thank the many photographers who have made their images available in the public domain or on Wikimedia Commons, whose work I acknowledge under the terms of the respective Creative Commons licences.

War stories cannot be told without the aid of maps. I offer my sincere thanks to Erin Greb who did a marvellous job of producing the specially-commissioned maps for me.

I have quoted extracts from several ancient authors' works whose voices lend authenticity to the narrative. For the translations of classical texts I used Aelius Spartianus' *Life of Hadrian* in the *Historia Augusta* translated by David Magie in the Loeb Classical Library, Harvard University Press (1921); Cassius Dio's *Roman History* translated by E. Carey in the Loeb Classical Library, Harvard University Press (1925); and Eusebius's *Ecclesiatical History* translated by Kirsopp Lake in the Loeb Classical Library, Harvard University Press (1926). The quotations from the *Torah* and other Old and New Testament books are taken from the Revised Standard Version unless otherwise stated in the endnotes; the *Midrash* by Reverend Samuel Rapaport, published by Routledge, London (1907); the *Babylonian Talmud* by Michael L. Rodkinson, published by New Talmud Publishing Company, Boston (1903–18); and the *Jerusalem Talmud* translated by Dr Moïse Schwab, published by Williams and Norgate, London (1886). The translations of the Ben Kosiba letters were taken from P. Benoit et al, *Discoveries in the Judaean Desert II: Les Grottes de Murrabba'at* (Oxford University Press, 1961); and Yigael Yadin et al, *The Documents from the Bar-Kokhba Period in the Cave of Letters: Hebrew, Aramaic and Nabatean-Aramaic Papyri* (Israel Exploration Society, 1989–2002).

Finally, I thank the many scholars who made their research available on Academia.edu, and Austin Public Library service in Austin, Texas for providing access to the phenomenal JSTOR.org ('journal storage') website, which greatly facilitated my desk research for this book.

List of Illustrations

List of Plates

List of Maps

Chronology

CE	Event
44	Death of Herodes Agrippa I, king of Iudaea; Romans impose control of Iudaea; riots in major cities.
66–73/74	First Jewish War.
66	Jewish rebels seize control of Jerusalem.
70	Siege of Jerusalem by T. Flavius (son of T. Flavius Vespasianus).
10 August	Destruction of the Second Temple, Jerusalem.
71	Triumph in Rome of T. Caesar Vespasianus for victory in the Jewish War.
72–73	Possible siege and capture of Masada by L. Flavius Silva.
73–74	Alternative possible siege and capture of Masada by L. Flavius Silva.
80	Opening of the *Amphitheatrum Flavium* (Colosseum) paid for from proceeds of sales of spoils of the First Jewish War.
98	
27 January	Death of Emperor Nerva; accession of M. Ulpius Traianus (Trajan) as emperor.
101–102	First Dacian War.
105–106	Second Dacian War.
110	Fire damages Pantheon, Rome.
115–117	Parthian War.
	Revolt of the Jewish diaspora (Cyprus, Egypt, Libya, Mesopotamia), aka Kitos War or War of Quietus.
116	Rutilius Rufus leads counterinsurgency against Jewish populations of Egypt.
	To quell Jewish insurrections, Trajan sends Q. Marcius Turbo to Egypt, C. Valerius Rufus to Cyprus and Lusius Quietus to Mesopotamia.

117–138	Reign of Imp. Caesar Traianus Hadrianus Augustus.
117	Hadrian serves as consul for the first time.
	Hadrian in Antiocheia, Syria as *legatus Augusti pro praetore*.
7 or 8 August	Trajan adopts Hadrian. Death of Trajan at Selinus, Cilicia.
9 August	News of Trajan's death reaches Hadrian at Antiocheia.
12 August	Hadrian acclaimed as *imperator* for the first time at Antiocheia.
	Q. Marcius Turbo sent by Hadrian to Mauretania to quell local rebellion.
	Lusius Quietus in Iudaea as *legatus Augusti pro praetore*. Second legion (VI *Ferrata*) transferred to garrison Iudaea.
	Hadrian given tribunician power for the first time.
118	
	Hadrian consul for second time.
9 July	Hadrian arrives in Rome.
	Trajan's conquests in Assyria, Mesopotamia and Parthia abandoned, except Armenia.
	Death of Lusius Quietus?
119	Hadrian serves as consul for third time.
	Hadrian tours Campania.
August –October	M. Paccius Gargilius Antiquus as suffect consul.
120	L. Cossonius Gallus in Iudaea as *legatus Augusti pro praetore*.
	Hadrian in Rome.
May-June	C. Publicius Marcellus as suffect consul in Rome. Legionary vexillations begin improving the road network of Iudaea; establishment of base at Legio/ Caparcotna in Iudaea for *Legio* VI *Ferrata*.
121–125	Hadrian's first tour of the Roman provinces.
121	Hadrian visits Tres Galliae, Germania Superior, Raetia, Noricum, Germania Superior.
122	Hadrian visits Germania Inferior, Britannia (Londinium, Vindolanda, commissions the Wall), Tres Galliae, Hispania Tarraconensis (Tarraco).

	Second Moorish revolt.
	M. Paccius Gargilius Antiquus in Syria as *legatus Augusti pro praetore*.
123	Hadrian visits Mauretania(?), Africa(?), Libya, Cyrene, Crete, Syria, the Euphrates frontier (Melitene), Pontus, Bithynia (meets Antinous for the first time), Asia.
124	Hadrian visits Thracia, Asia, Athens, Eleusis, Achaea.
	Q. Tineius Rufus in Thracia as *legatus Augusti pro praetore*.
125	Hadrian visits Achaea, Sicily; returns to Rome.
	Possible uprising in Britannia; Londinium destroyed.
126	Hadrian in Rome.
	Alternative possible uprising in Britannia; Londinium destroyed.
127	Hadrian in Rome.
May –September	Q. Tineius Rufus as suffect consul in Rome.
October –December	Sex. Iulius Severus as suffect consul in Rome.
128–132	Hadrian's second tour of the Roman provinces.
128	Hadrian visits Africa, Rome, Athens, Eleusis.
Winter	Hadrian in Athens.
129	Hadrian visits Asia, Pamphylia, Phrygia (23 July), Pisidia, Cilicia, Syria, Commagene (Samosata), Cappadocia, Pontus, Palmyra, Syria (Antiocheia, Bostra(?), Gerasa).
	C. Publicius Marcellus in Syria as *legatus Augusti pro praetore*.
130	Q. Tineius Rufus in Iudaea as *legatus Augusti pro praetore*.
	T. Haterius Nepos in Arabia moves to Iudaea as *legatus Augusti pro praetore*.
	Possible erection of triumphal arch erected at Tel Shalem
	Hadrian visits Iudaea (Caesarea, inspects progress at *Colonia* Aelia Capitolina on site of former Jerusalem, (Gaza), Arabia, Egypt.

30 October	Hadrian's lover Antinous drowns in the Nile River; city of Antinoopolis founded.
131	Hadrian holds tribunician power for fourteenth time. Sex. Iulius Severus in Britannia as *legatus Augusti pro praetore*.
	Hadrian visits Syria, Asia(?).
Winter	Hadrian in Athens.
132–136	Bar Kokhba War aka Second Jewish War led by *Nasi* of Israel, Shim'on Ben Kosiba.
132	Hadrian in Rome.
Summer	Possible start of the Jewish uprising in Judea: Jewish partisans led by Shim'on Ben Kosiba (at Herodium) seize villages and towns throughout Judea (except Aelia Capitolina).
	Rabbi Akiba declares Shim'on Ben Kosiba to be 'Bar Kokhba' ('Son of a Star') (?).
19 August	Last dated letter of Babatha Bat Shim'on of Maoza (found in 'Cave of Letters', Nahal Hever).
Autumn	Possible start of 'Year One' of Israel.
133	Jews from the Roman province of Arabia, the Galilee and Transjordan find refuge in caves in the Judean Desert.
	C. Publicius Marcellus arrives in Iudaea with *vexillationes* from Syria.
	T. Haterius Nepos arrives in Iudaea with *vexillationes* from Arabia.
Summer	Possible start of 'Year Two' of Israel.
Tishri	Alternative possible start of 'Year Two' of Israel.
134	Q. Lollius Urbicus arrives in Iudaea as *legatus imperatoris Hadriani* in *expeditione Iudaica* with *vexillationes* from Pannonia Superior.
	Sex. Iulius Severus arrives in Iudaea with *vexillationes* from Britannia and Moesia Inferior.
May –September	T. Haterius Nepos as suffect consul in Rome.
Summer	Possible start of 'Year Three' of Israel.
Autumn	Alternative possible start of 'Year Three' of Israel.

Winter	Hadrian in Rome.
135	Hadrian in Rome.
	Possible fall of Herodium.
	Shim'on Ben Kosiba moves field headquarters to Betar.
May	
–September	Q. Lollius Urbicus serves as suffect consul in Rome.
Spring	Siege of Betar; death of Eleazar of Modi'in.
Summer	Three years of Israel have passed.
9 *Ab*	Fall of Betar to the Romans; death of Shim'on Ben Kosiba; capture and slaughter of all inhabitants.
Autumn	Jewish insurrectionists flee to caves in the Judean Desert.
	Romans blockade refuge caves in Nahal Hever Canyon.
	Iudaea incorporated into Syria as Syria Palaestina.
	Dedication of Temple of *Venus et Roma* in Rome.
136	Hadrian in Rome.
	Hadrian granted tribunician powers for fourteenth time.
	Hadrian acclaimed *imperator* for second time.
	Triumphalia ornamenta awarded to Sex. Iulius Severus, C. Publicius Marcellus, T. Haterius Nepos and Q. Lollius Urbicus.
	Alternative possible erection of triumphal arch erected at Tel Shalem.
	Hadrian adopts L. Ceionius Commodus (L. Aelius Caesar).
	Mopping-up operations continue across the Judea; Ein Gedi destroyed; blockade of refuge caves in Nahal Hever Canyon.
	Sex. Iulius Severus appointed as *legatus Augusti pro praetore* of Syria Palaestina(?).
Autumn	End of blockade of refuge caves in Nahal Hever Canyon.
137	Hadrian in Rome.
	Trial and execution of Rabbi Akiba(?) in Caesaraea(?).
138	
1 January	Death of L. Aelius Caesar.

25 February	Hadrian adopts T. Aurelius Fulvus Antoninus (acting as joint emperor).
10 July	Death of Hadrian at Baiae; Hadrian's ashes kept at Puteoli.
11 July	Accession of T. Fulvus Aelius Hadrianus Antoninus Augustus Pius as emperor.
139	Completion of Hadrian's Mausoleum, Rome; Hadrian's ashes transferred to the Mausoleum.
145	Dedication of Temple of *Divus* Hadrianus in the *Campus Martius*, Rome by Antoninus Pius.
476	Fall of the Western Roman Empire.
1453	Fall of Constantinople was the capture of the Byzantine Empire's capital by the Ottoman Empire.
1840	Rabbi Dr Samuel Mayer's story 'Simon Barchocheba, Der Messiaskönig' published in *Israelitischer Musen-Almanach*.
1883	
5 May	First performance of Abraham Goldfadn's *Bar Kochba* in Odessa, Ukraine.
1887	Libretto and score of Abraham Goldfadn's *Bar Kochba* published in Warsaw, Poland.
1896	Theodor Herzel publishes *Der Judenstaat* making the case for the foundation of a Jewish state.
1897	Libretto and score of Abraham Goldfadn's *Bar Kochba* published in New York.
29–31 August	First Zionist Congress in Basel, Switzerland.
1898	
28 August	Max Nordau makes the case for the 'Muscular Jew' at the Second Zionist Congress in Basel, Switzerland.
22 October	*Jüdischer Turnverein Berlin 'Bar-Kochba'* founded.
1904	Libretto and score of Abraham Goldfadn's *Bar Kochba* published in London.
1905	Henryk Glitzenstein unveils his bronze statue *Bar Kokhba*.
1917	
2 November	British government issues the 'Balfour Declaration' announcing support for the establishment of a 'national home for the Jewish people' in Palestine.

1918–20	British Military Administration in Palestine.
1920–48	British Mandate for Palestine.
1937	
July	'Bar-Kochba International Sports Games' held in Berlin.
1945	
24 February	First performance of Abraham Levinson's adaptation of Jaroslav Vrchlický's play *Bar Kokhba* at the Ohel Theatre in Rehovot, Israel.
1946	
22 July	Militant Zionist paramilitary group *Irgun* blows up King David Hotel, Jerusalem.
1947–49	Palestine War (aka Israeli War of Independence).
1947	
11 July	4,500 Jewish refugees aboard the *Exodus 1947* depart Sète near Marseilles and sail to British Mandatory Palestine.
29 November	United Nations General Assembly votes for Resolution 181 partitioning Palestine.
1948	First Arab-Israeli War.
1948	
9 April	*Irgun* and *Lehi* attack Arab village of Deir Yassin.
14 May	Foundation of the State of Israel with its capital at Jerusalem.
1951	
Autumn	Discovery of correspondence from Shim'on Ben Kosiba and his subordinates in 'Caves at Wadi Murabba'at' in the Judaean Desert.
1956	
15 April	Benno Elkan's *Menorah* unveiled in a ceremony at the Knesset in Jerusalem.
1960	
15–28 March	'Expedition D', first archaeological explorations of caves in Nahal Hever Canyon in the Judaean Desert under Yigael Yadin, recovers correspondence between Shim'on Ben Kosiba and his subordinates from 'Caves of Letters'.

1961

12–31 March   Second archaeological explorations of caves in Nahal Hever Canyon in the Judaean Desert under Yigael Yadin, recovers of the 'Archive of Babatha'.

1967

5–10 June   Six-Day War.

1973

6–25 October   Yom Kippur War.

1982

11 May   *Lag B'Omer*: Burial of bones from the 'Cave of Horrors' and 'Cave of Letters' at Nahal Hever Canyon in a ceremony led by Israel's Prime Minister Menachem Begin; Yigael Yadin declines to attend.

2008

24 July
–26 October   *Hadrian – Empire and Conflict* exhibition at the British Museum, London.

2015

22 December   *Hadrian: An Emperor Cast in Bronze* exhibition opens at Israel Museum, Jerusalem.

2016

20 February
–18 June   *Bar Kokhba: Historical Memory and the Myth of Heroism* exhibition at Eretz Israel Museum, Tel Aviv.

27 June   *Hadrian: An Emperor Cast in Bronze* exhibition closes at Israel Museum, Jerusalem.

2017

11 August   The 1,900th anniversary of Hadrian's accession as Roman emperor.

2023

11 May   The 75th anniversary of the foundation of the State of Israel.

Roman and Jewish Names

Roman:

T. Haterius Nepos

This is the official name of the son of the military governor of the province Arabia Petraea from c.130 CE. It is preserved on an inscription (*CIL* XI, 5212 = *ILS* 1058) now in the Museo Archeologico (room 5) in Foligno, Umbria, Italy. His name embodies the key elements of Roman naming practice. Titus is his forename (*praenomen*) by which his family and close friends called him. In inscriptions, public records and narrative texts it was abbreviated. The standard abbreviations for common *praenomina* were as follows:

A.	Aulus	M'.	Manius
Ap.	Appius	P	Publius
C. or G.	Caius or Gaius	Q	Quintus
Cn. or Gn.	Cnaeus or Gnaeus	Ser	Servius
D.	Decimus	Sex	Sextus
L.	Lucius	Sp.	Spurius
M.	Marcus	T.	Titus
Mam.	Mamius	Ti.	Tiberius

Haterius is his clan or family name (*nomen gentilicium*) derived from *gens* Hateria. Many of these clans, such as the Claudii and Cornelii, were famous old families of Rome with proud traditions. The filiation or patrymonic of the father's *praenomen* is missing, but it might also have been Titus Haterius. To clearly tell men apart who had the same name, with their warped sense of humour, Romans often adopted a third name – a nickname – (*cognomen*), such as Rufus 'red-haired', Paulus 'shorty' or Brutus 'stupid'. Titus' *cognomen* is Nepos, a word which can mean 'grandson' but also 'spendthrift'.

Jewish:

Yeshua Ben Galgula

This is the official name of the camp commander at Herodium, the principal stronghold of the rebel Jewish state from 132 CE. It is preserved on papyrus letters (*Mur* 43–44) written in Hebrew from the president of Israel to his deputy, which were found in the refuge caves at Wadi Murabba'at near Ein Gedi. Yeshua is his first or given name (its modern equivalent is Jesus). Many traditional Jewish names are mentioned at the beginning of the *Book of Numbers*. Common in the second century CE were El'azar (Eleazar or Eliezer), Shim'on or Shimeon (Simon), Shmu'el or Shummai (Samuel), Yakof (Jacob), Yehonathan (John or Jonathan), Yehuda (Judah) and Yosef (Joseph). The Aramaic form 'ben' (alternatively the Hebrew 'bar') means 'son of'. The filiation or patrymonic is Galgula. This can also indicate the place from which the man came, such as Modi'in in the name of Rabbi Eleazar Ben Modi'in.

He [Hadrian] enjoyed peace, however, through the whole course of his reign; the only war that he had, he committed to the conduct of a governor of a province.

Eutropius, *Epitome of Roman History* 8.7

For The Redemption of Israel.

Inscription on a Jewish rebel *zuz* (silver coin)
issued in Year 1 of the Bar Kokhba War

Prologue

Stakes of glowing wood snapped in the heat of the raging bonfire. Shreds of flame from twisting plumes ripped into the dark sky. Curls of smoke vanished into the inky black of night, leaving just an acrid scent to betray their transient presence. A solitary voice began to sing. It was soon joined by others of people, young and old, seated around the festive fire and bathed in its flickering light. In Hebrew they cheerfully crooned to the song's catchy beat:

> There was a man in Israel.
> His name was Bar Kokhba,
> A tall, well-built, young and tall
> With glowing radiant eyes.

It was the eve of *Lag B'Omer*, the minor Jewish holiday between *Pesakh* (Passover) and the festival of *Shavuot* (Pentecost) in the month of May. The people gathered around the bonfire in northern Israel had learned the *Bar Kokhba Song* at school. Singing it was a tradition going back years, but it had not always been so. The original reason for the holy day was the death of a popular rabbi twenty centuries before. Yet somehow, to this memorialization of a respected sage, had been added the commemoration – even celebration – of the man who led a military campaign against the Romans at the time of the Emperor Hadrian.

The words of a verse left the lips of the happy singing throng:

> He was a hero.
> He yearned for freedom
> The whole nation loved him.
> He was a hero.

Yet *was* he? This is the quest for the truth of the man in the campfire song.

My investigation begins with the Roman whose name, to this day, many Jews still utter with the words 'may his bones be ground to dust'.

Chapter 1

'An Explorer of Everything Interesting'

'Click!'

A young couple stopped momentarily to take a selfie in front of the bust of a famous Roman emperor (fig. 1). It was a fine work of art indeed, and one certainly worth photographing. The greyish-white stone figure was bare-chested with his head turned slightly to the left. Large ringlets of hair formed a pronounced arc over the forehead, like a tiara.[1] With the pupils precisely drilled into the surface of the stone looking up and to the left, the eyes seemed almost to be squinting, as if focusing on an object far away in the distance. The nose was long and thick. The lips suggested a contemplative rather than a relaxed mood. The full moustache and neat beard, formed of distinct rows of thick, tight curls, hugged the cheeks and

Figure 1. The trademark beard and the curls of the hair on this portrait bust of Hadrian make him one of the most instantly recognizable of Roman emperors. The bust of his lover Antinous stands beside it at the British Museum.

jawline of the fleshy face. Out of the finest marble, the unknown ancient sculptor had carved the countenance of a strong but reassuringly sensible ruler. His subject was, of course, the very well-known Emperor Hadrian.[2] He was also the reason for my visit. I was on a quest to know more about him, his times and a war.

I was standing in the Wolfson Gallery – 'Room 70' on the plan – of the British Museum in the pulsating heart of London. Exquisite artefacts from the time of the Roman Empire surrounded me. Glancing at my wristwatch, I noticed that it was still on Texas time. I had flown to England two days before and forgotten to adjust it. Adding six hours to the time, I saw that it was a few minutes to 2.00 pm. I made my way to a discreet, almost hidden door at the end of the adjacent gallery. I pressed the button on the intercom and explained that I had an appointment with Dr Thorsten Opper, Senior Curator of Greek and Roman Sculpture. If anyone knew about Hadrian it was him. He had organized the *Hadrian: Empire and Conflict* exhibition in London in 2008.[3] Without doubt, it was one of the museum's best-ever special events and one that made a lasting impression on me. I had closely studied the book he had written for the exposition before our meeting.

A few minutes later I was greeted politely at the 'secret door'. I followed Thorsten Opper down the concrete steps of the fire-escape staircase. It felt as though I was walking behind the scenes of an epic film set, where usually hidden technicians worked to ensure the production on the other side of the wall went without a hitch. In the busy staff cafeteria, normally inaccessible to the public, we sat at a table. Over cups of coffee I excitedly discussed with this leading expert on Hadrian what was known of this memorable Roman and his times. As we talked, I flipped through pages of notes I had assembled during my preliminary research.

As ruler of the Roman world his full – and official – name was *Imperator* Caesar Traianus Hadrianus Augustus.[4] *Imperator*, which means 'commander', was once an honour bestowed on a general by his troops for leading them to victory in battle.[5] It was originally appended to the hero's name as public recognition for his achievements and carved on inscriptions, and sometimes shown on coins. Augustus (27 BCE–14 CE) brazenly co-opted it as his first name and, as he established his position of autocratic power, carefully controlled who could be granted use of it. By the time of Hadrian, the title had become the exclusive form of the Roman leader's name, gradually acquiring the regal and despotic connotations of the modern word 'emperor'. He also adopted the names Caesar and Augustus. Caesar was derived from C. Iulius Caesar – the Julius Caesar assassinated on the Ides of March 44 BCE – after which his great-nephew inherited the name. His successors also assumed it at the start of their reigns. The *cognomen* Augustus was an honorific title bestowed on Caesar's heir by the Roman Senate in 27 BCE for the respectful way he managed his relationship with them. It meant 'revered one' or 'one worthy of reverence'. Neither Caesar nor Augustus carried any formal power as such, but these names brought the bearer great prestige and authority (*auctoritas*). Hadrian inherited them from the deceased emperor Trajan (Traianus). Hadrian's full imperatorial name established his position in a long line of 'First Citizens' (*principes*), which set him apart from the ordinary Romans of his day.

Reconstructing his life and movements is more problematic. Opper reminded me of the sources and their limitations, which are always challenging for the historian of the ancient world. The first twelve Caesars were the subjects of biographies by a single writer, the famous Suetonius (C. Suetonius Tranquillus), whose gossipy accounts have come down to us virtually complete. Frustratingly, even though Suetonius was the most important administrator during the first five years of Hadrian's reign – a position in which he would have seen his employer's private and public correspondence and known a great deal about his life – he did not write a biography of the fourteenth Caesar.[6] Blame indiscretion: Suetonius was dismissed from Hadrian's service for being rather too familiar with his employer's wife.[7]

Instead, the most complete account we have is the *Vita Hadriani*, 'The Life of Hadrian'. This is the first of thirty books of what has come to be known collectively as the *Scriptores Historiae Augustae* or *Historia Augusta*. The titles mean 'Writers of the Histories of the Revered Ones' or 'Augustan History', but neither was the original name of the document since they were coined in 1603 by the classical scholar Isaac Casaubon. Its own ancient history is murky and still disputed by modern scholars. As a collection, it purports to describe the lives of most rulers from Hadrian through to Carinus (covering the period 117 to 285 CE).[8] It may have been written by one author, though six different men (the *scriptores*) are named.[9] The *Life of Hadrian* is ascribed to Aelius Spartianus, which may be his real name or a *nom de plume*. He seems to have lived at the time of Diocletian (who ruled 284–305 CE), though the 390s may be more accurate; either way, it means that the author wrote the book well after Hadrian's death.[10]

'When using it as a source for Hadrian's life and times we know that we have to be careful,' said Opper. Some of its author's claims are questionable, he explained, because the accuracy of them may be down to the way the biographer used his source material. Parts of the book may even have been written as satire.[11] One of these was Hadrian's own autobiography, since Spartianus refers to it but, regrettably, nothing of the original text survives beyond what he himself quotes.[12] There was an entry about Hadrian in the *Epitome de Caesaribus*, a history of the Roman Empire from Augustus to Julian written in the fourth century, which has survived in two dissimilar versions: one by Aurelius Victor, the other wrongly attributed to him and of unknown authorship.[13] Most importantly, there is also the commentary on events that took place under Trajan and Hadrian recorded by the chronicler Cassius Dio, who wrote during the reign of the Severan emperors (193–235 CE). The passages relating to the war I was researching only survive as a summary of Dio by an eleventh-century *epitomator* named Ioannis Xiphilinos, better known by his anglicized name of John Xiphilinus.[14] His summary is generally believed to accurately relate the words originally scribed by the earlier historian, or at least to omit few facts that were recorded in his source.[15]

Dr Opper reminded me, however, that 'evidence of events often missing from the surviving written sources could sometimes be found on inscriptions, or on coins, or deduced from artefacts uncovered by archaeology'. Like a jigsaw with several puzzle pieces missing, this diverse material can be assembled together to form an *impression* of Hadrian's life.

Our protagonist was born on 24 January 76 CE (where is uncertain) and named – nine days later, as was the custom – P. Aelius Hadrianus.[16] His father had come from Italica in the province of Baetica in the Iberian Peninsula.[17] The family was of senatorial rank and, by Roman standards, affluent.[18] Tragedy struck him early in his life when his father, Aelius Hadrianus Afer, died unexpectedly in 85 or 86 CE. The 10-year-old boy then became ward of his cousin, M. Ulpius Traianus.[19] Trajan's was an archetypal Roman success story, one all the more remarkable for not being Italian by birth.[20] His growing network of connections would help

Hadrian advance up the Roman public career ladder (*cursus publicus*). The military and civilian positions it encompassed were of increasing responsibility and designed to expose a young man to a wide variety of aspects of public service in the empire. For a few it would culminate in election to one of the two annually appointed consulships.[21]

A Roman in his late teens started his career in public service as a junior magistrate, typically working in a court of law. Preparing, handling and filing of paperwork – more correctly handwritten rolls of papyrus or thin sheets of wood – was the means by which the empire of the Romans was governed. Moving on, at age 20 Hadrian was appointed to his first army posting as one of a team of military tribunes of *Legio* II *Adiutrix* (c. 94/95 CE).[22] This took him far away from home as the legion was based in Pannonia at Aquincum (modern Budapest) on the Danube River. He likely secured the position because Trajan was then probably the imperial governor (*legatus Augusti pro praetore*) of the province, having been personally chosen by the reigning Emperor Nerva. While serving with the unit Hadrian made the acquaintance of Q. Marcius Turbo, who was a centurion at that time and with whom he struck up a friendship.

On 27 January 98 CE Nerva died and, by pre-arrangement, Trajan succeeded him, adopting the name *Imperator* Caesar Nerva Traianus Augustus.[23] Hadrian, now 22 years old, was related to the most important man in the empire. He was still ranked *tribunus militum*, but he transferred to *Legio* V *Macedonica* stationed at Oescus in Moesia Inferior.[24] Three years later (97–98 CE) he moved to Mogontiacum (modern Mainz) on the Rhine in Germania Superior to serve with *Legio* XXII *Primigenia*.[25] Trajan had himself been in this province six years before; Hadrian may have met officers and men who had undertaken an unspecified consular mission in the province, building relationships that would be useful later in life.

It was time to leave the army and take up a civilian position again. Hadrian moved to Rome where he served as one of the twenty *quaestores* responsible for managing public finances.[26] The Roman state extracted vast sums in taxes and tribute and spent them on the army, roads, public buildings and religious festivals. Keeping track of the cash and recording transactions in the ledgers was a labour-intensive task. Opportunities for errors or corruption were rife. Auditing the books was a constant process. Significantly, this seemingly tedious bureaucratic post granted him entry to the Senate. Though its responsibilities were greatly reduced since the heyday of the Republic two centuries before, nevertheless it acted as an advisory body to the emperor on a variety of matters and still passed decrees and rubber-stamped laws. As a member of the august assembly of some 300 men, Hadrian could study its inner workings, hear speeches given in support or against the passing of decrees and mix with the city's most influential citizens.

Trajan himself was away fighting the first of two wars in Dacia (101–102 CE).[27] His absence presented Hadrian with an opportunity to raise his profile. As one of the nominees of the emperor, Hadrian often read aloud Trajan's official communications in the Senate. Awkwardly, while speaking he 'provoked a laugh by his somewhat provincial accent'.[28] The episode was personally embarrassing, but rather than sulk and brood, Hadrian devoted time and effort to improving his speech 'until he attained the utmost proficiency and fluency'.[29] His next career move was the appointment to *curator actorum senatus* or *ab actis senatus* in which role he was responsible for drafting the official record of the Senate's transactions, published as the *acta diurna*.[30] Not long after he was elected as Tribune of the Plebs (*tribunus plebis*, 102 CE), a political appointment that carried the power of veto.[31] Emperor Trajan returned to Rome in triumph. Hadrian was promoted to serve as *praetor* (105 CE), a posting responsible for administering law and the courts.[32]

Having proved his competence at running civil service and judicial departments in Rome, Hadrian was ready to undertake a senior military position. Trajan appointed him *legatus legionis* of I *Minervia Pia Fidelis* (105–106 CE).[33] As legate, he was responsible for directing the legion of 5,600 troops more or less and its complement of officers. They were already on active service in the final stages of the Second Dacian War. It was a punitive war, intended to punish King Decebalus for having broken the terms of his peace treaty three years earlier. Active in what is now Romania, the war would test Hadrian's ability to command men in real combat operations, though it is unlikely that his legion was at the siege of Sarmizegetusa, during which the Roman forces destroyed the city and the king committed suicide.[34]

Trajan was evidently impressed by his cousin's performance in theatre. He presented him with a diamond, which he himself had previously received from Nerva.[35] Immediately following the war, Trajan assigned Hadrian to Pannonia Inferior as *legatus Augusti pro praetore* (106–108 CE).[36]

As military governor there, 'he held the Sarmatae in check, maintained discipline among the soldiers, and restrained the procurators [collectors of taxes], who were overstepping too freely the bounds of their power.'[37]

Precisely what he did to check the advances of the Sarmatae – people related to the nomadic Scythians living north of the Black Sea and considered highly dangerous – is nowhere explained, but having now established a track record of success in the field, Hadrian returned again to civilian life in Rome. In recognition of his achievements, from May to August 108 CE he was elected to serve as a suffect consul.[38] In this role he could convene meetings of the Senate and preside over them. He would be accompanied by a 'Secret Service' of twelve lictors who guarded his person with their ceremonial *fasces*, sharp axes wrapped in bundles of rods. He was still only 32 years old, much younger than the 45 years normally stipulated for this high appointment.

His progression continued relentlessly. After completing his short term in high office, he left Rome and went to Athens. There he served as *archon* (112–113 CE), the most senior administrative role in the ancient Greek city and was made a citizen.[39]

True to his nature, Trajan was ambitious for yet more military glory. To that end, in 113 CE he ordered Hadrian to Syria, then Rome's most easterly province bordering the Empire of Parthia, to take up the post of *legatus Augusti pro praetore*.[40] It was a significant promotion for Hadrian. There were four legions stationed in Syria; all were now under his direct command. Parthia had been Rome's nemesis for a century and a half and Trajan was intent on conquering it.[41] He needed a loyal deputy at his rear. Cousin Hadrian was his man.

Having completed his preparations, the emperor personally prosecuted the campaign.[42] Operations proved successful. Victories were quickly won, and Armenia, Mesopotamia and Babylonia fell under the taloned grip of the Roman eagles. The empire had now grown to its greatest ever extent. By his deeds, Trajan had proved himself unquestionably to be both a consummate administrator and a masterful commander. The Senate recognized his exceptional accomplishments when it declared him *optimus princeps* (the best ruler).[43]

As the newly-conquered territories settled, some communities long within the Roman Empire's own borders broke out in revolt.[44] While the emperor and his army were engaged on foreign soil, Jews in the diaspora and the eastern provinces seized the opportunity to settle old scores. The sources mention a man named Artemion who led Jewish rebels in attacks against the population of Cyprus; Cassius Dio states that 240,000 perished in the violence, a claim that seems wildly exaggerated.[45] As a proconsular province the island had no military garrison. Trajan sent one of his best commanders, Marcius Turbo, with units of infantry and cavalry aboard naval vessels and orders to restore order. Troops of *Legio* III *Cyrenaica* from Bostra and *Legio* XXII *Deiotariana* from Alexandria, as well as several auxiliary cohorts, took part in the counterinsurgency operations.

In the province of Libya in North Africa, Jewish rioters led by one Andreas (or Lukuas), who they believed was the messiah, attacked their non-Jewish neighbours.[46] They set public buildings on fire, including the sanctuaries of Apollo in Cyrene and of Asclepius at Balagrae. The rebels overturned and broke milestones along the road between Cyrene and its port, Apollonia, even tearing up the surface of the road to slow down any Roman troops arriving by sea from attempting to move inland. Dio claims that 220,000 were killed.[47] Marcius Turbo and his expeditionary force may have been involved in the fighting to subdue the rebels. To assist him, Trajan dispatched C. Valerius Rufus, tribune of *Legio* II *Claudia* from Moesia Superior. Several of the insurgent leaders slipped away, however, heading eastwards to foment trouble in neighbouring Egypt.

In Egypt, fighting between Greek-speaking Romans and Jews broke out in Alexandria on the Nile Delta and spread as far south as Thebes.[48] Like the desert sands, tempers were hot. Near Alexandria, Jewish rioters destroyed the shrine of Nemesis. The historian Appian (Appianus Alexandrinus) records in his *Roman History* how he narrowly escaped a mob of angry Jews; he lost his way at night while trying to find his ship, by accident found a trireme at dawn next day and only just managed to reach safety at Pelusium on the eastern side of the Nile Delta.[49] (Luckily for him, as the ship he was supposed to board was captured by Jewish rebels.) Assisted by peasants armed with farming implements, the non-Jewish population struck back. With what forces he had, Rutilius Rufus, the *Praefectus Aegypti*, led attacks upon the insurgents in person. His ability to deliver a decisive response was limited, however, because contingents of the units normally under his command had been seconded to campaign with Trajan. The remaining men of *Legio* III *Cyrenaica* and *Legio* XXII *Deiotariana* struggled to contain the situation.

Beyond the Euphrates, within the Parthian Empire, the Jews of Mesopotamia banded together with other resistance groups to impede the advance of Trajan's invading army.[50] The Roman commander-in-chief dispatched Lusius Quietus (a Moor of consular rank who had proved his worth at Nisibis and Edessa) to crush the opposition.[51] There is also a reference on an inscription found in Sardinia to an *expeditio Iudaica*, a 'Jewish Taskforce'.[52] Its meaning remains elusive. The Talmudic sources tell the story of two wealthy Jews, the brothers Pappus and Lulianus, who fomented rebellion but were slain on the orders of Trajan.[53] Quietus accomplished his mission with such violent ruthlessness that the *Midrash* records the 'Kitos War' – or the 'War of Quietus' – in phrases dripping with literary tears of sorrow.

Likely aware of the trouble brewing around him, while in Antiocheia (modern Antakya in Turkey) Hadrian received a letter with life-changing news on 7 or 8 August. He was informed that Trajan had adopted him as his heir.[54] On 12 August another letter arrived telling him that the *princeps* had died in Selinus (Gazipasa) in Cilicia.[55] When the news was made public, he was acclaimed *imperator* by the assembled troops.[56] He was 41 years old.

The cause of Trajan's death may have been entirely natural, but the timing and circumstances in which it occurred and the delay in announcing the adoption of his successor perplexed people at the time. Dio reports that:

> There was, to be sure, a widely prevailing belief that Trajan, with the approval of many of his friends, had planned to appoint as his successor not Hadrian but Neratius Priscus, even to the extent of saying to Priscus: 'I entrust the provinces to your care in case anything happens to me.' And, indeed, many assert that Trajan had purposed to follow the example of Alexander of Macedonia and die without naming a successor. Again, many others declare that he had meant to send an address to the Senate, requesting this body, in case aught befell him, to appoint a ruler for the Roman Empire, and merely appending the names of some from among whom the Senate might choose the best. And the statement has even been made that it was not until after Trajan's death that Hadrian was declared adopted, and then only by means of a trick of Plotina's; for she smuggled in someone who impersonated the emperor and spoke in a feeble voice.[57]

Hadrian's accession was also marred by alleged plots against his own life. The conspirators, among them four senior officers who had served with distinction under Trajan, were arrested on their return to Italy and summarily executed.[58] Several others, including the *praefectus urbi* (the chief magistrate responsible for the maintenance of law and order in the city of Rome), had designs of their own for seizing supreme power.[59] Hadrian initially showed them clemency (*clementia*), but later changed his mind in the case of one individual who had already been exiled under Nerva and condemned under Trajan.[60]

To ensure a favourable start to his principate, he gave the soldiers a cash donative of double the customary sum.[61] Hadrian had to be sure he could trust those around him. Spartianus states: 'He deprived Lusius Quietus of the command of the Moorish tribesmen, who were serving under him, and then dismissed him from the army, because he had fallen under the suspicion of having designs on the throne.'[62]

In contrast, the fortunes of the equestrian Marcius Turbo greatly improved. After he had first reduced Iudaea and then quelled an insurrection in Mauretania, Hadrian assigned him to the temporary command of Pannonia and Dacia and upgraded his authority to a rank equivalent to that of the prefect of Egypt.[63]

Hadrian then left Antiocheia to view for himself the remains of the deceased Trajan. On the journey from Selinus, the cortège was escorted by his widow Pompeia Plotina, his niece Salonia Matidia and P. Acilius Attianus, who had Hadrian's complete trust.[64] He received them, shared his condolences and sent them on to Rome by ship. Upon returning to Antiocheia he appointed Catilius Severus, *legatus Augusti pro praetore* to govern Syria. With the East secured (plate 4), he departed by way of Illyricum to Rome, where negative sentiment among the people and senators was growing.[65] In this Roman 'Game of Thrones' Hadrian had to firmly assert his right to rule early on, and to ensure that he could rely on the loyalty of the army.

Far from a *Pax Romana*, Hadrian inherited a world in turmoil: several provinces were in disorder or on the brink of civil unrest, and the newly-conquered territories still needed to be pacified.[66] A lifetime of military experience led Hadrian to conclude that the policy of imperial expansion aggressively pursued by Trajan and some of his antecedents was sheer folly. Rome's military resources were overextended. Now commander-

Figure 2. Hadrian extensively toured the provinces by land and sea. This coin shows an imperial transport being powered by oars. A sail could be raised when sufficient wind blew. The legend in Latin translates as 'Good Luck of Augustus'.

in-chief, he implemented a new policy based on containment.[67] Within hours of his acclamation by the troops, he abandoned most of Trajan's recent conquests, keeping just Armenia and Dacia.[68]

Consistent with maintaining control over Rome's chosen dominions, he travelled to the provinces to inspect the frontiers and installations and to meet the local civilian administrations and military units.[69] These state visits became a hallmark of his hands-on style of governance. They were celebrated on coins that circulated long after he had left (fig. 2). Hadrian made two grand tours of the provinces in his lifetime.[70] It was 'managing by wandering about' (MBWA) in the truest sense of the expression.[71] He set out on the first of these trips in 121 CE.[72] He travelled to the northern and western provinces and then those in North Africa, the Balkans, Anatolia and the Near East, returning to Rome in 125. In 128 he departed on the second trip, which took him to Anatolia, the Near East and Egypt. He was probably the most-travelled of any Roman emperor, with Caesar Augustus a close second.[73]

Wherever he went, Hadrian visited military camps and drilled the troops in every style of combat.[74] Under his command were an estimated 386,000 men-at-arms.[75] They were based at permanent camps, mostly sited on the nominal border of the empire (map 1). If he determined that the camp was in the wrong place from a tactical or strategic perspective, Hadrian simply ordered the unit to be relocated.[76] Arguably the most

Map 1. Roman Empire, 125 CE. (© *Andrein. CC-BY-SA 3.0*)

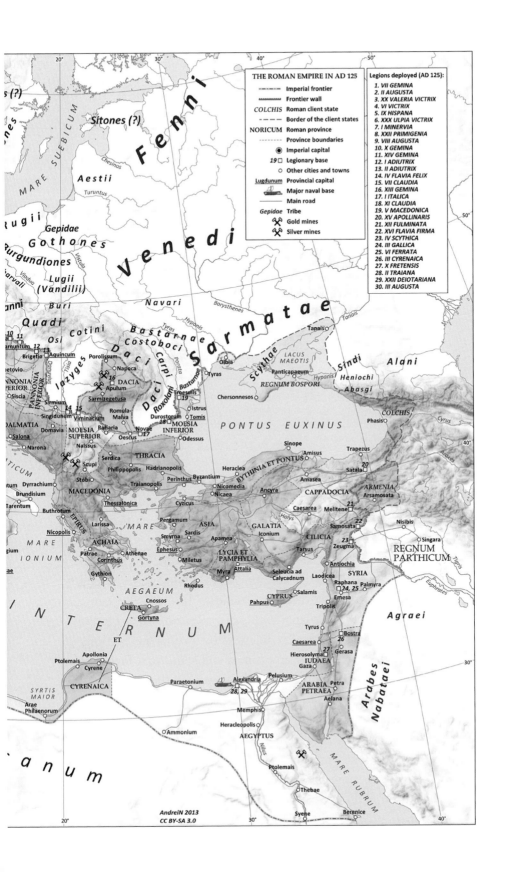

THE ROMAN EMPIRE IN AD 125

·-·-·-·	Imperial frontier
⌒⌒⌒	Frontier wall
COLCHIS	Roman client state
- - - -	Border of the client states
NORICUM	Roman province
------	Province boundaries
◉	Imperial capital
19☐	Legionary base
○	Other cities and towns
Lugdunum	Provincial capital
⛴	Major naval base
——	Main road
Gepidae	Tribe
⚒	Gold mines
⚒	Silver mines

Legions deployed (AD 125):

1. VII GEMINA
2. II AUGUSTA
3. XX VALERIA VICTRIX
4. VI VICTRIX
5. IX HISPANA
6. XXX ULPIA VICTRIX
7. I MINERVIA
8. XXII PRIMIGENIA
9. VIII AUGUSTA
10. X GEMINA
11. XIV GEMINA
12. I ADIUTRIX
13. II ADIUTRIX
14. IV FLAVIA FELIX
15. VII CLAUDIA
16. XIII GEMINA
17. I ITALICA
18. XI CLAUDIA
19. V MACEDONICA
20. XV APOLLINARIS
21. XII FULMINATA
22. XVI FLAVIA FIRMA
23. IV SCYTHICA
24. III GALLICA
25. VI FERRATA
26. III CYRENAICA
27. X FRETENSIS
28. II TRAIANA
29. XXII DEIOTARIANA
30. III AUGUSTA

AndreiN 2013
CC BY-SA 3.0

Figure 3. A view of Hadrian's Wall from Housesteads Fort reveals how its Roman architect exploited the landscape's natural features for maximum efficiency and impact. Although ostensibly a military barrier, it may have been intended to control movements of people and goods into and out of Roman territory.

audacious military infrastructure project he instigated was the eponymous wall in northern Britain (fig. 3). It established a demarcation line in the landscape from the fort of Maia at Bowness-on-Solway on the Solway Firth in the west to Segedunum at Wallsend on the River Tyne in the east.[77] All of the legions based in the province contributed the manpower to build the stone and turf barrier running '80 [Roman] miles in length, which was to separate the barbarians from the Romans'.[78] Begun in 122 CE and completed six years later, with a few adjustments to Hadrian's own initial design, it was exclusively manned by auxiliaries. Sections of Hadrian's Wall and many of the army camps still stand to a few courses of hand-cut stone, and parts of the deep ditch (*vallum*) that ran along the south side of the wall can also be seen in places. It is one of my favourite Roman sites anywhere in the world.[79] As was the case with so many structures he commissioned, Hadrian never saw it in its finished glory.

Spartianus claims that Hadrian 're-established the discipline of the camp, which since the time of Caesar Octavianus [Augustus] had been growing slack through the laxity of his predecessors'.[80] Indeed, a recurring theme on coins minted during his time is the image of the commander addressing a gathering of soldiers and their insignia in each of the praetorian provinces he visited.[81] In museums around the world, statues of Hadrian are often of the emperor presented as commander (*imperator*). Opper, who had published work on ancient sculpture, pointed out that in Roman times 'there were certain iconographic formulae that were rolled out again and again'. Thus, statues of Hadrian typically depict him standing with his right arm raised (as though about to call the troops to order), wearing the full panoply of cuirass (often elaborately decorated with scenes from mythology) over a fringed arming doublet from which hangs a cloak carefully draped over the left arm, and finely crafted officer's high boots on his feet.[82] Portrayed this way, Hadrian fitted into a long-established stereotype of the reassuringly strong national leader who wielded *imperium* on behalf of the Roman people going back to Augustus.[83]

Our biographical source asserts that Hadrian consciously chose to eat the same food (specifically mentioning bacon, cheese and sour wine) as the regular soldiers, to go on their route marches with them, to wear simple fatigues as they did during training exercises, to get to know them personally by name, and to visit them in hospital when they were sick.[84] By doing these things he won the affection of the rank and file and became a soldier's soldier (plate 5). He was rightly proud of his knowledge of military matters and was confident that he would notice the slightest irregularity during a review of the troops. Thorsten Opper reminded me that in 128 CE Hadrian travelled to Africa. On or around 1 July of that year he visited the military camp in Lambaesis (Lambeze-Tazoult in Algeria). An inscription was carved to record his address to the troops after they completed manoeuvres under his watchful gaze:

> You have built a lengthy wall, made as if for permanent winter-quarters, in nearly as short a time as if it were built from turf which is cut in even pieces, easily carried and handled, and laid without difficulty, being naturally smooth and flat. You built with big, heavy, uneven stones that no one can carry, lift or lay without their unevenness becoming evident.[85]

Buoyed by such well-executed displays, he could confidently follow the example of previous emperors when he wrote in his field reports to the Senate, 'if you and our children are in health, it is well; I and the legions are in health.'[86] Maintaining discipline (*disciplina*, plate 6) was crucial to the success of the Roman army which was the ultimate power behind the emperor.

Hadrian's surviving letters and speeches reveal him to have been a somewhat reticent man and always working tirelessly.[87] Spartianus states that he had a very good memory – perhaps a photographic memory – and had a talent for recalling names:

> Even without the aid of a *nomenclator* he could call by name a great many people, whose names he had heard but once and then all in a crowd; indeed, he could correct the *nomenclatores* when they made mistakes, as they not infrequently did, and he even knew the names of the veterans whom he had discharged at various times. He could repeat from memory, after a rapid reading, books which to most men were not known at all.[88]

He used this ability to review and retain information in the management of the army and its considerable – and sometimes frivolous – expenses.[89] He personally dictated his speeches to a secretary and gave opinions on all questions put to him. Multi-tasking was another of his abilities in that he could write, dictate, listen and converse with his friends, all at the same time.[90] Yet, for a man bearing the problems of the Roman world on his shoulders, he still managed to retain a sense of humour:

> He was also very witty, and of his jests many still survive. The following one has even become famous. When he had refused a request to a certain grey-haired man, and the man repeated the request but this time with dyed hair, Hadrian replied: 'I have already refused this to your father.'[91]

He made a jest while bathing in the public baths that became famous:

> On a certain occasion, seeing a veteran, whom he had known in the service, rubbing his back and the rest of his body against the wall, he asked him why he had the marble rub him, and when the man replied that it was because he did not own a slave, he presented him with some slaves and the cost of their maintenance. But another time, when he saw a number of old men rubbing themselves against the wall for the purpose of arousing the generosity of the Emperor, he ordered them to be called out and then to rub one another in turn.[92]

The statues show that Hadrian was a physically impressive individual: tall, elegant and strongly built.[93] Attempting to capture the essential Hadrian, the Christian writer Tertullian called him *omnium curiositatum explorator*, 'an explorer of everything interesting'.[94] What a striking epithet that is, and how insightful! He was a man of several innate talents and strong passions. He liked to be active, enjoying walking, riding and hunting (plate 7) from an early age, and trained regularly in the use of the spear (*pilum*) and the short sword (*gladius*).[95] His intellectual talents extended to debating, reading and writing (including composing epic and love poetry), as well as astrology, arithmetic, geometry and painting; he could play the flute and sing, about which he even boasted openly, even though Romans generally frowned upon performers of music.[96] He enjoyed theatrical and dramatic performances, invited performers to his banquets and befriended the most accomplished of their art.[97] He laid on lavish public entertainments, including beast hunts and gladiatorial combats that were always very popular with Roman spectators.[98]

One of his great passions was architecture. Following in the tradition of Augustus and Trajan he built, and he built big.[99] Opper said, 'Hadrian understood the powerful impact of architecture on the public psyche and used it to give substance to his vision of an empire united through cultural progress and religious traditions.'

In Rome, he restored several buildings originally erected by Augustus' right-hand man M. Agrippa, including the Pantheon (fig. 4), *Saepta Iulia* and the Baths which had fallen into disrepair, while on his overseas trips he often contributed to beautifying the cities he visited – several aqueducts and towns were named in his honour – or laid on public games and festivals.[100] It was said that 'he built something in almost every city'.[101] More than 130 cities received at least one benefaction from him, representing some 210 indications of imperial favour.[102] In general, Hadrian's visits brought goodwill and good fortune. This is the deeper significance of the message *Felicitati Augusti* – a phrase meaning 'For the Success of Augustus' or 'For the Happiness of Augustus' – inscribed on coins minted under Hadrian, and it accounts for the hundreds of statues and inscriptions of him found around Europe, Asia and Near East that were erected in gratitude for his benefactions.[103] These gifts had the effect of binding the local communities to him personally and encouraging the adoption of Roman norms and values.

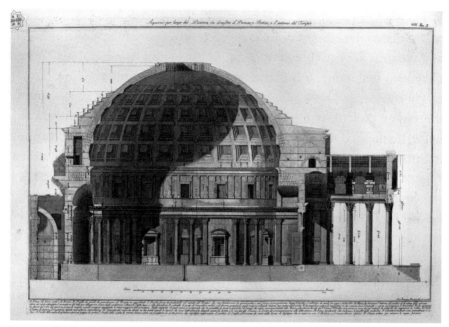

Figure 4. Hadrian rebuilt M. Agrippa's Pantheon with a coffered dome. It is still the world's largest unreinforced concrete dome. This architectural cross-section drawn by Francesco Piranesi in 1790 reveals the inner secrets of the innovative design conceived by Apollodorus and Hadrian.

It was while living in Athens that he developed a deeper love of Hellenic culture that had begun early in his life. Spartianus remarks that he then became deeply devoted to Greek studies to which his natural tastes inclined, so much so that some called him *Graeculus*, a word meaning 'Greekling'.[104] It was not intended as a compliment. Romans tended to look upon Greeks with distrust, a sentiment the poet Vergil captured in the famous line, 'I fear the Greeks, even when they bear gifts.'[105] Spartianus adds that, while living in Athens, Hadrian also began the practice of wearing a beard 'to cover up the natural blemishes on his face'.[106] 'That's the most common-sense version,' said Thorsten Opper, 'but I like the idea that, rather than a Greek philosopher's beard, it was a soldier's beard.' The facial hair also marked him out. Trajan was always clean-shaven, the preferred style of a Roman public figure for centuries. With his strikingly different appearance, Hadrian was, perhaps, making a statement that he was his own man.[107] Yet his philhellenism was backward-looking: he was nostalgic for an age that might have placed him in the Athens of Pericles, with its pantheon of violent and oversexed gods and goddesses, along with its esoteric philosophical and artistic obsessions.[108]

When not travelling, Hadrian retreated to a resort located near Tibur (Tivoli), 29 kilometres (18 mi.) east of Rome. It may have originally been a villa owned by his family; there were several families from Baetica in the region.[109] It became his personal 'project'. He started work on its redevelopment around 118 CE and, as the principal designer, transformed it into a palatial luxury estate. Set in the foothills of the Tiburtine Mountains, the *Villa Tiburtina* complex covered an area of at least a square kilometre (250 acres) and contained more than 30 buildings, each unique in design and decoration.[110] It was

> marvellously constructed, and he [Hadrian] actually gave to parts of it the names of provinces and places of the greatest renown, calling them, for instance, Lyceum, Academia, Prytaneum, Canopus, Poecile and Tempe. And in order not to omit anything, he even made a Hades.[111]

Many of the statues that furnish the ancient sculpture collections across Europe – not least the Musei Capitolini in Rome and the British Museum – came from excavations undertaken here in the sixteenth through to the nineteenth centuries.[112]

The private lives of Roman emperors fascinated the Romans every bit as much then as it does us today. It was said that Hadrian overindulged in the gratification of his desires.[113] As the most powerful and wealthiest individual in the Roman world, of course, he had the means to give them free rein. Yet he held them in check. Shaped by his extensive travels and life experiences, Hadrian developed into 'a pleasant man to meet and he possessed a certain charm'.[114] He could be generous to friends and he could even be inclusive in hearing different sides in an argument, but he could also be quick to criticize, vindictive and downright cruel at times.[115] On that point, Opper reminded me of a story recorded in the *Historia Augusta*:

> And once Favorinus, when he had yielded to Hadrian's criticism of a word which he had used, raised a merry laugh among his friends. For when they reproached him for having done wrong in yielding to Hadrian in the matter of a word used by reputable authors, he replied: 'You are urging a wrong course, my friends, when you do

not suffer me to regard as the most learned of men the one who has thirty legions!'[116]

He may have made the remark in jest, but the undertone of asserting his authority was clear. He was suspicious of his friends and not above listening to rumours about them, and ultimately regarded them as potential enemies. Several men of high standing are even reported to have been driven to commit suicide.[117]

It was time to wrap up the interview. I thanked Thorsten Opper, bade him farewell and returned to the Wolfson Gallery. I went back to the bust of Hadrian. Placed closely beside it was another portrait.[118] The ancient sculptor had captured in white marble a beautiful youth in his teenage years with a mop of thick hair, hanging down in long bunches over the brow, temples, ears and back of the neck, a blemish-free complexion, wide upward-curving eyebrows, a long slender nose and small, pouting lips (fig. 1). The portrait was instantly recognizable as Antinous. The pairing of the two sculptures by the curator was by design. The Roman sources imply that the boy was the emperor's lover – modern history books still euphemistically refer to him as the 'boy-favourite' – who deeply affected the older man's life.

Years ago, as a teenager, I read Marguerite Yourcenar's novel of the emperor. Written in French as *Mémoires d'Hadrien*, it was translated into English by her American lover Grace Frick and published three years later as *Memoirs of Hadrian*.[119] It became an international bestseller. Using the form of an autobiographical letter, the novelist produced an extraordinary book based on historical sources, which seemed to capture the mind and soul of the man. It made a lasting impression on me, especially the story of his love for the boy. Before leaving the United States, I had travelled to Hollywood, California to learn more about him. At The Counter on Sunset Boulevard I had met Anthony Nicias Subia. Preferring the Romanized form, Antonivs Svbia was a self-styled priest (*flamen*) of Antinous who had devoted years of his life to understanding the charismatic boy and his extraordinary relationship with Hadrian. In a corner of the busy, brightly-lit restaurant over a dinner of 'Old School' hamburgers and fries, we reviewed what was known of Antinous.

We began with Dio who writes that 'Antinous was from Bithynion, a city of Bithynia, which we also call Klaudiopolis.'[120] Antinous was a small-town boy, living a provincial life as a Greek-speaking freeborn citizen of his town. Likely not a Roman citizen, he was almost certainly not a slave. His birthday is preserved in an inscription: 27 November.[121] Antinous was likely in his early teens at the time Hadrian first encountered him. He was no skinny twink, however. Statues portray him as a somewhat fleshy but pleasantly proportioned athletic youth with a particularly pert bottom and a small, uncircumcised penis.[122]

Hadrian's personal life was, in a single word, *complicated*. Our sources may be unreliable, arguably prejudiced. Exaggeration of Hadrian's preferences and peccadilloes by ancient commentators cannot be ruled out. He had a close friendship with Plotina, whose support for his accession was crucial after her husband's premature death.[123] He was married to Vibia Sabina, his second cousin once removed, about whom little is written, but according to one statement their relationship seems to have been a fraught one: 'She used to say openly that, because she had judged his character inhuman, she had taken pains lest, to the bane of the human race, she become pregnant by him.'[124] They never had children; reasons are not given. Hadrian looked elsewhere for affection and sexual fulfilment. 'Indeed,' writes Spartianus, 'as for this habit of Hadrian's, men regard it as a most grievous fault, and add to their criticism the statements which are current regarding the passion for males and the adulteries with married women to which he is said to have been addicted.'[125]

Hadrian lived as a bisexual man but his natural orientation was *probably* homosexual, a point finally acknowledged by Thorsten Opper at the 2008 British Museum exhibition.[126] He was like his cousin Trajan, whose homosexuality is expressly noted by Spartianus. The original statement in the text is missing one or more words, but translates as 'And now he [Hadrian] became a favourite of Trajan's, and yet, owing to the activity of the guardians of certain boys whom Trajan loved ardently, he was not free from [...] which Gallus fostered.'[127] Is the implication here that they shared an interest in the same boys or perhaps harboured jealousies over younger lovers?

The extant sources do not specifically state what attracted Hadrian to Antinous.[128] His youth and beauty were obviously part of it. Yet the most powerful man in the Roman world could have had the pick of any young man or girl for his pleasure, so there must have been more to the relationship than pure lust. In ancient Rome, attitudes to same-sex and inter-generational relationships were very different than today. While there was no Latin word for 'homosexual', Romans did, nevertheless, recognize a variety of preferences in describing sex between men in their language.[129] As a phil-Hellene, Hadrian would have felt very comfortable openly forming a relationship with a boy. Two sources describe him as *paidika*, variously translated as a 'boy-favourite' or 'love boy'.[130]

Some were less accepting of his sexual orientation. Svbia told me of a comment written in the fourth century. In his summary of the lives of the emperors, Aurelius Victor includes the detail of 'foul rumours that he [Hadrian] had debauched young men and was inflamed by the notorious services of Antinous'.[131] Here Hadrian is presented as a sexual predator and Antinous as a willing participant and *agent provocateur*. This portrayal of their relationship dynamics may be truthful or entirely fabricated; the paucity of sources makes a clear determination difficult.

This, then, was the Hadrian who went to Province Iudaea in 130 CE. His visit would set in train a series of events that would end in catastrophe for both Jews and Romans. What did the Roman emperor do in the province? How was he received by the local population? What was the mood of the people after he departed? To find the answers to these and other questions I would need to travel to Israel.

Chapter 2

'Iudaea Recaptured'

The British Airways jet plane touched down on the tarmac of Ben Gurion Airport, Tel Aviv just after dawn on Sunday morning. Inside the quiet terminal building Israeli Immigration was polite and efficient. I picked up my compact, white rental car and committed to memory the security code that I would need to start the engine each time – a uniquely Israeli solution to car theft. Then I drove out of the airport complex and straight into a traffic jam. Israelis were going to work at the start of a new week. I had hit the Tel Aviv morning rush hour. It was the day most Americans and Europeans regarded as the day of rest, but in Israel the Sabbath had already passed with the rising of the sun.

Observing *Shabbat* on Saturday is a hallmark of Judaism, an ancient religion and culture characterized by several distinctive attributes.[1] Jews believe in one God, an incorporeal being, meaning that it is not composed of matter and has no physical form. Many consider the very word 'God' itself as sacred, referring to him as *YHWH* or *Yahweh*.[2] He is called *Eloha* ('God') or *ha-Elohim* ('the God') or *Elohim hayyim* ('the living God'), and also addressed directly as *HaShem* ('the Name') or more formally as *Adonai* ('my Lord'). *Shabbat*, the seventh day of the week, is a time to honour the Creator undistracted by busyness.[3]

Jewish people also believe that they demonstrate their faithfulness with the one God by praying, studying and observing the commandments set out in the *Torah*, meaning 'Learning' or 'Instruction'. These include specific dietary mandates (Hebrew: *kashrut*) and the requirement for boys to be circumcised (*brit milah* or *bris*) eight days after birth in accordance with the Covenant the patriarch Abraham agreed directly with God. The arc of the Jewish calendar is shaped by holy days, festivals and days of remembrance. Among the major ones are *Rosh Hashana*, the Jewish New Year lasting two days, which begins the period of 'Ten Days of Awe' and ends with *Yom Kippur*, the 'Day of Atonement'. During the year there is *Pesakh*, marking the Passover and Exodus of the Jews led by Moses from

Egypt in Pharaonic times; *Shavuot*, or Pentecost, commemorating the time God gave Moses the Law on Mount Sinai; and *Sukkot*, or Tabernacles, commemorating the period when the Jewish people wandered in the wilderness. This is Judaism as it is practised today. The question I sought to answer was this: what was life like for the Jewish people at the time of Hadrian?

The Jews living in 130 CE were following in the tradition of a culture and religion already well over a millennium old. The challenge for the modern historian is that before 586 BCE Jewish history almost exclusively comes from the Hebrew Bible.[4] It was written between c. 800–c. 400 BCE, but several of the books were not written earlier than the second century BCE.[5] Historians and biblical scholars constantly debate the factual basis of the stories told in the Bible. Archaeology has an important contribution to make in these ongoing discussions and inevitable controversies. To start my own investigation into life in Province Iudaea at the time of Hadrian, there was one place I had to visit.

Figure 5. An aerial view of the Israel Museum in Jerusalem, which is the largest museum in the country. The institution's archaeological collection is considered among the world-leaders of its kind. In the distance is the Knesset building.

My destination was the Israel Museum in Jerusalem. Navigating the slow-moving traffic from the airport, I eventually found and merged onto Highway 1. The drive on the motorway of freshly-laid blacktop took about an hour. The Israel Museum stands in Givat Ram, west of Jerusalem's Old City and right across from the Knesset building on Derech Ruppin Boulevard (fig. 5). Its proximity to where the members of parliament meet points to its importance in the country's life. Indeed, it is the largest cultural institution in the State of Israel. Where parliament deals with the myriad and complex issues of the present, the museum is dedicated to preserving and interpreting the past in all its messiness and complexity. It is probably most famous for the 'Shrine of the Book', a striking white dome that houses the so-called 'Dead Sea Scrolls', the oldest biblical manuscripts in the world. The museum is vast: its galleries cover some 20 acres. The website boasts that its Archaeology, Fine Arts and Jewish Art and Life wings feature 'the most extensive holdings of biblical and Holy Land archaeology in the world'.[6]

The galleries of the museum's Samuel and Saidye Bronfman Archaeological Wing trace the emergence of the Israelites – as the ancestors of the Jews are called in the Hebrew Bible – from around 1200 BCE.[7] They settled in the southern Levant (or Canaan) in small communities in Samaria and Upper Galilee. Since the first half of the second millennium BCE, a vibrant culture appeared in Canaan with populations living in cities – such as Ashkelon, Hazor and Megiddo – alongside farming society. In the eighth century BCE it seems probable that there was a Kingdom of Israel in the north and a Kingdom of Judah (Hebrew: *Yudah*) in the south.[8] Visitors to the Israel Museum can see for themselves royal inscriptions and seals bearing the names of men known from the Bible: kings of Israel named Yehoram, Yeroboam and Menahem; and kings of Judah named Ahaziyahu, Uzziah and Hezekiah. In the museum's collection is a particularly important inscription on a commemorative victory stele. It is the only proof outside the Bible confirming the existence of a king named David dating from this period.[9]

Israel lies at the intersection of three continents, serving as a natural crossing over which the armies of rival empires have marched.[10] In 732 BCE the Neo-Assyrian Empire – perhaps the world's first true empire occupying what is now northern Iraq, north-east Syria, south-east Turkey and north-west Iran – embarked on wars of conquest on its south-western border. The aggressor's actions were successful and the Kingdom of Israel fell to King Shalmaneser V (reigned from 727 to 722 BCE). In 722 BCE, after three years of hard campaigning perhaps under the king's more famous successor Sargon II (722–705 BCE), Assyria finally took Samaria.[11] Large numbers of Israelites were forcibly resettled elsewhere in the Neo-Assyrian Empire. They are the 'Lost Tribes of Israel' of the Bible.[12]

For 130 years the Kingdom of Judah remained independent. Then, in 598/597 BCE, Nebuchadnezzar II, king of Babylonia (reigned c. 605/604–562 BCE), dispatched his army to conquer it. Following a prolonged siege, in the summer of 587 or 586 BCE, on *Tisha B'Ab* (the 9th day of the month of *Ab* in the Jewish calendar) the city of Jerusalem was razed to the ground and the Temple to *Yahweh* (Hebrew: *Beit HaMikdash*) built by King Solomon (c. 961–c. 920 BCE) was burned.[13] The Jews refer to this as *churban*, the 'destruction'. This event marks the start of Jewish history.[14] Ever since, Jews have regarded *Tisha B'Ab* as the saddest day in the year on which they fast, deprive themselves of comforts and engage in solemn prayer.

Jewish history is filled with suffering. Much of the population of Judah was sent into exile in Babylon, a period the Jews call the 'Babylonian Captivity'. Hardly had fifty years passed after the exile when Cyrus II, king of Persia (known as Cyrus the Great, reigned 559–530 BCE), conquered Babylon. He permitted the Judahite exiles to return to their homeland and to rebuild their temple in Jerusalem. *Yehuda* (Judah) became a province of the Persian Empire. Official seals and coins on display at the Israel Museum bear the name of *Yehud*. A new Second Temple was completed in 515 BCE.[15] In the museum's collection is the 'Priestly Benediction' of the sixth century BCE, making it the oldest copy of a biblical text ever found.[16] Incised on two silver amulets, it dates from this turbulent period of history.

Though there were temples dedicated to *Yahweh* at Elephantine and Leontopolis in Egypt, the Temple in Jerusalem had become the main focus of Jewish religion.[17] Built on a hill, the Temple towered above the city. Daily rites and other sacrifices were held there on *Shabbat*, but especially during *Pesakh*, *Shavuot* and *Sukkot*.[18] Animals such as doves plus grains and liquids were offered. For Passover, a paschal lamb was slaughtered in the morning and a second one in the afternoon. So long as the Temple stood and priests observed sacrificial practices, Jews all over the world believed they were connected to it directly when their communities prayed in the morning or afternoon.[19] After prayers and the ritual killing, the meat was divided up while offerings (Hebrew: *korban*) were burned on the altar (*mishkan*) to *Yahweh*.[20] At these times with the bleats of sheep, streams of blood and the stench of entrails, the Temple must have resembled an abattoir. These festivals brought thousands of people into the Temple precinct. The priests (*kohanim*) had to be organized into groups to efficiently process the high volume of requests for blessings.[21] They were all men from the line of Aaron, whereas the clergy positions were held by Levites (male descendants of Levi).[22] The Levite clergy also provided music and sang the Hallel psalms to instrumental accompaniment.[23]

Persia was also conquered. In 330 BCE, Alexander III of Macedon (better known as Alexander the Great) seized Persepolis and brought down the mighty Persian Empire. Alexander unexpectedly died seven years later. His sprawling conquests were split up among his generals. Seleucus I Nicator and his successors ruled Judah. Exposure to the Greeks inevitably influenced and changed Jewish culture.[23] The museum has many coins, figurines, inscriptions, statues and ritual objects, as well as jewellery and funerary decorations attesting to the local population's adoption of Hellenistic ways from this time. In a display case is the 'Heliodorus Inscription' of 178 BCE. It is an order from the Seleucus IV Philopator to appoint an official in charge of temples and sanctuaries in the region, including the Temple at Jerusalem.[24] This move led to bans on religious Jewish practices and pillaging of the Temple. When Antiochus IV Epiphanes erected a statue of Zeus there in 168 BCE, a group of traditionalist Jews was outraged.[25]

A priest from Modi'in named Judah Maccabee (Yehudah HaMaccabee, also known as Judas Maccabaeus) and his four brothers decided to take action against their Hellenistic overlords.[26] A civil war ensued, the story of which is told in the books of the First and Second Maccabees. On the 13th of *Adar* 161 BCE the army of the Maccabees defeated the Seleucids at the Battle of Adasa near Beth-Horon.[27] Victorious, they established their own Jewish state: the kingdom of the Hasmoneans. Their re-dedication of the Temple in Jerusalem and the lighting of the *menorah* is an event still marked by the festival of *Hanukkah*, the Hebrew for 'dedication', the 'Festival of Lights'. From 152 BCE the Hasmoneans became the Temple's high priests, beginning with Jonathan Maccabee (Yonatan Apefus).[28]

Figure 6. A *perutah* minted by John Hyrcanus I, who was the son of Simon Thassi. The inscription in Palaeo-Hebrew on the reverse reads 'Yehohanan the High Priest and the Jews' Council'.

In an adjacent display case at the museum there is a collection of small bronze coins issued by leaders and high priests from this dynasty, among them John Hyrcanus I (Hyrkanos, 135/134–104 BCE, fig. 6) and his son and successor Alexander Jannaeus (103–76 BCE).[29]

In 69 BCE the brothers Aristobulus II and Hyrcanus II squabbled over who should succeed to the Hasmonean throne.[30] Aristobulus moved first and deposed his brother. The Roman commander Cn. Pompeius Magnus, who was in Syria at the time, received deputations from both sides and attempted to broker a settlement. Negotiations stalled, however, and Aristobulus and his supporters escalated tensions when they occupied the Temple in Jerusalem. Roman troops besieged the complex and, taking advantage of the Sabbath, seized it in 63 BCE.[31] Pompeius did something no other gentile had ever done: he went into the Holy of Holies, the holiest rooms of the Temple where the Ark of the Covenant (a gold-covered wooden chest containing the two stone tablets of the Ten Commandments) was kept, and inspected the sacred artefacts inside. Fortunately he disturbed nothing, but it was nevertheless a sacrilegious act by a gentile. When order was restored, the Temple was ritually purified according to Jewish law and Hyrcanus was installed as high priest.[32]

However, from 37 BCE the Romans exerted control of the area through their appointment of Hordos (Herodes) as the approved regent

Figure 7. This reconstruction of the Second Temple in the scale model of Jerusalem at the time of Herod the Great is a highlight of the Israel Museum.

over Judea.[33] Known as Herod the Great, he earned the epithet for his massive building works. It was a passion he shared with his Roman friend M. Agrippa, who was an ally of Jewry.[34] An enthusiast for city planning and engineering works in the Roman style, he enhanced the Temple Mount in Jerusalem by extensively rebuilding it between 25 and 10 BCE.[35] By enclosing the area of the Mount with four massive retaining walls and filling in the voids, Herod greatly extended the natural plateau and created a large flat expanse. Trimmed, rectangular stone blocks weighing many tonnes each were lifted into place using cranes and pulleys powered by the muscle of man and beast.

Herod's architects and engineers aggrandized the Mount with magnificent edifices (fig. 7).[36] The paved plaza was filled with courts and spaces for vendors to sell their wares to visitors, who might swell to 400,000 at Passover. To pay the vendors and the Temple tax required by Jewish law, money-changers exchanged worshippers' Roman and provincial coins for the *Didrachmon* or Tyrian *shekel* – the preferred currency – at designated tables.[37] An inscription carved into a limestone block from the parapet at the south-western corner of the Temple Mount is displayed in the museum. Translated from the Hebrew, it reads 'to the place of trumpeting…', indicating that it originally marked the location where a priest would stand and signal by his shrill trumpet blasts the beginning and ending of *Shabbat*.[38] The *Beit HaMikdash* itself was remodelled with decorated façades, engaged columns and even pinnacles.[39]

Among many cities and constructions, Herod also founded the new port city at Caesarea Maritima, built the palace complex at Masada, refurbished Betar and created a fortified residence-cum-mausoleum at Herodium. Despite a tempestuous family life, his death – an unpleasant one by all accounts – in 4 BCE ended what had been a relatively peaceful period.[40] Fragments from the mausoleum, alongside one of his three sarcophagi carved of reddish limestone, are on show at the Israel Museum.[41] They are surprisingly modest for a man of such great wealth and reputation.

Under Caesar Augustus (27 BCE–14 CE) the district of Judea became a Roman territory, administered by an equestrian-grade military prefect (*praefectus*) reporting to the governor (*legatus Augusti pro praetore*) of Syria.[42] The best-known is Pontius Pilatus. He was the fifth in that office, serving during the years 26 to 36 CE. He is described as a cruel and unsympathetic man, incapable of sensitivity to Jewish religious feelings. The only surviving contemporary inscription mentioning his name and title is in the Israel Museum. Though the stone is damaged, the infamous Roman's name carved into the block can still be picked out.[43]

The political arrangement between Romans and Jews was both uneasy and unpopular.[44] Tensions between them ran high. Jews also fought among each other. In the early years of Roman occupation rival Jewish leaders emerged and frequent rioting between factions required the intervention of Roman army units (which acted as police) to restore order. At this time there were three mainstream Jewish sects: the Pharisees, the Sadducees and the Essenes.[45] The Pharisees, numbering some 6,000 men, were conservative interpreters of the oral Law of Moses, seeing it as the sole source of divine authority, strictly observing the Sabbath and ritual purity; the Sadducees were men of the Jewish elite favouring the written *Torah*; the Essenes, numbering some 4,000, were monastic and apocalyptic in their world view and today known as the scribes of the 'Dead Sea Scrolls'.[46] A fourth sect had arisen called the Zealots (Hebrew: *Biryonim*), apparently founded by Judas of Galilee (also called Judas of Gamala). It seems to have been a religiously-inspired group intent on using violence against the Roman authorities.[47] Under Claudius (reigned 41–54 CE) there was an outbreak in the Galilee led by two sons of Judas, Jacob and Simon. It started in 46 CE and ended two years later when the ringleaders were caught and executed by the prefect of Iudaea.

While the people of the region were bound by a common Covenant, they were still divided along cultural lines.[48] In their use of domestic dining habits or burial preferences, archaeology shows that the urban elite of Jerusalem was quite different from the Jewish communities living in the Galilee, Gaulanitis or Judea. The aristocracy of Jerusalem greatly benefited from its close relationship with the Roman authorities. The *Kohanim Gedolim*, deputies, members of the supreme council and tribunal of the Jews, who together formed the Sanhedrin, lived in the upper part of the city in grand houses, equipped with all the latest modern conveniences and finest quality decor. The museum's collection has a fine ossuary, which once contained (according to the name engraved twice on the outside) the bones of High Priest Yosef, son of Caiaphas (c. 14– c. 46 CE), the same Caiaphas who was involved in the arrest and trial of Jesus of Nazareth.[49]

Silver coins in a glass case in the museum help tell the story of a rebellion that completely transformed the fortunes of Jews in Province Iudaea.[50] Caesarea became the first flashpoint in a major new war.[51] By 66 CE, the important posts of the coastal city's administration were taken by members of the non-Jewish Greek-speaking community. Meanwhile, the local Jewish population had a rented meeting-place in the city. They had tried for some time to buy a building of their own, but all their offers had been rejected by the owner and instead, over time, the property developer deliberately made access to their community centre more difficult by erecting commercial properties around it. The Jews petitioned Gessius Florus, the newly-appointed thirteenth prefect of Iudaea; he did little to intervene, but accepted their money nevertheless, 'then went away from Caesarea to Sebaste, and left the sedition to take its full course, as if he had sold a licence to the Jews to fight it out.'[52]

It took just one act of provocation. A pagan stood in front of the entrance to the Jewish meeting room, placed an earthenware pot on the ground and began sacrificing birds. The Jews were affronted by the blatant act of disrespect as it both polluted the place and transgressed their law.[53] Incensed by the insult, part of the offended group began remonstrating with the provocateur while another part left and sought the intervention of the Roman authorities. A Roman garrison commander, Iucundus, arrived and removed the offending pot but the damage was done. Rioting crowds overwhelmed the Romans. A deputation went to Florus for help, but the others evacuated the city and moved to another town, Narbata. Hearing of the slight, in retaliation one of the Jewish temple clerks named Eleazar Ben Hanania suspended offering prayers and sacrifices for the safety and wellbeing of the emperor at the Temple.[54]

Meanwhile, desperate for cash to fund his extravagant projects, Emperor Nero (reigned 54–68 CE) authorized his official representative to rob the Temple in Jerusalem of its riches. Florus felt insulted when some jokers carried around a basket and asked for donations for the governor who, they said, 'was destitute of possessions and in a miserable condition'.[55] Florus demanded the offenders be handed over, but when the city's population did not co-operate and his guards could not find them, he allowed the arrest and execution of people randomly hauled off the streets of Jerusalem. The patience of the local population snapped. In the autumn of 66 CE factions of the city's Jews united and butchered the Roman garrison.

Sent to deal with the popular uprising was Cestius Gallus, the propraetorian legate of Syria. His army was overwhelmed at Beth Horon – the very place where Judah Maccabbee defeated the Seleucid forces. The 'First Jewish War' had begun in earnest. The rebels established their own administration, exercised justice according to Jewish principles, and began minting coins. Rebel moneyers overstruck the silver Tyrian and Roman coins in the Temple strongboxes with their own symbols and messages. Many survive. On one side sacred objects appear, like chalices or the symbols of *Sukkot*, the closed frond of a date palm tree (Hebrew: *lulav*) and citron (*etrog*); on the other Hebrew inscriptions proudly announce '*Shekel* of Israel' (fig. 8), 'Jerusalem the Holy', 'The Freedom of Zion' or 'For the Redemption of Zion'.[56] These precious tokens with their messages of resistance sparkled under the museum's spotlights.

Emperor Nero dispatched Flavius Vespasianus to squash the rebellion. He was a battle-tested commander with a track record of success, including command of a legion during the invasion of Britannia two decades before. Joined by his son, Titus, working together the legates executed counterinsurgency operations in Iudaea. At the height of the war, they had under their command six full legions supplemented with auxiliary cohorts and contingents from up to six more legions, for a total force of perhaps 60,000 professional men-at-arms.[57] The rebels numbered

Figure 8. This coin was minted by the Jewish rebels during 66/67 CE of the First Jewish War. The legend in Palaeo-Hebrew on the obverse translates as '*Shekel* of Israel' surrounding a ritual chalice, with '[Year] One' above. On the reverse 'Jerusalem [the] Holy' surrounds a staff with three pomegranate buds.

an estimated 45,000 men, most of whom were non-professional, recruited from among the urban populations and peasantry.[58]

The Romans adopted a 'seek-and-destroy' strategy. Starting in the Galilee, the Roman army fanned out across the country, moving south. Whenever the Jews stayed within their walled strongholds, the Romans besieged them. At Jotapata (Yodfat) one of the rebel generals leading Jewish forces was Yosef Ben Matityahu. After forty-seven days the Romans took the fortified town and slaughtered the inhabitants. One of only two people to survive, Ben Matityahu was presented to Vespasian.[59] After hearing his story and prophesying great things for the Roman commander, the Jew was spared. He adopted the Roman name Flavius Josephus and wrote the most complete account of the Jewish War.

Titus reached Jerusalem in April 70 CE. The Roman army encircled the city with a circumvallation, established artillery positions and settled in for a long siege. The Jews and their leaders – among them Shim'on Bar Giora and Yohanan Ben Levi (John of Gischala) – resisted.[60] Having bombarded the city's walls with heavy ballista stones, on the 9th day of *Ab* (29 August) the Romans burst onto the Mount and pillaged the Temple.[61] The Ark of the Covenant was taken. Roman troops carried away the gold *menorah* and sacred artefacts to be star attractions in the great triumphal procession in Rome; an image of the event can still be seen carved on the Arch of Titus in the Roman Forum. Finally, they set the building alight. As its burning sacred timbers fell, the rebel state collapsed. One day – *Tisha B'Ab* – now marked two *churbanim*.[62]

In the aftermath the Roman soldiers desecrated the Mount, levering off many of the great blocks of stone laid by Herod's builders. The chunk of stone bearing the trumpet inscription was one of these; it was toppled from the parapet at the south-western corner of the Temple Mount and crashed down onto the street below. Three or four years later men under Flavius Silva's command surrounded Masada, then held by Eleazar Ben Simon and his rebels, and after a siege, seized it.[63] The only remains to have been found in the archaeological excavations at Masada are on display at the Israel Museum: they are the personal belongings of a man, a woman and a child, and a woman's braid.[64]

The casualties of the First Jewish War were appalling, but many of the living now found themselves enslaved:

The number of those that were carried captive during this whole war was collected to be 97,000; as was the number of those that perished during the whole siege (1,100,000), the greater part of whom were indeed of the same nation [with the citizens of Jerusalem], but not belonging to the city itself; for they were come up from all the country.[65]

Josephus wildly exaggerates the numbers; nevertheless, the impact on the small province was severe.[66]

After the capture of Jerusalem, Iudaea became a consular province independent of Syria. Its governor was now a *legatus Augusti pro praetore* with *Legio* X *Fretensis* at his disposal.[67] Following the War of Quietus around 115/116 CE, Province Iudaea was further upgraded in status.[68] A second legion – *Legio* II *Traiana Fortis* – established its base in the area to ensure there would be no further resistance.[69]

In the museum collection is indisputable evidence of the presence of *Legio* X *Fretensis* which set up camp in – or close by – the ruins of Jerusalem. One inscription marks the work done by a particular army unit. It is carved into a slab of limestone and reads '*Legio* X, *Cohors* IIX' (I noted with interest the novel use of 'IIX', rather than 'VIII', for the number '8').[70] Another inscription is more personal. It is dedicated to Ti. Claudius Fatalis, who held the rank of centurion *tertius hastatus* in *Legio* X *Fretensis*.[71] He was a native of the city of Rome who enrolled in the army when 19 years old. His career included service with legions stationed in Britannia, Pannonia Superior, Moesia Inferior and Cappadocia before finally arriving in Province Iudaea. He had found love in his final posting. The stela was erected by Claudia Ionice, the woman he freed from slavery and then married. He died young, aged just 42.

There are examples of Roman arms and armour too. On the shelf of a display case is a lump of rusted metal (plate 8), but closer inspection reveals it to be a coat of chain mail (Latin: *lorica hamata*), each link closed with a tiny rivet.[72] There are examples of contemporary weaponry (plate 9). There is the corroded blade of a short, two-edged sword (*gladius*) for close-quarter stabbing and thrusting, and once the pride and joy of a legionary soldier. A longer version lies below it. It is a *spatha* used by a cavalryman. Reported to have come from Mount Zion, Jerusalem, it is remarkable for still being in its scabbard (*vagina*), complete with the rings for attachment to the baldric. There is a complete legionary helmet (plate 10), also in remarkable condition. The trademark design, with integral neck-guard, brow-guard and articulated cheek-plates, features riveted cross-bars to strengthen the dome from direct blows to the head. It is often referred to as the 'Hebron Helmet', but the information card beside it reveals that it is actually unprovenanced.[73] This particular helmet is one of the most reproduced items of Roman military kit in books on ancient warfare. In the same display case is a particularly eye-catching helmet with a visor shaped like a young man's clean-shaven face.[74] There are slits in the eyes. The dome of the helmet is moulded to look like a mop of hair with thick curls, all realistically cast in bronze. It would have been worn by a cavalryman during military sports tournaments or parades.

Curiously, Josephus' prophecy came true. While in Judea, legate Vespasian had since become commander-in-chief (*imperator*, 22 December 69 CE). Promoting his military achievements, his new administration issued coins celebrating his victory over the Jewish rebels. The image on the obverse shows the distinct profile of the new emperor surrounded by his imperial titles and acclamations. The image on the reverse is pure propaganda. A distressed, wailing Jewish woman stands beside a palm tree. A gold piece (*aureus*) bears the message *IUDAEA RECEPTA* ('Iudaea Reconquered').[75] The coin was issued immediately after the fall of Jerusalem. It communicated unequivocally the *re*-subjugation of an old province and the crushing of an impudent people with their unconditional surrender. In the much more common depictions struck on lower denomination coins, the wailing Jewish woman sits dejected and a Roman commander stands over her. The inscriptions in Latin declare *IUDAEA CAPTA* ('[Province] Iudaea Conquered', fig. 9), *IUDAEA DEVICTA* ('Iudaea Defeated'), as well as *DE IUDAEIS* ('[Booty] from the Iudaeans'). The war spoils paid for a fabulous new public entertainment venue right in the centre of Rome: the *Amphitheatrum Flavium*, better known today as the Colosseum.[76] When Vespasian died his son Titus succeeded him and, when his turn came, his brother Domitian. As long as the Flavians ruled, Roman mints churned out '*Iudaea Capta*' coins, both to celebrate the family's consequential achievement and to intimidate other provincials who might be tempted to challenge their authority.

After a revolt, the Romans looked to those responsible to be punished with what has since been called a 'war indemnity'.[77] This might include

Figure 9. A *sestertius* minted after the First Jewish War by Vespasian bears the legend 'Iudea Capta' celebrating the capture of rebel Judea. Beneath a date palm, a bearded Jewish prisoner of war stands with his hands bound behind his back in front of a pile of weapons, while the personification of the Jewish province is shown in a gesture of mourning, seated upon a discarded cuirass.

crucifixion or enslavement for the offenders. Uniquely, a tax was imposed on Jews, collected by the *Fiscus Iudaicus* or 'Jewish Treasury'.[78] The tax penalty was exclusively imposed on Jews and all those actively living the 'Jewish life', by birth or conversion, who had supported the uprising, regardless of whether they were in Judea or the diaspora at the time; those who did not so identify were theoretically spared its imposition.[79] However, deciding who should pay could be troublesome:

> Besides other taxes, that on the Jews was levied with the utmost rigour, and those were prosecuted who without publicly acknowledging that faith yet lived as Jews, as well as those who concealed their origin and did not pay the tribute levied upon their people. I recall being present in my youth when the person of a man 90 years old was examined before the procurator and a very crowded court, to see whether he was circumcised.[80]

In effect, the tax previously paid by devout Jews to their Temple in fulfilment of the Covenant was renamed the Jewish Tax and deemed to be an ongoing war spoil. The proceeds went for the upkeep of the most important of Roman buildings, the Temple of Iuppiter Capitolinus right in the heart of Rome.

The destruction of the Second Temple in 70 CE changed Judaism forever. The required sacrificial rites and liturgies could no longer be performed; the blasts of the trumpets and *shofar* could be heard no more from the Temple Mount. As a direct consequence, there was no need for *kohanim* and clergy. The prominence of the Pharisees and Sadducees ceased; the Essenes also vanished.[81] Annual pilgrimages to Jerusalem were no longer possible, or even necessary.[82] With the Temple gone it seemed that an 'iron wall' now separated *Yahweh* from his 'Chosen People'.[83]

As I wandered from the gallery in search of coffee – museum visits can be thirsty work – I wondered what happened next. My question was soon answered. After the destruction of the Temple, the synagogue became the focal point of Jewish life. The Israel Museum has four full-scale, historic synagogues in its collection.[84] They each have the recognizable features of a synagogue. The centrepiece is the *aron hakodesh* or 'Holy Ark' where the *Torah* scroll is kept.[85] In front of it is the *bimah*, the raised platform from where the *Torah* is read and some services are delivered. Seats – if there are any – are arranged to keep men and women congregants apart. These are relatively modern developments, however. There had been meeting-places in towns with Jewish communities all over the Roman Empire – and outside it – even when the Temple stood; indeed, they date as far back as the exile in Babylon.[86] 'Synagogue' is actually a Greek word meaning 'place of assembly'; the Hebrew is *beit knesset*, meaning 'house of gathering'. First- and second-century synagogues had no uniform design or floor plan. Their purpose was to provide a place to study religious texts or just to bring Jewish people together. It was more like an informal bible study group meeting at someone's home rather than the elaborate building with its formal services of the later kind re-assembled in the Israel Museum.[87]

The Jews are known as 'People of the Book'. Writing around 94 CE, Josephus notes:

> We have not an innumerable multitude of books among us, disagreeing from, and contradicting one another [as the Greeks have], but only twenty-two books, which contain the records of all the past times, which are justly believed to be divine.[88]

Here he is referring to *Tanakh*, a word comprising the first letter of each of the three traditional subdivisions of the authoritative Hebrew and

Aramaic Texts: *Torah* ('Teaching'), *Nevi'im* ('Prophets') and *Ketuvim* ('Writings'). He explains:

> And of them five belong to Moses, which contain his laws, and the traditions of the origin of mankind, 'till his death. …The Prophets, who were after Moses, wrote down what was done in their times, in thirteen books. The remaining four books contain hymns to God; and precepts for the conduct of human life.[89]

Studying these texts was – and still is – an intrinsic part of being a practising Jew. Josephus observes:

> And how firmly we have given credit to these books of our own nation, is evident by what we do. …It is become natural to all Jews, immediately, and from their very birth, to esteem these books to contain divine doctrines; and to persist in them: and, if occasion be, willingly to die for them.[90]

One man reading the *Tanakh* might derive different insights to another reading the same text and interpret its meaning differently. There were even Jews who believed that, based on their reading of the Book of Daniel, there was not one true god but *two*.[91] The challenge of living by the *Torah* was that many of the codes and rules that were derived from it – such as on purity or intermarriage – were unclear or contradictory. Thus, there was a need for experts to offer interpretations and make rulings.[92] This has been the job of Temple priests, along with conducting sacrifices. After the war of 66–73 CE the Pharisaic Sanhedrin had been all but disbanded as the supreme authority over legal, legislative and political matters affecting the Jewish people.[93] Province Iudaea lived under a mix of common law based on *Halakhah* (the body of Jewish religious laws derived from the written and oral *Torah*), exercised through Jewish courts, with the Sanhedrin as the supreme court, overlaid by a legal system partly dating from the Seleucid era, augmented with contemporary Roman jurisprudence.[94]

The post-Jerusalem Temple era was an opportunity for an emerging group of teachers of the texts called rabbis. Think of Judaism and the word 'rabbi' surely comes to mind; it is a quintessentially Jewish occupation. The Hebrew word *rabbi* actually means 'my master'. The surprise is that the rabbis have no authority based in the Bible.[95] They may have arisen from among the scribes of village synagogues, but they do not seem to have been identified with the Pharisees. In the mid-first century they were a marginal group and, to some, they might even have seemed to be a sect.[96] With the unifying political and judicial infrastructure established around the Temple now gone, Judaism faced the real prospect of fracturing into myriad sects unless someone seized the opportunity, gave it direction and asserted their authority.[97]

That man was Rabbi Yochanan Ben Zakkai (c. 30 CE–c. 90 CE). There is a story in the rabbinic texts that during the siege of Jerusalem, the extreme Zealots seized a store of food and firewood that had been gathered over decades and destroyed it, thereby forcing their fellow countrymen to choose between certain death by starvation or resisting the Romans and the chance to live.[98] Realizing the prospects for the city were bleak, the rabbi made a plan to leave and attempt to negotiate with the Romans. By feigning his death and being carried out in a coffin for burial beyond the walls, Ben Zakkai succeeded in leaving the city. At a legionary camp he met Vespasian.[99] At the same time a messenger arrived to inform the commander that the emperor was dead and that *he* was the successor. Now emperor, Vespasian granted the rabbi a request. Ben Zakkai asked him to guarantee the safety of Jewish scholars gathering at Iamnia (modern Yavneh). The emperor consented.[100] It is a good story and whatever the historical truth, it was in the 'house of study' (*beit midrash*) at Yavneh that Judaism would be re-created for the post-Temple world.[101]

Ben Zakkai's teachings affected crucial aspects of Jewish religious life.[102] He taught his students that acts of kindness atoned just as meaningfully as sacrifices once did in the Temple. He entreated them that studying *Torah* was a key purpose of a good man and an essential way for him to serve God. He ordained that many of the rituals and regulations formerly confined to the Temple should now be adopted more broadly. He also maintained that authorized scholars of the sages and rabbis could make basic decisions regarding practice and instruction wherever circumstances compelled them to sit in session.[103] The rabbis had begun their grab for power.[104]

Ben Zakkai left Yavneh and founded a new study group at Bror Hayil when Rabban Gamaliel II arrived.[105] He was the son of Shimon Ben Gamaliel I, the last leader or president (*nasi*) of the Sanhedrin in the last war.[106] The arrangement suited the Romans who sought stability and order first and foremost. Any proclamation Gamaliel issued to improve life among Jews required Roman approval, likely that of the imperial

Figure 10. Emperor Nerva closed the 'Jewish Treasury', the repository of the proceeds from the punitive tax on Jews which provided revenue to repair and maintain the temples on the Capitoline Hill in Rome.

propraetorian legate.[107] When Domitian died, an independent-minded senator named Cocceius Nerva took his place. One of his first acts in 96 CE was to address an old injustice. 'No persons were permitted to accuse anybody of adopting the Jewish mode of life,' writes Cassius Dio.[108] It was considered such an important reform that it was celebrated on coins. *FISCI IVDAICI CALVMNIA SVBLATA*, 'the wrongful accusation of the Jewish Tax [or Treasury of Iudaea] is removed', proclaims the legend on a *sestertius* minted that year (fig. 10).[109] Scholars still debate the precise meaning of the text. One interpretation is that not only those living the Jewish lifestyle or non-devout Jews – such as the new gentile Christians or Christians living according to the Laws of Moses – would no longer have to pay the special tax or be subjected to public embarrassment to prove their status, but any and all Jews were exempted.[110]

Though Gamaliel was from the House of Hillel, a family considered Jewish royalty, he nevertheless worked hard to prevent a split in the community. There were many arguments, and passions ran high. Indeed, it was said that students of Hillel and Shammai argued so forcefully against each other that they would 'make the *Torah* into two *Torot*'.[111] Gamaliel's historic contribution to Judaism was to reject the teachings of the scholar Shammai championed by Rabbi Eliezer Ben Hyrcanus, and to centralize and unify Judaism around the version of Hillel the Elder.[112] One outcome was agreement about the manner of prayer to ensure uniformity in the act of worship.[113]

Yet there were strains among the men gathered at Yavneh. One of the first men to challenge Gamaliel's authority was Rabbi Akiba Ben Yosef.[114] Of his background next to nothing is known: the details of the year he was born, his birthplace, his parentage and early life are all lost to history and the truth may never be known.[115] Some speculate that he was born around 50 CE, making him a young man when the destruction of the Second Temple occurred. There are stories about him in both Babylonian and Jerusalem versions of *Talmud*, but they cannot be independently verified.[116] One version tells the story that, one day, when aged 40 with a wife and son and still an illiterate and uneducated man, he stood at a well, contemplated his life and decided there and then to devote himself to studying *Torah*.[117] The motivation was, according to one tradition, the mythic Prophet Elijah who visited him and his wife, after which she said to Akiba, 'Go – be a rabbi.'[118] Thereafter he studied with Rabbi Eliezer and Rabbi Joshua for twelve years. After twenty-four years had passed, so the tale goes, he returned to his wife.[119]

Traditional Pharisaic Judaism was backward-looking. Reforming it was not enough for Akiba: he wanted a revolution.[120] Where the Pharisees had derived their power and influence from their positions in government, and the Sadducees theirs through the Temple, its institutions and rituals, the rabbinic sages would become the ultimate authority on *Torah* because they were the means by which Jews could understand it.[121] The rabbis claimed authority over oral *Torah* – the national law given by God – and determined what it did and did not allow in every aspect of life, from marriage to money.[122] Akiba argued with his peers for his vision of Judaism to prevail; as the compiler and editor of *Talmud* he selected or rejected material from what was available as it suited his purposes, making it canonical in its own right, and in doing so he created rabbinic Judaism and made *Talmud* the declaration of its authority.[123] In the post-Temple era, Jews would need to be mindful to obey *rabbinic* laws and regulations, which were often more stringent than *Torah*.[124] Law was not made in Heaven but by rabbis on Earth; *their* word was the Law.[125] Eventually rabbis would replace the Temple priests and daily rabbinic services at synagogues would take the place of Temple observances and liturgies.[126] The rabbis would also assume the role of prophets, and even decide when the messiah had come.[127]

In the meantime, Akiba had assembled a large following of students. His stature as a rabbinic scholar had increased substantially, causing tensions at times with his own teacher Rabbi Eliezer.[128] A star pupil, Akiba was eager to learn and was reputed to be forgiving and modest, though he could sometimes appear to lack compassion.[129] Strong-willed, confident and resolute, Akiba knew his own mind and was unimpressed by social status or personal wealth. What mattered to him was the *Torah*. Gamaliel recognized Akiba's great intellect, which he came to see first-hand before and during a visit to Rome; he even learned to respect his tendency to question convention and rebel against it.[130]

Akiba's lasting contribution to Judaism would be to create a new method of interpreting Jewish oral law by systematizing the *Halakha*.[131] He arranged the works of interpretative material on the oral *Torah* into what would become the *Midrash* (meaning 'textual interpretation', a body of rabbinic commentaries seeking to clarify ambiguities in the Hebrew Bible) and the *Mishnah* (meaning 'study by repetition', the first authoritative written collection of the oral traditions).[132]

We are told that Rabbi Akiba left Yavneh to lead a *beit midrash* of his own at Bene Berak near Jaffa.[133] By the time of Gamaliel's death in 114 CE, there was a small network of *Torah* study groups in villages and towns across Iudaea, each led by a rabbi having a personal connection directly to a sage at Yavneh.[134] This network of rabbi-led groups embedded in communities in Province Iudaea would help them assert their influence and power throughout the province.[135] It would be no easy task. In 130 CE they were few in number, perhaps less than sixty individuals operating in Iudaea at this time, and they had limited influence.[136] The rabbis would have to earn acceptance of their authority in a country where most Jews did not recognize it.[137]

Leaving the Israel Museum, I realized that on the eve of Hadrian's state visit in 130 CE the pain of the First Jewish War was still felt, and the evidence of destruction of that time was visible. The future of mainstream Judaism in Iudaea without the Temple still seemed uncertain. The old power structure was in disarray. A small but motivated group of rabbis sought to take the lead in shaping its future, but their success was not assured. Resentments between Jews and non-Jews remained. For many people life was still a daily struggle, made harder by the demands of the imperial administration and the presence of outsiders enforcing their rules. They were the same circumstances that had led to rebellion before, only now they were much worse.

Chapter 3

'At Jerusalem He Founded a City'

Nineteen centuries before I arrived in Israel by air, Hadrian had entered the region by road. He often travelled by sea, but the itinerary for this leg of his trip called for a route overland. I imagined that he was very likely to have been the cause of congestion on many an ancient road. Like any modern head of state, a virtual mobile city accompanied him on his official journeys. He travelled with thousands of men and women. Along with his close travel companions Sabina and Antinous was an imperial entourage: hand-picked adjutants, secretaries and physician; the emperor's security detail of Household Cavalry (*Equites Singulares Augusti*) and two – or more likely four – Praetorian Cohorts, perhaps up to 5,000 men combined; a constant stream of messengers bringing official correspondence from Rome and taking back his written replies; and slaves of every kind, some attending to the imperial family's personal needs, including his barber, cooks and servers, porters for carrying their baggage, and others for minding the pack animals and driving the carriages and waggons.[1]

Travel in the Roman world was time-consuming and dangers lurked. Going by sea meant having to plan to arrive at a destination before the shipping lanes were effectively closed in late autumn and winter. Hadrian had left Rome in early 128 CE, boarding a galley at Portus and traversed the Mediterranean Sea – *Mare Nostrum*, 'Our Sea', as the confident Romans thought of it – to reach Africa. Having completed his business there, he sailed to Athens where he spent the winter months. While in the Greek city he dedicated the new Temple to Olympian Zeus (*Olympiou Deos*) that he had ordered to be finished during his last visit and an altar erected in his name.[2] Afterwards, long a benefactor of the city, Hadrian accepted the title 'Olympios' and received divine honours in the Temple.[3] At Eleusis just outside Athens in September of that year, he and Antinous were initiated into the ancient cult of Demeter and Persephone.[4] The following spring, Hadrian, his boy and his retinue departed for Asia, crisscrossing Anatolia to visit the provinces of Pamphylia, Phrygia, Cilicia, Syria, Commagene, Cappadocia (where he received slaves for service with the army), Pontus and Syria again.[5] He is known to have been in Apamea in Phrygia on 23 July 129 CE.[6] Always the disciplinarian, 'as he went about the provinces, he punished procurators and governors as their actions demanded, and indeed with such severity that it was believed that he incited those who brought the accusations.'[7]

As political and military leader of the *Res Publica* – or 'Commonwealth' – he diligently conducted his duties by befriending kings and potentates from beyond the frontiers, with whom he exchanged diplomatic gifts, and exercised his civic duties when he met with local dignitaries from communities within the borders. Now twelve years into his reign, he would reward loyalty with benefactions and exert the soft power that his presence brought to any who wavered.[8]

Hadrian visited Palmyra, the exotic, semi-autonomous city on the border of his empire. An ancient Las Vegas located in the Syrian Desert, its economic prosperity depended on the trade passing between the neighbouring Roman and Parthian superpowers.[9] Despite the precariousness of its position, the Palmyrene community was plenty wealthy and enjoyed a hedonistic lifestyle. Hadrian was fortunate to visit it in its heyday during happy times. The people welcomed him as a 'second founder' of their famous city and renamed it *Hadriana* Palmyra in his honour.[10] In response, he declared Palmyra a 'free city' and assigned an officer (*curator*) to manage the treasury. It was a truly impressive place, blending Greek and Roman architecture for its public spaces with local Arabic styles for its domestic residences. Even in its ruined state, it has become a major tourist attraction in Syria in modern times. People have wandered upon the paved stones of its Colonnade Street, admired the wedge-shaped triumphal arch, given impromptu performances in its theatre to test out its acoustics, and ogled at the gigantic Temple of Zeus or Baal Shamin set in its vast peristyle sanctuary (originally paid for by Hadrian).[11] That stopped abruptly when the terrorist group DAESH/ ISIS seized the archaeological park, systematically destroyed its precious artefacts with hammers and explosives, and on 15 August 2015 murdered Khaled al-Asaad who had devoted his life to preserving its legacy.[12]

The precise sequence of cities Hadrian called on during 129 CE is uncertain, despite years of careful study by scholars.[13] He likely stopped at Antiocheia on the Orontes (modern Antakya, Turkey) in Syria in or after July.[14] It is recorded that the city celebrated a *panegyris Hadriane*, a 'Hadrianic festival' in his honour.[15] One of the largest and most sophisticated cities of the empire, many high-ranking Romans before him had sojourned there when touring the eastern part of the empire; Hadrian himself last visited in 117 CE.[16] Since his decision to pull back the frontier to the Euphrates River, the city of Antiocheia had become the administrative centre of the East, the *de facto* second capital of the Roman Empire.[17]

Archaeology provides some clues about his onward itinerary. From Syria he certainly passed through Roman Arabia. Coins were minted, inscribed with the message *ADVENTUI AUG(USTI) ARABIAE*, 'Augustus' Arrival in Arabia', using his honorific title.[18] His *legatus* in Arabia was T. Haterius Nepos who, as a courtesy, would certainly have met up with Hadrian and accompanied him on at least part of the journey. The imperial train may have stopped at Damascus, though this is undocumented. An inspection of *Legio* III *Cyrenaica* at its military base at Bostra (Bostra al-Sham) is possible, even likely given that Hadrian was commander-in-chief, but there is no direct evidence for it. Continuing southwards, the party would have reached Gerasa (Jerash). A visit by him in person to this city is suggested by an inscription dated to the autumn into the winter of 129 CE.[19] The inscription states that the *Equites Singulares Augusti* wintered there, which would strongly imply that Hadrian was in Gerasa as well.[20] So enthralled were the town's citizens by the emperor's visit and so willing to advertise to the world their loyalty and commitment to the great leader that they erected a monumental triumphal arch, which still stands almost 21 metres (68.9ft) tall.[21] Even in its ruined state, this ancient city – now in Jordan – can take your breath away. With paved streets impressively lined with decorative columns, it boasted a unique oval forum, a theatre, baths, public fountains and temples. The city appealed to his cultural sensibilities and he decided to stay there for the winter.[22] Leaving the city in the spring of 130 CE, the emperor's entourage trekked south, reaching Philadelphia and perhaps Petra too.[23] Then the imperial caravan must have turned west.

In the early months of 130 CE, Hadrian's retinue was in Province Iudaea. It was then a minor province, covering roughly the same area as the island of Sardinia or the state of New Hampshire; it was squeezed between Syria in the north, the Mediterranean Sea in the west and Arabia Petraea in the

Figure 11. A *sestertius* minted 130–133 CE by Hadrian celebrates the arrival of the emperor in Province Iudaea. He is shown standing beside an altar, raising his right hand and holding a scroll in his left hand, facing the personification of Iudaea who is surrounded by boys carrying palm fronds.

south and east. As Hadrian travelled through the province, the citizens of the towns turned out to welcome him. Many received benefactions, which was cause for celebration. Marking his visit to the province, commemorative coins were struck by decree of the Roman Senate and bore the legend *ADVENTUI AUG(USTI) IUDAEAE*, 'Augustus' Arrival in Iudaea' (fig. 11).[24] The image in the centre of the coin is Hadrian wearing a *toga* standing before an altar while a lady, standing opposite him, makes a ritual offering. Three small children stand beside her, each holding a palm frond. The woman is the personification of Province Iudaea and the scene evokes the unity of the emperor with his subjects in appeasing the gods.

Eventually he reached the provincial capital. Formerly Caesarea Maritima, after the First Jewish War Vespasian and Titus re-established it as *Colonia* Prima Flavia Augusta Caesarea, indicating that it was the first of its kind in Iudaea.[25] A *colonia* was a specific type of urban settlement founded under the *ius Italicum*, a privilege set in law granted to a few select communities in the provinces which treated their land as if it were in Italy. It was normally intended for honorably discharged legionary troops, where each man received a tract of land to farm or a lump sum in cash (*praemia*) in lieu, on which they were exempted from paying land taxes; Caesarea had not originally been inhabited by retired soldiers.[26] A *colonia* was also a microcosm of the *Res Publica* of Rome itself. It was a self-governing community with magistrates – *duumviri, aediles* and *decuriones* – having term-limited roles and responsibilities clearly defined in law, each elected by the male Roman citizens from within its constituency.[27] The first such city had been established in Italy, but with expansion of Roman dominion *coloniae* were carefully sited all over the empire, especially in provinces or in border country still undergoing pacification. The retired soldiers living there would be informal ambassadors of Rome, promoting the Roman way of life, speaking the empire's official languages of Latin or Greek, developing the local economy with an infusion of money and raising families – perhaps fathering sons who would follow in their hobnail-booted footsteps to join the legions in their own right. In the event of an insurgency among the local indigenous population, the city's Roman inhabitants would readily defend what was theirs and had the training and experience to do so.[28]

The high standard of living enjoyed by the city's inhabitants is still evident, as I found out when visiting the archaeological park myself on a boiling hot June day.[29] Caesarea had been founded and developed by Herod the Great in 22 BCE. He chose an excellent location for his port city right on the edge of the coast (plate 11). When Herod built, he built on a grand scale. He constructed a deep-sea harbour, creating moles out of hydraulic concrete, an amazing material that actually hardened in sea water.[30] Projecting out into the azure-blue Mediterranean, they provided shipping with a safe berth for stevedores to unload and load the cargoes. The handiwork of the king's civil engineers can still be seen submerged beneath the salty foam when the crashing waves recede.[31]

Beside the harbour, with its arrays of warehouses, was the city itself. Caesarea grew rich on the back of international trade.[32] It was an example of how a Roman city was supposed to work. Laid out in a grid pattern, the streets formed blocks (Latin: *insulae*) for residential and commercial buildings, as well as public spaces and temples, all within a defensive city wall. It might once have been home to 100,000 people.[33] The streets were paved with low-maintenance flagstones on top, while drains beneath carried wastewater and raw sewage away from the city into the sea. Fresh water was brought over a raised aqueduct to a distribution point on the north-east of the city from the springs at Shummi, located on the southern side of Mount Carmel about 10 kilometres (6 mi.) away.[34] Complete arches, which supported the lead-lined channel carrying the water, can

Figure 12. The aqueduct at Caesarea was maintained by men of the legions stationed in the province. It brought fresh water to the seaport city, which was the administrative capital of Iudaea.

still be seen (fig. 12). The arcade constructed of hand-trimmed blocks emerges out of a beach of finest sand, ending abruptly at a tarmacked area where sunbathers nowadays leave their cars. At its maximum extent, the aqueduct continued on to the city where the water was distributed through underground pipes of clay or wood to public fountains, bath-houses and the homes of the wealthy in the city.

Running water was just one of Caesarea's many public amenities. In the city there was a hippodrome, a long racetrack with stadium seating running north-south along the coast.[35] Here the population thrilled as they watched chariot races and athletic competitions. Outside the city there was an amphitheatre where spectators could watch the Roman blood sports of gladiatorial combats and wild beast hunts.[36] On the other side of town there was a theatre with tiered seating. Up to 4,000 spectators could comfortably attend live performances of dramas, comedies and pantomimes (a favourite form of entertainment among Romans).[37] Some 2,000 years later concerts are played here in the summer months by local and international singers and musicians against the dramatic azure-blue backdrop of the Mediterranean Sea and the radiant glow of the setting sun.

In Caesarea the imperial legate occupied the *praetorium*. Rectangular in shape and arranged around two inner courtyards, by 130 CE it was an office complex covering some 12,000 square metres (129,167 sq ft), about the area of one and a half football pitches. The upper building was expanded on its eastern side to add more space. The legate's private suite in the lower building, formerly the summer palace of the king, was built on a concrete promontory projecting into the sea.[38] The foundations are still visible when the tide recedes. Though now a ruin, armed with a floor plan and a little imagination it is possible to reconstruct the building in its former glory. The dining rooms, baths and bedrooms were once colourfully decorated with painted walls and their floors were covered with mosaics. A semi-circular room with a colonnade and a balustrade once offered a breathtaking panoramic view of the sea. The constant splash of waves against the rocks below provided an ambient soundtrack to life, while cooling, negative ion-rich breezes coming off the sea provided relief from the heat in an age without air conditioning. There was even a freshwater pool for swimming. It was an ideal place in which a busy governor could relax after a hard day at the office or touring his province. Amidst this opulence Hadrian sojourned. We know he did so because an inscription and statue to honour his visit was set up by the *beneficiarii* working in the office of the governor (*officium consularis*).[39]

At the time of his visit, Hadrian's representative in Province Iudaea was Q. Tineius Rufus.[40] A *consul suffectus* in 127 CE, Rufus had been recently appointed to the position.[41] He commanded an army – and a disproportionately large one at that for such a small province – of some 11,200 men-at-arms, assuming the two legions were at full strength. Replacing *Legio* II *Traiana Fortis* around 120 CE, *Legio* VI *Ferrata* was now stationed at Tel Shalem in the Beth Shean Valley where it could patrol northern Iudaea; *Legio* X *Fretensis* was still encamped in or near Jerusalem, from where it could patrol southern Iudaea.[42] The highly-trained, heavily-armed legionaries undertook the more demanding tasks required for ongoing pacification and assimilation, but also carried out police work. Many literate and numerate men of these legions were seconded to work in the *praetorium*, providing Rufus with an all-military staff to run his administration.[43] Others better suited to physical work undertook the construction or repair of the public infrastructure such as the aqueducts or roads. Additionally, there were several auxiliary units,

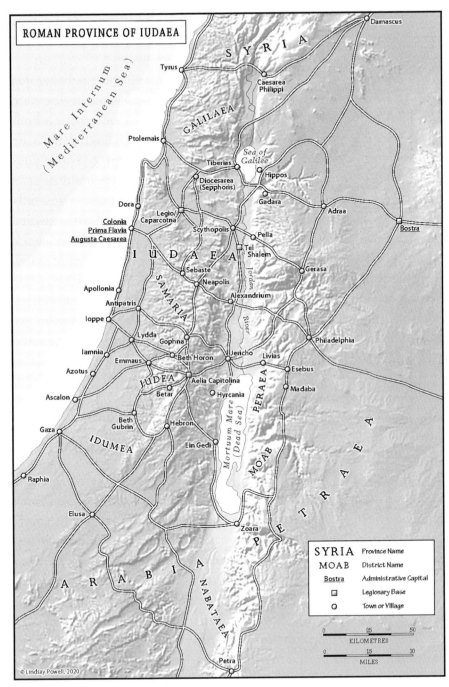

Map 2. Roman Province of Iudaea. (© *Lindsay Powell*)

non-citizen troops who performed security duties operating from forts located around the province. Among them were units of Thracian infantry and combined Gallic and Thracian cavalry and archers.

In Province Iudaea all roads led to Caesarea (map 2).[44] They connected it to the urban centres of its three administrative districts. In the north roads linked Caesarea to the affluent cities of the district of Galilaea (Galilee); among them Diocaesarea (modern Zippori), and Tiberias on the shores of the Sea of Galilee (Kinneret), and eastwards to Scythopolis (Beth Shean) and Gerasa (Jersah in Jordan).[45] In the central district of Samaria, a road connected Caesarea with Sebaste (Sebastia) and Flavia Neapolis (Shechem, modern Nablus).[46] Here native Samaritans mixed with Jews and Christians who all believed in one god and lived alongside others believing in many gods. Though they shared the tribal patriarch Abraham with the Jews, the Samaritans claimed theirs to be the true religion of the ancient Israelites.[47] On the hill of Gerizim, near Shechem, stood the remains of their holy temple.[48] It had been destroyed in the second century BCE and never rebuilt. A long-standing enmity existed between Jews and Samaritans. The Samaritans often sided with enemies of the Jews and *vice versa*. Hadrian would almost certainly have been briefed on local sentiments in advance.

South of Samaria, bordered in the east by the Dead Sea, was the district of Judea. Consulting a map of roads in Roman times, I saw that the road along the Mediterranean coast (the region of Philistia in the Bible) linked Caesarea with the cities of Apollonia (Arsuf), Ioppe (Yafo), Azotus (Ashdod), Ascalon (Ashkelon) and Gaza (Gaza City). A highway ran inland to connect Antipatris (Rosh ha-Ayyin), Lydda (Lod), Hebron, Jerusalem and Hierichous (Jericho).[49] A series of local roads connected the many smaller towns, such as Betar (Kirbet el-Yahud). Trackways linked numerous villages and market towns – such as Emmaus and Tekoa (Tuqu') – to farms scattered across the area. A road from Jerusalem via Bethlehem led directly to a community situated on the left bank of the briny Dead Sea at Ein Gedi. Beyond the east bank of the Dead Sea lay the districts of Peraea and Moab. South of Judea lay Idumaea.

Expanding the road network after the brutal War of Quietus seems to have been one of Hadrian's first priorities in 117 CE. Roads facilitated troop movements and were a means of control. Having just stamped out the fires of rebellion across the diaspora, he could not afford an uprising in the Jewish homeland itself, which might then spread out again. Legionaries were deployed to carry out the skilled work. Surviving milestones (all of them dated to 120 CE and 129/130 CE) indicate that at least twelve new roads were constructed in the densely-populated regions of Galilaea and Samaria with a recorded history of unrest.[50] The strategy had worked. By the time of Hadrian's visit there had been no significant trouble in the region.

Having completed his review in Caesarea, Hadrian then headed out into the province. A few more details of Hadrian's itinerary are contained in the *Treatise on Measures and Weights* written by Epiphanius of Salamis.[51] The original text was written in a now lost Greek text, but it has survived in a Syriac translation:

> And, approaching other places in order from that of the Romans, he must inspect them, for he was a man who loved to see places. So, he passed through the city of Antiocheia and passed through [Coele-Syria] and Phoenicia and came to Palaestina – which is also called Iudea – forty-seven years after the destruction of Hierosolyma. And he thus went up to Hierosolyma…[52]

I could relate to the observation that Hadrian 'was a man who loved to see places'. To rule his vast empire, he had to be fully acquainted with facts on the ground; for myself as a historian field research is how I too seek out the essential truths of a story.

In the early second century, the shortest route went inland from the coast, going south-east to Sebaste, then on to Neapolis past Mount Gerizim, where the road turned south to Gophna, finally entering Jerusalem by its north gate. Nowadays the most direct route is to take Highway 2 from Caesarea to Tel Aviv, and once there enter Highway 1 – a fine two-lane motorway furnished with new blacktop – to reach Jerusalem on its western side. The journey of 121 kilometres (75 mi.) took me a mere 1 hour 42 minutes. Hadrian's entourage, perhaps moving at an average of 12 Roman miles per day by the longer route would have taken several *days* to cover the same distance; there would be stops along the way to dine and rest, to meet local officials, to pay respects to their gods and to take in the sights. For both the ancient and modern traveller the journey is uphill; a gentle slope characterizes the first miles, which trek across the Judean *Shephelah*, but the incline steepens considerably over the final miles to the city.

Jerusalem is situated in the Judean Mountains on the southern spur of a plateau. The historic Old City sits some 760 metres (2,490ft) above sea level.[53] Its natural setting is dramatic, with the Mount of Olives to the east and Mount Scopus to the north-east. When Hadrian saw it, as in biblical times, the city was surrounded by forests of almond, olive and pine trees. The underlying geology is limestone, the product of compacted skeletal fragments of marine organisms deposited hundreds of millions of years ago; like much of Texas, the area of Jerusalem was long ago under a prehistoric ocean teeming with life. Used as a construction material, any buildings incorporating the locally-cut, coarsely crystalline *meleke* stone have a pale but appealing off-white colour like a milky coffee.[54] It was a favourite material of Herod's builders who used it extensively.

Arriving from the north, Hadrian may have crossed the sacred city limits (*pomerium*) through a ceremonial portal of an arch straddling the approach road.[55] It had long since vanished, but there is fragmentary evidence of its presence. The Romans typically inscribed public buildings and monuments with dedicatory inscriptions and, true to form, one adorned this now lost structure. The stone slab had long since broken into several pieces. A large segment had been found in the nineteenth century and was in the possession of the Studium Biblicum Franciscanum Museum, the first museum in Jerusalem. Remarkably, excavators of the Israel Antiquities Authority working in a cistern in the north of Jerusalem had found another large fragment in October 2014.[56] For the first time in 1,886 years the two pieces were reassembled (plate 12) for a special exhibition at the Israel Museum, Jerusalem where I was able to examine it closely myself. It was likely the work of an army stone mason. Its letters were fine and neatly inscribed, competent rather than grandiose, and were likely originally picked out with red paint to stand out so they could be read from a distance. In translation the text reads:

> For *Imperator* Caesar Traianus Hadrianus Augustus,
> Son of Divine Traianus, Conqueror of the Parthians, Grandson of
> Divine Nerva,
> High Priest, Holding the Tribunician Power Fourteen Times,
> Consul Three Times, Father of His Country.
> *Legio* X *Fretensis*[57]

Crucially the references to the number of times Hadrian held the tribunician power and consulship have enabled archaeologists to date the inscription to 129/130 CE. The inference is clear: a visit by Hadrian had been expected well in advance and the legionary legate had hung out the banner to officially welcome his commander-in-chief.

What Hadrian saw from that moment on is a matter of conjecture. Flavius Josephus, who had seen the city after the siege of 70 CE with his own eyes, describes it as 'so thoroughly levelled by those digging it up to the very foundations, that those who saw it could not believe it had ever been inhabited.'[58] Writing three centuries later, Epiphanius offers a rather fanciful, more faith- than fact-based description:

And he found the temple of God trodden down and the whole city devastated save for a few houses and the church of God, which was small, where the disciples, when they had returned after the Saviour had ascended from the Mount of Olives, went to the upper room. For there it had been built, that is, in that portion of Zion which escaped destruction, together with blocks of houses in the neighborhood of Zion and the seven synagogues which alone remained standing in Zion, like solitary huts...[59]

What can be said with reasonable certainty is that both accounts confirm the ruinous state of the *postbellum* city. Evidence of that destructive siege can still be seen in Jerusalem today. Wandering the streets of the Old City and passing through a security check I eventually came to the Western Wall Plaza and, a little further on, arrived at the Western Wall Excavations. A series of walkways and steps take the visitor down to the ground beside the Temple Mount. Here runs a stretch of *meleke* limestone retaining wall, neatly dressed in Herodian style. At the base of it were piles of rubble made of fallen blocks, some weighing between 2.7 and 4.5 tonnes (3 and 5 tons).[60] They had been deliberately pushed off the top of the curtain wall at the end of the siege of 70 CE.[61] It was testament to the thorough way in which the victorious Roman soldiers had carried out their orders issued by legate T. Flavius. Sixty years later, for Hadrian it represented a marvellous opportunity for urban renewal, offering him a blank canvas to create a fresh, new work of art – one of his own conception to rival the great cities in Asia and Syria that he had just visited.

Historians have long presumed that Hadrian visited the city in 130 CE and only then, having seen its ruinous state, decided to rebuild it.[62] They have based their dating on Cassius Dio's comment (as epitomized by Xiphilinus), 'at Jerusalem he founded a city in place of the one which had been razed to the ground.'[63] The remark occurs in the context of Hadrian's advancing travels when he arrived in Province Iudaea; viewed alone it is a reasonable interpretation. However, others argue that they disregard Epiphanius' account stating that the order to rebuild was issued as early as the start of his reign, perhaps during a visit while he was *en route* to Alexandria.[64] While scholars may be divided, archaeological evidence now tends to support the Christian writer's assertion. Excavations conducted inside modern Jerusalem in the north-western part of the Western Wall Plaza of the Old City strongly suggest that the city was already being rebuilt when Hadrian arrived.[65] Digs at the Eastern *Cardo* reveal that the streets of the new Roman city had been planned and its main thoroughfares had been laid out and paved during the early years of Hadrian's reign; that is to say, about *a decade before* his visit in person in 130 CE.[66] Coins commemorating the foundation of Aelia Capitolina showing Hadrian as a priest ploughing the *sulcus primgenia* ('aboriginal furrow') to define the city's *pomerium* were minted locally and have been found in hoards that *pre-date* the war of 132–136 CE (fig. 13).[67] Rather

Figure 13. An outline drawing of the image and text on a bronze *as*. It shows Hadrian ploughing the *pomerium* or sacred boundary line during the rite officially 'Founding *Colonia* Aelia Kapitolina'. The *vexillum* or military flag in the background represents the veteran status of the colony's new inhabitants.

than to officially commission the work, it now seems that Hadrian's stop at the city was actually intended to inspect the progress being made on his grand design.

The city he planned was a *colonia*, doing for Jerusalem what Vespasian had done for Caesarea.[68] It was to be here that veterans of the two legions stationed in Province Iudaea could look forward to spending their years after active service. By design this would be a city built by Romans for Romans. The essential Jewish character of Jerusalem would be erased. As in the city of Rome, the important central feature of a *colonia* was its 'capitol'. It was a place where one or more temples to the Roman gods Jupiter, Juno and Minerva would stand. In the regenerated city of Province Iudaea the capitol's location was surely what is now called the Temple Mount (plate 14), perhaps even the exact spot where the Second Temple once stood.[69]

The name of the city would also change. In the words of Cassius Dio:

> At Jerusalem he founded a city in place of the one which had been razed to the ground, naming it Aelia Capitolina, and on the site of the temple of the god he raised a new temple to Jupiter.[70]

It was a masterpiece of Roman branding.[71] 'Aelia' connected the city to Hadrian's family (his *nomen gentilicium* was Aelius) as its mortal benefactor. Vespasian had chosen *Prima* for Caesarea, but for Hadrian *Secunda* was not an option. He went one better. In choosing 'Capitolina' he connected the place to the hill in Rome upon which stood the temple of Iuppiter Capitolinus – dedicated to Jupiter, Juno and Minerva, forming the 'Capitoline Triad' – as its divine benefactor.[72] The name bound together Rome's leading family and its pre-eminent gods. No one hearing it for the first time would ever know this had been the once famous City of David dedicated to the singular god of the Jews.[72]

Hadrian's decision to build a Roman edifice on this spot sacred to Jews was bound to be contentious. 'You do not rule the Holy City and the Temple,' one story relates.[74] Yet in this urban development of his own conception it seems there could be no room for ancient relics associated with a troubled past; it was all about creating a new future and making a fresh start. It is a point Epiphanius notes when he writes that 'Hadrian made up his mind to (re)build the city but not the [Jewish] Temple.'[75] Preserved in this same document is the name of the man Hadrian put in charge of his building programme: Aquila (or Akylas).[76] Born in Sinope on the coast of the Black Sea, he was apparently related to the emperor and by trade a Greek-speaking interpreter who knew Hebrew.[77] One might imagine Hadrian and his architect wandering around the Temple, as Pompeius Magnus had done in 63 BCE, except now the building was a charred ruin.

The natural topography of the location and the presence of two large man-made impediments – the buttressed mount in the south-east of the city and the military camp of *Legio* X *Fretensis* somewhere in the south-west – may have imposed unusual constraints on the architect laying out the city's streets (fig. 14). Hadrian's – or his architect's – solution was novel. On the north-west side he located a grand gateway.[78] That spot is now covered by the towering Damascus Gate, built in 1537 under the rule of Suleiman the Magnificent, Sultan of the Ottoman Empire.[79] On the day I came to Jerusalem, large crowds were passing hurriedly under the pointed arch. It was the start of Ramadan, observed by Muslims in Israel as in the world over and a reminder of how multi-cultural this city continued to be. Armed police and soldiers stood quietly in the background; it was a scene that might have been true of the same place 2,000 years before.

When first constructed, the ancient Roman gateway was a freestanding structure, unattached to a city wall. Something of its former grandeur can still be seen. Hurrying through the gate, the visitor would miss it. Tucked almost out of sight to the left of the sixteenth-century building was a staircase to a lower level. A wooden sign with a Roman soldier painted on it pointed the way. A flight of steps took me several metres below the present-day street level. At the bottom was the very ground upon which Hadrian and his staff walked in 130 CE. The arch in front of me was once the left-side portal used by pedestrians. Carved bases show that engaged columns flanked the entrance. A recessed semicircular arch at the top completed the restrained architectural design, but as a structural measure it helped spread the crushing weight of the stone above; it was a technique perfected by Roman builders over centuries. There was once a matching arched portal on the right side of the large central gateway used by wheeled vehicles and animals. Some Herodian-style dressed stones could be identified in the gateway.[80] The ruined city provided Hadrian's construction crews with a ready-made quarry. Building material finished by earlier generations of stonemasons was recycled and repurposed for Aelia Capitolina. It would

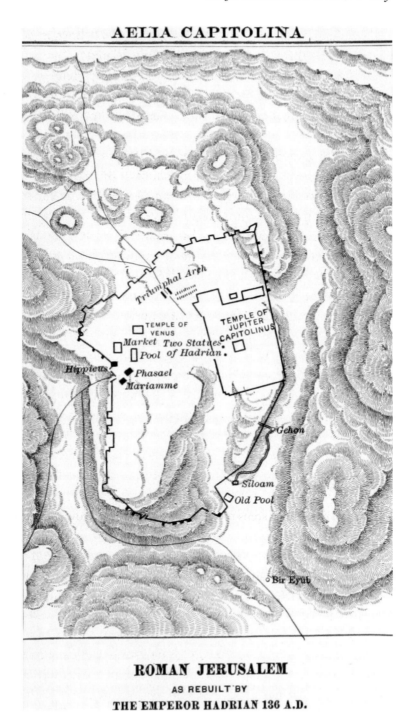

Figure 14. This plan of Aelia Capitolina drawn in 1899 shows the principal features of the new *colonia* in the context of the local topography and the location of the Temple Mount. Excavations have since identified several more buildings and streets.

happen again. Embedded above and to the right of the pedestrian arch in the later gateway there is a fragment of an inscription, which ends with the words 'by decree of the decurions of Aelia Capitolina'; it may have been part of the large slab that was mounted over the central archway.[81]

Behind this main gate, the Roman architect created a semi-circular paved plaza. Some of the flagstones of the plaza can still be seen in the museum, a few bearing decorative parallel grooves (plate 13).[82] In the centre was a tall column, perhaps 22 metres (72.2ft) high, upon which stood a statue of the new city's founder.[83] From here several streets radiated out, rather like the Place Charles de Gaulle (also aptly known as the 'Place de l'Étoile') in Paris. The main street, called the *Cardo Maximus*, ran north-south from the plaza down the Tyropoeon Valley to the Siloam Pool, while a second *Cardo* ran north-west/south-east.[84] Hadrian radically adapted the traditional chequerboard plan of a typical Roman city. Where the east-west street or *Decumanus Maximus* intersected the *Cardo* was normally the location of the *forum* (a large rectangular place for open markets with adjacent covered buildings for hearing court cases). Hadrian's city was different: it had not one *forum* in the centre, but two *fora* located in separate places.[85] Throughout the new *colonia* were colonnaded streets, temples, pools, shops, residences and perhaps a circus for chariot-racing.[86] Aelia Capitolina rose phoenix-like in a spectacular transformation of a war-torn ruin, resulting in a cityscape to rival Antiocheia, Gerasa or Palmyra for architecture and amenities. This was Hadrian as the *restitutor*, the 'restorer'. Indeed, as contemporary Pausanias writes, 'as for the sanctuaries of the gods that in some cases he built from the beginning, in others adorned with offerings and furniture, and the bounties he gave to Greek cities, and sometimes even to foreigners who asked him.'[87]

Satisfied with what he had seen, in the late spring or start of summer Hadrian and his retinue left the great building site behind them. He would never return. A few kilometres south-west of the city, the road took them through the Judean Hills and past Betar, a minor hilltop town refurbished years before by King Herod. At Mamre (Ramet el-Khalil), just north of Hebron (el-Khalil), Hadrian ordered the great public market repaired; it had been destroyed during the First Jewish War.[88] It was famous for the great oak tree associated with Abraham which grew there.[89]

The tour thus far had been a resounding success. Hadrian had been welcomed and fêted wherever he went and, in return, he had bestowed benefactions and recognitions. Statues were erected to Hadrian, and a shrine to his sacred spirit (*Hadrianeum*) was built in Caesarea, and other cities followed its lead.[90] The imperial party eventually reached Gaza on the coast. Nowadays the principal city in the Gaza Strip, being under the control of Hamas and subject to a total blockade by Israel and Egypt, was inaccessible to me on my research trip. Back in 130 CE it was an open, cosmopolitan, Hellenized city, a terminus on the trade route between the Mediterranean and Indian Ocean. Through its role in the distribution of aromatics, incense and spices it enjoyed great wealth and was adorned with temples and statues to gods and goddesses, as well as a gymnasium, hippodrome and theatre, and even a school of rhetoric.[91] Delighted by the emperor's visit, his hosts celebrated a *panegyris Hadriane* for their honoured guest.[92] Indeed, the city's magistrates went one step further: they reformed the local dating system, establishing a new era by counting the years since Hadrian's visit.[93]

By July or August Hadrian and his followers were in Aegyptus, the Roman province of Egypt.[94] His official duties in Alexandria done, he found time for rest and relaxation. On one occasion he went lion-hunting with Antinous riding by his side, an event that was immortalized in a poem.[95] He went on a cruise down the Nile River. At Thebes he stopped to view the famous singing 'Colossi of Memnon' – actually massive twin stone statues of Pharaoh Amenhotep III – which were already 1,480 years old when the Roman emperor saw them.[96] Then tragedy struck. In late October, Antinous fell off the imperial barge into the Nile and drowned.[97] Retrieved from the water, he could not be resuscitated. In despair, it was later reported that Hadrian 'wept over [the body] like a woman'.[98] Channelling his grief, Hadrian made a dramatic gesture. On 30 October he founded a new city on the east bank of the Nile, a few miles from Hermopolis, which lay on the opposite bank; he called it Antinoopolis, 'Antinous-city'.[99] There he inaugurated a cult to the deceased boy.[100] A new god – the last of the ancient world – had been born. In the months and years that followed, portrait busts and statues of Antinous authorized by Hadrian would appear in shrines across the Empire for his worship and veneration.[101]

In the evening I reviewed my notes. As always, the research led to yet more questions. Top of my mind, however, as I dined at a crowded restaurant in Rehavia in Jerusalem, I wondered how the native Jewish population reacted to the visit of Hadrian to their historic city.

Chapter 4

'Son of a Star'

When I returned to my hotel room I turned on the TV. A reporter on location was speaking directly at the camera, the microphone gripped firmly in his hand. He was speaking in Ivrit (modern Hebrew), which I do not, but I could sense that the story was grave. Checking on the BBC News website I learned that during the evening there had been an attack at a shopping centre in Tel Aviv.[1] Gunmen had shot dead three people and injured eleven at the popular Max Brenner Café in the Sarona Market. The two shooters, both 21 years old and from Yatta in the West Bank, had been dressed in business suits, sat down and ordered desserts, then they stood up, pulled out their improvised rifles and started shooting at the diners. When one of their guns jammed, they fled the scene of carnage. They were found, arrested and charged. Later I would learn that the official indictment filed by the Tel Aviv District Prosecutor's Office stated that the men were inspired by watching propaganda videos produced by the terrorist organization Islamic State (ISIS/DAESH), although neither received aid or instruction from or pledged allegiance to it.[2]

What would make a man so angry that he would take up a weapon and kill people for an idea? Answering the question is crucial to understanding the Bar Kokhba War. In short, it is complicated: the ancient evidence is dubious; modern scholars are divided.

For Appian, a contemporary historian of the war, destroying the ancient city was the crux of the problem, writing that:

> The Jewish nation alone resisted, and Pompeius conquered them, sent their king, Aristobulus, to Rome, and destroyed their greatest and to them holiest city Jerusalem, as Ptolemy, the first king of Egypt, had formerly done. It was afterward re-built and Vespasian destroyed it again, and Hadrian did the same in my time.[3]

The later Roman historian Cassius Dio expresses the same view, concluding that 'This brought on a war of no slight importance nor of brief duration, for the Jews deemed it intolerable that foreign races should be settled in their city and foreign religious rites planted there.'[4] The reference to alien religious practices in the text specifically includes the erection of a temple to Iuppiter Capitolinus on the Temple Mount (which Dio mentions earlier in the text) and with it the desecration of the Holy of Holies, effectively banishing the god of the Jews.[5] That alone would be a particularly egregious public insult as the rabbinic texts show. The Roman rite of establishing the *pomerium* of the city, what the Jewish population saw as the 'ploughing of Jerusalem', they considered sacrilegious.[6] The *Mishnah* records 'the city was ploughed up; Rufus, may his bones be crushed, ploughed the Temple building.'[7] (The Rufus here is Q. Tineius Rufus, the governor personally appointed by Hadrian.)

In the Hebrew texts, however, there is a suggestion that Hadrian himself had actually agreed to rebuilding the Temple of *Yahweh*. In the story preserved in *Midrash*, the emperor is approached by a delegation of Cutheans (the name in Hebrew used for the Samaritans), 'in the days of Rabbi Yehoshua Ben Hananiah the evil kingdom (Rome) decreed to rebuild the Temple.'[8] The primary cause for complaint was that Hadrian suddenly broke his promise. His official word was supposed to be his imperial bond. Though the parable stresses the peaceful outcome, in Jewish eyes the act of betrayal by the head of state would be an insult, a double-cross. Amplifying the hurt, it would have been galling to witness the official promotion of the new Antinous cult complete with statues, shrines and even coins bearing the boy-god's profile.[9]

At first glance it seems an odd thing for Hadrian to have agreed to do. However, the suggestion that he did so exists in other written sources. The Patriarch of Constantinople – writing at the end of the fourth century CE that the duty of all Christians is to hate the Jews – also mentions Hadrian's intention to rebuild the Temple.[10] There are other Christian sources that also state the same thing.[11] In the *Epistle of Barnabus*, believed to have been written between 70 and 130 CE, there is a curious passage which states:

Furthermore, he says again, 'Behold, those who tore down this temple will themselves build it.' It is happening. For because of their fighting it was torn down by the enemies. And now the very servants of the enemies will themselves rebuild it.[12]

Some scholars take this to refer to the Temple being constructed by the Romans.

In his plan for Aelia Capitolina might Hadrian have perhaps envisaged temples to the Capitoline Triad *and* the Jewish God all standing together on the Mount? If so, there is no mention of it in any extant texts. While they suggest there was support at the highest echelon of Roman society for building a Third Temple, there is, as yet, no archaeological evidence to substantiate the claim. The latest discoveries appear only to confirm that work to construct a Roman *colonia* over the ruins of the City of David, Solomon and Herod the Great was already under way by 130 CE; what was happening on the Temple Mount at that time remains a mystery.[13]

Another cause mentioned in a Roman source is a ban on circumcision. In his *Life of Hadrian*, Aelius Spartianus writes 'at this time also the Jews began war, because they were forbidden to practise circumcision.'[14] He is the only source stating it was a cause of the war. The Jewish texts specifically mention it too, but they place the timing of the ban to *after* the war, inferring that it was a consequence.[15] Circumcision is a defining feature of Judaism; the act of *brit milah* is a central duty of a male Jew in honouring the Covenant which the patriarch Abraham agreed with *Yahweh*.[16] In contrast, for the Romans circumcision was considered equivalent to castration. It was a practice outlawed under the *Lex Cornelia* enacted by Domitian and affirmed by Nerva and, under that law, deemed to be on a par with murder. If Hadrian did ban the practice outright, he may not have been specifically targeting the Jews on religious grounds, however. There were other people in the empire who engaged in the practice, among them the Arabs of Nabataea, Egyptians (at least high-ranking priests), and the Sarmatians.[17] Himself a gay phil-Hellene, Hadrian quite possibly considered it a barbaric custom, no less than a 'mutilation of the genitals' (*mutilare genitalia*), inflicting a wound that spoiled the aesthetics of the male body.[18] The Jews would certainly have interpreted the prohibition as a direct attack on them. Yet even on the point of this purported ban, there is disagreement among scholars about whether it occurred around the time of Hadrian's visit or much later, or whether it happened at all.[19] The emperor's assumed personal revulsion at the practice notwithstanding, even if the ban was implemented, it is not beyond doubt that it was enough to cause a violent uprising among those impacted by it.

Also reported to have been banned by Hadrian was study of the *Torah*.[20] Now that the *batei midrash* were the only places open for believers to study the Five Books of Moses, a ban would be particularly harsh. The problem with this claim is that it too likely did not happen. It appears in rabbinic texts probably written well after the time they describe and may have been superimposed on the past.

Jews were also told to 'desecrate *Shabbat*' by working on the day of rest.[21] This too would represent an attack on a defining feature of Judaism, the duty of every Jew in honouring the Covenant Abraham agreed with *Yahweh*. The weekly holy day was a sore issue especially in communities with a majority of Greek-speaking gentiles, who resented the fact that the Jews made no effort to conform to their norms for working, worshipping and celebrating festivals.

Economic or political issues may have been underlying causes for an uprising. The imposition of the *Fiscus Iudaicus*, which intentionally singled out those living the 'Jewish lifestyle', had a material cost on the local population, taking cash from the local economy and redistributing it far away. The burden would fall heaviest on the poorest members of the Jewish community, 'the people of the land' (Hebrew: *am ha'aretz*). After 66–70/74 CE there had been confiscations of land, initially from direct supporters of that rebellion.[22] By 130 CE the condition of leaseholders had worsened; rabbinic texts mention their oppression by landowners who used violence to assert their control and extract payments.[23] A man living in Judea might well have asked 'What have the Romans ever done for us?':

> Rabbi Yehuda and Rabbi Yose and Rabbi Shimon were sitting, and Yehuda, son of converts, sat beside them.
>
> Rabbi Yehuda opened and said: 'How pleasant are the actions of this nation, the Romans, as they established marketplaces, established bridges, and established bathhouses.'
>
> Rabbi Yosei was silent.
>
> Rabbi Shim'on Bar Yohai responded and said: 'Everything that they established, they established only for their own purposes. They established marketplaces to place prostitutes in them; bathhouses, to pamper themselves; and bridges, to collect taxes from all who pass over them.'[24]

Yet it seems some managed to hold onto their wealth or found means to improve their personal prosperity, men such as Rabbi Tarfon, Rabbi Eleazar Ben Azariah and Raman Gamaliel II.[25] That itself might have fostered resentment among the less well-off in Judea.

The biggest changes to occur post 70/73 CE were administrative and military.[26] Upgraded to a proconsular province and having two legions supported by several professional, non-Roman auxiliary units meant the presence of Roman troops would have been much more visible – even intrusive – to the local population than in earlier times.[27] Increased contact exposed Jews to Roman culture, but it came with a greater risk of misunderstandings and frustrations, or abuses. The story in the *Talmud* about the angry residents of Tur Malka ('King's Mountain'), a real or imagined community located somewhere in the Judean Hills, illustrates the point:

> One day a troop [Hebrew: *gunda*] of Roman soldiers passed by there while a wedding was taking place and took the rooster and hen from them. The residents of the city fell upon them and beat them. The soldiers came and said to the emperor: 'The Jews have rebelled against you.' The emperor then came against them in war.
>
> Among the residents of the King's Mountain there was a certain man named Bar Daroma who could jump the distance of a *mil*, and he killed many of the Romans, who were powerless to stand up against him.
>
> The emperor then took his crown and set it on the ground as a sign of mourning. He said: 'Master of the Universe, if it is pleasing to You, do not give over that man, a euphemism for himself, and his kingdom into the hands of only one man.'[28]

Obliterating the Temple site, a ban on circumcision and the study of the Books of Moses, desecrating the Sabbath: it could be inferred that Hadrian was deliberately and calculatingly seeking to undermine the very foundations of Judaism. For the Jews it would seem as though the oppressive times of Antiochus IV Epiphanes had returned. A devout man believing such news to be true – whether fact or fake – might be motivated to take up arms to defend his people, faith and culture. Factor in economic hardship and intrusions by soldiers of a 'foreign occupying power' traipsing about in his own homeland, and that man might turn motivation into action. History is filled with insurrections sparked by much less.

In 168 BCE Judah Maccabee had stepped forward to save his people from injustice and ignominy.[29] In 130 CE the man with a cause was Shim'on Ben Kosiba: Simon Son of Kosiba.[30] Written in Aramaic book hand his name is spelled שמעון בן כוסבא, '*SM'WN BN KWSBH*'.[31] We know it to be so because seventeen letters bearing the name were recovered from caves near the Dead Sea between 1952 and 1961, one of which, remarkably, is signed by Shim'on himself![32] Strangely, he is not named at all in Cassius Dio's account, the most complete chronicle we have of the war; indeed, neither does he appear by his real name in the rabbinic nor Christian literature.[33]

Like so many characters of the ancient world, he is an enigma to us today. Key biographical facts elude us. When and where he was born is unknown. A date of sometime around 90–95 CE seems possible, which makes him a whole generation after the calamitous First Jewish War. A rabbinic text refers to him as 'a certain man from the south' and 'the southerner' (presumably the district of Judea).[34] The patronymic may indicate that his father was called Kosiba, or that he came from a place of the same name.[35] Another rabbinic source suggests that he was an only son. He was raised as a Jew and he was likely married, though nothing is known about his wife.

Assuming he was born in the 90s CE, Ben Kosiba would have been in his 20s during the so-called War of Quietus (115–117 CE). Scholars are still divided on whether the conflict spread to Province Iudaea.[36] News of the rioting by Jewish communities in Cyprus, Cyrenaica, Egypt and Mesopotamia would, however, have reached Caesarea as official communiqués sent to the governor's office and by way of scuttlebutt from seafaring merchants. It would have spread from there inland to cities and villages across the province. The local response seems to have been one of indifference. Apparently, Province Iudaea remained peaceful in the last years of Trajan's reign. Distant memory of the First Jewish War of 66–70/74 CE may have tempered any desire to foment trouble as the people of Ben Kosiba's time still lived with its consequences.

In the religious texts Ben Kosiba appears out of nowhere as the fully-formed rebel leader (fig. 15). He may not have been the initiator of the war, perhaps instead rising to prominence through success as a war leader.[37] To

Figure 15. Rabbinic texts portray the Jewish warlord as a *gibbor*. This woodcut by Isac Friedlander (1890–1968) conveys the strength and toughness of the man. Rabbi Akiba stands behind him.

Roman writers he was 'murderous and bandit-like'.[38] The Jewish writers portray him as a man of extraordinary physical strength. It was said he was able to 'catch the missiles from the enemy's catapults on one of his knees and hurl them back, killing many of his enemies'.[39] He could strike a man dead with a single kick of his foot.[40] The Jews called a powerful champion, a man able to perform such great feats of strength and courage, a *gibbor*. The biblical Samson (of Delilah fame) and Judah Maccabee and his brothers were all renowned *gibborim*; the less famous Bar Deroma of Tur Malka would also fit into this mould. Although Ben Kosiba is not specifically referred to this way anywhere in the texts, the implication was there nevertheless. A seemingly unbreakable spirit drove this leader in the battle against the gentile foe; but fearlessness could so easily become arrogance. A quick temper and overconfidence were also character traits of this strong but temperamental warrior leader.

Ben Kosiba was literate. He was educated in Jewish scripture and his letters use Talmudic terminology. His surviving messages to front-line commanders and troop units are on display in the Israel Museum.[41] They reveal that he could be an uncompromising and harsh leader. He demanded complete obedience from his deputies and subordinates. Today he might be called a micro-manager in the way he detailed missions and closely followed progress of their implementation. He personally criticized and reprimanded those who failed to carry out his orders, often using sarcasm to make his point. Where he learned the arts of war is not known. Yet he appears to have been a charismatic leader too, a man who others would follow into battle. He addressed his fellow fighters – in Aramaic, Greek or Hebrew – as 'brothers', perhaps suggesting that his followers were organized as a fellowship.[42] A letter written in Greek provides an example of its usage:

> Aelianos to Yonathes the brother, greetings.
> Simon Kosiba has written to me that you must send the
> … needs of the brothers….
> [Aelia]nos. Be well, my brother![43]

Curiously, the name Kosiba was inserted above the line of text after Ailianos had completed the letter; presumably he realized that Simon was a very common name and, to ensure Yonathes understood that message came from the commander-in-chief, he added in the patronymic. The insertion is written in the Greek characters $X\tilde{\omega}\sigma\iota\beta\alpha$ informing us that the name was pronounced 'Chō-si-va'.

Written evidence in the form of a deed suggests that Ben Kosiba was in the premier leadership position in May 133 CE and had probably already been in power for several months before that date, perhaps as early as 131.[44] On correspondence his name is frequently used in conjunction with the title *Nasi Yisrael* (or *Nasi 'al Israel*).[45] His decision to use the title was highly significant. The designation asserted his political claim to *national* supremacy grounded in a religious hope to re-found the homeland for the Jewish people.

Yet why Israel and not Judea or Zion?[46] Judea – as *Yudah* – is found in the Hebrew Bible. Judea only came into common use from the second century BCE.[47] It was the name the Romans took for their province down to Ben Kosiba's time. The rebels of the First Jewish War, however, usually invoked the memory of Zion, which referred to the sacred hill in Jerusalem. Traditionally, Jerusalem was always located in Judea.[48] 'Israel', in contrast, did not encompass Jerusalem – or Caesarea, Bethlehem, Hebron or Masada, for that matter – because it applied only to the area of Samaria and some adjacent territories. Israel of the *Torah* was the ancient Kingdom of Israel, as distinct from the Kingdom of Judah. The area they occupied was identified in the biblical texts by the pharaonic moniker 'Land of Canaan'. The events in the books describing the wars of the Maccabees did not occur in the 'Land of Israel'. Neither Philo of Alexandria nor Josephus refers to the region this way. The name Israel first gained commonplace usage from the time of Ben Kosiba.[49] It was the designation that he, or his supporters, consciously chose to frame their aspiration for national independence with a Jewish identity. Thereafter 'Land of Israel' appeared frequently in rabbinic and Christian texts instead of the contemporary geographic name Palestine, but it did not define a region with fixed political borders.[50] For Ben Kosiba, Israel was a revolutionary idea, the dream of a Jewish nation where Jerusalem would be taken back from the occupying power which was, at that very moment, actively working to erase it. As its president he would strive to achieve national redemption.

The Jewish sources write that the rebel leader found support among the sages and rabbis, and one in particular: Rabbi Akiba. The connection is fundamental to the claim of fulfilment of a prophecy about the messiah (Hebrew: *Moshiakh*). In the Jerusalem *Talmud* is this story:

יז אֶרְאֶנּוּ וְלֹא עַתָּה אֲשׁוּרֶנּוּ וְלֹא קָרוֹב דָּרַךְ כּוֹכָב מִיַּעֲקֹב
וְקָם שֵׁבֶט מִיִּשְׂרָאֵל וּמָחַץ פַּאֲתֵי מוֹאָב וְקַרְקַר
כָּל־בְּנֵי־שֵׁת:

Figure 16. The text of Numbers 24:17, here written in square Hebrew book hand, states that 'there shall step forth a star out of Jacob, and a sceptre shall rise out of Israel'. Rabbi Akiba is alleged to have cited it to justify his identification of the King Messiah with Shim'on Ben Kosiba.

Rabbi Shim'on Bar Yohai taught, 'Akiba, my master, expounded, *'A star shall come forth from Jacob'* (Numbers 24:17), [to mean] 'Koziba has come forth from Jacob.'

When Rabbi Akiba would see Bar Koziba, he would say, '*This is the King Messiah!*'[51]

The full text of Numbers 24:17 (fig. 16) reads:

> I see him, but not now;
>> I behold him, but not near;
> A star shall come forth from Jacob,
>> A sceptre shall rise from Israel,
> And shall crush through the forehead of Moab,
>> And tear down all the sons of Sheth.[52]

According to scriptural prophecy the King Messiah's coming will be accompanied by the sign of a star or comet. To connect Ben Kosiba with the prophecy, Akiba engaged in clever word play. The Hebrew word for 'star' (כּוֹכָב, *kokab*) is close enough to the sound of the rebel's real name, Kosiba; in Hebrew it requires changing just a single letter to make it sound like *kokhba*.[53] He also substituted the Aramaic word *ben* (son) for the Hebrew word *bar* (son).[54] Thus, בן כוסבא, Ben Kosiba, 'Son of Kosiba', became בר כוכבא, ('*BR KWKBH*'), Bar Kokhba, 'Son of a Star' – the 'star' of the prophecy.[55] By itself Akiba's support would be a positive endorsement of Ben Kosiba as the leader for the Jews to follow. If true, Akiba's recognition of him as the 'Bar Kokhba', the man who would fulfil biblical messianic prophecy, was quite extraordinary.[56]

The Hebrew word *Moshiakh* simply means 'anointed one', someone picked to fulfil a certain destiny.[57] The title could be bestowed on someone who had attained a position of greatness and nobility in Jewish society. The 'King-Messiah' (Hebrew: *Melekh HaMoshiakh*) is a fundamental idea in Talmudic literature reserved for the Jewish leader who will redeem Israel in the End of Days.[58] While there is no direct reference to a messiah in the Hebrew Bible, there is in its verses a yearning belief in the coming of a man who will redeem the 'Children of Israel'.[59] He is a warrior king who will rid Israel of its mortal foes, bring the scattered tribes back to the 'Promised Land', rebuild the Temple and establish the Kingdom of God in the new Jerusalem.[60] He must be a descendant of the line of King David and rule justly.[61] The time when all this occurs on Earth – and specifically *not* in Heaven – is referred to as the 'Period of the Messiah' (*Yamot HaMoshiakh*).[62] It is a time expounded in great detail in the Fourth Book of Ezra (Esdras), written around the time of Ben Kosiba, which stresses the events to come in '*this*' world'.[63] Terrible violence will precede that age; so terrible that a rabbi living in the third century CE wrote 'May the Messiah come speedily, but not while I am alive.'[64]

Support for Akiba's assertion that Ben Kosiba was the King Messiah was not universal among the sages and rabbis at Yavneh and *batei midrash* elsewhere.[65] There had been pretender messiahs before, though none had actually exclaimed 'I am the Messiah'.[66] Preserved in the rabbinic texts is memory of argument and disagreement between them. Responding to Akiba's declaration 'This is the King Messiah!' is this exchange, 'Rabbi Yohanan Ben Torta said to him, "Akiba, grass will grow on your cheeks and still the Son of David will not have come."'[67] Modern scholars note that problematical is the fact that Akiba's exclamation is written in Aramaic and may be a *later* insert into the Hebrew text.[68] For sages opposing Akiba now was not yet the time of the messiah but, instead, the moment for Jews to commit to following *Halakhah*.[69]

Reviewing the sources, the twelfth-century Jewish philosopher Maimonides (Moshe ben Maimon) commented:

> It should not occur to you that the King Messiah must bring wondrous signs or perform marvels or invent new things or revive the dead or anything like what the fools say. It is not so. For Rabbi Akiba, one of the wisest of the Sages of the *Mishnah*, was King Ben Kosiba's arms-

bearer and said that he was the King Messiah. He and all the Sages of his generation thought that he was the King Messiah.[70]

In the biblical texts all warriors of distinction had an 'arms-bearer'.[71]

If Akiba was Ben Kosiba's left-hand man, his right-hand man may have been a certain Eleazar the Priest (El'azar HaKonen).[72] There are several candidates for which Eleazar he could be: Ben Azariah, Ben Harsum or HaModai (of Modi'im). Identification is difficult with scholars championing one or the other.[73] Where Ben Kosiba would be the military leader, Eleazar would be his high priest. It was not a new idea. A warrior and clergyman working together in partnership had precedent dating back to the prophet-priest Ezekiel (c. 662–570 BCE), who lived during the Babylonian captivity.[74] Might *and* Right would sweep the Jews to victory.

Ben Kosiba's choice of formal title as *nasi* rather than king was deliberate. It carried the pre-eminence of national leadership, but not the full prestige of royalty, yet it drew on older associations.[75] In biblical times the titles could be interpreted as equivalent.[76] The only time Bar Kokhba is referred to as 'king' in rabbinic sources is, in fact, Akiba's own 'King Messiah' exclamation.[77] Nevertheless, some in his time may have interpreted Ben Kosiba's posture and messaging as messianic.[78] For the Jews, the conflict that would follow would be a war of necessity. The rabbis of Akiba's circle created the legal concept of *Milhemet Mitzvah*, a 'holy war' required by *Torah*, a war of obligation that every Jew must fight.[79] As a war to defend the nation's interests, Akiba's declaration meant that Jews of Judea *had* to unite behind his King Messiah. Their refusal would lead to a trial on a capital crime before the seventy-one members of the Sanhedrin, even though their approval of the war was not required.

Why Ben Kosiba believed he could succeed where so many had failed is a mystery. We may speculate that he looked to Jewish History and that he was inspired by the successes of the Maccabees. It took the brothers seven years (167–160 BCE) to defeat the Greeks in the field, and a further eighteen for Simon Thassi (Shim'on the Hasmonean), the last surviving son of Judah Maccabee, to permanently take Jerusalem from them.[80] Crucially they demonstrated how waging a guerrilla war against a professional army could work, at least initially, by leveraging the advantages of agility and mobility over heavily-armed opponents.[81] Simon was declared ethnarch ('ruler of the people') in 141 BCE, the Hebrew original of that title probably being *nasi*.[82]

Had Ben Kosiba been a student of History, he would have surely realized that the odds of success were weighed heavily *against* him. Unlike the Seleucids, the Romans were accustomed to dealing with rebellions. Some were so disruptive that the names of their ringleaders have been preserved by Roman chroniclers and historians: Viriathus in Lusitania (147–142 BCE); Q. Sertorius (80–72 BCE) in Hispania Citerior and Ulterior; Vologases in Thracia (13 BCE); Bato of the Daesidiates and Bato of the Breuci in Illyricum (6–9 CE); Tacfarinas in Africa (15–24 CE); Aedemon and Sabalus in Mauretania (40–44 CE); Boudicca in Britannia (60/61 CE); Shim'on Ben Giora in Province Iudaea (66–70 CE); and C. Iulius Civilis in Germania Inferior (69–79 CE). Yet in all that time only *one* had been successful in ousting the Romans from the disputed territory. He was Arminius, often known today as 'Herman the German'. In Germania (9 CE) he famously destroyed three legions at Teutoburg.[83] Perceived by the Romans as a military disaster (*clades*), the shockwaves spread. The Romans abandoned their territory across the Rhine and, despite several attempts, it proved too difficult and too expensive to regain. This was not the case with Iudaea.

While contradictions and open questions remain, the textual and archaeological clues prove beyond a doubt that Shim'on Ben Kosiba existed and that he was a figure of historical importance. He was a man from Judea, a devout Jew, with a burning desire to take his country back. He was willing to kill and die to achieve it. Perhaps it was the sheer force of his personality and the appeal of his vision rather than any single grievance which drew people to rally to his call for cessation from Rome.[84] Ben Kosiba, who some may have called Bar Kokhba, was the man who would lead his people in the daring attempt to establish a Jewish nation in defiance of Hadrian.

Chapter 5

'For The Redemption of Israel'

Nasi Shim'on Ben Kosiba had a grand vision, but there were complicated pragmatics to consider. The moment he declared home rule he would be fighting professional, well-equipped, well-provisioned Roman troops. To win his war of independence, he needed a strategy, an army and the means to hold on to his gains. Archaeology has provided firm evidence about the military and administrative aspects of the revolution. From letters found in caves in the Judean Desert it is clear that the 'camp at Herodis' was a key base and that Ben Kosiba may have even established his centre of operations there.[1] Herodium (or Herodion) still exists. It is now a national park and lies 12 kilometres (7.5 mi.) to the south of Jerusalem. I decided to investigate the site for clues.

Figure 17. Destroyed during the First Jewish War, Ben Kosiba commandeered Herodium and used it as his headquarters. From letters the head of camp is known to have been Yeshua Ben Galgula.

After breakfast, I set off from my hotel taking Route 60 south. Seeing Herodium for the first time makes an immediate impression. It rises dramatically out of the expansive flat, sandy brown plain (fig. 17) and stands separate from the hills of the Judean Desert. Of all of them it is the highest peak and is 758 metres (2,487ft) above sea level. The approach road to the historic site winds about two-thirds of the way up the steep, cone-shaped hill and terminates in a car park. From there one enters Herodium on foot.

The hill, or motte, is all the more remarkable when one realizes it is partly man-made.[2] The man who had the idea to erect it was, as the name implies, Herod the Great. Built between 23 and 15 BCE, on the top once stood his circular, seven-storey, fortified palace (plate 15).[3] It is an exquisite example of advanced military architecture of its day. Josephus writes:

> This fortress, which is some 60 *stadia* distant from Jerusalem, is naturally strong and very suitable for such a structure, for reasonably nearby is a hill, raised to a (greater) height by the hand of man and rounded off in the shape of a breast. At intervals it has round towers, and it has a steep ascent formed of 200 steps of hewn stone. Within it are costly royal apartments made for security and for ornament at the same time. At the base of the hill there are pleasure grounds built in such a way as to be worth seeing, among other things because of the way in which water, which is lacking in that place, is brought in from a distance and at great expense. The surrounding plain was built up as a city second to none, with the hill serving as an acropolis for the other dwellings.[4]

In recent years, archaeologists have exposed its interior plan and their excavated finds are still on view to visitors. The remains of one of the towers of dressed blocks of stone stands above the ruins. In the central, circular space (plate 16) are the cut stones marking the foundations of the peristyle courtyard with its partially standing columns, luxury living quarters and even a bathhouse.[5] Contained deep inside the motte of Herodium are giant vaulted cisterns which held potable water to serve the needs of its royal guests. To entertain them there was a theatre embedded into the exterior slope. Herodium was also intended to be Herod's final resting place; an elaborate sepulchre was located into the side of the hill, only discovered by archaeologists in 2007, parts of which are now displayed in the Israel Museum.[6]

In 130 CE Herodium was a ruin, but Ben Kosiba saw its potential as his forward command post. I could imagine him standing on the parapet, surveying the view before him. Herodium's height gave the rebel leader panoramic views (plate 17) across Aelia Capitolina, Bethlehem, the Judean Desert, the Dead Sea and as far as the mountains of Moab. He was not the first to appreciate its advantages, even in its incomplete state. Herodium had been commandeered before by the rebels of the First Jewish War who built a synagogue in the courtyard and dug tunnels into the base of the hill to enable them to hide from the Romans.[7] It was a futile endeavour. In 71 CE Titus' army seized the building and destroyed it. Some fifty-nine years later, Ben Kosiba's men cleared away the rubble in the central courtyard and erected a workshop – its walls still standing up to several courses of trimmed, rectangular stone blocks – with a smithy (Latin: *fabrica*) and seven hearths (*tabuns*).[8] Meanwhile, his engineers created a new network of tunnels inside with arched ceilings hewn into the living rock, supported where necessary with stone or timber, and wide enough for several men to stand shoulder to shoulder (plate 18); now equipped with artificial lighting and handrails they appear rather like the corridors of a modern subway system. When new, they led to sally ports flanking Herod's sepulchre to the outside from which his men could suddenly emerge, engage in hit-and-run attacks, rob or destroy the baggage train (*impedimenta*), and then retreat back into the safety of the motte.[9] It was a formidable HQ from which to direct a war. We even know the name of Ben Kosiba's camp commander at Herodium from surviving letters: Yeshua Ben Galgula.[10]

Ben Kosiba needed an army of tough, motivated fighters who would devote themselves to the cause and face the great dangers ahead with him. In the Jerusalem *Talmud*, *Ta'anit* there is an account of his recruitment policy:

> Ben Kosiba was there, and he had 200,000 troops who had cut off their little fingers. The sages sent word to him: 'How long are you going to turn Israel into a maimed people?'
>
> He said to them: 'How otherwise is it possible to test them?'
>
> They replied: 'Anyone who can uproot a cedar of Lebanon while riding on his horse will not be registered in your army.'
>
> So there were 200,000 who were qualified one way, and another 200,000 who were qualified the other way.[11]

There were objections to this brutal treatment of new recruits. Conceding the point, a man might be exempted from serving if he was 'faint-hearted':

> Then the officers shall go on addressing the troops and say: 'Is anyone afraid or fainthearted?' (Deuteronomy 20:8).
>
> Rabbi Akiba says: 'afraid or fainthearted' is to be understood literally, that he cannot stand in the battle lines and see a drawn sword.
>
> Rabbi Yose the Galilean says: 'afraid or fainthearted' this is the one who is afraid because of the transgressions he has committed; therefore, the *Torah* connected all these [other categories of those who return home] with him that he may return home on their account.[12]

Any man with a deformity could also be exempted.[13] It is difficult to determine the historical truth of these rabbinic writings. The numbers of men must be exaggerations. Far-fetched as they seem, they may yet preserve a kernel of truth about the harshness of service in Ben Kosiba's army.

The army of Israel, like Judah Maccabee's, was not professional.[14] It was a militia comprising primarily farmers with townsfolk joining their ranks, perhaps in mixed units of light infantry, skirmishers, archers, slingers and mounted troops according to their skills and means.[15] A militiaman was assigned to a camp (Hebrew: *mahane*).[16] Nothing is known of their size or organization beyond the fact that each camp had a commander or 'head' (*rosh hamahanaya*). The rebel warrior was equipped for asymmetric warfare, primarily ambushes and 'hit-and-run' attacks. He would prize lightweight personal protection to preserve his advantage of agility. What armour the warrior could find was worn over a short tunic of homespun wool or linen. Remarkable examples of coloured fabrics – in up to thirty-four hues – have been found preserved in the refuge caves at Ein Gedi beside the Dead Sea and can be seen in the Israel Museum.[17]

In the Judean Desert an entire segment of scale armour was found, consisting of four rows, each made of six overlapping scales, perhaps once part of a coat of scale armour (the Roman *lorica plumata* or *squamata*). Exploring the 'Cave of the Spear' in the Wadi Marrazah, north of Ein Gedi, archaeologists found a single thin, rectangular copper plaque, about the size of a postage stamp, with two holes pierced in the upper corners for thread to tie the scales together.[18] Another scale was found at the Teomin Cave on the lower slopes of the Judean Mountains.[19]

Sturdy, well-made footwear was essential in the varied terrain of Judea to keep a soldier mobile. Iron hobnails from the soles of open leather boots or military-style sandals have been found at several sites, including Herodium and several refuge hideouts, such as the 'Sabar Caves'.[20]

For his personal defence the Jewish soldier would likely carry a shield (Hebrew: *magen*) with a handgrip behind a protective central boss. A shield would be essential in one-to-one combat, where it could deflect direct hits from a Roman *pilum* or *gladius*. Several men could gather together in tight formation and form a defensive shield wall. A fragment of a wooden plank shield was discovered in one of the refuge caves near Ein Gedi. The business card-sized piece of wood has an acute-angled edge at the top, but it is sadly not large enough to enable conservators to reconstruct the shape of the whole object of which it was originally part; it could have been hexagonal, oval or round.[21] A row of holes drilled or punched into the upper edge suggests that a strip of leather was stitched around the edge to protect the perimeter of the buckler. A shield could be used as an offensive weapon too, using the boss to punch or the edge to stab at an opponent.

The simplest weapon was also one of the most lethal. A stone picked up from the ground could be thrown and concuss or kill the man it struck in the head. A highly effective way to increase the range and accuracy of a thrown stone was to use a sling.[22] It was also easy to make. Two lengths of twine were attached to a small cradle or pouch into which the pebble, stone or shot (made of moulded clay or lead) was placed. Then the slinger placed his finger through a loop on the end of one cord, and his thumb and forefinger held a tab at the end of the other cord. The slinger would rotate the loaded weapon in an arc several times and release the tab at a precise moment informed by experience. The famous story in the Book of Samuel describing the duel in which David 'put his hand in his bag and took out a stone, slung it, and struck the Philistine on his forehead' and killed Goliath illustrates how deadly the weapon could be.[23] Its great advantage was its simplicity, in that it could be made at very low cost from readily available materials, combined with its ease of use, meaning that a soldier could become a proficient user after just a few hours of training.

The bow and arrow was a crucial weapon of Ben Kosiba's army. Archery was widely practised in the region for hunting and banditry and is often mentioned in rabbinic texts.[24] A trained archer could fire several arrows a minute, both with precision and over great distance. The Israel Museum has many specimens of arrowheads on display recovered from sites dated to the Bar Kokhba War context. There are the simple flat, leaf-shaped arrowheads made of copper alloy, which were found in the 'Caves of the Spear' near Ein Gedi. Armour-piercing arrowheads of the three-winged (trilobate) design (plate 19) – the most common type at this time and in this region of the world – were found in several other locations.[25] They were made in a variety of profiles including straight, tapering, barbed and round. A cache of twenty-eight arrowheads were found at Herodium and twelve in the 'Har Yishai Caves' at Ein Gedi.[26] Eleven of them were found in near-perfect condition. The profile of four of the blades were drawn back, while seven were 'cut' towards the sharpened end. Behind each blade was a long, narrow tang, which was used to push it into the wooden shaft. Amazingly, one was still attached to the shaft of the arrow and tightly wound with a strip of sinew to ensure the bond. Arrows made of iron were found at Herodium.[27] A near-complete arrow with its upper shaft and its trilobate blade still in place was found near the entrance of the 'Cave of Letters' at Nahal Hever. A further thirty specimens of this style of arrowhead have been found at Horbat 'Eqed, as well as others in caves in the Nahal David and Nahal Arugot areas.[28] These arrows were probably shot with a composite bow, which was popular in this area and time. A grip made of bone from an ibex (a species of wild mountain goat endemic only to this region) was found at Herodium.

For close-quarter fighting, there was a variety of edged weapons. Spears could be utilized to stab or slice an opponent at close quarters or thrown as missiles at an enemy located tens of metres away. Bronze and iron blades were found in the 'Cave of the Spear', so named because several specimens were found inside.[29] Consistent with hand-crafted weapons made by different metal-workers, they all varied in breadth and length but they were generally flat, leaf-shaped design blades and nailed to a long wooden shank.[30] Roman ammunition for artillery weapons (plate 21) could also be retrieved and repurposed.

Judean metal-workers – such as those working at Herodium – could make forged iron or steel swords and daggers as good as any. The Jewish war fighter might even resort to using domestic cutlery; their iron blades could still inflict deadly wounds. They could be easily concealed in the folds of a tunic. Four kitchen knives and a meat chopper with wooden and bone handles in a basket (plate 34), as well as farming tools such as an iron sickle, were found at the 'Cave of Letters'.[31] The curved knife called the *sica* was often used by bandits (for which reason they acquired the name *sicarii*) in this region.

One cunning way in which Ben Kosiba could secure arms and equipment for his men was to exploit an apparent loophole in the Roman military supply chain. The army of occupation in Province Iudaea consumed very large quantities of clothes, equipment and food, as well as raw materials such as iron and leather. They were primarily paid for through taxation and by requisitioning items from the local population, but the free market also had an important role in augmenting the supply of goods.[32] The legions themselves fabricated military equipment at facilities within the walls of their camps. *Legio* X *Fretensis* had a manufacturing plant at Aelia Capitolina making roof tiles.[33] For metal weapons such as arrowheads, spearheads, daggers and swords, Ben Kosiba turned to local Judean metal-working contractors servicing the Roman army's needs and involved them in a subterfuge: 'They purposely made of poor quality such weapons as they were called upon to furnish, in order that the Romans might reject them and they themselves might thus have the use of them.'[34] In time, as he scored victories, Ben Kosiba's soldier would supplement his kit and weaponry with captured Roman gear.[35]

While the insurrectionists made their preparations, their strategy was to give the Romans the impression that it was 'business as usual' in Judea. Cassius Dio writes: 'So long, indeed, as Hadrian was close by in Egypt and again in Syria, they remained quiet.'[36] Between 130 and 132 CE, the rebel army gathered matériel and trained out of view of Roman scouts and troops on police duty, all while gathering field intelligence. One day, however, when Bar Kosiba decided the time was right, it would reveal itself. Gazing out from the walls of Herodium, I wondered what factors the *Nasi Yisrael* considered as he contemplated the day he would launch his revolution.

War was coming. Cassius Dio, the Roman chronicler who meticulously recorded omens as well as accounts of actual events, wrote that 'the people had had forewarning before the war', noting 'For the tomb of Solomon, which the Jews regard as an object of veneration, fell to pieces of itself and collapsed, and many wolves and hyenas rushed howling into their cities.'[37]

Leaving Herodium and joining the main road I found myself in rush-hour traffic again. Misreading the signs, I made a couple of wrong turns and realized I was still driving away from Jerusalem. I turned the car around and headed back in the direction of the city. Then, instead of taking the slip road, I carried on driving straight on only to now find myself in East Jerusalem.

The main street was crowded with traffic. The scene was chaotic. Some drivers seemed not to be following basic road rules and had just left their cars and lorries in the road or double-parked. Without hesitating, I instinctively slammed on the brakes. I could not believe what I had just seen. On the road in front of the car ahead of me I could see the legs of a small boy. It looked as though the driver had knocked down a child! The driver leaped out to see what had happened. Quickly a crowd gathered around. One man dived into the car to grab his car keys so that he could not make an escape. A lot of bad-tempered shouting ensued. In the meantime, the boy got up from the road and dusted himself down. Within the safety of my car all I could do was to ensure the doors were locked. Then from behind a lorry honked its horn. In the rear-view mirror I could just see the lorry driver. He was getting out of his cab and waving his arms around and shouting in Palestinian Arabic. He still had deliveries to make and this crowd was blocking his way. Within minutes the crowd dispersed, the car in front drove to the side and I was able to continue my journey.

My pulse gradually returned to normal, but with a heightened sense of alertness I now drove *very* cautiously. At that moment it occurred to me that this type of incident could mark the start of a riot. With tensions high, an accident or misunderstanding occurring at just the wrong moment could spark unrest and, if mishandled, could lead to a popular uprising, or such an incident could be contrived, set up to become something bigger. The twenty-first century already has numerous examples. In the first century, Josephus recorded the provocative event at the community centre that incited rioting in Caesarea and led to the First Jewish War. How the Second Jewish War began, however, is lost to history. Clearly the Bar Kokhba War had been carefully planned long in advance. If there was a single trigger event, it was likely not an accident. It certainly was timed to begin while the emperor was distracted and on his travels. As Cassius Dio writes, when Hadrian 'went farther away [from Egypt and Syria], they openly revolted'.[38]

One day between the spring and summer of 132 CE – perhaps during the month of *Iyyar* – the Jewish insurgents executed their plan.[39] It is tempting to imagine Ben Kosiba turning to his crowd of followers and using the same words as Mattathias Hakohen Ben Yohanan (Mattathias Maccabeus) when he struck down a Greek official presiding over the ritual sacrifice of a pig, thereby unleashing the struggle to overthrow the Seleucids. 'Follow me,' said Ben Yohanan, 'all of you who are for God's law and stand by the Covenant!'[40] His revolutionaries quickly established toparchies, semi-autonomous administrations in each town and village that declared for him. They appear to have been based on the pre-existing Roman jurisdictions. From the letters they are known to have included Betar, Ein Gedi, Herodium, Ir-Nahash (Kirbet Natash near Herodium), Kiryat 'Arabaya, Jericho and Tekoa.[41]

Each rebel community was managed jointly by a civilian administrator (Hebrew: *parnas*) working together with a militia commander or liaison who reported directly to Ben Kosiba, from whom they would exchange written dispatches to share intelligence and instructions.[42] The *parnasim* ensured compliance of weights and measures, authorized contracts, adjudicated in civil disputes and oversaw the minting of coins.[43] Several rectangular lead weights have been found but almost all are unprovenanced, which is problematic because it casts some doubt on the authenticity of the artefacts and certainly reduces what they can tell us about the past.[44] One example, found in a documented archaeological context at Horbat Alim, is on display at Israel Museum (fig. 18). Around a six-petal geometric rosette set within two concentric circles, the inscription in Aramaic reads: 'Shim'on Ben Kosiba, *Nasi* of Israel, and his *Parnas* Shim'on Dsnw, *prs*.'[45] The reference to *prs* may signify *peras*, meaning 'half', this being its weight; in this example, it is the equivalent of sixty Tyrian *shekels* or one *maneh*.

They also authorized land leases. When the rebels seized land formerly occupied by a Roman landlord, the *parnas* saw to its return to the previous owners, but in many cases the administrator controlled the plots himself and leased them from Ben Kosiba.[46] In this case, farmers were considered his tenants. The *parnas* collected the annual rent from tenants leasing the land. A document reveals that Hillel Ben Garis sub-leased land in

Figure 18. Each community in Ben Kosiba's Israel had a civilian administrator. This steelyard weight from Horbat Alim was approved for use by *parnas* Shim'on Dsnw and weighs 803.6 grammes (1lb 12oz).

Ir-Nahash personally belonging to the *Nasi*.[47] Whether a tax was paid into the national treasury to support the revolutionary state is not clear, but a tithe of agricultural products, such as the four species, was taken for the harvest festival of *Sukkot*.[48]

Ben Kosiba's operational strategy worked remarkably well and the region was soon 'devastated'.[49] Encouraged by these early successes, he needed a mass medium to communicate his success. His new administration took existing Roman coinage out of circulation and over-stamped it with its own images and messages.[50] Dies were made by skilled artisans to approved designs. There was no central mint, however. Coins were reprocessed at community workshops and mobile mints, though how the process was managed is not known; perhaps residents brought their Roman coins to a moneyer and exchanged them for the new legal tender.[51] It comprised the highest denomination full *shekel* by converting the *tetradrachma*; the half *shekel* (or *sel'a*) from the *didrachmon*; the *zuz* replaced the *denarius* and provincial *drachma*; and the *perutah*, which became the new small change, taking the place of the *sestertius, dupondius* and *as*.[52] Re-striking existing Roman coins literally obliterated the graven images of gods and goddesses, the emblems of conquest and victory, and especially the profile of the emperor's head.[53] One of the Ten Commandments expressly states: 'You shall not make for yourself an image in the form of anything in heaven above or on the earth beneath or in the waters below.'[54] The new coins defiantly showed Jewish symbols: the seven-branched palm tree with dates, harp, lyre, trumpets, wine jug, a bunch of grapes, and the four plants – the *arava, etrog, hadas* and *lulav* – associated with the thanksgiving festival of *Sukkot*.[55] The regime's public messaging sought to decisively assert the new state's distinctively Jewish identity. The choice of these images communicated that Ben Kosiba's regime was ideologically rooted in the *Torah*.[56] Israel was proudly independent of Rome and its gods.

Mimicking Roman types, the coins bore legends or slogans; however, they were not written in Latin or Greek characters but in palaeo-Hebrew.[57] It was an early form of cursive script, which was already long obsolete by 132 CE. In using this archaic form of lettering, the new regime was celebrating the great antiquity of Judaism and connecting itself with the glory days of King David, following in the tradition established by the Hasmonaean rulers and collective leadership of the First Jewish War who had used it on their coins.[58] However, for everyday use scribes in Ben Kosiba's administration wrote legal documents and military correspondence in the elegant Aramaic square, calligraphic book hand in which Ivrit is still written. It was the script in which the Hebrew Bible and the derivative commentaries were written; promoting it as the 'official font' gave all official documents issued under Ben Kosiba a decidedly priestly look.[59] The earlier letters are written in Aramaic, the later ones in Hebrew.[60] In fact, says one scholar after having studied hundreds of texts, the *Nasi* of Israel *required* book hand for Hebrew documents; it is the way his own letters and all contracts were written.[61] One, given the modern reference '*Mur* 43', is actually *signed* by him.[62]

The way the official documents were written offers insights about how the language was spoken at the time. The scribes wrote phonetically, combining the definite accusative with the noun. Thus 'the camp' would be written 'thcamp'.[63] There are other oddities in the documents suggesting that vernacular Hebrew speakers who normally wrote in Aramaic struggled to write in the mandated Hebrew script. They often wrote with spelling errors by omitting letters in words because when speaking they did not pronounce them, or spelled the words differently because of the way they pronounced them, such as nasalizations.[64] Correspondents sometimes mixed Hebrew and Aramaic words or phrases in sentences, or included new words, or used old ones with new meanings.

Documents preserve the new, official form of dating correspondence adopted by administrators and scribes: 'On the first of *Iyyar*, Year One of the Redemption of Israel by [the hands of Shim]'[o]n son of Kosiba, *Nasi* of Israel.'[65] It echoed in a very deliberate manner the messaging of Simon Thassi of 142 BCE.[66]

Ben Kosiba's moneyers struck their first coins with the same slogan (plate 22): *'YEAR ONE: FOR THE REDEMPTION OF ISRAEL.'*[67] For the rebels it must have been thrilling to hold in the palms of their hands tangible evidence of their daring achievement. They were part of something big. It was affirmation expressed in gleaming metal that the Israel of Saul, Solomon and David described in *Torah* had been re-established in their own lifetimes! They now had control over their own sovereignty.[68] Where the messaging on the coins struck by Zealots in the earlier war had declared for the Zion, Ben Kosiba deliberately appealed for a much grander vision.[69]

The most impressive coins issued by Ben Kosiba's mints were the silver *shekelim* or *sela'im*. On the obverse was a depiction of the front elevation of a large building. Pairs of great columns flank an open arched doorway, revealing the Ark of the Covenant inside the flat-roofed, tetra-style building. It may be the Temple frontage or an entranceway to the great Temple courtyard (fig. 7).[70] A ladder-like object lies on the ground in front of the Temple, which may represent the twelve steps that once led up to the Temple door. On either side of the image are palaeo-Hebrew letters spelling the name 'Shimeon' and the mysterious 'Eleazar the Priest' (plate 23).[71]

Liberating Jerusalem from the Romans and rebuilding the Temple appear to have been central policy objectives of Ben Kosiba's mission. Scholars continue to debate whether Ben Kosiba's forces actually succeeded in doing so. Coins may provide the answer. Of the 15,000 or so coins found at archaeological excavations in Jerusalem, only *four* of them were specimens overstruck by the Bar Kokhba War administration; if the city had been taken by the rebels it would surely be reasonable to expect to find many more there?[72] The conclusion must be that Jerusalem was not captured by Ben Kosiba.[73] Consistent with waging a *Milhemet Mitzvah*, the coins communicated the *nasi's* aspirations and were intended as propaganda but not as a celebration of an actual achievement.[74]

Thousands of these bronze and silver coins have been found over the years, often as single specimens, but sometimes in hoards. Researchers use the distribution pattern of coin finds – often found in caves – to determine the geographical extent of the rebellion led by Ben Kosiba (map 3).[75] Coins serve as a proxy for which communities accept the tokens as legal tender for buying and selling goods. They have been found all over Judea, from the area around Jerusalem (north, north-east, south-east and south-west), the western Jerusalem Hills, Bethlehem, Beit Guvrin, Hebron, Herodium and in caves near Ein Gedi beside the Dead Sea.[76] What they show is that the Galilee, which had been central to the First Jewish War, Samaria and Transjordan, as well as the Greek-speaking coastal cities such as Gaza, were *not* involved in the new conflict, though people from those regions may have fled to Israel.[77] Other attempts to map the extent of the revolt trying to locate places named in the rabbinic literature have been unsuccessful for the most part.

In this holy war, Ben Kosiba's strategy was to play to the strengths of the guerrilla fighter. He knew the weaknesses of his professional trained opponent. He had all the advantages of local knowledge of the terrain, as well as surprise and agility. His militiamen could appear out of nowhere, ambush Roman troops on the march, wreak havoc and quickly disappear. Cassius Dio writes:

> To be sure, they [the rebels] did not dare try conclusions with the Romans in the open field, but they occupied the advantageous positions in the country and strengthened them with mines and walls in order that they might have places of refuge whenever they should be hard pressed.[78]

Archaeologists nowadays refer to these as 'hiding complexes'. More than 390 have been discovered, located in more than 150 places in Judea.[79] They are found as far north as Kirbet Seilun (north of Ramallah and Jericho); south as far as Hahal Nattir (near Beer Sheva); west as far as el Meghara (between Ashdod and Bet Shemesh); and east as far as Kirbet Bani Dar

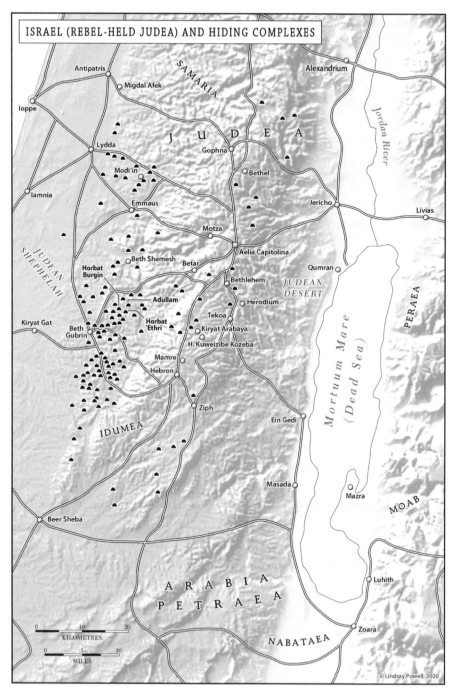

Map 3. Israel (Rebel-held Judea) and hiding complexes. (© *Lindsay Powell*)

(near Hebron).[80] Each of these underground systems is unique in the way their architects combined vertical shafts, interlocking chambers, openings for ventilation and light, and even niches for oil lamps. I was keen to examine some of these 'advantageous positions' and 'places of refuge' for myself. It was time to take to the hills: the Judean Hills.

About an hour's drive – 35 kilometres (22 mi.) – south-west of Jerusalem lie the excavated remains of two fortified Jewish farmsteads that took part in the Bar Kokhba War. At the interchange on Highway 1 I took Route 38 and headed south. A few miles along it the going slowed as traffic navigated contraflows set up by construction workers who were widening and resurfacing the road. It reminded me how, 2,000 years ago, Roman soldiers expanded and maintained the road network across Province Iudaea by order of Hadrian in the aftermath of the War of Quietus. Today mechanized equipment does the heavy work of drilling and digging, filling in the layers of aggregate and laying the blacktop. In those days they did the back-breaking work by hand using the *dolabra* – the legionary's versatile combination pickaxe and mattock – and wicker baskets. While they form the arteries to commerce and trade, then as now, roads were also the means by which troops and supplies could move quickly to conflict zones.

Eventually I saw the sign for Adulam-France Park (Parc de France-Adoulam). It had been established as a nature reserve managed by the Israel Nature and National Parks Protection Authority in 1994. Across its 12,350 acres a winding road network connects the points of natural and historical interest. I followed the roadside markers bearing a small icon of an Ionic column capital, pointing the direction to the archaeological sites. The landscape is achingly beautiful, of fields gently undulating over grassy marl-covered soft chalk and dotted with clusters of trees. This is the *Shephelah* (*Shfela*), meaning 'lowlands'. It is a transitional region in south-central Israel of soft-sloping hills stretching over 10 to 15 kilometres (6.2 to 9.3 mi.) between the Judean Hills and the Mediterranean coast. Since the Late Bronze Age farmers have planted crops and grazed animals here. It has been farmed ever since. During the First Jewish War partisans had fortified their villages and fought the Romans. They suffered greatly when they lost.

After several miles driving over the twisting, stony country lane the incline steepened and eventually I could drive no further. I had come to the end of the road. The marker pointed to the left. Above me was Adullam. From this point the site could only be reached on foot. At the top of the hill I could see the outlines of stone walls that had once been the large square and rectangular buildings of a settlement. It is a surprisingly important place: it is mentioned in the Book of Genesis and listed as one of the cities conquered by the Israelites.[81] Judah Maccabee came here with his men when returning from his war with the Idumaeans.[82] Two centuries later its occupants sided with Ben Kosiba. Constructed of roughly finished stone blocks, Adullam would have been imposing in its heyday. Today the site feels forlorn and abandoned. Long grass and weeds grow in and between the ruined buildings, making identification of the site's features difficult to the untrained eye. Adding to the confusion, on the east side of the summit are ruins of several houses of an Arab village from the Ottoman period, which were later reduced to rubble. On the crest of the hill a long wall of large, regular blocks rises to several courses. At ground level there is a small stone arch of rough-hewn stones. It was large enough for me to crawl through. Inside I found a chamber large enough for several people to gather. The cool air in the enclosed, shady space offered pleasant relief from the heat of the sun.

Back outside again, I walked through a clearing in the trees growing over a sloping ledge. The view from the site looking east impressed me. Beneath, a vast sweep of land ranged across a wide valley. The place fitted Cassius Dio's description of how Ben Kosiba fought his war. I recalled Cassius Dio's words. The occupants of this stronghold in its 'advantageous position' could watch for Roman troop movements. They could either take 'refuge' behind the thick stone 'walls' or launch attacks by sweeping down the hillside. Signs warned visitors of the risk of falling into hazards hidden in the ground and openings to caves; these could be the 'mines' the Roman historian mentions. Atop the steep hill the stronghold would be difficult for the Romans to stage a counterattack. Little wonder that Judah Maccabee decided to retreat to this particular place.

A car ride away in the same National Park is Horbat 'Etri. The remains of this fortified farmstead or village lie on a long ridge. In 2004 and 2016 archaeologists fully excavated and mapped the site. Happily, the conserved remains of its buildings have been left exposed for visitors to safely explore. In their report the archaeologists recorded that an ancient road, 2 to 5 metres (6.6 to 16.4ft) wide, delimited by two walls and constructed of medium-sized fieldstones, ran the length of the brow of the hill that extended south-east of the ruin.[83] This road connected Horbat 'Etri to Horbat Shua' (Khirbet Umm es-Suweid), a village located at the top of the nearby hill located to the south-east.[84] Horbat 'Etri had been occupied during the war of 66–70/74 CE and was then abandoned, but in the decades following it had been reoccupied and repaired. A metal sign with a reconstruction drawing etched on it (fig. 19) shows that the village was a collection of rectangular buildings arranged around a courtyard; a building erected across the middle of the space divided it into two enclosed spaces. The two-storey, flat-roofed buildings each contained a series of small, regular-shaped rooms for family living and the storage of goods. The archaeologists noted that the most impressive feature was a 'public building' containing a courtyard, a large *mikwa* (a ritual bath) and a vestibule.[85] This opened into a rectangular hall with three pillars across the centre. They interpreted this structure to have been a *beit knesset*. It was in use until the end of the Bar Kokhba War.[86]

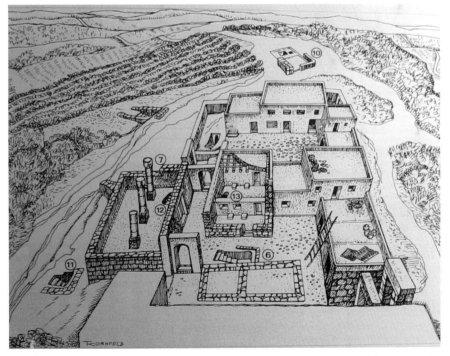

Figure 19. This imaginative, partial reconstruction of the village at Horbat 'Etri shows the buildings arranged around a split courtyard. They include a winepress (10) and community meeting room or synagogue (12), as well as access to hiding places (6 and 11).

In ancient times the Judean *Shephelah* was known for its wine production as well as for growing a variety of grains.[87] Horbat 'Etri was a working farm producing figs and wine. Round and square holes and channels cut into the rock suggest there were once three wine presses operating here.[88] Grapes were gathered in from the surrounding countryside and poured into vats. The farmers would tread the fruit with their bare feet to release the juice which drained to a settling pit and collecting vat. The must or pulp was put into baskets for transfer to a screw press to squeeze out the remaining juice. Containerized and allowed to ferment, the wine would be stored and then decanted for sale in pottery amphorae.

Horbat 'Etri occupies a fine, defensible location. Its high elevation meant that residents could survey the surroundings unobstructed for unwanted intruders. The excavators identified watchmen's huts on the terraces close to the village.[89] There were narrow portals into the village, which were likely gated. The construction of the buildings' stout walls made of stones (plate 26) would offer its residents some protection in the

Figure 20. This is the entrance to a hiding space beneath the village at Horbat 'Etri. It is marked (11) in Figure 19. Some of the entrances to the rock-cut caves like this one are visible from the steps, while others are completely disguised.

event of a raid. However, the site contains a secret. Below the buildings
are cavities. Caves form naturally in the local limestone, but the residents
here dug out the rock beneath their homes to form burrows where goods
could be stored in the cool subterranean air, or people could hide in
times of trouble. There are several of these at Horbat 'Etri with shafts cut
into the floors of rooms, but some are accessible by steps (fig. 20) which
go down to openings in the ground.[90] Many are simple round dugout
chambers, but under two of the buildings they are better described as
rooms, being longer in length with squared angles in which people can
stand, and connected by tunnels.[91] The caverns on the eastern side date
to the Bar Kokhba War.[92] There is also a burial system of caves with a
vestibule and walls of funerary slots.[93] Some of these spaces were created
during the First Jewish War but were re-dug by Ben Kosiba's rebels to
enlarge them. Their existence corroborates a statement made by Cassius
Dio that the Jewish rebels 'might meet together unobserved underground,
and they pierced these subterranean passages from above at intervals to
let in air and light.'[94]

Not far from Horbat 'Etri is the contemporary village at Horbat Burgin
(Khirbet Umm Burj).[95] The burrows are even more elaborate there

Figure 21. Some of the tunnels in the hiding complex at Horbat Burgin are high enough for
a man to stand up in. To move through others a man must crawl.

(fig. 21), with winding shafts so narrow that a man must get down on his hands and knees in order to crawl through them.

In their heyday these places were filled with the myriad sounds of farming life: the bleating of goats, the threshing of wheat, the groan of winepresses, the shouts of farm workers and the laughter of children. Apart from the occasional chatter of visitors, today they are silent.

After leaving Adulam-France Park that day I checked into Neve-Shalom (Wahat as-Salam) near Latrun.[96] Sitting outside under the clear night sky and surrounded by the dark outlines of the hills of the Judean *Shephelah*, I could see the sparkling lights of Tel Aviv on the horizon. In the middle distance the fields were still. I reflected on the day's findings. This was rebel country in 133 CE. It was an astonishing feat for Ben Kosiba to engage the people of Judea in a conspiracy and commit them to keeping a secret until it was time for the revolution he had planned to burst forth. The people who followed Shim'on – perhaps believing him to be the King Messiah – did so because they shared his vision of a free Israel. He had delivered. 'Year One' had been a success.

Yet Ben Kosiba knew the Romans would respond and when they did, they would come hard and heavy. The matter was now personal. Hadrian would not let up until he had taken back what was his. Ben Kosiba would fight to keep it.

Chapter 6

'Do Not Help or Hinder Us!'

Over breakfast I re-read my well-thumbed copy of Book 69 of Cassius Dio's *Roman History*. What struck me was the provincial authority's dismissive initial response to the latest Jewish uprising. Dio writes: 'At first the Romans took no account of them.'[1] Occurring in the same region as the First Jewish War, it was a remarkable reaction. I reasoned that Roman military officials in cosmopolitan Caesarea perceived them as minor disturbances that could be handled by the centurions and tribunes deployed throughout the province. That was, after all, their job. Intelligence reports from the units dealing with the trouble, however, continued to flow into the governor's office.[2] Only then did the perception of the unfolding events change. Briefed by his adjutants, Tineius Rufus must have realized that he was no longer facing a low-level, localized problem:

> Soon, however, all Iudaea had been stirred up and the Jews everywhere were showing signs of disturbance, were gathering together and giving evidence of great hostility to the Romans, partly by secret and partly by overt acts.[3]

As the provincial governor, Rufus' primary objective was to keep his province *pacata atque quieta*, 'pacified and quiet'.[4] He was imbued with power (*imperium*) coming direct from Hadrian with which, as the emperor's deputy, to restore order, using military force if necessary.[5] Rufus had substantial resources at his disposal. Assessing the situation, he would need to decide which legions and auxiliary units to deploy and where to deal with the insurgency. Rufus' slow response had already lost him valuable time and by the end of 132 CE the situation was getting worse, much worse. He would soon have to officially notify his commander-in-chief: *imperator* Hadrian.

To find out more about how Hadrian responded to the troubles in Iudaea I had arranged to meet David Mevorah, Senior Curator of Hellenistic, Roman and Byzantine Periods at the Israel Museum. His department was staging a special exhibition entitled *Hadrian: An Emperor Cast in Bronze*. It brought together the only three metal statue busts of the emperor to survive from the ancient world. Having signed in at the reception and attached my gold visitor's badge, I was met by a cheerful member of the department and taken behind the scenes of the great institution. We walked through storerooms piled high with artefacts awaiting conservation or being held until a suitable time arose to display them in the museum's archaeological gallery. Some had never been seen by the public. I was introduced to Mevorah in his office and he immediately made me feel very welcome. He liked to be called Dudi.

'Hadrian is one of the characters of history I'd love to meet,' said Mevorah. He explained how the emperor had great energy, a keen intellect and wide-ranging interests. As Opper had done in London, he ran through his military, architectural and even poetic achievements with me. 'He spied on his friends and he had insecurities,' added the curator with a grin.

Mevorah then offered a fascinating insight. He said, 'Hadrian was the best student of Augustus.' It was a remark that resonated with me because, at the time I was researching this book, I was finishing *Augustus at War: The Struggle for the 'Pax Augusta'*.[6] The heir of Iulius Caesar had established many of the practices continued by his successors, not least creating a standing, professional army and forming the legal and administrative framework which managed the provinces. To ensure its continuing efficient operation, Hadrian spent years travelling Rome's dominions and legionary camps. Augustus dealt with military policy challenges, including launching wars of necessity and wars of choice, but at the end of his life 'the ocean and remote rivers were the boundaries of the empire'.[7] Heeding that smart advice, more than a century later Hadrian abandoned many of the lands conquered by his predecessor, bringing the borders back almost to the same configuration as Augustus had left them. Public image mattered very much to Augustus, who used statues, coins and buildings to project his pre-eminence and strength. Hadrian adopted the same practices. 'Hadrian was a master of propaganda,' said Mevorah.

He escorted me to see the special exhibition he had organized. In a large room, its walls and ceiling painted black, spotlights shone down on three objects inside glass cases. They were spaced apart to form a triangle. As a backdrop there was a floor-to-ceiling photograph of Hadrian's Wall meandering over a grassy escarpment. The overall effect was dramatic. I focused on the artefacts. One bust (plate 3) I recognized immediately. It was the head found by London Bridge in the River Thames in 1848. Normally at the British Museum, where I had seen it many times, the trustees had lent the bronze head to the Israel Museum for this event under Thorsten Opper's supervision. The second of the busts (plate 2) had been loaned by the Musée du Louvre. It was an unprovenanced find and largely unknown outside Paris; I had certainly never seen it before. The third bust was from the Israel Museum's own collection.

All the portraits clearly represented one man, yet they were not identical and differed in subtle details such as the profile or shape of the nose or dressing of the hair. In that regard it was the same with coins of Hadrian. The curator explained that the portrait busts were displayed high up rather than at eye-level, as this was how they were intended to be seen in ancient times. There was a particular spot where a viewer was intended to stand and admire the work. Each of the over-life-size statues, polished to look lifelike, originally stood upon plinths and the viewer *looked up* at them; their eyes, made of coloured glass, once stared over and past the viewer at some faraway horizon.

The bust from Tel Shalem (plate 1) was normally the centrepiece of the Israel Museum's Samuel and Saidye Bronfman Archaeological Wing. It was found by a New York stockbroker and occasional amateur archaeologist on 25 July 1975 while he was searching for ancient coins with a metal detector – the find of a lifetime if ever there was one![8] Mevorah said that the head was likely cast in a workshop in Italy, while the torso was probably of local Judean manufacture, possibly recycled from an earlier statue.[9] He had a theory about it. When it was found in the Beth Shean Valley in 1975, the condition of the head and torso – though missing the arms and legs – strongly suggested that it was deliberately buried in the ground. It had probably served a ritual function in the camp of *Legio* VI *Ferrata*, perhaps either standing outside in the centre of the courtyard of the headquarters building (Latin: *principia*), or inside the building surrounded by the legion's sacred standards (*signa*). One working theory is that the legionaries suddenly found themselves under attack from Jewish insurgents. To prevent the statue from falling into enemy hands and being defaced by them, soldiers were ordered to dig a hole and bury it. The camp then appears to have been evacuated soon after.

'The clash here [in Judea] was not intentional,' suggested Mevorah, 'Hadrian did not understand the deeply religious aspect of the Jews.' He was curator of the *Cradle of Christianity: Jewish and Christian Treasures from the Holy Land* exhibition at the Israel Museum in 2000.

Mevorah had no reason to suspect Cassius Dio's reason for the rebellion. In founding Aelia Capitolina the curator argued that the emperor was trying to establish a 'cultured place' that would be crucial to life in the future of Iudaea, but in doing so he was severing the Jews' ancient connection to Judea. Once rebellion broke out, Hadrian had to prevent it spilling over to neighbouring Arabia Petraea, Syria and Egypt. He did not need a repeat of the War of Quietus. 'Huge unrest somewhere had repercussions everywhere,' said Mevorah.

He had no doubt that Hadrian would have learned about the rebellion soon after it erupted. 'He was not delayed in getting information,' he said. As a military man Hadrian understood the need for early containment and a swift end to the revolt. The usual response to rebellion was *vastatio*, a punitive action intended to show that resistance to Roman rule would not be tolerated.[10] Tiny as it was, a hostile independent state like Ben Kosiba's Israel could not be allowed to exist within Rome's *imperium*. 'His decisions were not limited to this small space,' Mevorah said. Others must be deterred too. 'It's not just the people in Judea,' he said, 'it's everyone.' He pointed out that the war in Judea was not his only experience of rebellion.

The author of the *Life of Hadrian* writes:

> There were no campaigns (*expeditiones*) of importance during his reign and the wars (*bella*) that he did wage were brought to a close almost without arousing comment.[11]

There was evidently more than one military operation, but the statement then does not disclose what or where the others occurred. For clarification we have to look for answers in other sources. One is a casual reference in a letter. Writing in 162 CE to Emperor Antoninus Pius, M. Cornelius Fronto remarks how under his grandfather Hadrian a large number of soldiers were killed 'by the Britons'.[12] An uprising in Britannia is nowhere else mentioned in the extant written record.[13] Archaeology, however, now provides some tantalizing evidence.

Buried under the city of London is a layer of ash caused by a fire, which devastated most of the Roman city.[14] Whether it was an accident or arson is not known. An attack on Londinium may also explain how the decapitated bronze head of the emperor ended up in the Thames. A large number of skulls from young males were also found by the ancient stream at Walbrook, which once flowed through Londinium to the Thames River. There are several working theories to explain their fate, one of which is that they are trophy heads belonging to executed captives. Soon after 120 CE a Roman fort was constructed at Cripplegate in the north-west corner of the city along with a new military road. Remains of the west gate and a substantial section of the fort wall can still be seen in the London Wall underground car park. These provide compelling evidence to suggest that there was a significant problem of civil unrest in Province Britannia during 128/130 CE, years during which Hadrian reigned.[15] It would have fallen to his governor, then Cn. Minicius Faustinus Sextus Iulius Severus, to deal with the crisis.[16] The cost in Roman lives was high and memorable enough for a friend of one of the emperor's successors to recall it more than thirty years later. There may well have been other incidents that we do not know about.

In 132/133 CE Rufus had to regain control of his province, and quickly. It would surely have been personally embarrassing for Rufus to have to ask for assistance from his colleagues, but it was now about bringing to bear overwhelming force to crush the rebellion. It was no longer an uprising, but now a conflict with a name: *Bellum Iudaicum*, 'Jewish War'.[17] 'Then, indeed,' writes Cassius Dio, 'Hadrian sent against them his best generals.'[18] He had thirty legions at his disposal (map 1). The evidence points to several legions being involved, many travelling over great distances to reach Judea. Rather than entire legions, detachments (*vexillationes*) were drawn, generally comprising multiples of cohorts.[19] The organization of the legion – going back to C. Marius in the first century BCE, and later refined by Augustus and Hadrian himself – allowed for these self-contained units of 480 men to break off from the main body as and when required to deal with a military contingency. The main advantage of this design was that *vexillationes* could be scaled according to need without committing entire legions. They marched under their own unit flag (*vexillum*).

Building a Roman order of battle and a campaign map for the Bar Kokhba War is challenging.[20] The evidence is fragmentary and comes almost entirely from archaeological and epigraphical sources.[21] An inscription documenting a soldier's or officer's career, for example, may include the legion he was attached to or campaign he fought in. A shard of a brick or roof tile stamped with a unit's name seemingly places it in a known location, but the material may have been brought in from a factory run by another unit elsewhere. Some associations are the result of inference or informed guesswork. The process is like a detective working on a cold case trying to track the movements of suspects at a crime scene while relying on an old box of forensic and circumstantial evidence where a lot of it has gone missing.

Legio X *Fretensis* (fig. 22), encamped inside or close by Aelia Capitolina, was the unit nearest to the combat theatre and it would already have been committed in full.[22] Its centuries and cohorts would already have been active across the district on training manoeuvres and police duties, and have taken the first casualties of the Bar Kokhba War.

Legio VI *Ferrata* was stationed in the north of Province Iudaea, but the evidence for its participation in the war is slight.[23] A *vexillatio* moved

Figure 22. A roof tile (*tegula*) made at the factory operated by 'LEG X FR'. The stamp of manufacture includes the legion's bireme and boar emblems.

from its camp at Tel Shalem south of Beth-Shean/Scythopolis, where the bronze head of Hadrian (plate 1) was buried, to Caparcotna (also called Legio), which suggests that the legion was mobilized but appears to have remained within Galilee and Samaria.[24] Its manoeuvres may have prevented the spread of any unrest in the districts. Curiously, a centurion's tombstone has been found at Sebaste and dated to Hadrian's era, but how he died is not disclosed, and if it was a violent death it may in any case have been in a local Samaritan disturbance.[25]

Legio III *Gallica* marched from its home base camp at Raphanaea in Syria into the war zone.[26] Leading the column was C. Quinctius Certus Publicius Marcellus, the *Legatus Augusti Pro Praetore* of Syria; with three legions under his command he could afford to release one to Iudaea.[27]

Legio II *Traiana Fortis*, or more likely a *vexillatio* of it, arrived from Egypt in the south-west.[28] It had seen service in Iudaea before. Founded by Trajan for his Dacian War in 105 CE, the legion was later transferred to Arabia Petraea by the emperor after his campaigns in Parthia and from there to Iudaea. Sometime around 120 CE Hadrian then rotated it with VI *Ferrata* and moved II *Traiana* to Alexandria.

Legio III *Cyrenaica* provided a *vexillatio* from its base at Bostra in neighbouring Arabia Petraea to the east with provincial commander T. Haterius Nepos arriving in person.[29] He had a colourful past. Among many political and military positions held during his career, when Hadrian turned 43 Nepos was the procurator of the *ludus magnus* in charge of training gladiators and organizing games for public occasions in Rome.[30] When visiting Egypt at dawn on 18 February 121 CE he went to the Colossus of Memnon and heard the famous stone statue sing, which was the occasion for setting up an inscription.[31] At the outbreak of hostilities in Iudaea he assessed that the Jews in his own province posed no threat. It was a risky move, however. *Legio* III was the only legion stationed in Arabia Petraea.[32] The unit had seen combat in the Parthian War and was likely called upon to squash unrest during the War of Quietus.

Legio XII *Fulminata* based in Melitene, Cappadocia sent a *vexillatio*.[33] It is listed with X *Fretensis* and II *Traiana* on an inscription.

Legio V *Macedonica* arrived from Troemis, Moesia Inferior as a *vexillatio*.[34]

Legio XI *Claudia*, also from Durostorum, Moesia Inferior, provided soldiers for a *vexillatio*.[35] In the Bar Kokhba War it campaigned alongside *Legio* V *Macedonica*.

Legio X *Gemina* from Vindobona, Upper Pannonia was also represented in Province Iudaea as a *vexillatio* under the command of Q. Lollius Urbicus.[36] His inscription defines his position as 'legate of commander Hadrian in the Jewish Taskforce'.[37] The implication is that Urbicus was Hadrian's chief deputy but perhaps, rather than *the* legate, it may perhaps be read as *a* legate of the emperor.[38] He was assisted in this task by equestrian tribune Sex. Attius Senecio.[39]

The participation of several other legions has been proposed by different scholars based on creative reconstructions and readings of inscriptions, or pure guesswork. They include *Legiones* VIIII *Hispana* and XXII *Deiotariana*, either or both of which some authorities contest was wiped out during the Bar Kokhba War, but with little hard evidence to support their arguments.[40]

Around half the men-at-arms in Hadrian's army were professional non-Roman citizen troops.[41] These allied troops (*auxilia*) were organized into three types of unit: infantry *cohortes peditata* ('cohorts of foot') 480 or 800 men strong; cavalry *alae* ('wings') 512 or 768 men strong; and mixed *cohortes equitata* ('cohorts of horse') of 480 infantry and 128 cavalry or 800 infantry and 256 cavalry.[42] Several were stationed in Province Iudaea and operating specifically in the district of Judea.[43] A document cast in bronze honourably discharging an auxiliary soldier – nowadays called a 'diploma' – has been found dated to 139 CE that mentions fifteen units, of which five are believed to have fought in the Bar Kokhba War.[44] They are *Ala Gallorum et Thracum*; *Ala* VII *Phrygum* from Syria; *Cohors* I *Flavia C R.E.* from Syria; *Cohors* V *Gemina C R.*; and *Cohors* I *Sebastenorum C R.* from Syria.[45] Other units that may have been active in Judea during the war include *Cohors* III *Bracaugustanorum* from Britannia; *Cohors* IIII *Bracaugustanorum* from Syria or Province Iudaea; and *Cohors* I *Montanorum* from Pannonia Inferior or Moesia Superior.[46] Adding their numbers to the expeditionary army in Judea may have been *Cohors* I *Breucorum C R.* from Raetia; *Cohors* III *Lingonum* from Britannia; *Cohors* I *Claudia Sugambrorum* (*Veterana*) *E.* from Moesia Inferior; and *Cohors* I *Hispanorum M. Eq.* from Britannia.[47] A stamped roof tile from Hebron appears to attest to the presence of *Cohors* I *Thracum Milliaria* there, while a papyrus states that the unit – or a detachment – was located at Ein Gedi in 124 CE.[48]

Scholars still argue about the role of *Classis Syriaca*, the navy unit stationed in Syria at Seleucia Pieria on the Mediterranean Sea. Its involvement in the war is suggested by an inscription honouring its equestrian prefect (*praefectus Classis Syriaca*).[49] There are several possible explanations. The fleet may have transported troops from Britannia or Moesia Inferior or Pannonia Superior from embarkation points to Caesarea or Ioppe. It may even have patrolled the Sea of Galilee (Hebrew: *Kinneret*) or Dead Sea, perhaps intercepting and blockading rebels or supplies sailing in and out of Ein Gedi. Marines might have joined the land army as a fighting force in its own right, replacing Roman casualties. Men of the *Classis Misenensis* at Misenum may also have been transferred to Province Iudaea to join *Legio* X *Fretensis* but, again, the evidence is open to interpretation.[50]

Determining the precise numbers of Roman troops that Hadrian committed to the *expeditio Iudaica* is extremely difficult based on what little information is available.[51] Complicating matters, they probably did not all arrive in the theatre of operations at the same time. The combined force of legions, *vexillationes* and auxiliaries may have been in the range of 30,000–50,000 professional soldiers, but that is an informed guess. If so, this represented almost a tenth of the entire standing army.[52] Hadrian made a big investment in blood and treasure, but it was necessary to break the rebel leader's hold on his Province Iudaea. Determining their movements is just as difficult based on what little information we have. The extensive road network, recently expanded by Hadrian, would certainly have expedited their logistics and pre-determined their manoeuvres. They traversed the rebel-held territory, but many of their strongholds were off-road, making access particularly challenging to heavy infantry.

With this force, the Romans launched an aggressive 'shock-and-awe' counter-insurgency campaign. Eusebius records that:

> As the revolt of the Jews at this time grew much more serious, Rufus, governor of Iudea, after an auxiliary force had been sent him by the emperor, using their madness as a pretext, proceeded against them without mercy, and destroyed indiscriminately thousands of men and women and children.[53]

Yet it is a rule of war that 'no plan survives contact with the enemy'.[54] The surge of more men and matériel appears to have had little impact, at least initially. The militia army of Israel was seemingly able to take on Hadrian's highly-trained soldiers and hold their own. The Jews were neither shocked nor awed. Buoyed by their early victories, his men continued to launch surprise attacks upon unsuspecting Romans from their underground hide-outs. The rabbinic sources record that when the army of Israel went into battle against the Romans, the men shouted:

> Master of the Universe!
> Do not help or hinder us![55]

It was gutsy, bordering on the profane. The war cry was a twisting of the words of Psalm 60:

> Who will bring me to the fortified city?
>   Who will lead me to Edom?
> Is it not you, God, you who have now rejected us
>   and no longer go out with our armies?
> Give us aid against the enemy,
>   for human help is worthless.
> With God we will gain the victory,
>   and he will trample down our enemies.[56]

The Talmudic source portrays Ben Kosiba with the headstrong confidence of a *gibbor*, revealing an arrogant trait in the leader's personality.[57]

Before we parted, I asked David Mevorah his opinion of Ben Kosiba and the Bar Kokhba War. 'Bar Kokhba was erased from history, he's not a hero,' he said, 'but there's so much we don't know.' He remarked that the rabbinic sources give dramatic descriptions of the catastrophes that befell the Jews. Referring to the letters, it was clear to Mevorah that 'he's not an intellectual, he's a brute.' He added that he knew Greek but did not know Greek philosophy. Ben Kosiba was leading a rebel nation at war.

Our time together was up. Mevorah had another meeting to attend and we said our polite goodbyes. I remained behind to explore the gallery further.

Mevorah had presented a stark assessment of the Jewish warlord. Nevertheless, it was clear to me that during the first years Ben Kosiba's strategy of fighting a nationwide guerrilla war worked. His men followed his orders and went into battle. There is a story in the *Midrash* that may contain a memory of a real event about two militiamen who faced the Romans in the Judean valley:

There were two brothers in Kefar Haruba, who did not allow any Roman to pass there, because they killed him.

They said: 'The conclusion of the whole matter is that we must take Hadrian's crown and set it upon our own head.'

They heard that the Romans were coming towards them; and when they set out against them, an old man met them and said: 'May the Creator be your help against them!'

They retorted: 'Let him neither help nor discourage us!'[58]

By the summer of 133 CE, the rebel nation could celebrate an anniversary. The Jewish moneyers began issuing a new series of coins in celebration. The accompanying slogan read: '*YEAR TWO: FOR THE FREEDOM OF ISRAEL.*'[59] The die-makers now added a symbol about the image of the Temple on the silver *sela'im* (fig. 23); some interpret it to refer to the star in the rebel leader's moniker Bar Kokhba but, in fact, it is a cross or rosette.[60] Gone is the name of Eleazar the Priest.[61] One piece dated to the 'Second Year', found in the 'Har Yishai Cave', was struck over a Roman coin which had a countermark of *Legio* VI, presumably *Ferrata* at Caparconta/Legio.[62]

Ben Kosiba was eager to share news of his victories. Jewish tradition banned display of graven images, but there was a visual vocabulary that could be used for messaging. The Hasmonaean John Hyrcanus I had

Figure 23. A silver *sela* struck in 133/4 CE bears the name 'Shim'on' in Paleo-Hebrew arranged around the tetra-style façade of the Temple of Jerusalem. Visible inside is a show bread table or the Ark of the Covenant in chest form with a semicircular lid and short legs. On the reverse, the legend reads 'Year Two For The Freedom of Israel' surrounding a *lulav* and *etrog*.

displayed military symbols on his coins. One of these was the palm branch.[63] Tied with a fillet (a length of cloth), the palm frond was a symbol of triumph used by the Greeks. Simon Thassi was greeted with waving palms in celebration of his capture of the fortress of Akra at Jerusalem from the Seleucid garrison in 141 BCE.[64] His arrival was also accompanied by 'harps and cymbals and stringed instruments, and with hymns and songs because a great enemy had been crushed and removed from Israel'.[65] Single palm fronds (fig. 24) as well as stringed instruments appear on Ben Kosiba's smaller silver coin issues.[66] While the *lulav* was used in the religious festival of *Sukkot*, its appearance on Ben Kosiba's coins may also signify his victories over the Romans and their ousting from Israel.

News of Ben Kosiba's successes travelled beyond rebel-held territory. Cassius Dio writes: 'Many outside nations, too, were joining them through eagerness for gain, and the whole earth, one might almost say, was being stirred up over the matter.'[67] Volunteers and mercenaries arrived from neighbouring Arabia Petraea and Nabataea, not always drawn to the conflict by glory but for cash or a share of the war spoils.[68] Support for Ben Kosiba's army came from an unexpected place. According to rabbinic sources Rabbi Akiba's students were keen to enter the fight. Some '12,000 pairs' arrived from Bene Berak.[69] It was the thirty-third day of

Figure 24. This silver *zuz* struck in 133/134 CE bears the name 'Shim('on)' in Paleo-Hebrew within a wreath of thin branches wrapped around eight almonds, with a medallion at the top and tendrils at the bottom. On the reverse an upright palm branch is surrounded by the legend 'Year Two For The Freedom of Israel'.

the Counting of the Omer (Hebrew: *Lag B'Omer*) on the eighteenth day of the month of *Iyyar* and they argued with one another.[70] Tragedy struck when they came down with a mysterious plague and all but five students died. The story may be a parable and have little to do with the war, but the date would come to have lasting significance.[71]

The Christians, however, adamantly refused to assist in the rebel leader's cause. They already had a messiah, Jesus, a Jew from Nazareth who they called the 'Son of God'.[72] Their mission was not to establish a new Israel, but to prepare for the 'Kingdom of Christ'.[73] Jesus had taught them to pray, 'Your kingdom come. Your will be done. On earth as it is in heaven.'[74] Ben Kosiba's Christian contemporary portrays the Jewish rebel leader as a trickster (fig. 25):

> ... just as that famed Barchochebas (Βαρχωχεβας), the instigator of the Jewish uprising, kept fanning a lighted blade of straw in his mouth with puffs of breath so as to give the impression that he was spewing out flames...[75]

Ben Kosiba decided that if they were not for him, they must be against him. Justin (quoted by Eusebius) writes:

> For in the late Jewish war Barchochebas, the leader of the Jewish rebellion, commanded that Christians alone should be visited with terrible punishments unless they would deny and blaspheme Jesus Christ.[76]

Eusebius remarks in his description of the events of the second year of the Bar Kokhba War:

> Chochebas, leader of the Jewish sect, killed the Christians with all kinds of persecutions [when] they refused to help him against the Roman troops.[77]

Orosius too writes:

> In this way, he [Hadrian] avenged the Christians, whom the Jews, under the leadership of Chochebas, were torturing because they would not join them against the Romans.[78]

Yet there were many Christians who lived by the Laws of Moses (Hebrew: *Talmidei Yeshua*), 'Messianic Gentiles', for whom this forced

Figure 25. Christian writers describe the Jewish warlord as a trickster. In this engraving, published in the Netherlands in 1784, he is shown breathing fire beside Rabbi Akiba. The Dutch caption reads 'Barchochebas the seducer'.

split with their Jewish brothers and sisters represented a terrible personal rent. Akiba's declaration that Ben Kosiba was the King Messiah may have been deliberate to bring about this final break because they rejected the authority of the rabbis.[79] On principle they could not possibly fight when called to join the *Milhemet Mitzvah*. Conscience notwithstanding, as a practical matter, commander-in-chief Ben Kosiba needed men who believed in his cause.[80] He could not afford to have a fifth column working to undermine it.

For those living in Israel, life went on with a renewed purpose. People expressed their patriotic confidence in the rebel state by conducting business and making contracts with Ben Kosiba:

> On the 20th *Shevat* in Year Two of the Redemption of Israel by Shim'on Ben Kosiba, *Nasi* of Israel. In the camp situated in Herodium Eleazar Ben ha-Shiloni said to Hillel Ben Garis: I, of my own free will, have leased from you some land which I have taken on lease in Ir-Nahash; I have leased it from Shim'on, the *Nasi* of Israel, for five years. [...]
>
> I have leased it from you today until the end of the year before the sabbatical year. The rental, which I hereby pay to you, every year: fine and pure wheat, four *kor* and eight *se'ah*, tithed, [...], which you shall measure out on the roof of the storehouse in Herodium every year. (This agreement) is binding for me in this form,
>
> Eleazar Ben ha-Shiloni on his behalf,
Shim'on Ben Kosiba by his word.[81]

The dating convention in this legal agreement mimics the Roman style: 'In the fifteenth year of the reign of Tiberius Caesar' or 'Hadrian's year 17'.[82] Another example is: 'On the fifth of *Elul*, Year [?] of Shim'on Ben Kosiba.'[83] There is no doubting here that Shim'on has supplanted the Roman emperor as head of state.[84]

In the display cases of the Israel Museum are a selection of letters found in Cave 5/6 (the so-called 'Cave of Letters') of Nahal Hever and the caves at Wadi Murabba'at, both in the desert valleys located near Ein Gedi. They offer an unrivalled glimpse into everyday life in Ben Kosiba's Israel.[85] There were occasions when, even not fighting each other, the opponents were still physically very close. An epistolary affidavit survives that evokes the stress of the time. It was written on behalf of both of the *parnasim* of the town of Beth Mashiko to the *rosh hamahanaya* at Herodium. The civil administrators explained that a soldier had unlawfully taken a cow from a resident of the village, a man named Ya'akob Ben Yehudah, who had purchased it. The administrators claimed the animal back on the man's behalf. The claimants had to explain that they could not petition Ben Galgula themselves in person because 'the Gentiles are near us'.[86] It was just too dangerous for the claimant and all the witnesses to travel beyond the village because they might run into units of Roman soldiers stationed nearby. Fortunately for the *parnasim* and the claimant, Ya'akob Ben Yosef the scribe was also a militiaman; he travelled alone and carried the affidavit by hand to Ben Galgula himself in Herodium. As a soldier he could be trusted to deliver it.

Found concealed in a crevice inside a leather purse were six contracts belonging to Eleazar Ben Shmuel, a farmer from Ein Gedi.[87] The signed and witnessed contracts document the land and property he bought or leased. In the spring of 'Year Two' Eleazar Ben Shmuel paid the sum of 650 *zuzim* to lease land in Ein Gedi in a document prepared by Masabala, the military co-commander of the town.[88] Making the initial payment on the negotiated lease in the autumn, he fulfilled the contract.

Discovered in the same cave was a cache of documents – private papers – belonging to Babatha Bat Shim'on.[89] In all, there are thirty-five documents including marriage contracts, land deeds and bills of sale, written in Aramaic, Nabatean and Greek on papyrus. They had been carefully wrapped in a package kept inside a fine leather case and then placed in a crevice deep inside the cave to be retrieved at a later time. Most of the documents are well preserved on account of the dry, desert conditions and have been read and studied in detail.[90] Significantly they are precisely dated, ranging from the years 94 CE to 132 CE.

They tell Babatha's poignant life story. She had had her unfair share of family troubles. In 124 CE a court assigned guardians for her orphaned son Yeshua.[91] In 125 CE Babatha subpoenaed Yeshua's guardians to charge them with inadequate maintenance.[92] Then she had to depose them.[93] She was from a wealthy family and had married a man called Yudah Ben Eleazar who, the documents inform us, owned three date orchards near Ein Gedi.[94] In 128 CE her husband took out a 300 *denarii* interest-free loan from his wife.[95] He died just two years later and, as his widow, Babatha took the orchards in settlement of the outstanding loan, but there was

a contester. Yudah's first wife Miriam, who lived in Ein Gedi, brought
a court action against Babatha over her former husband's property in
131 CE.[96] Encouraged by the success of Ben Kosiba's rebellion, she was one
of the Jews living in Roman-controlled Arabia Petraea who took the life-
changing decision to flee to Israel. Babatha abandoned her comfortable
residence in Mehoza (modern Maoza, Jordan) for an uncertain life in the
oasis town beside the Dead Sea, which was now under the control of the
nasi. While war raged in the Judean Hills above them, the two litigants
felt confident in the local *parnas* – approved by Ben Kosiba – to continue
to conduct their legal business in the seaside town.

On the Roman side, progress in taking back territory seized by the
rebels was painfully slow. An indication of how grave the Roman emperor
assessed the situation is preserved by Cassius Dio:

> Hadrian in writing to the Senate did not employ the opening phrase
> commonly affected by the emperors: 'If you and our children are in
> health, it is well; I and the legions are in health.'[97]

The 'first of these' best commanders – and the only one specifically named
by Cassius Dio in his entire account of the Bar Kokhba War – was Sex.
Iulius Severus.[98] At the time he was the *Legatus Augusti Pro Praetore* of
Britannia who had recently put down the revolt there. He was ordered to
march to Province Iudaea without delay. It is reasonable to conjecture that
Severus was accompanied on the march of 5,000 kilometres (3,106 mi.)
by a bodyguard from his own province. Inscriptions attest to men from
Britannia operating in Judea: the legionary centurions C. Ligustinius
Disertus and Q. Albius Felix of *Legio* XX *Valeria Victrix* from Deva
(Chester); *Legio* VI *Victrix* from Eboracum (York); M. Censorius
Cornelianus as overseer (*praepositus*) of *Cohors* I *Hispanorum M. Eq.* from
Maryport; *Cohors* III *Bracaugustanorum* from Melandra Castle; and M.
Statius Priscus with *Cohors* IV *Lingonum* from Wallsend.[99]

The careers of three centurions from Britannia provide a glimpse
into the operational workings of the army. Albius Felix served all of his
early career with the Deva-based legion as adjutant to the praetorian
prefect (*cornicularius praefecti praetorio*) and was promoted up, rather than
through appointment by a direct commission, to become *primipilus*, the
most senior of all the centurions.[100] Ligustinius Disertus, whose *cognomen*
means 'eloquent' or 'fluent', took a very different path.[101] He served a

full term with the praetorian cohorts in Rome, during which he was a *beneficiarius* of the *praefectus praetorio*. After his contracted sixteen-year term he retired honourably but decided to remain in the army as an *evocatus Augusti*, a 'soldier retained in service by the Emperor', in effect a reservist.[102] Now likely still in his mid-30s, he was appointed as a legionary centurion with XX *Valeria Victrix*, during which time he was temporarily assigned to IIII *Scythica* at Zeugma on the Euphrates and then returned to his original unit on the Dee River. Another centurion, T. Quintius Petrullus, described as 'from Britain' (*domo Britannia*), served with *Legio* III *Cyrenaica*.[103] He died aged just 30 at the army camp in Bostra. This was a remarkably young age for a centurion, which suggests that he had entered the army by a direct commission rather than had risen through the ranks. Yet what was *he* doing in Arabia Petraea? The fragmentary inscription gives no indication. Taken together, the inscriptions all seem to point to Iulius Severus taking with him an away team of trusted individuals, perhaps known for their special skills or leadership abilities. As a *legatus Augusti* he had personal authority to make appointments without having to refer to Hadrian, though the appointment of legionary legates did require imperial approval.[104] These men had possibly come to his attention during the uprising in Britannia in the late 120s CE. On arriving in the combat zone, Severus reassigned them to different units. As his appointees they likely would each have had a place on the legionary legate's leadership advisory committee (*concilium*) and contributed their valuable expertise and insights to the discussions.

Transfers were not limited to officers from the island province. From Gallia Narbonensis, M. Censorius Cornelianus, who was equestrian rank, became a centurion in *Legio* X *Fretensis*.[105] This might appear at first glance to be a demotion for Cornelianus, but it was quite common practice.[106] Part of *Cohors* I *Hispanorum M. Eq.* may have remained with him or have been deployed elsewhere in the combat theatre.[107] Far from a rigid organization, in wartime the component parts of the Roman army could be split off and re-assembled to suit operational needs of the commander leading the expedition.

How the senior command structure worked in practice in this campaign is nowhere explained. The visiting commanding officers would normally have retained their ranks, but reported to Tineius Rufus as the governor of Province Iudaea only for the duration of the war. Appointed by the emperor and with a proven track record of success in crushing rebels, however, Iulius Severus may have assumed overall command of military operations in Judea, which would mean subordinating the host governor Rufus along with the other legates.[108] Both men were proconsuls and *legati Augusti* and so of equal status. Severus and Rufus could have worked jointly together with the other legates subordinated. Where this places Lollius Urbicus – self-styled *legato imperatoris Hadriani* – in the command hierarchy is unclear. Perhaps he was Hadrian's 'chief of staff' working behind the scenes solving problems, mediating disputes between the legates and dealing with issues before they were brought to the emperor's attention.[109] Hadrian was in Rome on 8 April 133 CE; whether he returned to Province Iudaea to direct operations himself is unclear from Roman sources.[110] It is, however, stated affirmatively by some of the rabbinic sources.[111] As Caesar Augustus had done, Hadrian did not need to lead the war from the front. Being the military leader, he set the goals and expectations of the war, and provided inspiration and motivation; as the manager of the war he planned, organized, coordinated, controlled the resources and delegated authority to use them.[112] The Bar Kokhba War was a campaign that Hadrian's legates would fight on his behalf.

The war reached its height in the latter half of 134 CE and first half of 135 CE.[113] Iulius Severus had joined the counterinsurgency campaign at a crucial time. Two years had passed and the Romans had little to show for their efforts. The Jewish militia was fighting a very effective asymmetric, guerilla-style war, while the Romans were applying their usual tried-and-tested doctrine of massive force. Severus changed it. From that point on the Romans adopted a new strategy:

> Severus did not venture to attack his opponents in the open at any one point, in view of their numbers and their desperation, but by intercepting small groups, thanks to the number of his soldiers and his under-officers, and by depriving them of food and shutting them up, he was able, rather slowly, to be sure, but with comparatively little danger, to crush, exhaust and exterminate them.[114]

His centurions would have to improvise to secure their objectives on the ground. They led their men, sometimes with words of encouragement, sometimes with the sting of the vine staff. Training, discipline, experience, grit and determination now took over. They had learned to operate in the

Figure 26. Despite its defensible position and stout construction, the village at Horbat 'Etri was stormed by the Roman army under the command of Iulius Severus and destroyed.

chaos of the battlefield. By one means or another they would take down the rebels.

The fortified farms and villages across Judea were tested as never before. Archaeological finds illustrate the effectiveness of Severus' new, methodical approach. One by one they fell. The complex at Horbat Zalit was surrounded by a glacis on a spur overlooking Nahal Eshtemo'a on the southern slopes of the Judean *Shephelah* (about 1.5 km (1 mi.) south-east of modern Meitar).[115] Evidence points to a violent end. From the high vantage point of the watchtower a guard could see the Roman army coming and sounded the alarm. Below, in the courtyard and surrounding rooms, the residents stopped their work and prepared to defend themselves. Working at the site in 1983 and 1984, archaeologists found a hoard with Roman coins as well as overstruck specimens.[116] They believe that the farm served as a mint producing coins for the rebel administration and that, when attacked, the coin-maker hurriedly stashed away the pile, fully intending to recover it later.

Horbat 'Etri, some 32 km (20 mi.) to the north, faced the inevitable arrival of the Roman army (fig. 26). When the soldiers stormed the place the residents fought back, but the Romans overwhelmed them. Archaeologists working at the site from 1999 to 2001 found a burned layer right at the centre of the site at floor level: evidence of an extensive fire.[117] A *zuz* of the Ben Kosiba regime, which showed scorch marks, was

found in this layer, confirming the date to be contemporary with the Bar Kokhba War. The village's *mikwa* was used as a makeshift burial plot. It contained the skulls and bones of at least twelve individuals (seven adults, including females and males, four adolescents and a foetus). They tell a harrowing tale. It seems that the defenders had been brutally slaughtered during the capture of the settlement. During conservation cut marks were identified on a neck vertebra, indicating that at least one individual had been beheaded by the blow of a sword. The bones also showed evidence

Figure 27. Overstruck on a *denarius* of Trajan, this silver *zuz* is attributed by scholars to Year Three of the war (134/135 CE). The name 'Shim'on' in Paleo-Hebrew appears with a bunch of grapes. On the reverse the legend 'For the Freedom of Jerusalem' surrounds two upright trumpets.

that the bodies had been left exposed in the open air for a considerable time and they began to decompose in the heat. Later they were picked up and unceremoniously dumped in the *mikwa* along with bowls, casseroles, cooking pots, jars, jugs and oil-lamps. When the buildings were set alight, two silver coins fused together and some of the glass vessels deformed in the intense heat. Despite its burrows, caves and escape tunnel (plate 27), neighbouring Horbat Burgin was similarly overrun.[118]

Deception is one of the highest skills in warfare, requiring great creativity to fool the enemy. A rabbinic text may contain a recollection of the Romans' use of the tactic to capture rebels:

Hadrian – *may his bones be crushed* – set up three garrisons: one in Emmaus, one in Kefar Lakatia, and one in Beit El in Judea.

He said: 'Whoever attempts to escape from one of them will be captured in another.'

He also sent out heralds to announce: 'Wherever there is a Jew, let him come forth, because the king wishes to give him assurance of safety.'

The heralds proclaimed this to them, thereby capturing the Jews. Thus, it is written: '*And Ephraim is become like a silly dove, without understanding.*'

[Hosea 7:11].[119]

The rebel nation entered another year. By the summer of 134 CE, the Jewish moneyers began issuing a new series of coins. The slogan each coin carried now read (fig. 27), '*FOR THE FREEDOM OF JERUSALEM*'.[120] Omitted from this message was the number of the year (plate 24). That raises an interesting question: did the rebels believe the revolution would endure and they no longer needed to count the passing years, or was there a dawning realization that its days were numbered? The harsh truth for Shim'on Ben Kosiba and his followers was that, after three years of struggle, Aelia Capitolina remained firmly in Roman control. Freeing the city and rebuilding the Temple still remained a dream (plate 25). For the *Nasi Yisrael* it was still a motivator, an ideal around which to rally his besieged nation.

Observing the festivals was crucial to binding its citizens and army together in common cause. As a devout Jew himself, Ben Kosiba actively encouraged religious observance. He personally planned ahead for the holy days. A letter survives from him written in Aramaic requesting supplies for the festival of *Sukkot*:

> Shim'on to Yehudah Bar Menashe in Kiryat 'Arabaya.
>
> I have sent to you two donkeys, and you must send with them two men to Yehonathan Bar Be'ayan and to Masabala [Bar Shim'on], in order that they shall pack and send to the camp, towards you, palm branches and citrons. And you, from your place, send others who will bring you myrtles and willows. See that they are tithed [literally 'set in order'] and send them to the camp.
>
> The request is made because the army [or crowd] is big.
>
> Be well.[121]

The men in Kiryat 'Arabaya presumably did not have pack animals available to spare; Ben Kosiba had to provide the means to transport the items himself. It also implies that if he did not send the donkeys the farmers might not execute the order and thus spoil his *Sukkot*. The last line of the letter is intriguing. It may indicate that the garrison at Kiryat' Arabaya itself was large, or that the camp was hosting militiamen coming from different locations just for the special occasion (also known as the 'Festival of Ingathering'), in which case the numbers were greater than usual.[122]

In another remarkable letter the writer Soumaios requests Yohanathan Ben Baianos and Masabala to urgently supply palm fronds and citrons 'for the camp of the Jews'.[123] The items are needed 'as quick as possible – do not do otherwise'. He apologizes for writing in Greek 'because of no means having been found to write it in *Hebraesti*'.[124] The letter, concluding with a repeat of the warning 'and do not do otherwise', was delivered by one Agrippa who was expected back in time for the festival.

Ben Kosiba's deputies relayed field intelligence to their commander-in-chief. Shim'on Ben Mattaniah, writing in Hebrew perhaps from his camp at Kephar Baru, reports that events had gone badly for some of the 'brothers', but 'we were not among them'.[125] One Elisha was planning an important mission. Ben Kosiba dictated a confidential letter in Aramaic to a scribe:

> Shim'on Ben Kosiba to Yehonathan Bar Be'ayan.
>
> Peace!
>
> [My order is] that whatever Elisha tells you, do to him and help him and those with him [or: in every action].

Be well.[126]

Perhaps Yehonathan had a special skill he could use to help him accomplish it. What happened after is not known.

As the rebellion came under pressure from Roman incursions, cracks appeared within his base. Maintaining the commitment, cohesion and discipline of the militia units became Ben Kosiba's primary concern. Without them the rebel state would quickly collapse. The strains of command showed. Ben Kosiba had a quick temper. He wrote angrily to his co-commanders at Ein Gedi on the Dead Sea:

> Shim'on Ben Kosiba to the men of Ein Gedi, Masabala [Bar Shim'on] and Yehonathan Bar Be'ayan:
>   Peace!
>   In comfort you sit, eat and drink from the property of the House of Israel, and care nothing for your brothers.[127]

The last part of the letter conveys the reality of how Ben Kosiba's troubles were mounting:

> …they have [fl]ed [to] your father…
> … to the fortress of the Hasidim…
> …till the end…
>   …they have no hope…
> …And my brothers in the sou[th]…
> …[Many] of these were lost by the sword…
> …these my brothers…[128]

Despite threats, some of his camp commanders seemed willing to ignore his orders altogether, resorting to desertion or even defection:

> Shim'on Ben Kosiba to Yehonathan and to Masabala…
>   Let all men from Tekoa and other places who are with you, be sent to me without delay. And if you shall not send them, let it be known to you, that *you* will be punished… [129]

Perhaps because he could not always trust his deputies to execute his orders, there were occasions when Ben Kosiba had to address them himself. 'Get hold of young men and come with them,' he demands of his two commanders in Ein Gedi in a letter, 'I shall deal with the Romans.'[130]

1. Bronze bust of Hadrian from the camp of *Legio* VI *Ferrata* at Tel Shalem in the Israel Museum. The head was likely cast in Italy, the torso in Iudaea.

2. Bronze bust of Hadrian of unprovenanced location now in the Louvre.

3. Bronze head of Hadrian found in the Thames, London now in the British Museum. The style betrays its local craftsmanship.

4. The sun god Sol looks east ('Oriens'), while Hadrian looks west ('Occidens').

5. Emphasizing his own army background, this *aureus* shows Hadrian in military dress standing between legionary *signa* while holding a spear.

6. Hadrian believed in enforcing *disciplina militaris*, the doctrine that the army should be run efficiently and strictly but frugally. This coin celebrates 'Augustan Discipline'.

7. Hadrian riding while carrying a spear in a *decursio*, the precision military exercise which required the cavalry to ride closely in a circle.

8. Now fused together by rust, the individual riveted links originally made a complete, form-fitting coat of chain-mail body armour.

9. A double-edged legionary *gladius* and a longer cavalry *spatha* still in its scabbard. With these weapons the Roman army built and maintained its empire.

10. Roman legionary's helmet, complete with its original cheek plates. The bars across the dome help protect the wearer from direct downward blows.

11. Aerial view of *Colonia* Prima Flavia Augusta Caesarea shows the aqueduct, harbour, circus, theatre and *praetorium*.

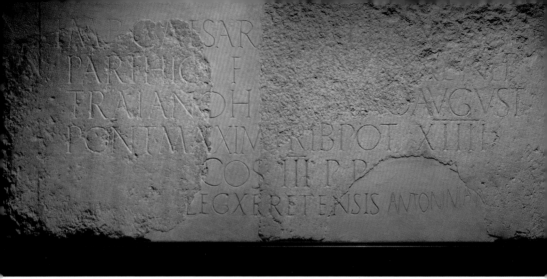

12. Inscription set up by the men of *Legio* X *Fretensis* to coincide with the official visit of Hadrian to Aelia Capitolina in 130 CE.

13. The paved area below the Damascus Gate, Jerusalem is the actual level of Hadrian's *Colonia* Aelia Capitolina. It formed part of the semicircular piazza behind the gateway.

14. Originally the location of the Temple of *Yahweh* in Jerusalem, Hadrian may have erected a temple to the Capitoline Triad on the Mount in Aelia Capitolina.

15. Ben Kosiba was based at Herodium for a time and may have directed the rebellion from here. It was a formidable defensible location built to withstand a siege.

16. Jewish rebels built a smithy and hearths within the ruins of the upper fortress to fabricate arms, armour and ammunition for the war effort.

17. From the parapet of Herodium, Yeshua Ben Galgula, head of the garrison, had a commanding view of the Judean Desert and Judean Hills.

18. Jewish sappers excavated new and larger tunnels inside the motte of Herodium, enabling troops to store equipment and launch ambuscades.

19. Rebel militiamen used bows, often with armour-piercing trilobate arrow-heads, several of which have survived still attached to their wooden shafts.

20. Spear blades varied in size and shape. This fine specimen was found in a refuge cave in the Wadi Marrazah, north of Ein Gedi.

21. This pyramid-shaped bolt tip, found still attached to its original wooden shaft, may have been ammunition for a Roman *catapulta* that was retrieved and repurposed by men of Ben Kosiba's militia.

22. 'Shim'on *Nasi* of Israel' written in Palaeo-Hebrew script appears on a bronze coin (*perutah*) with a palm branch set within a wreath. On the reverse, the legend around a lyre reads 'Year One Redemption of Israel' (132/133 CE).

23. The text in Palaeo-Hebrew script on this *perutah* reads 'Eleazar the Priest' arranged around a seven-branched palm tree with two bunches of dates. The reverse-side text reads 'Year One Redemption of Israel' placed around a bunch of grapes.

24. Prevented by the Second Commandment from displaying graven images, rebel moneyers used symbols from Jewish culture. This *zuz* from 'Year Three' (134/135 CE) features a bunch of grapes and a lyre.

25. *Sela* from 'Year Three' with the name 'Shim'on' shows the doors of the Second Temple open to reveal a showbread table. On the reverse, 'Freedom of Israel' surrounds a *lulav* and *etrog*.

26. The Jewish community at Horbat 'Etri in the Judean *Shephelah* produced fruits, vegetables and wine. Below ground level were storage spaces and hiding-places.

27. Beneath the village at Horbat Burgin tunnels connect hiding-places. Carved into the limestone, this walkway example has three niches for oil lamps.

28. View of Battir-Khirbet al-Yahud, which may have been ancient Betar, the site of Ben Kosiba's last stand. The terraces are part of an ancient irrigation system fed by natural springs.

29. Archaeological excavations have revealed a defensive circuit wall with buttresses and towers at Battir-Khirbet al-Yahud, which date to the time of the Bar Kokhba War.

30. The harbour town of Ein Gedi on the Dead Sea thrived by trading balsam, dates and bitumen. It was one of the last strongholds loyal to Ben Kosiba.

31. Caves occur naturally in the limestone geology of the canyons around the Dead Sea. They have provided places of refuge in troubled times.

32. Caves high up in the Nahal Hever Canyon provided a last place of refuge for those desperate to flee the Romans at the end of the Bar Kokhba War.

33. A bronze bowl and its original rope found in the 'Cave of Letters'. Refugees brought their personal effects and valuables with them.

34. People taking refuge in the 'Cave of Letters' brought household items like these knives and keys, hoping to return to their homes after the war.

35. 'IOVI VICTORI', 'Iuppiter the Victorious', sits naked to the waist on his throne. He holds a victoriola in his extended right hand and a sceptre of kingship in his left.

36. Winged Victory holds an eagle in her right hand and a palm frond in her left. This coin was likely minted to celebrate the end of the Bar Kokhba War.

37. 'VICTOR IA AVG', the personification of 'Augustan Victory', strides forward, holding up a wreath in her right hand and a palm frond in her left.

38. 'SECVRITAS', the personification of 'safety', sits at ease holding overflowing cornucopias, suggesting the bounties accruing from times free of struggle and strife.

39. While in Rome, and inspired by classical period statuary, Henryk Glitzenstein cast his statue *Bar Kokhba* (1905). He depicted the Jewish warlord as a 'muscular Jew'.

40. Poster celebrating the tenth anniversary in November 1910 of *Jüdischer Turnverein Berlin 'Bar Kochba'*, the Berlin branch of the 'Bar Kochba' Gymnastic Movement.

Feſtſchrift

zur Feier des 10 jährigen Beſtehens

der Lehrlings = Abteilung

des J. T. V. **Bar Kochba** Nov. 1910.

41. 'Bar Kochba' rides over abandoned Roman arms with his soldiers in this artwork by Arthur Szyk (1927). The artist was inspired by Byzantine and Mediaeval art styles.

42. 'Bar Kokhba' is the figure in exotic armour on the left side of Arthur Szyk's exquisitely illustrated frontispiece to *Visual History of Israel* (1949).

Plate 43. Definitive stamps issued by Israel Post soon after the founding of the new state. Each design includes the image of a coin struck during the Bar Kokhba War. The series ran for several years, with increasing denominations printed to keep pace with hyper-inflation.

Plate 44. 'Bar Kokhba' is depicted as an archer on this stamp for Israel Post designed by Asher Kalderon (1961).

Plate 45. *Mur.* 43 (signed by Ben Kosiba) is part of the 'Ancient Letters' series of commemorative stamps designed by Meir Eshel (1984) and issued by Israel Post.

David Mevorah had told me that Ben Kosiba 'was too absorbed in fighting to be worried about economics'. Yet it has been said that 'amateurs study tactics, armchair generals study strategy, but professionals study logistics'. Securing food supplies was a continuing concern to him. A letter in Aramaic survives, revealing how he worried about the delivery of a shipment of wheat, and how demanding he could be of his co-commanders in Ein Gedi to secure it. Mevorah had included it in the exhibition about Hadrian as a memento of the war he fought. Unlike the others, the letter is written in ink on a trimmed wafer of wood, folded down the middle to form two columns, and is of a type well-known from the Roman fort at Vindolanda in Britain.[131] The first reads:

> Shim'on Bar Kosiba, *Nasi* of Israel to Yehonathan [Bar Be'ayan] and to Masabala [Bar Shim'on]:
>> Peace!
>> You are [ordered] to inspect and [to] seize the wheat that Hanun [or Tanun] Ben Yishmael has [brought?], and send me one *se'ah* of it. And place it under guard for fear of it being stolen. If you do not do this accordingly (know) that retribution will be exacted from me, and send me the man immediately under guard.[132]

It continues into the second column:

> And any man of Tekoa who is found with you, the houses in which they dwell shall be burned down, and from you I shall exact retribution. [As for] Yeshua, son of the Palmyrene, you shall seize him and send him to me under guard. And seize the sword which is upon him and send it (to me). Shmu'el Bar Ammi.[133]

In another letter he worries about a man who leased land from him:

> Shim'on Ben Kosiba, *Nasi* of Israel to Yehonathan [Bar Be'ayan] and to Masabala [Bar Shim'on]:
>> [My order] is that you send me Eleazar Ben Hitta immediately before the *Shabbat*. [... his wheat and fruit shall be confiscated] and if anyone oppose you send him to me and I shall punish him. [...] See that the herds do not trample and destroy the trees or else – a severe punishment. [...] And as for the spice orchard let no one get anywhere near it.[134]

The reason for Ben Kosiba's annoyance with Eleazar Ben Hitta is not known. The urgency of the request is determined by the fact that travel is not permitted on the Sabbath day; Ben Hitta had to get back before it.[135] His directive tone is that of an autocrat or a king demanding complete obedience.[136]

It would seem from the letters that the military commanders at Ein Gedi either did not fully appreciate the gravity of their predicament or chose to ignore it, instead clinging to hope. Life went on as normal in the small seaside town. Several men gathered in a scribe's shop to sign an agreement about sharing fields with Eleazar Ben Shmu'el on 'the twenty-eighth *Marheshvan* of the Third Year of Shim'on ben Kosiba, *Nasi* of Israel', which dates the document precisely to 6 November 134 CE.[137] He also invested in a house in Kefar Baarou. Others put their money into houses for private rental. Their investments indicate that they still believed in the long-term viability of Israel. For others it was speculation. Over time, the price of property in Ein Gedi had fallen. Those with cash could buy houses at a discount in relative terms and earn a reasonable return from rents. The inflationary pressures belied the good health of the economy. The future of Israel was actually becoming ever more uncertain.

It was clear that I needed to go to Ein Gedi to understand its importance in Ben Kosiba's world. However, there was another site I had to visit first.

Chapter 7

'A Fence Consisting of the Slain'

By the start of 135 CE the tide had turned. Ben Kosiba's 'big army' was struggling to resist the Roman onslaught masterminded by Iulius Severus. At an unknown date the leader of the insurrectionists left Herodium. David Mevorah had told me that some of the tunnels in the great motte, which were buttressed by wooden supports, had been set on fire by the Romans and they 'burned the rebels out'.[1] Charred wooden beams as well as ash and soot were indeed found during excavations. The fire was so intense in the entrance hall that the rock turned to lime. Its loss was a setback, but the rebel leader and some of his supporters survived. Roman sources are silent on the subject of Ben Kosiba's movements. Rabbinic sources, however, state that the Jewish resistance removed to 'Betar where Bar Kozeba was located'.[2]

Yet where was Betar?[3] As with so many details of the Bar Kokhba War story, scholars still debate the matter. Writing in Greek, Eusebius offers us a clue: 'The war raged most fiercely in the eighteenth year of Hadrian, at the city of Biththira [$B\eta\theta\theta\eta\rho\alpha$], ...situated not far from Jerusalem.'[4]

There are a number of candidates in Israel and Palestine for the ancient city, but the leading contender is a village now called Battir.[5] It lies 11 kilometres (7 mi.) south-west of Jerusalem and 6.4 kilometres (3.1 mi.) west of Bethlehem. The site has drawn archaeologists, explorers and historians for centuries seeking to answer what role, if any, it played in the Bar Kokhba War.[6] Yigael Yadin was convinced it was the site of Betar.[7] David Mevorah had warned me that there was not much to see there today. Nevertheless, I wanted to get a sense of the place which is so important to this story. Travelling to Battir means crossing the so-called 1949 Armistice Agreement Line or 'Green Line'. One way to reach it is to drive south-west from Jerusalem following the winding Route 386 to Havatika in Israel until it intersects the 375, which goes to Husan in Palestine. Leaving the town the first left turn is a long straight road heading north which terminates at Battir. Adjacent to it, to the north-west, is Khirbet al-Yahud – Arabic words meaning 'Ruin of the Jews'. The name is grimly apposite.

The natural setting of Battir is as dramatic as it is beautiful (plate 28).[8] The surrounding hillsides are scored with parallel lines that, at first glance, seem to be natural, geological courses. In fact, they are man-made cultivation terraces, created by centuries of farming activity in the Rephaim Valley. Fed by seven springs, water hydrates the terraces through an irrigation system that dates back to Roman times. Rising 250 metres (820ft) out of the Judean *Shephelah*, the steep hill upon which Battir and Khirbet al-Yahud sit is an ideal site for a stronghold. Today, the Palestinian village overlooks a section of the Jaffa-Jerusalem railway laid in the valley below in Ottoman times. In the second century CE Betar was a stop on the important Aelia Capitolina-Gaza road, connecting the great city to the coast. In the late-nineteenth century, a milestone was found inscribed with the name of Hadrian with the date 130 CE and the number 'VIII', this being the miles counted from Aelia Capitolina.[9]

The top of the hill at Battir and the adjacent Khirbet al-Yahud would offer the defenders relatively flat ground on which to establish their base. Crucially it was defensible. The hill slopes to the north, falling steeply 150 metres (490ft) to the Nahal Sorek in the valley floor. The residents of the town were supplied with fresh drinking water from natural springs in the valley, likely supplemented by rain captured in one or more cisterns cut into the rock. Rabbinic sources describe Betar as a large city.[10] The pre-war population has been estimated to have been between 1,000 and 2,000 people.[11] Some of the interior buildings were constructed of rectangular ashlar blocks; they may have been mansion houses of a style found elsewhere in Province Iudaea.[12] The blocks are dressed with a recessed border along all four front-facing sides like a reversed-out picture frame, a style popular at the time of Herod the Great and similar to the finished blocks in the Western Wall, Jerusalem. Betar seems to have been a smart but quiet town thriving on its income from agriculture and official travellers stopping on their journeys for refreshment or to exchange horses.[13]

That changed abruptly with the Bar Kokhba War. The town likely steadily filled with displaced people fleeing the advancing Roman army. By the summer of 135 CE it may have looked more like a shanty town or refugee camp, with every available space between the existing buildings occupied by temporary shacks and tents. One Talmudic source records: 'There were 400 synagogues in the city of Betar, and in every one were 400 teachers of children, and each one had under him 400 pupils.'[14] The numbers are almost certainly exaggerated, but they do convey a sense of the high concentration of people trapped there. Jostling for space were men of Ben Kosiba's army. The *Talmud* records: 'Eighty [thousand] battle trumpets assembled in the city of Betar' – again likely an inflated number of soldiers, but confirmation that Jewish militiamen were at Betar in some strength.[15]

The town of 4 hectares (10 acres) was unwalled at the start of the war.[16] Preparing for the Roman threat, the defenders of Betar erected a stout wall. The rough, often careless construction of the circuit wall hints at the speed at which the builders had to work. The first detailed survey of the site was conducted by W.D. Carroll in 1923–24.[17] He photographed, measured and mapped its identifiable features, including seven buttresses or towers, a gate on the north side and a blocked gateway on the south-western side.[18] There was extra strengthening along the south-south-eastern segment of circuit wall. Carroll noted that the town was accessible via a rock-cut approach road on the south-eastern side, and that there was a dry moat or fosse measuring c. 10 metres wide by c. 35 metres long and 5 metres deep (c. 32.9ft x c. 114.8ft x c. 16.4ft) running east-west at the southern end of the town, probably to stall an attack from that side.[19] By the time Carroll had finished his investigation he was convinced that Battir was the Betar of the Bar Kokhba War.[20]

In 1984 archaeologists from Tel Aviv University led by David Ussishkin were able to investigate the site anew. They too noted that 'specific attention was given to strengthening the south-eastern corner where the approach was easiest.'[21] The team excavated two sections of the circuit wall, in particular the external buttresses – three semi-circular and one rectangle-shaped – along the south and west sides to understand how they were built. They found that in order to create a continuous line following the contours of the hill Ben Kosiba's engineers had to demolish several existing buildings that stood in their way in a few places. Blocks from these Herodian-Roman-era buildings were recycled, laid directly on the bedrock to build the lowest courses of the rectangular tower and wall of the new defensive structure.[22] The archaeologists noted that surviving sections of the inner wall survived to 4m (13ft) of its estimated original height of 5 metres (16.4ft), which was likely the same on the front face.[23] Most of the material used to build the inner and outer wall were worked field stones with an infill of rubble, loose stones and earth. Some of the excavated buttresses and segments of wall can still be seen (plate 29). Even as ruins they are impressive. They validate Eusebius' description of the resulting structure as 'a very secure fortress'.[24] Ussishkin was also convinced that Battir was the Betar of the Bar Kokhba War.[25]

Within these walls the defenders made ammunition. They chipped rocks of flint or limestone – whatever hard materials they could find – to make round sling stones. Thirty-eight were retrieved by the archaeologists; the specimens ranged in size from 5 centimetres to 9 centimetres (2in to 3.8in), and in weight from 110 grammes to 650 grammes (4oz to 23oz).[26] They were stored in piles beside the new defensive wall, ready to unleash at a moment's notice. The archaeologist from Tel Aviv writes in his report that on the top of the rectangular tower they found a cache of twenty-two sling stones which they speculated was the ammunition of the defenders manning the tower.[27] The stones were found c. 1.50 metres (4.9ft) lower than the upper inner edge of the tower, suggesting to the researchers that there was originally a balcony in the centre of the tower surrounded by a protective balustrade. The defenders also amassed an arsenal of iron arrows; two badly-preserved specimens of the trilobate design were found on a semi-circular buttress.[28] They were prepared as best they could be.

From his command centre at Betar, Ben Kosiba personally directed operations.[29] Having lived through the fall of Herodium, he knew what was coming. His leadership skills were now sorely tested. The rabbinic sources portray the *Nasi* of Israel under great pressure and not handling it well:

In the city was Rabbi Eleazar of Modi'in, who continually wore sackcloth and fasted, and used to pray daily: 'Lord of the Universe, sit not in judgement today!' so that Hadrian thought of returning home.

A Cuthean went [to the Roman emperor] and found him and said: 'My lord, so long as that old cock wallows in ashes, you will not conquer the city. But wait for me, because I will do something that will enable you to subdue it today.'

He immediately entered the gate of the city, where he found Rabbi Eleazar standing and praying. He pretended to whisper in the ear of

Rabbi Eleazar of Modi'in. People went and informed Bar Koziba: 'Your friend, Rabbi Eleazar, wishes to surrender the city to Hadrian.'

He sent and had the Cuthean brought to him and asked: 'What did you say to him?'

He replied: 'If I tell you, the emperor will kill me; and if I do not tell you, you will kill me. It is better that I should kill myself and the secrets of the government be not divulged.'

Bar Koziba was convinced that Rabbi Eleazar wanted to surrender the city, so when the latter finished his praying, he had him brought into his presence and asked him: 'What did the Cuthean tell you?'

He answered: 'I do not know what he whispered in my ear, nor did I hear anything, because I was standing in prayer and am unaware what he said.'

Bar Koziba flew into a rage, kicked him with his foot and killed him. A heavenly voice issued forth and proclaimed: 'Woe to the worthless shepherd, who deserts the flock! May the sword strike his arm and his right eye!' [Zechariah 11:17]

It was intimated to him: 'Thou hast paralyzed the arm of Israel and blinded their right eye; therefore shall thy arm wither and thy right eye grow dim!'[30]

As in all campaigns before this one, the Romans determined that the leader of the insurrection had to be captured or killed. If he were taken alive he could be paraded as a living trophy in the emperor's anticipated victory parade or triumph in Rome. Since Ben Kosiba was now holed up in Betar, taking it became the strategic imperative. Two legions struck out from the rest of the expeditionary force in the direction of the target. They established their marching camps on the south-east side of the valley which, crucially, overlooked Betar. Both are of the signature playing-card shape favoured by the Roman camp prefect (*praefectus castrorum*), though the one on the left – at 8.3 hectares (20.5 acres) – is more than three times larger than the one on the right.[31] They could have accommodated a full legion and a *vexillatio* of around 1,800 men respectively. Other legionary or auxiliary units may also have been involved. Study of aerial photographs has revealed up to four other camps at distances of 1.5 kilometres to 4 kilometres (1.0 to 2.5 mi.) away from Betar. One is on the same west-east alignment as the 'main' legionary camps, just located further east, but three are sited on high ground well to the south forming a second arc radiating west to south-east.[32] The combined size of the camps suggests a Roman presence of some 10,000 to 12,000 men-at-arms, making it a much larger force than had been assembled at the famous siege of Masada.[33]

The Roman commander-in-chief needed an end to the war. 'For three and a half years the emperor Hadrian surrounded Betar,' says a passage in the *Midrash*.[34] Eusebius is less precise, writing only that 'it lasted a long time'.[35] Siegecraft was a forte of the Roman army. One stratagem was to blockade the defenders so that they could not be relieved from outside and eventually, their resources used up, they would starve and surrender. This approach required patience and time. Iulius Caesar had used it at Alesia.[36] The other stratagem was to directly assault the stronghold, breach the walls and take on the defenders in street-to-street fighting. Flavius Silva had executed it at Masada.[37] This approach required siege equipment and risked the lives of the troops making the final assault.

Both approaches required the objective to be sealed within a palisade, rampart and ditch (*circumvallatio*). In rabbinic literature it is described vividly as 'a fence consisting of the slain'.[38] The present state of the circumvallation is extremely poor and has vanished for most of its length. It has been variously incorporated into modern property or agricultural development or been destroyed by them.[39] Traces of the wall constructed of field stones were initially identified from field work and study of aerial photographs.[40] A line was observed across the top of the hill opposite Battir on the north-west side with flanking walls running down the slope of the hill at each end forming a C-shape (map 4). This arrangement offered three advantages: it sealed off the town from the north-west while allowing the Romans to control access along the Aelia Capitolina-Gaza road; it provided a guard on the south-eastern hilltop using the two *vexillatio* camps; and it exploited the natural profile of the valley in between. The defenders could not now get out without risk of being captured, and any relief troops coming to their rescue could not get in.

Roman soldiers located and seized a spring (fig. 28) in the valley floor to prevent the rebels from using it. We have a Frenchman to thank for recording this detail. On 9 August 1874 the intrepid explorer and archaeologist Charles Clairmont-Ganneau hurriedly trekked to Battir in search of an important artefact he had been advised could be found there. In the book describing his travels and discoveries he writes about what he saw below a rock escarpment (fig. 29):

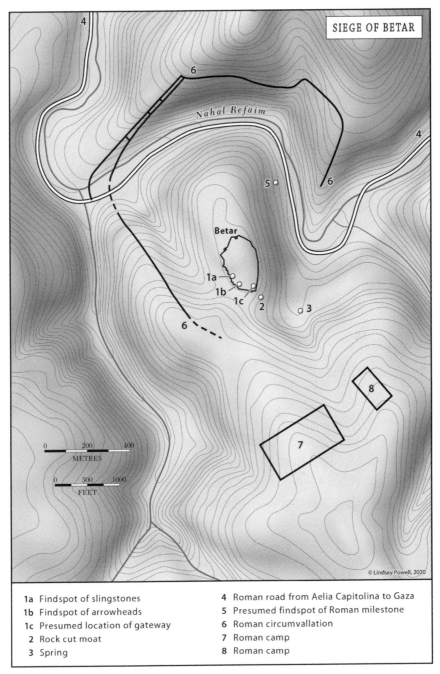

SIEGE OF BETAR

Nahal Refaim

Betar

1a
1b
1c
2
3
5
6
7
8
4

0   200   400
METRES

0   500   1000
FEET

© Lindsay Powell, 2020

1a Findspot of slingstones	**4** Roman road from Aelia Capitolina to Gaza
1b Findspot of arrowheads	**5** Presumed findspot of Roman milestone
1c Presumed location of gateway	**6** Roman circumvallation
2 Rock cut moat	**7** Roman camp
3 Spring	**8** Roman camp

Map 4. Siege of Betar. (© *Lindsay Powell*)

Figure 28. The natural spring at Battir drawn by A. Lecomte Du Noüy. Natural springs were the primary sources of potable water to the town.

At its foot runs an ancient road leading to the spring, a very plenteous one. Its water is received by an old channel, partly hewn out of the rock, and bordered by enormous blocks of stone, which originally must have completely covered it. At the mouth of this watercourse on the left-hand wall of rock is the inscription which I wished to examine.

Our inscription is neither Byzantine nor Greek, but Latin and Roman. It consists of five or perhaps six lines, set in a rectangular frame which measures about 0.50m x 0.35m. Unfortunately, it is much perished, and I was not able to make it all out. This is all the more to be regretted, because the inscription, which undoubtedly dates from the Roman Empire, might possibly have enabled us to set at rest the extremely vexed question of the identity of Bettir with Barcocheba's stronghold.[41]

At the site he took a cast of the inscription and then sketched it as best he could, allowing for the 'deplorable condition of the original', which he presented in his book (fig. 30):

Figure 29. The Escarpment at Battir drawn by A. Lecomte Du Noüy while accompanying Charles Clermont-Ganneau in 1874 on his explorations. It may have been used by the Romans during the siege of the town.

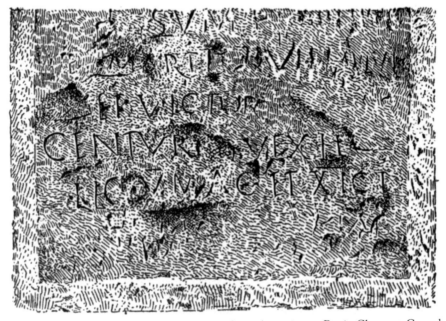

Figure 30. From a cast of the inscription made at the spring at Battir, Clermont-Geraud identified the inscribed names of two legions: V *Macedonica* and XI *Claudia*.

In the first two lines I can only make out a few more or less doubtful letters here and there. The restorations which might be suggested for them are too conjectural for me to discuss. It is probable that this part contained an account of some work accomplished by the personages mentioned in the second part. Considering the position of the inscription, this work was probably connected with the watercourse, with the distribution of water.[42]

Clermont-Ganneau interpreted the inscribed letters to be:

> ...SVM...
> ...MARII ■ ■ V
> ETVICTOR
> CENTVR ‹ VEXILL.
> LEG. V. MAC. ET. XI. CL[43]

He interpolated the abbreviated and fragmentary text to read '*et victor, centur(iones) vexill(ationum) leg(ionis) V Mac(edonicae) et XI Cl(audiae)*': 'There can be no doubt that the inscription speaks of the centurions commanding two detachments of the Fifth Legion, surnamed "The Macedonian", and of the Eleventh Legion, surnamed "The Claudian" (Pia, Fidelis).'[44] Here was indisputable proof of two identifiable legions at Betar!

He indulged in some speculation and applied deductive reasoning to complete the missing text:

> What comes before this is very hard to recover, from the dilapidated state of the inscription. One might, with M. de Villefosse, whom I have consulted on this subject, conjecture it to run thus:
>   ... V(alens) et Victor, centuriones, etc.,
> making it give us the names of two Roman officers. Perhaps, however, it would be better to adopt the view of M. Cagnat, who has also been good enough to give me his advice upon this difficult matter, and consider that the text began with some formula of dedication to the great gods of Rome and to Victory, such as *explendi gratia*:
>   Jovi summo, Juoni, Marti .... Et Victor(iae Aug?).
> In this case, the centurions would not be mentioned by name, but only in an anonymous collective fashion. With regard to the last point, at any rate, I admit that I prefer the second view.[45]

In 135 CE, these two legions and their support troops engaged in a textbook siege. Prevented from leaving Betar by the circumvallation, 'the rebels were driven to final destruction by famine and thirst.'[46] At the start of the assault, to break the will of the defenders, the Romans would likely have unleashed a fusillade from ballistas and catapults at positions on the higher ground of the south-western and southern hills. Experiments with re-enactors and full-size reconstructions of tension and torsion artillery weapons prove that a trained crew could precisely shoot at target objectives located hundreds of metres away and reload iron-tipped bolts or shaped stones several times a minute.[47] Remarkably, the Roman army had not undertaken a full-scale siege since the Battle of Sarmizegetusa Regia (106 CE) during the Dacian War.[48] New machines or tactics may have been deployed on this occasion. A few scholars have proposed that in a letter and treatise, believed to be addressed to Hadrian, the author Apollodorus suggested innovative ideas for siege machines better suited to hill-fort warfare, and specifically for the Bar Kokhba War.[49] It is a bit of a stretch, but it is an intriguing idea.

The rabbinic texts purport to capture something of the resilience of the rebel leader and his quick reflexes in response to incoming projectiles: 'He would catch the missiles from the enemy's catapults on one of his knees, and hurl them back, killing many of the foe.'[50] Even if the text makes a fantastical claim about Ben Kosiba's abilities, it does preserve the memory of the use of artillery by his enemy.

No after-action review or ancient historian's account survives to tell the story of the last stand of the soldiers of Israel at Betar. Instead, we have rabbinic texts which present cameos – echoes, perhaps, of real events. When the town was deemed safe enough to approach, Roman troops climbed up the steep hill. The Romans may have assaulted the town from the south-western side or the gates on the south-eastern side, or both simultaneously. Attacks on multiple fronts would distract the defenders and divide their resources. The Jewish militia may have rushed out to intercept the attackers. One rabbinic text mentions men 'who went down to the rampart of Betar', which may refer to the dry moat on the southern side of the fortified town.[51] Unlike Masada, there is no evidence of a ramp for a siege tower.[52] The final Roman advance may have been quick. The piles of small, hand-cut stones found by Ussishkin and his team attest to the ammunition never having been thrown in anger.

The Romans burst into the town. A general slaughter ensued in the streets. The *Talmud* records:

> When the enemy entered there, they pierced them with their staves, and when the enemy prevailed and captured them, they wrapped them in their scrolls and burnt them with fire.[53]
>
> Eighty thousand Romans entered Betar and slaughtered the men, women and children until blood flowed from the doorways and sewers. Horses sank up until their nostrils, and the rivers of blood lifted up rocks weighing forty *se'ah*, and flowed into the sea, where its stain was noticeable for a distance of four *mil*.[54]

How Ben Kosiba performed in his last minutes is nowhere recorded. We do not know if he died fighting or if he was taken alive. *Talmud* offers this version of events:

> His head was brought to Hadrian, who asked: 'Who killed him?'
>
> A Cuthean came forward and said: 'I did.'
>
> Hadrian told him: 'Go and bring his body.'
>
> He went and brought it, and they found a snake curled around his neck.
>
> Hadrian declared: 'Had his God not killed him, who would have been able to do so?'[55]

It was a dramatic end for the man Rabbi Akiba allegedly called 'Son of a Star', but an entirely fictional one since the Roman commander-in-chief was not there.[56]

By a quirk of fate, Betar fell on *Tisha B'Ab* in the Jewish calender.[57] It was the day of *churban*: the same day on which the First Temple in Jerusalem had been razed by Nebuchadnezzar II in 587 BCE, and on which the rebuilt Second Temple was destroyed by Titus in 70 CE.

Mopping-up operations began. There were no Geneva Conventions then to mitigate the harsh treatment of defeated soldiers or captive civilians at the hands of victorious troops. Atrocities were inevitably committed. The memory of that harrowing day has been preserved in the Jewish religious texts:

> Rabbi Yohanan said: 'The brains of three hundred children were dashed upon one stone, and three hundred baskets of capsules of

phylacteries were found in Betar, each capsule having a capacity of 2,130 litres.'[58]

It has been taught that Rabbi Eleazar the Great said: 'There are two streams in the valley of Yadaim, one running in one direction and one in another, and the Sages estimated that at that time they ran with two parts of water to one of blood.'[59]

In a Baraitha [rabbinical tradition] it has been taught: 'For seven years the gentiles fertilized their vineyards with the blood of Israel without using manure.'[60]

Rabban Bar Hanah said in the name of Rabbi Yohanan: 'Forty times twenty-four phylactery boxes were found on the heads of the victims of Betar.'[61]

Betar had fallen. The *nasi* was dead and with him the House of Israel. Yet the war for many of the insurrectionists was still not over. Refugees from across the rebel state had fled eastwards, as far away from Roman troops as they could go. To learn about their fate, I now needed to go to Ein Gedi.

Chapter 8

'They Were Sitting in a Cave'

It was already dark when I reached the Youth Hostel at Ein Gedi and the automatic security gate closed behind me with a loud 'clunk!' My room was in a block high up at the rear of the campus. The stillness of the place was palpable; it was a welcome respite from being constantly on the go for the last several days. After a restful sleep, next morning I walked out on to the balcony to take in the view. It was early, but the heat was already rising. In the distance, through the shimmering haze, I could just make out the hills of Jordan. In the middle distance lay the famous Dead Sea. The Hebrew name for it is *Yam Ha-Melah*, 'Salt Sea'.[1] Modern tourists come here to float in its briny water and enjoy cures for skin ailments, as well as to breathe in the oxygen-rich, allergen-free, salt sea air. In Ben Kosiba's day these were not the reasons people settled here. They came to make money.

In the early-second century CE Ein Gedi was a small but thriving town covering 1.6 hectares (4 acres).[2] Lying 430.5 metres (1,412ft) below sea level, it was the lowest inhabited place on earth. The town was able to survive in the desert, which is one of the harshest wastelands in the world, because it was an oasis with four springs supplying fresh water (plate 30). The population of approximately 1,000 Eingedites lived relatively well and in comfort. Their high-quality houses – some multi-storey, some with courtyards – were densely packed together.[3] Owner-occupiers and renters lived cheek by jowl. It was a majority Jewish community and a synagogue is mentioned located next to a courtyard building.[4] There was even a bathhouse, in operation at least during the years the Roman army had a presence in the town; *Cohors* I *Thracum Milliaria* was at Ein Gedi in 124 CE with quarters on either side of a street.[5]

Ein Gedi was unabashedly a commercial town (map 5). There were workshops, groves and a market. The townsfolk thrived on a variety of cash and consumption crops including citrons, palm fronds, pomegranates, salt and sulphur.[6] Fresh fish, such as catfish and tilapia, were caught in

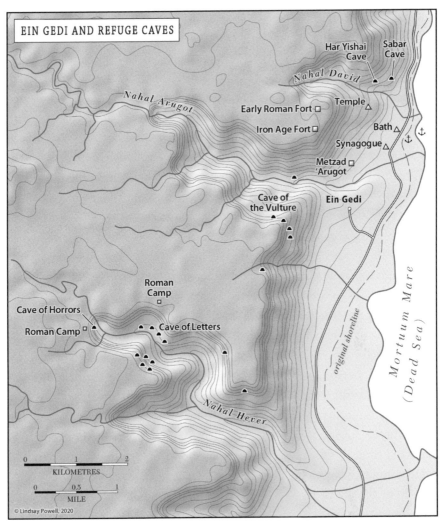

Map 5. Ein Gedi and refuge caves. (© *Lindsay Powell*)

the local springs or the Jordan River.[7] The dates of Iudaea grown here were world-famous. Polymath Pliny the Elder describes the dates' 'rich, unctuous juice' as possessing 'a milky consistency' with 'a sort of vinous flavour, with a remarkable sweetness, like that of honey'.[8] Ben Kosiba had understood the value of the land and its produce; it is why he leased it to tenants. The town's highly lucrative perfume industry was based on the production of *balsamum* or *laudanum* (*Commiphora gileadensis*), an aromatic resinous substance exuded by various trees and shrubs that were cultivated in orchards beside the town.[9] Pliny noted that it was 'a plant that has been only bestowed by Nature upon the land of Iudaea'.[10] The perfume manufacturing techniques were carefully-guarded trade secrets.[11] Processed and bottled, the resulting fragrance was an expensive luxury product – literally worth more than its weight in gold – was exported overseas (likely via Gaza).[12] Ben Kosiba had known its value too; it is why he ordered that his deputies treat Eleazar Ben Hita's balsam plants with the utmost care, despite arresting the man.[13]

Located beside the Dead Sea, Ein Gedi had a harbour, though it has yet to be identified.[14] At the height of the war, Ben Kosiba wrote in Hebrew to his commanders in the town ordering them to deal with the consignment from 'a ship in your place and in the harbour [Hebrew: *mahoz*]'.[15] Anchors have been found on the beach of a small bay, about 1 kilometre (0.6 mi.) north of Ein Gedi, an area so far without Hellenistic or Roman remains. One of them, dating to the Roman period, originally weighed 130 kilos (286lb); it was constructed of timber cut from a jujube tree, reinforced with lead, iron and bronze, and was found with some of its ropes made of date palm fibres still attached, complete with a reef knot.[16] It would have come from a large ship, at least 7 metres (23ft) long. To seal the gaps between the planks in hulls of sea-going ships ancient boat-builders used bitumen. Ein Gedi was one of the few known sources of the rare commodity. Blocks of almost pure bitumen occasionally bobbed up in the Dead Sea, a fact also recorded by Pliny.[17] It was packaged and exported from the town. Some boats used on the Dead Sea were actually quite simple affairs made from locally-grown reeds.[18]

Where the 'small bay' of the ancient harbour probably lay is now far away from the modern shore. The level of the Dead Sea has sunk in recent years at the astonishing rate of 1 metre per year.[19] In Ben Kosiba's time, the water reached up to the footings of the cliffs in some places. Consequently, there was no road along the shore from the north-western end. A road connected Ein Gedi to Aelia Capitolina by traversing the west-side brow of the Jordan Rift Valley. It was by this route that the Roman army arrived.

By late 135 and into early 136 CE, Ein Gedi's fortunes had changed dramatically.[20] The correspondence between *Nasi* Ben Kosiba and the town's two military officers, Yehonatan Bar Be'ayan and Masabala Bar Shim'on, ended abruptly with the siege of Betar. When news of the fall of the stronghold reached the oasis town, its inhabitants were suddenly on their own. Perhaps they hoped to make a getaway across the Dead Sea to Moab or beyond. Their numbers swelled with battle-weary soldiers fleeing the Romans. Everyone now had to fend for themselves. Anticipating the worst, some had already taken action and left town. Babatha Bat Shim'on and Yehonatan Bar Be'ayan were among them.

Finding Ein Gedi abandoned, the Roman soldiers destroyed it. They knew who they were looking for and where to find them. Eusebius writes:

> No high tower, no fortified wall, no mightiest navy and not the most diligent in commerce could overcome the might of the Roman army; and the citizens of Iudaea came to such distress that they, together with their wives, their children, their gold and their silver, in which they trusted, remained in underground tunnels and deepest caves.[21]

The soldiers then fanned out in search of their prey.[22] The fatal game of cat and mouse began.

In the Judean *Shephelah*, at the first sign of danger, communities such as at Horbat 'Etri, had gone underground into their hiding complexes.[23] In the Jordan Rift Valley below the Judean Desert, instead people looked to the canyons directly behind them for shelter. On the western shore of the Dead Sea some of the cliffs rise almost 310 metres (1,017ft). They were formed over millennia by seasonal streams eroding the sedimentary rock. Caves are a feature of this starkly beautiful landscape. They reach deep into the rock, with 'passages', 'halls', 'chambers', 'cavities' and 'niches' created by fissures and rock-falls (plate 31). These had provided humans with habitation since the earliest times and they had been used as places of refuge in the First Jewish War.[24] The townsfolk would withdraw to the caves in times of danger and emerge again after the threat had passed. They were accessible via difficult mountain tracks known only to the local people.

For a few kilometres either side of Ein Gedi, there are several ravines and gorges. To the untrained eye the caves are hard to find from ground level. Scanning the sedimentary layers, eventually one sees a dark spot. It is a cave entrance. Some twenty-nine caves have been identified in the north Judean Desert. Directly to the north of Ein Gedi in the ravine of the Wadi Murabba'at are four caves. Over the years clay, silt, sand, sediment and boulders from fallen ceilings, and collapsed cave walls, filled the depressions, sealing in and preserving any artefacts left there by the occupants.[25] In 1952, after Bedouins first found fragments of papyri and reported them to the Rockefeller Museum, archaeologists discovered in 'Cave 2' a cache of documents in Hebrew and Greek, including biblical texts and letters from Ben Kosiba.[26] They had been secreted away by men from Herodium, perhaps deputies of the *nasi* himself.[27] In the adjacent Wadi Murrazah, in the 'Cave 84 Complex' – also known as the 'Cave of the Spear' – people from Ein Gedi and Tekoa hid together.[28] Some of the occupants were evidently militiamen. Among the finds was a spear point, on account of which archaeologists assigned the moniker to the find-spot. It was a unique design; there was no equivalent from other Jewish or Roman examples. The archaeologists described it as having 'a narrow elongated blade, rhomboid in section, tapering to a point that is square in section.'[29] Remarkable was that it had a distinct V-shaped notch on one side, suggesting that it had taken a direct hit from another weapon in the heat of battle – the soldier wielding it had used the spear to intercept a sword blow. Pieces of baskets and rope, remnants of food including barley seeds, a cooking-pot lid, an oil lamp with traces of soot, shards of pottery and glass, and the key to a jewellery box were also found. A silver coin re-struck with dies used during the Bar Kokhba War confirmed that it dated to the 'Second Year'. Another bore the legend 'For The Freedom of Jerusalem', meaning that it was struck in the Third Year or 134–135 CE.

Closer to Ein Gedi, above the Nahal David springs, the 'Cave of the Pool' had been known for some time, but two other caves have been recently explored and documented. In the small 'Har Yisahi Cave' archaeologists found the telltale burn marks of two fires.[30] They recovered several bronze coins, broken potsherds, pieces of glass, a jug and five cooking pots, pieces of textiles, bits of twined baskets, and many trilobate arrow-heads, as well as their shafts and reeds, all dateable to the Bar Kokhba War period. Two fragmentary documents written in Greek were also retrieved. Having been brought by the occupants into the cave with much thought and effort, the artefacts seemed to have been hurriedly abandoned. The scatter of pottery and glass fragments suggested to the archaeologists that humans rather than animals were the cause and speculated that Roman soldiers had entered the cave and created the disarray.

The larger 'Sabar Cave 184' nearby produced yet more remarkable finds.[31] Bronze coins minted in the 'Third Year,' corroded together inside the remains of a cloth pouch, were found with silver coins issued under

Nero, Vespasian, Trajan and Hadrian – testament to how long coins circulated in the Roman world. Digging further, the archaeologists found trilobate arrow-heads, a link of chain, a bent iron blade perhaps used as a scythe, an iron knife, a piece of cloth, various glass bowls and potsherds, as well as date and olive pits. The archaeologists speculated that an Engedite had used the cave to hide his cash, or took refuge there in person, but never returned to collect it.

I tried to imagine how militia and civilians, friends and strangers, young and old, drawn by fear and fate, all managed to live together in these caves. A shared faith, community, family ties and necessity bound them. They were urbane, sophisticated people used to creature comforts. Under such extreme and awful conditions of life in a cramped cave, how could these people possibly survive? It would be a test of endurance and resolve. They could only hope that the future would be better. After all, the Jews had suffered – and survived – torments before.

The refugees may have initially used ropes to rappel down the cliff faces. The other way was to climb up. When I visited the Nature Reserve next to the Youth Hostel, to get a better view of Ein Gedi I climbed up the south face of Nahal David. It was not, Rabbi Akiba may have agreed, for the faint-hearted. A good sense of balance was essential, and a clear head for heights. For most of the length of the path there was no handrail, only rough-hewn steps in the rock – where they existed at all – smoothed by the thousands of visitors who had climbed them before. I had almost reached the top, but the combination of height and the heat of midday had taken their toll. I shot the photos I needed (plate 30) and then began my descent, *carefully*. Elsewhere in the Dead Sea region access through the ravines is by rough pathways formed by the feet of hikers. Walking and climbing them can be dangerous; there have been deaths among visitors falling from the cliffs in recent years.

Behind Ein Gedi lies the valley of the Nahal 'Arugot. Archaeologists have explored a cave there situated 200 metres (656ft) below the cliff edge, which could only be accessed using a rope anchored at the top, hence the name 'Cave of the Rope'.[32] If used during the war, the refugees left no traces. The 'Cave of the Vulture' similarly produced no finds.[33] All the caves in the Dead Sea area are now strictly off limits to casual visitors. Indeed, the Unit for the Prevention of Antiquities Robbery and the Cave Research Unit of the Israeli Antiquities Authority (IAA) try to protect them from illegal excavations and lootings which occur all too frequently. Just weeks before I arrived in Israel, teams of archaeologists and volunteers conducted an emergency dig in a cave because it had been raided by robbers.[34] There are thirty-four more caves with evidence of human use and most of them have yet to be explored by scientists, but they are already known to looters.

Today expert guides offer personal tours of the canyons, pointing out the caves from a safe distance (plate 32). A stout pair of hiking boots or a 4x4 SUV is needed to handle the uneven rocky trackway from Ein Gedi to reach the top of the Nahal Hever (Wadi Habra) canyon which lies to the south of the town. It is worth the trip. The panoramic view from the cliff edge is spectacular, looking down the entire length of the deep gorge and out to the Dead Sea. In 136 CE, a Roman officer could really feel that that he commanded the world from up here.

The Nahal Hever canyon was a favoured place for refugees of the Bar Kokhba War. Ten caves – originally named Caves A to J – have been explored. Identified in 1953, exploration of the 'Square Cave' on the north side of the canyon two years later produced no finds.[35] 'Cave B', explored again in 2014 following reports of robbery, similarly revealed no evidence of human occupation.[36] The 'Cave of Letters' (fig. 31), on the north side of the canyon, however, proved to be an archaeologist's dream. It was where they found the archives of Babatha Bat Shim'on, Eleazar Ben Eleazar, Eleazar Ben Shmuel and Bene Hananiah. The collected correspondence between the *Nasi* of Israel and his militia commanders at Ein Gedi was found here too. The carefully-folded sheets of papyrus and wooden slats were neatly stacked and tied together with two strings, one thick and one thin; it would seem that Yehonatan Bar Be'ayan – and perhaps Masabala Bar Shim'on too – brought the letters with them when taking refuge in this cave.[37] There were fragments of scrolls from the *Torah*, including books of Psalms and Prophets, all carefully written in Biblical Hebrew.[38] Babatha and the other elite members of local Jewish society had brought their finest possessions with them: a woven basket was found with a set of bronze bowls (plate 33), cups and incense burners; a bronze jug with its decoration scored to make it *kosher*; three glass platters including, arguably, the finest clear glass bowl to survive from the Ancient World; fine, patterned cloths in many colours; a waterskin packed full of cosmetic items, and nearby a handheld mirror.[39] It is clear that they came always

Figure 31. A view of one of the entrances into the so-called 'Cave of Letters' in the Nahal Hever Canyon. Refugees from Ein Gedi and elsewhere hid here hoping to escape from the Romans and re-emerge after the war.

intending to leave and re-establish their lives anew. They even brought their front-door keys (plate 34).[40]

At the western end of the canyon in the 'Cave of Horrors', which was smaller than the 'Cave of Letters', conditions were cramped and unsanitary.[41] The occupants had brought their possessions with them too, both luxury and utilitarian: combs, fish nets, gaming pieces, glass bowls and jugs, nails, needles, tooled leather, wooden boxes and cash.[42] They hid the Greek and Hebrew documents as best they could, but there was no space to bury the larger items. Instead, they lit a fire in the centre of the cave, broke up the glassware and utensils, and threw their treasures onto the pyre. Was it an act of despair or of defiance?

The Roman army, meantime, had set up two camps, one on either side of the Nahal Hever canyon. One stood on the ledge above the 'Cave of Letters' (which archaeologists call 'Camp A') on the north side, the other above the 'Square Cave' or 'Cave of Horrors' ('Camp B') on the south side.[43] Soldiers in each encampment could watch activity in the cave on the opposite side of the canyon and relay messages to their colleagues; they could harass the people trapped in the cave directly below and prevent their escape; additionally, 'Camp B' also controlled access to the only available source of water.[44] Enough survives of 'Camp A' for us to understand its design and function. Using field stones, the troops set up a {-shaped perimeter wall with a clavicular gate at its centre. The enclosed space was around 1,250 square metres (13,455 sq ft). Inside the secure compound there was a *principia*, comprising three rooms from which the camp commandant and his staff could direct operations. There were hearths or ovens for baking bread. There was a walled-off space, presumably for supplies. The soldiers set up their *contubernium* tents and arranged stones around them forming low-walled 'cubicles', either to anchor the tent pegs in the dry ground or to protect the occupants from the chill desert wind. The goatskin tents, perhaps ten in number, were arranged back-to-back in two irregular-shaped clusters. It is likely that a *centuria* of eighty men was barracked at 'Camp A', perhaps from *Cohors* I *Thracum Milliaria*, which is known to have had a presence at Ein Gedi in 124 CE.[45] The impression they give is one of semi-permanence. This was not a temporary overnight camp; it was designed with weeks or even months of occupation in mind. The Romans would be here for as long as it took to eliminate the last of the insurgents. Time was now on their side.

As at Betar, the Romans let thirst and starvation to do their dirty work. There would be no escape for the fugitives. A dramatic tale is told in *Midrash*:

It happened to one group who took refuge in a cave.

One of them was told: 'Go and fetch a corpse of one of those killed that we may eat.'

He went forth and found the body of his father and hid it and marked it, and buried it, then returned and said: 'I did not find any [corpse].'

Figure 32. A view looking out from the 'Cave of Letters' to the Dead Sea. Archaeologists found the personal possessions and household items that the refugees had taken with them. They included letters and contracts, many of which have been preserved in the dry desert conditions.

They said: 'Let another go forth.'

One of them went out, and followed the stench of that corpse and brought it back. They ate it and the teeth of the son became blunt.

He asked: 'Whence did you bring that corpse?'

And was answered: 'From such and such corner.'

He asked further: 'What mark was on it?'

And was answered: 'Such and such a mark.'

He said: 'Woe to this child; he ate the flesh of his father.'[46]

The 'Cave of Horrors' finally revealed its grim secrets when thoroughly excavated in 1960–61. The remains of some forty individuals were unearthed.[47] They included women and children. There were no signs of violent struggle or cannibalism, however, categorically disproving the story in *Midrash*, and a reminder that the rabbinic texts cannot always be taken at face value. They had slowly starved to death. As people died, the living carefully and respectfully buried the bodies deep within the cave. Two skeletons, one of a 6- or 7-year-old child, the other of a middle-aged adult male, were found in caves in Nahal Mishmar.[48] As for the 'Cave of Letters' (fig. 32), the skeletons of the occupants were found by archaeologists, including jawless skulls carefully placed in woven baskets.[49] They were mostly female in the ratio of eight women to three men.[50] The fact that the skulls were placed in a basket suggests that someone – a survivor? – later returned to re-inter them. In the neighbouring Nahal Seelim (Wadi Seiyal), where there were no Roman camps, there is also evidence of re-interment and of stocking caves.[51]

When it was clear to the Roman soldiers above that the people trapped in the caves in Nahal Hever were no longer alive, they rolled up their goatskin tents and marched out of their camp. A garrison remained in the area of Ein Gedi to ensure there would be no further disturbances.[52]

'This, then, was the end of the war with the Jews,' writes Cassius Dio.[53]

Chapter 9

'He Liberated Syria Palaestina from the Enemy'

Sipping a hot mint tea at a café in Mamilla Mall just outside Jerusalem's city walls, I reflected on the outcome of the Bar Kokhba War. By the end of 135 CE Hadrian and his legates had won and mopping-up operations were concluded the following year. Roman law and Roman order were finally restored to Province Iudaea. Eusebius writes: 'In accordance with the laws of war [Rufus] reduced their country to a state of complete subjection.'[1] This was the very definition of *pax* to the Romans, 'peace born through victories'.[2] Or in the emotive words which Tacitus put into the mouth of a defeated British king, 'where they make a wasteland, they call it peace.'[3]

It had taken three and a half years to do so.[4] The cost in blood and treasure was high. 'Very few of them in fact survived,' writes Cassius Dio of Jewish losses.[5] The statistics he compiled for casualties and damages make for grim reading:

> 50 of their most important outposts and 985 of their most famous villages were razed to the ground. 580,000 men were slain in the various raids and battles, and the number of those that perished by famine, disease and fire was past finding out. Thus, nearly the whole of Judea was made desolate.[6]

Dio's numbers are almost certainly overstated and by orders of magnitude. They do, however, convey the catastrophic impact on the region which had been engulfed in the years of conflict. In the rabbinic texts the question is asked: 'How many battles did Hadrian fight? Two teachers gave an answer. One said it was fifty-two and the other fifty-four.'[7] In another fable Hadrian turns to Aquila and says, 'See how much I have humiliated it (the people of Israel), how cruelly I have chastised it.'[8] A statuette is identified by some as Hadrian with the defeated Jewish warlord (fig. 33).

Figure 33. A marble statuette from Egypt depicting a Roman emperor with a seated captive. Some identify the beard and hairstyle of the victor with Hadrian and the long-haired defeated figure with 'Bar Kokhba'.

Significantly the losses were not all on the rebel side. Dio adds, 'Many Romans, moreover, perished in this war.'[9] Writing to Emperor Antoninus Pius twenty-six years after the Bar Kokhba War, M. Cornelius Fronto remarks: 'Under the rule of your grandfather Hadrian what a number of soldiers were killed by the Jews.'[10] Loss of Roman life was unforgivable under any circumstances. It was particularly egregious when the perpetrators were supposed to be subjugated peoples. The casualties were blemishes on the emperor's reputation and still remembered a generation later.

Roman civil law was surprisingly imprecise on the issue of sedition as a crime and lacked a legal concept for it.[11] It was considered with high treason (*laesa maiestas*) as an injury (*iniuria*) on the dignity of the Roman people, but only later in the Empire's history would it encompass aspects such as counterfeiting coins, which clearly Ben Kosiba had done. In the past, the punishment for rioting or violent breach of the peace in Iudaea was often death by crucifixion, but there are no reports of its prescription for participants in the Bar Kokhba War.[12] Rather, in a form of social engineering, an oft-used post-war policy was the forcible removal of troublemakers from a former conflict zone, in particular the men of military age.[13] The captives of the Bar Kokhba War were stripped of their rights and freedoms and reduced to the status of slaves (*servi*). Enslavement of prisoners of war was considered a benefit to them as 'commanders order captives to be sold and so spare (*servare*) them rather than be killed'.[14] In Hadrian's eyes he was showing clemency (*clementia*); the captured Jews ought to be grateful as the alternative was a lot worse. They were taken to the slave market held annually at Mamre near Hebron, by tradition the site of the ancient Terebinth-Eloh tree.[15] As if by prescience, the market had recently been repaired at Hadrian's request. According to Jerome so many men, women and children were offered for sale that the price of a human fell to the amount paid for horse feed – four Jews for just a single measure of barley.[16] 'Hadrian's market' was talked about for centuries. Any unsold slaves were sent to Gaza to be auctioned there, while others were shipped off to Egypt, adding their numbers to the Jewish diaspora. They would never be able to cause trouble in Judea again.

It is reported that Jews were forbidden to wear *tefillin*, eat *matzah* on Passover, light candles on *Hanukkah*, appoint judges, ordain rabbis (Hebrew: *semicha*) or gather to teach *Torah*.[17] Hadrian reportedly banned any Jews from entering his new, urban creation:

> The whole nation was prohibited from this time on by a decree, and by the commands of Hadrian, from ever going up to the country about Jerusalem. For the emperor gave orders that they should not even see from a distance the land of their fathers. Such is the account of Aristo of Pella.
>
> And thus, when the city had been emptied of the Jewish nation and had suffered the total destruction of its ancient inhabitants, it was colonized by a different race and the Roman city, which subsequently arose, changed its name and was called Aelia, in honour of the emperor Aelius Hadrian.[18]

It is also reported that 'before its gate, that of the road by which we go to Bethlehem, he set up an idol of a pig in marble, signifying the subjugation of the Jews to Roman authority.'[19] Rather than a spiteful anti-Semitic insult, however, the animal – a boar – may simply be the totemic emblem of resident *Legio* X *Fretensis* (fig. 22).[20]

Hadrian changed the status of the Jewish homeland too. Before the war, Iudaea had been a stand-alone proconsular province; after the war, it was absorbed into neighbouring Syria. The new, combined regional authority was renamed, recalling another name coined by the Greeks: Syria Palaestina. It is shown for the first time in the archaeological record on the metal discharge document issued to an auxiliary infantryman from 139 CE.[21] The name of Palestine has endured to the present day.

The two legions in the former Province Iudaea remained in the region. *Legio* VI *Ferrata* now established its permanent base at Caparcotna/Legio in the Jezreel Valley.[22] Its location gave the legion direct control of the Galilee and Samaria. *Legio* X *Fretensis* continued to encamp at Aelia Capitolina. From there it had direct access to the desert, hills and plains of the Judea and Transjordan. Additionally, fifteen auxiliary units – comprising three *alae* and twelve *cohortes* – supported the legions.[23]

The successful conclusion of the war was the occasion to issue rewards and recognitions to those fellow citizens who had helped Hadrian win it. He was generous to officers and rankers for acts of valour and derring-do, offering them an array of military decorations (*dona militaria*).[24] The courageous legate of *Legio* X *Fretensis*, whose name is sadly lost, received the double distinction of a *corona muralis* and *corona vallaris*, respectively a crown awarded to the first soldier who climbed the wall of a besieged city and entered by force, and a crown awarded to the first soldier who climbed the parapet of an enemy camp.[25] While serving with *Legio* III *Cyrenaica* as military tribune (*tribuni militum*) Popilius Carus Pedo received unspecified *donis militaribus* from Hadrian.[26] Equestrian officers were decorated too. M. Statius Priscus received a *vexillum*, a unit flag; Sex. Cornelius Dexter accepted a *vexillum* and a *hasta*, the spearhead being an award given for voluntary single combat with the enemy.[27] Several centurions were recognized. Octavius Secundus of *Legio* X *Fretensis* received a *corona aurea*, a golden crown awarded to a soldier for killing an enemy in single combat and holding the ground to the end of the battle.[28] M. Sabidius Maximus of *Legio* XI *Claudia* received a *corona muralis.*[29] Q. Albius Felix with *Legio* XX *Valeria Victrix* received the award of the *hasta pura*, a highly-prized ceremonial spearhead apparently made without iron, as well as a *corona aurea* in an unspecified Hadrianic campaign, presumed to be the Bar Kokhba War.[30] C. Nummius Constans received a *corona aurea*, though it is unclear whether he was serving with *Legio* III *Cyrenaica* as centurion or II *Traiana* as *primipilus* at the time it was merited.[31]

It is said that the auxiliary troops at the Roman camp at Beit Guvrin were rewarded with an amphitheatre for blood games (*munera*) or military parades as the gift of either the grateful governor or the emperor. It is a nice interpretation, but one that may not actually be true. It is certainly an impressive building, one that would have been expensive to erect; it was so well built that it is still in a good state of preservation. Based on ceramics and coins found during excavations undertaken between 1981 and 1986, however, the amphitheatre likely dates to the late second-third centuries CE, well after the end of the war.[32]

Hadrian was known to be much less generous in his distribution of rewards to his direct reports. Like Augustus before him, he *expected* them to perform in difficult circumstances. The victorious legates of the Bar Kokhba War, however, were the rare exceptions. Lollius Urbicus received the *corona aurea* and *hasta pura* from Hadrian.[33] Triumphal ornaments (*triumphalia ornamenta*) were granted to Publicius Marcellus, Haterius Nepos, Iulius Severus and Lollius Urbicus.[34] The distinction entitled them each to ride their horses in a military parade along the *Via Sacra* in Rome; it was less grand than the full triumph with a victor's chariot (since Augustus exclusively reserved that for the emperor), but nevertheless a highly coveted recognition.[35] It was all the more remarkable because this honour had not been granted to so many senators for a single campaign since the war to suppress the Great Illyrian Revolt (6–9 CE).[36] Each commander was also honoured with a statue mounted on an inscribed base in his home city.[37] Not content with just a statue on a plinth, Publicius Marcellus went one better than his colleagues and erected his own monument in Aquileia.[38]

Hadrian rewarded his deputies with political positions as well.[39] The equestrian Haterius Nepos, who may have suppressed a rebellion of Jews in Arabia Petraea before he joined the campaign in Iudaea, was elected suffect consul in 134 CE. Lollius Urbicus was elected suffect consul for

135 or 136. Iulius Severus, who had brilliantly led the counterinsurgency to a successful conclusion, may have remained in the region, becoming the first *legatus Augusti pro praetore* of the new province of Syria Palaestina. The equestrian Statius Priscus was adlected into the Senate, opening a new world of career opportunities for him.[40]

Everyone on the Roman team was a winner – all except one. For Tineius Rufus there were no rewards, only regrets. He disappears from recorded history after 132 CE. Ironically, he gained an immortality of sorts in the Talmudic texts as the villain of the story. His son, Q. Tineius Sacerdos Clemens, however, was spared any stain on his family's reputation and he would go on to become consul in 158 CE and later assume one of the pontifices.

Hadrian had generally declined military distinctions for himself, but this time he relented.[41] Sometime between 5 September and 9 December 135 CE, Hadrian received the second imperatorial acclamation of his career, which is generally believed to have been for the victory in Judea.[42] From then on he would use the form '*IMP[erator]* II' on coins, official documents and inscriptions. In Rome a colossal statue of Hadrian or a small triumphal arch was raised with an inscribed slab measuring c. 2 metres (6.6ft) long.[43] Significantly it stood at the western end of the *Forum Romanum* in Rome beside the Temple of the Deified Vespasian and Titus, the victors of the First Jewish War. Though only the right-hand-side block containing a few words of five lines of text now survives, the formulaic style of Roman public statements means reconstruction of the full inscription is possible. One attempt hails Hadrian for 'fighting with great enthusiasm' (*summo pugnandi ardore*) and records how his army 'liberated Syria Palaestina from the enemy' (*Syriam Palaestinam ab hoste liberaverit*). It should be noted that '*[a]dore*' and '*[hos]ste liberaverit*' were among the few words still surviving; the rest are informed guesses.[44]

There is another war-related monument that has perplexed scholars for years. In 1976, six fragments of an inscription written in Latin were discovered near the camp of *Legio* VI in Tel Shalem.[45] Its exquisitely-carved lettering – 41 centimetres (16in) high in the first row and 24 centimetres (9.5in) in the second – rivals anything erected in Rome itself for size, including the Pantheon and Arch of Titus. Estimates of the full dimensions of the original slab suggest it was 10 to 11 metres (33 to 36ft) in length. The only structure that could carry an inscription that big would be a triumphal arch. There is now nothing of the structure left to see. One argument is that it was constructed to mark Hadrian's visit to Province Iudaea in 130 CE; the other is that it celebrated the Roman victory over the Jewish rebels (following a possible but unlikely return by Hadrian in 134/135). Which option is the right answer – assuming one of them is correct – turns on a reconstruction of the text and whether it mentions the tribunician power fourteen times or the tribunician power twenty times, and includes that important second imperatorial acclamation along with some additional text to complete the inscription.[46]

The proposed solutions are certainly clever. There are good arguments in support of either version. The significance of the tribunician power is that it dates the inscription to no earlier than 130 CE (before the war), whereas the imperatorial acclamation dates it to no earlier than 135 CE (after the war). However, the suggestion that the inscription was raised by *Legio X Fretensis* is debatable.[47] The arch stood in the region patrolled by *Legio VI Ferrata*. If any legion would erect the victory monument it would surely be the local unit based in Tel Shalem. Had the unit's operations stopped the uprising gaining traction in the Galilee, that would be a good justification for the commemorative building. The proposed inclusion of 'SPQR' presupposes the backing of the Roman Senate for the arch.[48] It is conceivable that, understanding the significance of their victory, the three field commanders (now consuls and ex-consuls) personally lobbied their colleagues for its construction.[49] There was precedent. Commemorating Germanicus Caesar's life and achievements, in 20 CE the Senate voted for triumphal arches to be erected in Rome, at Mogontiacum on the Rhine and on Mount Amanus in Syria.[50] The magnificent arch at Gerasa was similarly built when the city swelled with pride for having received Hadrian in person. Until more pieces of the inscription are found, the presumed victory memorial remains an elusive structure.

There was also a triumphal arch in Aelia Capitolina itself. The arch still stands, at least in part, some 350 metres (1,148ft) north of the Damascus Gate.[51] Known today as the 'Ecce Homo Arch', it straddles the busy Via Dolorosa. Navigating a path through the crowds of pilgrims to see it, my first impression was that the positioning of the archway seemed rather odd. The explanation is that the arch was not planned that way, as excavations revealed in the 1860s (fig. 34). Originally free-standing, later buildings expanded, eventually incorporating its ancient fabric into

Figure 34. The so-called 'Ecce Homo Arch' as it appeared when excavated in Jerusalem in 1864. It was actually Hadrian's triumphal arch which straddled the *Decumanus* street – nowadays called the Via Dolorosa – from the Eastern Gate of Aelia Capitolina.

their own. There were originally two smaller arches flanking the main archway (fig. 35).[52] One was integrated into a monastery for Uzbek dervishes in the Order of the Golden Chain, but when the monastery was demolished the arch went with it. The other one on the north side became part of the Ecce Homo Basilica, continuing into the Convent of the Sisters of Zion where its footings beneath the foundations can still be seen. Many Christians believe the Ecce Homo Arch is the location where Jesus was sentenced, but the structure itself was built a full century *after* the crucifixion.[53] The triumphal arch was the grand entrance-way on the east-west *Decumanus Maximus* into Hadrian's magnificent city, located below the north-west corner of the Temple Mount.[54] There was a large area of paved stones outside it. For those entering the new *colonia*, visitors would have been in no doubt that this was a Roman city. When completed it could have been as large as the Arch of Hadrian in Gerasa, or the later Arch of Constantine beside the Colosseum, and perhaps surmounted by

Figure 35. A reconstruction drawing of how the 'Ecce Homo Arch' may have appeared when first built. The triumphal arch comprised a high central archway for vehicles flanked by two smaller arches for pedestrians with decorative apertures and alcoves. The upper storey and inscription was robbed for its stone in later times.

bronze statues and trophies.[55] The inscription that would have graced the entablature on the side of the attic has long since vanished. Fragments may yet be found, perhaps as material reused in another building.

After the First Jewish War, Vespasian, Titus and Domitian were very keen to let the world know of their victory, minting coins announcing *Iudaea Capta.* Where the Flavians went for overt propaganda in a big way, Hadrian's approach was much subtler. The omission of any references to Iudaea (or Iudea) on his gold and silver coinage issued after the war may have been a deliberate policy of not drawing attention to it.[56] Instead, one issue (plate 35) shows a figure of an enthroned god Iuppiter holding a sceptre in the left hand and a Victoriola (a miniature Victory) in the right.[57] Another (plate 36) shows Victory holding an eagle in the right hand and a palm frond in the left. Yet another design, issued both as a gold *aureus* and a silver *denarius*, shows the winged goddess Nemesis-Victory, poised and striding right, holding a laurel branch; a variant (plate 37) has Victory striding towards the viewer, holding a palm frond.[58] The accompanying legend *Victoria Aug(usta)* is generic and could apply equally to the suppression of the Jews or Britons. For ordinary Romans the end of war meant freedom from anxiety and the opportunity for prosperity (plate 38). Rebel coins, meanwhile, with their exotic Jewish images and strange writing, were taken out of circulation. Some specimens found their way back to Roman army camps with returning troops – war spoils (*praedia*) and souvenirs of a mission accomplished.[59]

The remaining years of the emperor's life were stressful. The consensus view was that 'Hadrian was hated by the people, in spite of his generally excellent reign.'[60] Hadrian was not a well man. Cassius Dio writes that as a result of his great loss of blood, he became consumptive and this in turn led to dropsy, an old name for oedema.[61] Medications, charms and magic could not cure him of his chronic illness, and it is reported that he contemplated suicide to bring an end to his suffering.[62] He moved to the upscale seaside resort of Baiae on the Gulf of Naples to recuperate.[63] Reflecting on his life and knowing that his death was imminent, he composed a poem:

> *Animula, vagula, blandula*
> *Hospes comesque corporis*
> *Quae nunc abibis in loca*
> *Pallidula, rigida, nudula,*
> *Nec, ut soles, dabis iocos.*[64]

The Latin is rich with meaning, the rhythm and meter distinctly paced, rendering a faithful translation into English very difficult. This one captures well the sentimentality:

> Oh, loving Soul, my own so tenderly,
> My life's companion and my body's guest,
> To what new realms, poor flutterer, wilt thou fly?
> Cheerless, disrobed, and cold in thy lone quest,
> Hushed thy sweet fancies, mute thy wonted jest.[65]

Then his life ended. *Imperator* Caesar Traianus Hadrianus Augustus died on 10 July 138 CE. Cassius Dio informs us that, 'he had lived 62 years, 5 months and 19 days, and had been emperor 20 years and 11 months'.[66] Heart failure is suspected.[67] Even in death there was no rest. Hadrian had built a great mausoleum for himself in Rome (fig. 36). Bigger than the dynastic tomb Caesar Augustus had constructed, it was not yet complete.[68]

Figure 36. Hadrian built a mausoleum for himself beside the Tiber in Rome. It was extensively reworked in later centuries and is now known as the Castel Sant' Angelo.

Hadrian was temporarily buried at Puteoli (Pozzuoli) on an estate that had once belonged to Cicero.[69] When the mausoleum was finally ready the urn containing his ashes was placed inside. The edifice still stands – albeit in substantially modified form – on a bend in the Tiber River close to the Vatican City; it is now called Castel Sant' Angelo. The Senate received a proposal for his deification, but there was opposition. The Conscript Fathers only consented when T. Antoninus – his adopted son, heir and successor known as Antoninus Pius – advocated for the motion in person.[70] A temple dedicated to *'Divus* Hadrianus' (*Hadrianeum*) was built at Puteoli and another in the Campus Martius, Rome in 145 CE.[71]

In Aelia Capitolina, erected upon the Temple Mount, there was a powerful symbol of Roman victory, strategically located for maximum effect. Cast in bronze and glittering with gold leaf was 'the statue of the mounted Hadrian, which stands to this very day on the site of the Holy of Holies'.[72] Jerome was writing in the fourth-fifth centuries CE, meaning that the equestrian statue had already been in that place for almost 200 years. Where the followers of the *Nasi* of Israel had once obliterated the images of Roman emperors every time they overstruck Roman coins, the statue of a man made god now effaced the most sacred space of the Jews, which Ben Kosiba had failed to secure.

The Roman victor had outlived the Jewish warlord by just three years. Shim'on Ben Kosiba had achieved a certain notoriety in life, but in death the rebel became something much more potent: a *legend*.

Chapter 10

'Son of a Lie'

Having checked out of my hotel on King George Street in Jerusalem, I headed to my rental car. By coincidence, the car park was on Rabbi Akiba Street. White text on the blue retro-reflective street sign (fig. 37) explained in Hebrew that Rabbi Akiba was:

> Of the greatest *Tannaim* and *Mishnah* scholars, [he] taught 24,000 students.
>
> Of the Ten Martyrs.[1]

By tradition – which means according to rabbinic sources since there are no Roman accounts – Akiba was a wanted man. He was eventually arrested by Tineius Rufus on some administrative offence, but not an actual crime.[2] Assuming the event to be historically true, some scholars

Figure 37. The sign on Akiba Street in Jerusalem declares the famous rabbi was one of the ten *tannaim* who are still held in the highest esteem by Jews in modern Israel.

argue that it occurred during the Bar Kokhba War, while others contend that it happened after. The story goes that Akiba was taken to Caesarea where he was imprisoned for a long time.[3] He was visited by his students from Bene Berak and other rabbis, including Shim'on Bar Yohai.[4] They insisted that he teach them *Torah*, but Akiba deemed it too dangerous. Yohai persisted, threatening to report him to the Romans for it, which would lead to a criminal charge. Akiba relented. Later the students were forbidden by the Roman authorities from visiting their teacher, but they took to disguising themselves to deceive the guards in order to meet with him.[5]

Akiba was interviewed by Rufus on several occasions. He is reported to have discussed charity, *brit milah*, observance of *Shabbat* and other subjects.[6] Rufus also allegedly had an affair with Akiba's wife which, while introducing a love interest sub-plot to the story, seems far-fetched.[7] Finally, Rufus sentenced the rabbi. It was to be a dreadful punishment by scourging. The terminals of the multi-thong Roman whip (*flagrum*) were made of lead and designed to tear the skin.[8] Preparing for his torture, he recited the *Shema*.[9] His hands tied and back exposed, the Roman torturer applied the *flagrum* with deliberate strokes. Even as Akiba suffered terrible agonies from being flayed alive, he uttered his prayer quietly and calmly. Perplexed by his remarkable composure *in extremis* since he appeared to feel no pain, Rufus asked him whether he was a sorcerer. The rabbi replied:

> I am neither a sorcerer nor a mocker, but I rejoice at the opportunity now given to me to love my God 'with all my life', seeing that I have hitherto been able to love Him only 'with all my means' and 'with all my might'.[10]

Akiba uttered the verse, 'Behold the cause of my joy' and, as he spoke the last word, he expired.[11] His students bore his brutalized body and buried him on one of the highest hills in Tiberias overlooking the Sea of Galilee.

Scholars still debate why Akiba supported Ben Kosiba in the first place.[12] It is entirely possible that the rabbi did not, that the men never met and that the whole story is just that, a story. One theory is that the tradition took root because the rabbis, then a small, emerging but ambitious group in Jewish society, wanted to be seen as involved in important events in history, the point being that the rabbis were not just witnesses to history but active participants in it.[13] That need trumped any reputational damage with which the negative outcome might taint any individual like Akiba. The pairing of a great leader with a rabbi was a *topos*, a way of making a historical event part of the present and elevating the role of the rabbis in a form of literary time travel: rabbis – like the fictional Dr Who – could appear in key events of the past. This is why there is a story that Rabbi Yochanan Ben Zakkai met Vespasian. In other words, Rabbi Akiba appears with a prominent figure of his day – Ben Kosiba – and has influence over him by declaring him the King Messiah.[14] Similarly, the supporting literary conceit placed Rabbi Akiba and Rabbi Yohanan Ben Torta together in the same room, though they too likely never actually met. Rabbis could appear with famous people to shape important decisions, even if they occurred in the past.

There is another possible explanation. According to rabbinic sources Ben Kosiba's militiamen charged into battle shouting, 'Master of the Universe! Do not help or hinder us!'[15] In backing Ben Kosiba, Rabbi Akiba made him the warrior in his revolution to assert the power of the rabbis. Conceived as a *Milhemet Mitzvah*, a 'holy war', the permission of the Sanhedrin was not required and the entire Jewish nation would be obliged to fight. The law was 'not made in Heaven' but by the rabbis, who claimed sole authority to make it, and even if it proved wrong, it was *still* right: 'Whether they are announced properly or otherwise, the proclamation makes them holy.'[16] Ben Kosiba was Akiba's King Messiah simply because *he* had decided so, with or without God's blessing.[17]

Akiba's martyrdom ensured his place in Jewish history. Many other rabbis were allegedly rounded up too and executed by the Romans under orders from Hadrian.[18] Among the 'ten martyrs' referred to on the street sign, not all were captured and executed at the same time. Indeed, some were killed in the aftermath of the First Jewish War.[19] Their names are still celebrated. A liturgical poem (*Midrash Eleh Ezkerah*) about the ten martyrs is recited twice a year and can be found in the *Machzor* or prayer book of Yom Kippur.

According to another tradition, Akiba's student Shim'on Bar Yohai (also known affectionately as 'Rashbi') fled to a cave to escape the Romans. His son Eleazar was with him and they hid together. Nuts from a carob tree and fresh water from a well sustained them. After twelve years had passed, they emerged. Bar Yohai now rejected all occupations and insisted that everyone study *Torah*. He was inspired by God to write down the mystical

Figure 38. The tomb of Rabbi Shim'on Bar Yohai in Meron draws large crowds of orthodox Jews each year on *Lag B'Omer*.

text called *The Book of Radiance* (*Sefer haZohar*) in Aramaic, which had been first given to Moses and until then shared orally.[20] He was buried at Meron in the Galilee. He is still celebrated every year on *Lag B'Omer* (fig. 38) with bonfires and the singing of kabbalistic songs.[21]

After the Bar Kokhba War, Judaism relocated its centres of learning to the Galilee and Babylonia.[22] Akiba's students completed the *Midrash* and secured their teacher's place in the narrative; work on the *Mishnah* continued apace in Jewish academies (Hebrew: *Gemara*), becoming one of the defining achievements of the period.[23] From now on rabbis would drive the destiny of Judaism. As descendants of David they considered themselves the natural and legal leaders of the Jewish community and reached an uneasy arrangement to be so with the Romans.[24] Rabbi Gamaliel II became *Nasi Yisrael*, inheriting his father's patriarchy.[25]

During the years following Hadrian's reign, the rabbis contemplated how the uprising could have gone so wrong. In the pages of the Jerusalem *Talmud* and the *Midrash Lamentations* the sages argued over whether Bar Kokhba was really a military hero or a failed *gibbor*, or whether he was a

King Messiah or an imposter.[26] Many of the rabbis who came after Akiba castigated the leader of the Jewish insurgency. His direction had been a catastrophe for the Jews of Judea. Reflecting the disillusionment, his name underwent a transmutation for a second time. Ben Kosiba, כו בנסבא, ('BN KWSBH') or 'Son of Kosiba', became Ben Koziba, בן כוזיבא, ('BN KWZBH') or 'Son of a Lie'.[27] This is how his name is spelled in the rabbinic texts and reproduced in the extracts from rabbinic texts quoted in this book: rereading them with this insight casts the protagonist in a wholly different light. The search for meaning in defeat and exile became a key theme. The loss of the Temple in one war, followed by the loss of their most important city and homeland with so many lives and livelihoods sacrificed for one man's arrogance in a second war, suggested to the rabbis that they had been rejected by their own god.[28] They rationalized that it was not the military superiority of the Romans that had led to their defeat (the Romans were merely the instruments of God); no, the Jews had abandoned *Torah* and the military defeats and the suffering they brought were God's means to force his people back to it in order to redeem and save themselves (Israel would be vindicated and all those who had celebrated the nation's losses would then be punished).[29] After the Bar Kokhba War Judaism changed from a religion that resisted its conquering overlords to one that, instead, adapted to accommodate and to seek redemption in other ways, all while staying true to its core beliefs. The Jewish messiah, who was still to come, was described less in terms of a fearless warrior king and more in terms of a good student of *Torah*.[30] The sword was discarded in favour of the word; *Mishnah* replaced Messianism.

Beyond Judea in the years immediately after the fall of Betar, Judaism itself did not come under attack from the Roman authorities. Through the second and third centuries CE Jews were free to assemble, pray and observe their customs.[31] Indeed, it was considered a *licita religio*, an 'approved religion' on account of its antiquity and body of literature, though that phrase was not a legal term.[32] Hadrian's heir and successor Antoninus Pius (138–161 CE) lifted some of the onerous restrictions on the Jews, especially on them entering Aelia Capitolina, though he forbade them to proselytize.[33] Septimius Severus (193–211 CE) and Caracalla (198–211 CE) were said to have 'greatly loved the Jews'.[34] Julian the Apostate (361–363 CE) even 'planned at vast cost to restore the once splendid temple at Jerusalem' and 'entrusted the speedy performance of this work to Alypius of Antioch, who had once been vice-prefect (*pro praefectis*) of Britannia.'[35] There were unexpected problems in building the Third Temple:

> But, though this Alypius pushed the work on with vigour, aided by the governor of the province (*provinciae rector*), terrifying balls of flame kept bursting forth near the foundations of the temple, and made the place inaccessible to the workmen, some of whom were burned to death; and since in this way the element persistently repelled them, the enterprise halted.[36]

No further work was attempted then, or since.

The Bar Kokhba War was always an issue specific to Judea, Ben Kosiba's Israel.[37] The uprising had been firmly dealt with, its ringleader killed and his supporters removed from the scene of the crime. Jews living in the rest of Syria Palaestina and elsewhere in the empire, however, thrived. The Jews even assimilated Roman cultural norms into their traditions and ceremonials: the *Seder* meal eaten at *Pesakh*, for example, became much more like a Roman symposium banquet; study of *Torah* became analytical in the same way that Romans read Homer's works, even assigning numbers to the books of the Hebrew Bible to match those of the *Iliad* and *Odyssey*; Roman rhetorical techniques were applied to the *Midrash*; Roman gods – such as Sol Invinctus and Zeus-Helios – appeared in the mosaic floors and wall decorations of synagogues.[38]

It is often claimed that Judea was depopulated after the war. There is some evidence that Jews no longer lived in Akraba, Betar, Gophna and Herodium, but they did continue to live in Lod, the region south of the Hebron Mountain and along the Mediterranean coast.[39] Archaeological evidence also points to recovery at some of the former hiding complexes. If not returning Jews, the inhabitants were Roman veterans (from the new *colonia* at Eleutheropolis) or Christians. After 200 CE until the fifth century, Horbat 'Etri was renovated, the four wine presses were put back into operation, and one of its late-Roman pagan owners was likely buried in a nearby cave.[40] Horbat Burgin too recovered and a new mosaic floor was laid, on which pottery dated to the Late Roman period was found, and a cistern was dug in one of the disused burial caves.[41] A Byzantine-era Christian burial cave was dug at Horbat Tannim.[42]

Drawn by the prospect of making money, people once again returned to Ein Gedi. These entrepreneurs *were* Jewish, perhaps descendants of the inhabitants at the time of the Bar Kokhba War. In the third century CE they built a grand, new *beit knesset*. It can still be visited. Today the remains lie protected beneath a sculpted roof canopy. The floor is superb – arguably the loveliest of any synagogue in the Roman world. Within a large square, intersecting circles of petals surround a central square comprising exotic birds. The three proud benefactors who paid for it had their names permanently set in the mosaic: Yose, Ezron and Hazikin. In an adjacent vestibule, the mosaic included Aramaic text warning any inhabitants that they would be cursed if they started quarrels, slandered their neighbours before Gentiles, stole, or broke the vow of not 'revealing the town's secret', presumably the trade secret of making *laudanum*.[43] Some features of the modern synagogue can be discerned in the design and floor plan. At the northern end – facing Jerusalem/Aelia Capitolina – is a *bimah* on which the portable ark once stood and from where the *Torah* was read out, and a semicircular niche – the *aron hakodesh* – for storing the scroll between services.[44] A place for public reading and study of the *Torah*, this expensive building was clearly the vibrant centre of the reborn community's religious life.

Jewish men also enrolled in the Roman army. Romano-Jewish soldiers – whether as volunteers or conscripts – saw service in Dacia and Pannonia, as well as Asia Minor, Egypt and Syria.[45] Jews served on the eastern front at Dura Europos, defending Rome's interests from the rival Sassanian Empire, and worshipped in the local synagogue until enemy troops overran the town after a siege in 256 or 257 CE.[46] The declaration of Christianity as the official religion of the Roman Empire in Theodosius I's Edict of Thessalonica in 380 CE would, however, gradually lead to the end of Jews serving in the military.[47] Faced with increasing discrimination and state-authorized persecution in their own country, many Jewish soldiers sided with enemies of the Christian-led administration or supported usurpers like Maximinus and Eugenius, or even deserted to the Persians. Theodosius I agreed to rebuild a synagogue in Callinicum in Mesopotamia in 377 CE, much to the dismay of Saint Ambrose; however, he also passed a law banning Jews from serving as military officers.[48] It was followed by an edict from Theodosius II in 410 CE expelling Jewish soldiers from units serving on the eastern frontier, which was later extended to include Italy and the Gallic provinces in 425 and then applied right across the Empire from 439.[49] The Christian theologian and Church Father St Augustine of Hippo (Aurelius Augustinus Hipponensis, 354–430 CE) wrote about the Jews in his *City of God Against the Pagans* (*De Civitate Dei Contra Paganos*). He asserted that they had been chosen as a special people and that they had been scattered in a fulfilment of prophecy.[50] Though Augustine considered Jews followers of a mistaken faith – a 'sect' – and to be spared forcible conversion to Christianity, nevertheless he wrote that they were inferior to Christians. They were certainly now second-class citizens in the Roman Empire, while it lasted.

When the Germanic leader Odoacer overthrew Romulus Augustus in 476 CE, the Roman Empire effectively ceased to exist in the West. In the East, around 530 CE during a wave of persecutions of Jews, which took place under the Emperor Justinian I, the synagogue at Ein Gedi was destroyed by fire.[51] It was never rebuilt. The split between Jews and the myriad Christian sects, which had begun after the destruction of the Second Temple and been exacerbated by Ben Kosiba's rebellion, now became an unbridgeable chasm that saw Christians increasingly asserting their rights while denying Jews theirs.[52]

To be successful in the emerging post-Roman Europe Jews had to be circumspect in their relations with their neighbours.[53] They were often appreciated for their business acumen and trading connections. There were people and places that actively welcomed Jews, such as the Holy Roman emperors of the Carolingian Dynasty, and the cities of Speyer, Sevilla and Toledo which granted them certain privileges. Those settling in towns along the Main and Rhine rivers became known as 'Ashkenazi' from the Hebrew word for the German-speaking world, while those in the Iberian Peninsula became known as 'Sephardic'.[54]

However, over time the Jews in general became a 'rejected people'.[55] On account of the Church's own rules on usury, in Northern Europe Jews saw a way to make a living in banking and money-lending, and soon came to be resented for it. As the great cities arose, the burgeoning Christian merchant class sought to remove the Jews from their control over commerce and trade. Their influence on Christians was also feared by some leaders of the Church, which worked tirelessly to seek out and eradicate heresies of all kinds.

Jewish communities suffered terrible anti-Semitism sanctioned by official rules and regulations. Hundreds of shameful incidents are recorded in Europe's history books. In 1095 Pope Urban II exhorted Christians to march to Jerusalem and seize the Church of the Holy Sepulchre, then held by the Muslims. The following year, First Crusader bands traipsing through the Rhine Valley turned on 'the enemy within', calling the Jews the 'Christ-killers'.[56] The year 1096 saw many Jews martyr themselves rather than be subjected to extreme mob violence. During the Black Death, in 1298 anti-Jewish rioters killed thousands of Jews in some forty German towns. Random attacks continued for decades after, the perpetrators citing 'well poisoning' as the justification for acts of summary justice, though the truth was more often motivated by leading townsfolk eager to seize Jewish property. In England in 1290, King Edward I imposed limits on usury and the professions in which Jews could participate. Later the same year all Jews were officially banished from the kingdom. Expulsions occurred across France, Germany, Portugal, Sicily and Spain for the next 251 years. Jews had little choice but to look east for their peace and prosperity. In particular, Ashkenazi Jews went to Poland and built new lives there.

Sephardic Jews lived under different rules imposed by their new Muslim overlords who arrived in Syria-Palestine, Egypt, North Africa and Spain in the seventh and eighth centuries CE.[57] Following a siege in 637 or 638 CE, Jerusalem was conquered by the Muslims who seized it from the Sassanids of Persia who had themselves taken it from the Eastern Roman Empire just twenty-three years earlier. While the Prophet Muhammed tolerated the Jews, as he did Christians, they were both regarded as 'infidels' and subject to payment of tribute and discriminatory regulations in order to be accorded the status of 'protected people' (Arabic: *ahl ad-Dhimma*).[58] The regulations excluded Jews from serving in public office. Instead Jews took up professions as doctors, scribes and teachers. In the Muslim world the physician was particularly highly regarded, which led to some trusted Jews being elevated to high-level administrative positions in the government bureaucracy.[59] With the establishment of the Ottoman Empire at the end of the thirteenth century, many Jews were well-placed to prosper. The Empire, which encompassed Western Asia, North Africa and South-Eastern Europe, was home to one of the largest Jewish populations in the world until 1918.[60] The Jews living in Palestine under the regime were well-integrated and well-treated; indeed, they were trusted and valued members of society.[61] The Christian Roman Empire in the East continued for almost 1,000 years longer than its lost Western half. When the Turks captured Constantinople in 1453 its territories were absorbed into the Ottoman Empire.

Thus, in both the Christian and Muslim worlds, Jews were seen as the 'other'. It did not help that nineteenth-century German Classicists consciously – or deliberately – ignored the Jewish people, effectively writing them out of Ancient History.[62] Jewish writers always had to preserve and retell the stories about their own past. In communities across the Western world Jews closely studied their books. Rabbis continued to debate the whys and wherefores of Bar Kokhba – or Ben Kosiba – and Akiba. The writings of rabbis and Jewish philosophers like Rashi (Solomon Bar Isaac, 1040–1105), Ibrahim Ibn Daud (c. 1119–c. 1180) and Maimonides (Moses Ben Maimon, 1135–1204) merged these ideas, creating the unified tradition of Bar Kokhba as the *Moshiakh* based on his military victories.[63] Isaac Abravanel (1437–1508) saw Bar Kokhba as an agent appointed directly by God and endowed with what might today be called 'superpowers'.[64] During the sixteenth century the ideas were again unbundled, with the political theme becoming separated from the messianic, but now the stories were overlaid with visions and values from the places and times of the writers, such as rabbinic scholar and chronicler David Gans (Dovid Solomon Ganz, 1541–1613).[65] Each author has contributed his insights which, in turn, have added nuance and complexity to the legend.

There is still more to tell in this story. To learn about the unlikely hero I needed to go to Tel Aviv.

Chapter 11

'He Was a Hero'

Like Britain's King Arthur, the story of Bar Kokhba has been retold so many times through the ages that today the historical fiction has become completely disconnected from the historical truth.[1] To better understand this process of transformation and the role the Bar Kokhba story played in founding the State of Israel I drove to the Eretz Israel Museum. Located in Ramat Aviv, a suburb located north-west of Tel Aviv, it is the third-largest museum in Israel and its lush campus spreads over some 20 acres. It was hosting *Bar Kokhba: Historical Memory and the Myth of Heroism*. Due to end that week, I had tried to meet exhibition curator Sara Turel, but a scheduling conflict prevented it; however, she had kindly arranged for me to meet knowledgeable museum guide and native Telavivian Michal Bentovim.

As we entered the darkened room, Bentovim told me, 'A lot of Israelis who come to this exhibition only know about Bar Kokhba from what they were taught at kindergarten or in the lower grades at school.' She explained that the exhibition curator had set out to 'deconstruct the myth of Bar Kokhba'. Being neither Israeli nor Jewish, I was in for a series of surprises.

The exhibition began with what archaeology has revealed about the real man. Rebel coins, documents and other artefacts recovered from the 'Cave of Horrors' and 'Cave of Letters' were displayed and explained; by now I knew these well. Bentovim then took me directly to see the panel in the far right-hand corner of the exhibition space. It was an enlarged photograph of the first page of a story written about the Jewish rebel leader (fig. 39). The font was the instantly recognizable German blackletter or Gothic font made famous by Johann Gutenberg. I could just about decipher the words *Simon Barchocheba, Der Messiaskönig*. Subtitled a 'Historical Novella from the First Half of the Second Century', it was written by Rabbi Dr Samuel Mayer (1819–82) and published in *Israelitischer Musen-Almanach* or *Almanac of the Jewish Muses* of which Mayer was the editor. I

IV.

Simon Barcocheba, der Messias-König.

Historische Novelle aus der ersten Hälfte des zweiten Jahrhunderts.

Im Menschenherzen gibt es viel Gedanken,
Doch nimmer wird der Rathschluß Gottes wanken.
Sprüch. Salom. 19, 21.

1. Traurig und wehmüthig schaute die Festung Bethar von der steilen Felsenmasse herab. Die Graben und Cysternen waren aufgeschüttet und die Mauren und Wälle zerstört. Die Zeug- und Vorrathshäuser waren leer. Die Zinnen der Thürme erglänzten blutroth im Golde der flammenden Sonne. Die hohen Pforten waren nicht geschlossen und die riesigen Thore nicht gesperrt. Römische Soldaten schritten stolz durch die Gassen der weitläufigen Festungsstadt, oder sie schauten auf Trümmern in das schöne Land

Figure 39. Published in 1840, Dr Samuel Mayer's *Simon Barcocheba, der Messiaskönig* established the modern tradition of the captured heroic Jewish leader who fights a lion in the arena and rides it to Betar to lead a final battle with the Romans.

had never seen this document before. Published in 1840 in Dinkelsbühl, a picturesque market town in Bavaria, the rabbi's creative fiction, while based on real events, established the basic outline of the story for the modern era.[2] 'This is the earliest version of the modern Bar Kokhba story,' said Bentovim.

Written in the romantic-historical style that was in vogue, Mayer's novella tells the tale of the Jewish hero's exploits against Turnus Rufus and how, betrayed by the Cuthean Papos, he is captured and destined to die as a gladiator in the circus in Jerusalem but, defeating a lion in the arena, the King Messiah escapes and rides upon the snorting animal with lance in hand, sword tucked in his belt, and leads his army of thousands to fight the Romans at Bethar.[3] This is the first time the lion enters the folkloric tale. It is, of course, complete nonsense, yet the story proved popular with readers. It soon spread the legend of Bar Kokhba as a Jewish superhero – and his lion – across the diaspora.

Music was another way in which the Bar Kokhba legend was propagated. On 5 May 1883, the Russian-born Jewish poet Abraham Goldfadn (1840–1908) and his troupe presented the new opera *Bar Kochba: Or The Last Hour of Zion* for the first time in Odessa, Ukraine.[4] The libretto was written in Yiddish. The story is an equally fanciful contrivance, blending historical and invented characters framed in a fully Western European-style five-act melodrama consisting of fourteen *tableaux*. He had written other well-received operas with Israelite themes, which had been performed in Moscow (1881) and St Petersburg (1881 and 1882). *Bar Kochba* was – very loosely – based on real events. The prologue and first act are set in Betar, the second, third and fourth acts switch to Caesarea, and the penultimate and final acts return the drama to Betar. With rousing marches, solos, duos and songs for a chorus, all set to memorable tunes, it was intended to be a crowd-pleaser. The cast includes Bar Kochba ('a young hero'), Asaria ('his general'), Rabbi Eleazar ('an old, learned man'), Dinah ('his daughter'), Turnus Rufus ('a Roman Governor') and Serefina ('his wife'). The main cast is joined by 'corps of Sanhedrin Priests, Levites, Guards, Indians, Assyrians, Jewish and Roman soldiers, [and] People'. The opera features eighteen musical pieces, the highlights of which include 'Eleazar Mourning', a duet sung between Bar Kochba and Dinah, a 'Coronation March', a 'Chorus before Caesar', 'Bar Kochba's Triumphal Solo' (fig. 40), 'Bar Kochba Among the Beasts' and 'The Grinding Mill'.[5]

The story is set '60 years after the destruction of Jerusalem', viz. 130 CE, and opens on *Tisha B'Ab*. The plot weaves the fearless heroism of *gibbor* Bar Kochba, the consuming fears of a rabbi who wants accommodation with the Romans, and the vying of three rivals for the love of a noble

Figure 40. The aria 'Rabbi Eleazar Mourning' from Abraham Goldfadn's popular Yiddish operetta *Bar Kochba*. First performed in the Ukraine in 1883, this is the score and English libretto printed as sheet music in New York City fourteen years later.

BAR KOCHBAS TRIUMPHAL SOLO.

(SIEGESLIED VON BAR KOCHBA.)

Tbl. 7 .4 -3

woman betrothed to the hero, which then leads to a false accusation. The friend-turned-villain Papus ('a Samaritan Jewish jewellery pedlar'), who becomes a spy for the Romans, has two arias all to himself: 'Papus' Revenge Song' and 'Papus' Deceit'. The ending is not a happy one: Dinah is imprisoned, Bar Kochba stabs Eleazar to death, the Romans defeat his soldiers, he commits suicide and his rebellion collapses in blood and flames. A Jewish captain takes his revenge on Papus.

The opera was a hit with its intended audience, as well as an emerging activist group eager to establish a Jewish homeland.[6] It touched a raw nerve in other circles, however. Odessa was located in Tsarist Russia. A decree (Russian: *ukaz*) of 14 September 1883 banned performances of Yiddish theatre. Tsar Alexander II had been assassinated two years before and pogroms had since become common.[7] Goldfadn's *Bar Kochba* was seen by critics as a comment on contemporary events, encouraging a national Jewish consciousness and sedition. It was denounced – perhaps by enemies of Yiddish theatre, the Russian Orthodox Church, or even the fearful Jewish elite in the capital – and taken off stage. Yet the opera reached a wider audience when it was published in sheet music format in Warsaw in 1887. Copies were taken overseas. Translated into English and 'arranged by H.A. Russotta for piano', an edition went on sale in New York in 1897 and separately another 'arranged by Prof. A Garfinkel for piano, violin or voice' appeared in London in 1904. There was a live performance of a translation by Professor E. Dorf (who 'has lectured in the finest places of education on Science') by the Russian Opera Company in New York.[8] In Act 2 Rufus has Bar Kochba enchained, but then the prisoner breaks them. The production featured a suitably spectacular special effect:

> A rainbow of coloured flame of fire explodes out of the hero's helmet (done by a chemical preparation of Prof. Dorf), which has such a fearful impressive effect upon the [Roman] warriors that they all tremble in their cowardice.[9]

Now free, the *deus ex machina* appears and Bar Kochba jumps into the sea and escapes, 'on the back of a monstrous fish, passes by the castle to the great astonishment of the Romans, who thought him to have committed suicide – and declares war against the Romans.'[10] Anything, it seems, is permissible in the world of historical opera.

In the visual arts, images of Bar Kokhba appeared on household items from table plates to mantelpiece ornaments. Arthur Szyk (1894–1951) applied to the subject his mastery of miniature painting and calligraphy, and unique artistic style.[11] Inspired by the illuminations of mediaeval books, he painted images of the *nasi* (1927, plate 41) as a general in military panoply of crested helmet, cuirass, long sword and bronze shield, his scarlet red cloak billowing behind him, and riding a white horse. He developed the theme further in a deck of playing cards decorated with images of *Princes of Israel* which he designed in the 1930s. In the series Bar Kokhba represents clubs. Here he clutches a sword in one hand, a shield in the other and wears elaborately decorated and coloured armour. The bearded face bears a frown. It is a look fit for a King Messiah.

By the late nineteenth/early twentieth century the Ottoman Empire was considered the 'sick man of Europe'.[12] France, Russia and the United Kingdom had designs on its lands. The Ottomans capitulated and ceded some to the European powers. Palestine, however, remained in the Empire. It had a majority Muslim population with Christians forming the second-largest group and the Jews a distant third by religious affiliation. That began to change. Between 1881 and 1904 Jewish emigrants from Eastern Europe and the Yemen settled in Palestine in what became known as the First *Alliyah* or 'agricultural migration'.[13]

Watching these developments from Austria-Hungary, it became evident to Theodor Herzl (1860–1904), a Jewish journalist, that there was now only one way to solve the 'Jewish problem' and anti-Semitism in particular. He set out his argument in *Der Judenstaat* (*The Jews' State*) published in Leipzig and Vienna in 1896. Subtitled *Versuch einer modernen Lösung der Judenfrage* (*Proposal of a Modern Solution for the Jewish Question*) he explained the basis for re-establishing the historic Jewish state.[14] The following year he founded the Zionist Organization (ZO). At its first world congress Herzl argued for 'a home for the Jewish people in Palestine secured under public law'. It met every two years for the next half-century. Speaking at the Sixth Zionist Congress on 26 August 1903, Herzl proposed British East Africa as a safe haven for Jews, an idea first proposed by the British.[15] Herzl had taken some considerable persuading to even consider it. On the day the reaction from the delegates was one of consternation. An investigatory committee of the ZO travelled to Africa and reported on its findings at the Seventh Zionist Congress. The 'Uganda Scheme' motion was roundly rejected. For Zionists there could

Figure 41. The face of Bar Kokhba as imagined by Henryk Glitzenstein. The sculptor presents the Jewish leader as a naked athlete inspired by ancient Hellenistic models. The subject is a modern vision of the 'muscular Jew'.

only ever be one true Jewish homeland and it was in Palestine. Herzl died prematurely of a heart attack, aged 44, possibly brought on by the stress of the intense criticisms he had faced.

The ugly caricature of the Jew among Europeans since mediaeval times was typically of a greedy or miserly rogue with exaggerated facial features and an odd fashion sense.[16] He was also the victim, the convenient scapegoat for society's failings. In the late nineteenth century anti-Semitism and oppression of Jews was evident everywhere in Russia, Romania, Galicia and even France where the notorious Dreyfus Affair (1894–1906) was widely reported in the newspapers. The Jewish community needed a positive image to counter this perception. *Muskeljudentum* was the response. The 'Muscle Jew' was 'invented' by Max Nordau (1849–1923) in his speech to the Second Zionist Congress in Basel on 28 August 1898.[17] He envisaged the modern Jew as both strong in his healthy body as well as fit in his moral bearing, a Jewish take on *mens sana in corpore sano*. It proved a powerful motivator to a minority eager to improve its standing in a prejudiced world.

Across Europe sports clubs were founded.[18] Jewish men and women eagerly joined them to take part in gymnastics or football and to compete as teams. The brand name adopted by many organizations was 'Bar Kochba'. The first was the *Jüdischer Turnverein 'Bar-Kochba'*, (fig. 40) founded in Berlin in 1898.[19] Others soon followed across Germany as well as Hungary, Palestine, Poland, the Ukraine and what would come to be known as Czechoslovakia. The 'Bar Kochba Association' even published its own newspaper. To promote membership and competitive events, posters presented fit athletes in new and dramatic ways using contemporary art styles. Photographs from the time capture the evident pride of members. In one taken around 1910 seventeen members dressed in white athletic kit in various poses balance precariously yet symmetrically on gym apparatus in Berlin. Bar Kochba scouts organizations for boys and girls were also founded where members played football or went on hikes and group outings. In a pre-war photograph from Antwerp men, women and children, all smartly turned out, sit in a formal group around a placard bearing their association's name, while in another dated to 1926 the young members of Bar Kochba Legion V of Tartu, Estonia sit or lean propped up on elbows, each wearing uniform caps and neckerchiefs, their smiling faces conveying the joy of a happy occasion shared together.

One of several artists trying to depict the 'muscular Jew' was renowned Polish-born sculptor Henryk Glitzenstein (Hanoch Glicenstein, 1870–1942).[20] While living in Rome he made a statue in bronze of Bar Kokhba (1905, fig. 41), inspired by Hellenistic or Roman models.[21] Military paraphernalia is not shown on the artwork; in fact, without knowing the title of the piece it would not be immediately apparent that this was the Jewish warlord. The tall, young man with a lean physique is naked, captured in the moment of stretching his right leg in the manner of an athlete preparing for a race (plate 39). In accordance with the Covenant, he is appropriately circumcised. The bearded face leans forward and slightly upward, while the enamel eyes express intense concentration. Nowadays it normally stands in the sculpture gardens of the Museum of Art at Kibbutz Ein-Harod.[22]

The decades following the foundation of the ZO brought enormous and profound change. In 1914, the Ottoman Turks made the strategic mistake of siding with the Kaiser. The British War Cabinet began to actively consider the future of Palestine. British Jewry, led by Chaim Azriel

Weizmann (1874–1952), lobbied their own government for action.[23] The tangible result of that was one of history's most important letters. Dated 2 November 1917 and signed by Arthur James Balfour (1848–1930), it became known as the 'Balfour Declaration'. The letter stated, 'His Majesty's government view with favour the establishment in Palestine of a national home for the Jewish people, and will use their best endeavours to facilitate the achievement of this object.'[24]

With the war in Europe still raging, in the last month of that year British troops commanded by Field Marshal Edmund Allenby (1861–1936) entered Jerusalem; his army included three battalions of the Jewish Legion raised from Jewish volunteers from around the world.[25] When Imperial Germany lost the First World War in 1918, the dominions of its Ottoman alliance partner became war spoils and they were divided up among the victors. From 1923, Mandatory Palestine came under the British by a resolution of the League of Nations.[26]

In the 1920s and 1930s Jews fled Europe and arrived in Palestine in ever-growing numbers. There was a recognition that achieving the goals of the ZO would take more than lifting dumb-bells and that political outreach and even armed resistance would be necessary. Appealing to the promoters of Zionism was the iconic image of Bar Kokhba as the courageous leader who refused to accept defeat. Militant Zionists, like Polish-born David Ben-Gurion (David Grün, 1886–1973), saw in him a hero who could inspire younger Jews who were being asked to fight to establish their own homeland. There were more than twenty youth movements bearing the ancient warlord's moniker by the outbreak of the Second World War.[27] The Alliance of Revisionists-Zionists, led by Ze'ev Jabotinsky (Vladimir Jabotinsky, 1880–1940) from the Ukraine, named their militant youth movement after Betar, the place of Ben Kosiba's last stand.[28] It held the UK accountable for delivering on the promises of the Balfour Declaration.

Zionists needed a holiday. The Jewish calendar was already blessed with several holy days. Finding one that tied in with the Bar Kokhba narrative was the challenge. Traditionally *Tisha B'Ab* was the day on which Betar had fallen – the same dismal day on which the First and Second Temples had been razed. That was a time to mourn, not a time to celebrate. Based on a rereading of *Talmud*, *Lag B'Omer* was chosen. It was also the day on which ended the plague that had decimated Rabbi Akiba's 24,000 students. As those disciples had gone to support Bar Kokhba's war effort a connection had been found.[29] Bar Kokhba became the focal hero of the day. That *Lag B'Omer* was already marked with a memorial gathering, festive bonfires and group singing in Palestine in honour of the Jewish mystic Rabbi Shim'on Bar Yohai's life was seemingly overlooked, or rather it was appropriated. Though also known as 'Scholars' Day', Akiba's students and Bar Yohai too were soon forgotten. Among secular European Jews *Lag B'Omer* became a whole day of fun activities and competitive sports mainly aimed at families and children. Playing with bows and arrows also tied the event into a manufactured tradition of commemorating the rebellion led by Bar Kokhba. When they emigrated to Palestine, they brought this 'tradition' with them. 'This story is invented,' said Bentovim, 'all of its rituals come from different places, from sixteenth-century Europe, from the diaspora.'

Outdoor events and bonfires are settings for happy gatherings and for singing. Levin Kipnis (1894–1990), a children's author and poet, wrote the song that became the signature tune of the *Lag B'Omer* tradition. He took Israel Benjamin Levner's *Bar Kokhba: Historical Novel on the Destruction of Betar* (1905), which rewrote Mayer's story, and published *Bar Kokhba and the Lion* (1929), which Mordechai Zeira set to music.[30] In translation the lyrics read:

> There was a man in Israel.
> His name was Bar Kokhba,
> A tall, well-built, young and tall
> With glowing radiant eyes.
>
> He was a hero.
> He yearned for freedom
> The whole nation loved him.
> He was a hero.
>
> One day an incident occurred,
> What a sad incident it was!
> Bar Kokhba was taken captive
> And was put in a cage.
>
> How horrible was this cage
> In which a lion raged.
> As soon as it spotted Bar Kokhba,
> The lion attacked him.

But you should know Bar Kokhba.
How courageous and daring he was.
He dashed and jumped on the lion
And raced out as fast as an eagle.

Over mountains and valleys, he cruised,
The banner of liberty up his arm.
The whole nation applauded him:
Bar Kokhba, *hurray!*[31]

'Every child in Israel still knows this song,' said Michal Bentovim.

During the interwar period the Bar Kochba sports groups continued to meet and compete. Lilli Henoch (1899–1942), the world record-holder in the discus, shot-put and 4 x 100 metres relay events, herself trained in the women's section of the club in 1924.[32] By 1930 *Bar Kochba Berlin* was one of the largest Jewish organizations in the world (fig. 42) counting more than 40,000 members from 24 countries.[33] In Gdansk, Poland the Bar Kochba Association built its own boat-house for its rowing team. The last recorded event, taking place in Berlin in July 1937, was the 'Bar-Kochba

Figure 42. Members of the *Juden Sportverein 'Bar-Kochba'* attending an athletics competition in Germany in 1932. It was one of several active Jewish sports clubs using the ancient warlord's moniker across Europe before the outbreak of the Second World War.

International Sports Games' with the participation of Hakoach Vienna.[34] Jewish athletes had been prohibited from representing Germany in the 1936 Berlin Olympic Games. Now, in their crisp, new kit, Jewish athletes proudly competed in track and field sports – such as handball, hockey, javelin, shot-put and relay racing – in Olympic-style tournaments of their own. Photographers were there to capture exciting moments during the great occasion. Open displays of Semitic athletic prowess, however, offended Aryan political dogma. Jewish sports ended in Germany on *Kristallnacht* ('the Night of Broken Glass'), 9/10 November 1938.[35] Jews unable to escape Germany and its occupied territories suffered appalling atrocities under the Nazi government and its Axis partners in the Second World War. Hitler's anti-Semitic prejudice was championed by his henchman, Adolf Eichmann, who masterminded a very different solution to the *Judenfrage*, which directly caused the deaths of an estimated 6 million European Jews in the Holocaust (Hebrew: *Shoah*).[36]

In Palestine the residents of the Jewish settlements (*Yishuv*) worked their farms, while the British assisted with infrastructure.[37] Many in the *Yishuv* tried to help Jews escaping from Axis Europe, but they were limited by restrictions on immigration under the British Mandate. This angered the *Yishuv*'s militia groups who began to sabotage the British-managed infrastructure in the area and continued their efforts to bring in immigrants illegally. A source of inspiration was the ancient rebel commander. In 1945, on 24 February, the first performance of Abraham Levinson's adaptation of the play *Bar Kokhba* by Czech poet Jaroslav Vrchlický (Emil Freud) took place at the *Ohel* Workers' Theatre in Rehovot.[38] People travelled from all around Palestine to watch the show with its dramatic stage sets and exotic costumes. Panned by several critics for its bleak message and stiff acting, nevertheless the *Yedioth Ahronoth* newspaper urged teachers to take their students, calling it a 'must-see' and a 'manifesto for our youth!'[39]

In the Second World War many Jews enrolled with the British armed forces to fight the Nazis. Hopes had been high that the British would honour the Declaration of 1917 and found a Jewish state but it was not to be and, enforcing the rules, they actively blocked Jewish immigration during 1945. In July 1946 militant Zionist paramilitary groups blew up the Central Police HQ at the King David Hotel in Jerusalem, indiscriminately killing Arabs and British as well as Jews. In July 1947,

4,515 refugees aboard the *Exodus* were denied disembarkation in Palestine by the Mandatory authority, marking a low point in British-Jewish relations.[40] When Germany surrendered in 1945 and the revelation of the ghastly horror of the death camps was fully revealed, however, there was an international outpouring of sympathy towards the Jewish refugees and growing support for a Jewish homeland. In 1947 the United Nations adopted 'Resolution 181 (II). Future government of Palestine', a proposal for a partitioning of Palestine into Arab and Jewish sectors.[41]

The reality on the ground was messier. To create a new nation for one people meant taking land from those already there. Initially buying packets of land from Arabs, the continuing settlement by Jewish immigrants greatly added to the need for homes. Jewish paramilitary groups – the *Hagenah*, *Irgun* and *Lehi* – fought Arabs and British in a guerrilla campaign, which became known as the 1947–49 Israeli War of Independence. Menachim Begin, who led the *Irgun* (the organization which broke away from the *Hagenah*), evoked Bar Kokhba when he spoke on the radio in 1948: he equated the new Hebrew army to the soldiers of the warlord and talked of how 'the spirit of ancient heroes' and 'the rebels of Judea' would accompany the modern resistance fighters in smiting the enemy and liberating the long-suffering Jewish people.[42] Jewish fighters attacked the Arab village of Deir Yassin, a massacre that became a rallying cry for the displaced population of Arabs in Palestine.[43] When the last of the British sailed out of Haifa and Mandatory Palestine ended at midnight on 14 May 1948, the new Jewish state was declared by David Ben-Gurion, who became the first prime minister – the first national leader since Shim'on Ben Kosiba.[44] The name chosen for the new state was not Judea or Zion but Israel, the same name Shim'on had chosen. Dr Chaim Weizmann, who had helped broker the Balfour Declaration, was sworn in as president three days later.[45] The president of the United States of America, Harry S. Truman (1884–1972) officially recognized the nation as legitimate at eleven minutes after midnight local time, the first country in the world to do so.

It was a story 4,000 years in the making. In the exquisitely illustrated *Visual History of Israel* (1949, plate 42) by Arthur Szyk Jewish history came vividly to life. Like a modern *Book of Kells*, the cover art vibrates with colour and meaning. The blue Shield of David (Hebrew: *Magen David*) dominates the design. Szyk populates the spaces around the six-pointed star with notables of the nation's history. Bar Kokhba sits to the left dressed in full armour and carrying a round shield with a blazon of the six-pointed star. Directly above him is King David, while King Solomon is located on the top right and the prophet Ezekiel faces him on the right. The Hebrew text written both above and below Bar Kokhba and Ezekiel proclaims: 'Praise be Your God, our God, King of the Universe, who had kept us alive, sustained us, and enabled us to commemorate this time.'

Ben-Gurion's appeal to the countries bordering Israel for 'peace and neighbourliness' was met with the cry for war. On 15 May 1948, the Arab League members Egypt, Lebanon, Saudi Arabia, Syria and Transjordan sent air and ground forces to attack the fledgling state. The move backfired. Before the war the borders of the State of Israel did not encompass Jerusalem. During the First Arab-Israeli War Jewish troops of the newly-created Israel Defense Forces (IDF) seized Jerusalem.[46] Only after a second truce was held, negotiated in November, did a tenuous peace return. On 3 April 1949 an armistice agreement signed between Israel and Jordan divided Jerusalem in two and the 'Green Line' – the colour used to draw the boundary on maps following the course of the cease-fire of the previous year – became permanent. In an historical irony, the city that the *Nasi Yisrael* had failed to capture now lay within the new border, but the city he had defended and died in now lay on the other side of it.

The Israelis declared West Jerusalem as their capital city and set up the parliament (Hebrew: *Knesset*) there. Bar Kokhba has an honoured place close to the political heart of modern Israel. In the garden outside the Knesset building in Givat Ram stands a *menorah*. Measuring 4.3 metres high by 3.5 metres wide (14.1ft x 11.5ft) and weighing 3.6 tonnes (4 tons), it is the work of sculptor Benno Elkan OBE (1877–1960) who escaped from Nazi Germany to the UK in 1933. Cast at the Morris Singer Foundry in London, the bronze sculpture was erected at a formal ceremony in Israel in April 1956.[47] It was a gift of one nation to another. The accompanying inscription in English explains that the idea of presenting the *menorah* was conceived by Members of Parliament of the United Kingdom in appreciation of the establishment of a democratic parliamentary government in the State of Israel. The gift was paid for through many small cash donations from British citizens as well as financial support from the leading banks and large industrial concerns.[48]

Figure 43. The *menorah*, which now stands in a garden near the Knesset, Jerusalem, was a gift of the British people to the State of Israel. Among the notable figures and events featured on it, sculptor Benno Elkan portrays Bar Kokhba as a hero who gallantly fought and died for his nation.

Elkan's *menorah* was modelled after the golden seven-lamp candelabra that once stood in the Temple in Jerusalem. It comprises thirty reliefs of characters and events, which Elkan believed were the most important and significant in the Hebrew Bible and Jewish history. The Ten

Commandments are here, and Jacob and Abraham, the Maccabees and Rabbi Yochanan Ben Zakkai, and so too the Warsaw Ghetto Uprising and the Foundation of Israel. On the inner branches King David is paired with Bar Kokhba. Both men were warlords, but where David is shown in the moment of triumph holding the severed head of Goliath after their famous duel, Bar Kokhba is displayed in his tragic moment of infamous defeat at Betar (fig. 43). It is an unexpectedly bleak depiction. The mortally-wounded commander has dropped his helmet and sword, and his hand clutches his chest as he gasps for breath. A comet – recalling Numbers 24:17 – flies over his head.

Memory of Bar Kokhba was sustained in Israel through public education. Kipnis' *Bar Kokhba and the Lion* song was reproduced in the nursery school textbook published by Levin Kipnis and Yemina Tchernowitz in 1947.[49] Another version in the book of Jewish holidays and memorial days by Z. Ariel, M. Blich and N. Persky became the most widely-used schoolbook during the 1960s and 1970s.[50] Thus, generations of Israeli children were taught about Bar Kokhba's military success, but nothing of his ultimately tragic failure. The justification was that the Roman Empire finally fell but the Jewish nation rose and survived, which was a good thing.[51]

Everyday items also kept the Bar Kokhba legend alive, from calendars to tableware, novels to postcards.[52] Coins from the Bar Kokhba War period were reproduced by the Israel Post Office on several of its definitive stamps (plates 43a–43d), which appeared from 1951 and continued to be printed for a decade or more. A coin with the citron appeared on the 8.5 Israeli Pound stamp, the bunch of grapes on the 15 Israeli Pound, the Temple façade on the 100 Israeli Pound, while the lyre was reproduced on the 125 Israeli Pound stamp; the increasing prices of postage reflected the growing problems of hyperinflation that gripped the economy during the 1960s and 1970s, reaching 1,000 per cent in the second half of 1984.[53]

The discovery of the 'Bar Kokhba Letters' in 1960 was celebrated in the highest echelons of government. Prime Minister David Ben-Gurion ordered that a medal be issued and one be given to each of the participants in the expedition. The Israel Coins and Medals Company was commissioned to strike these special 'Bar-Kochba Medals'.[54] The handsome metal disc was designed by the painter and graphic designer Jakob Zim (Yakob Cymberknopf, 1920–2015), who had survived the concentration camp at Buchenwald and come to Palestine in 1945. It depicts an archaeologist

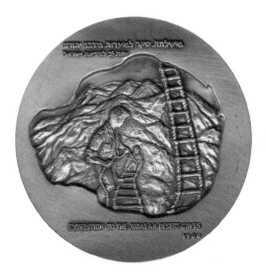

Figure 44. Designed by Jakob Zim, the obverse of the silver 'Bar Kokhba Medal' commissioned by Israeli Prime Minister Ben-Gurion depicts an archaeologist climbing a rope ladder and entering the 'Cave of Letters'.

Figure 45. The reverse of the silver 'Bar Kokhba Medal' shows the tied bundle of letters of Ben Kosiba found in the 'Cave of Letters' with the emblem of the State of Israel.

climbing a rope ladder and entering the 'Cave of Letters' on the obverse (fig. 44), with the cache of letters of Ben Kosiba with the emblem of the State of Israel on the reverse (fig. 45). Specimens can still be found on sale in some coin shops and on eBay. In 1961 the Israel Post Office responded to the discovery by printing a 0.40 *shekel* stamp with the image of 'Barcochébas' (plate 44) as part of its commemorative series *Moadim Lesimcha – Héros D'Israël* issue.[55] Imitating a modern mosaic or stained-glass window, the artist Asher Kalderon depicts the warlord as a kneeling, helmeted figure holding a bow and arrow.[56] The *se-tenant* stamp features a lion rampant. A letter of Ben Kosiba appeared on the 1.60 *New Israeli Shekel* stamp in a series celebrating 'Ancient Letters' issued in 2008.[57] Designed by Israeli artist Meir Eshel ('Absalon', 1964–93, plate 45), it shows a letter written by Ben Kosiba to Ben Galgula found in the Murabba'at Caves, which are featured in the background.[58] The word 'Kosiba' written in book hand appears just above the perforation line of the *se-tenant* tab.

The year 1961 was particularly notable in Israel and the time for national celebration. Key moments in history came together. On 21 April, the thirteenth anniversary of the foundation of the country, Ben-Gurion addressed the *Knesset*:

The discovery of the remains of the armies of Bar Kokhba by our young researchers, and the capture of Adolf Eichmann and his standing trial in Jerusalem are the two events that the *Bar Mitzvah* year of the State of Israel has bequeathed to Jewish history ... events whose marks will be etched upon us for years to come. The events are: (a) the meeting of the 1948 War of Independence in our time, with the fighters for the independence of their people and their homeland some 1,830 years ago in the Judean Desert that overlooks the Dead Sea; (b) Jewish law in the capital of the State of Israel against the exterminator of European Jewry.[59]

Yigael Yadin published a popular account of his discoveries in Nahal Hever a decade later. The book entitled *Bar-Kokhba: The rediscovery of the legendary hero of the second Jewish Revolt against Rome* brought the revolutionary leader 'out of the shadows of legend and restored to Jewish history a real-life hero of the people'.[60] A former leader in the *Haganah* at the time of the British Mandate who went on to direct key military operations during the Arab-Israeli War of 1948, he was an archeologist, a politician and a master of self-publicity. Professor Yadin had previously published a best-selling book in 1966 about his excavations at Masada. His latest volume turned archaeology into an adventure-cum-historical detective story in which 'the reader can himself experience the excitement of discovery taken at the moment when the finds were made.'[61] (It certainly caught the imagination of *this* writer!) The emphasis was, as the title suggested, on the heroic. Yadin presented Bar Kokhba as:

> a figure who, though shadowy, looks as great among national heroes as Arthur or Ulysses, through his fame in Jewish legend as the guerrilla leader of the Second Revolt against Hadrian's Rome – the revolt that for an intoxicating moment recaptured the Holy City before the legions fought their way back into it.[62]

Through words and pictures, he relished telling the story of the discoveries of the contracts and letters of 'a pathetic heap of skeletons, probably refugees from Roman pursuit' as he phrased it, and of the domestic items found in the 'Cave of Letters' and 'Cave of Horrors'.

Despite these spectacular yet poignant finds, children in Israeli schools continued to be taught fairytale versions of the story.[63] In Miri Tselelsohn's illustrated *The Son of a Star: Bar Kokhba's Legend for Children* (1982) a star appears when Bar Kokhba is born.[64] Instead of riding to support the Jewish rebels who are fighting the Romans, at the end of his life the lion carries Bar Kokhba up into the sky towards the star. In this example, curiously Christian-inspired messianic messaging trumps the historical one of resistance and the struggle for freedom. Even as the twenty-first century approached, the Jewish warlord was still being depicted in colourful illustrations by Rinat Hoffer fighting a lion in the arena and then riding it to make his escape in *Lag Boamer – The Bar Kokhba Revolt* (1995) written by Noga Tenenbaum.[65]

This unquestioned jingoistic hero worship jarred with another professional soldier who denounced the 'Son of a Star'. Dr Yehoshafat Harkabi (1921–94) pointed out that Shim'on Ben Kosiba had abjectly failed in his mission. The former chief of Military Intelligence of the State of Israel reflected on the war of 132–136 CE for what it could tell modern armed forces commanders and politicians. In his book *The Bar Kokhba Syndrome* he reviewed the historical record and observed how the ancient commander had planned to start a war but – crucially – had not planned how to end it. 'In war,' he writes, 'the main thing is to win the last battle, not the first.'[66] His concern was how Jews had come to admire his error of judgement and how this still influenced Israel's national thinking. In admiring the Bar Kokhba War, 'we are forced into the position of admiring our destruction and rejoicing over a deed amounting to national suicide,' Harkabi told *The New York Times*.[67]

In his controversial book he posited that political and military leaders who perceive their situation as desperate may make decisions that risk national suicide. The Bar Kokhba War was based on impulse, not on rational thinking; its leader could have anticipated the calamitous outcome of the war, but apparently he did not.[68] Furthermore, Ben Kosiba failed in observing the prime directive of 'Love of Israel' (Hebrew: *Ahavat Yisrael*), which means ensuring that no harm comes to its people.[69] Here was a lesson for leaders of his own day. Since its foundation, Israel had survived attacks from its Arab neighbours: the Six-Day War in 1967 during which it extended the country's borders; and the Yom Kippur War in 1973 after which the Jewish state realized its limitations. That led to Israel accepting a peace brokered by the United Nations, consummated in the 1978 Camp David Accords when then Prime Minister Menachim Begin shook hands with Egyptian President Anwar Saddat.[70] In matters of national security regarding the Palestinians there was still tension between 'government hawks' and 'military doves' to whom Harkabi's message was directed. Jewish culture and tradition had survived, he argued in the book, because the Jews of the Galilee and the diaspora did *not* take part in the Bar Kokhba War.[71] It could be said that Harkabi's scathing critique began the much-needed process of re-assessment of Bar Kokhba and his war in modern Israel, and of debunking the myth of the problematic ancient leader. This new analysis undoubtedly tarnished the image of a man so long regarded as a hero.

Bar Kokhba remained a cherished, visionary figure for many in Israel, however. Harkabi's thesis met fierce opposition from Dr Israel Eldad (1910–96), a professor of Jewish history, a politician and a former active member of *Lehi*. Eldad perceived the Bar Kokhba letters as the last messages of the general of Israel (Ben Kosiba) intended to be discovered and read by the latest (Yigael Yadin), 'as if by personal delivery' and 'from army to army, and commander to commander'; moreover, they were also a miraculous sign affirming that Israel was destined to be reborn in the twentieth century.[72] In his book *The Controversy: Destruction of the Second Temple and the Bar Kokhba Revolt and its Lessons* (1982) Eldad challenged Harkabi's basic methodology and arguments.[73] He contended that Harkabi wrote with the benefit of hindsight. Ben Kosiba had believed that establishing Israel then was a realistic prospect, Eldad argued, just as Theodor Herzl had believed, and he was ultimately proved right.[74] The ancient commander may have reasonably expected Jews in the diaspora to revolt, he suggested, though in the event they appear not to have responded. Eldad also argued that it was a mistake to compare the revolt against Rome with Israel's political and military policies in dealing with the Palestinians.

The publication of Harkabi's and Eldad's books came at a time of elevated partisanship in Israeli politics. In the 1980s Bar Kokhba was politicized in a way that proved divisive with the public. The last exhibit in the exhibition was a video newsreel. The black-and-white film was a television report about how the remains of twenty-five people found inside the caves beside the Dead Sea were returned to Nahal Hever and reburied on the ridge directly above the 'Cave of Horrors'. They had been held in storage by the Israel Antiquities Authority since their discovery in 1960. Chief Rabbi Schlomo Goren declared the bones to be those of Jewish resistance fighters, though nothing was ever published that supported the claim.[75] On 11 May 1982, Prime Minister Menachem Begin presided at a controversial ceremony and was accompanied by the Chief Rabbi, President Yitzhak Navon, Defence Minister Ariel Sharon, Foreign Minister Yitzhak Shamir and other leaders and dignitaries who were flown in by helicopter.[76] A road had been laid at a cost of $250,000 – an extravagant amount for a single event – to enable the invited dignitaries to attend the ceremony at the top of the canyon.[77] Along the route the VIPs were met by twenty-four demonstrators wearing Roman-inspired costumes and carrying placards with the words 'You're making a laughing-stock out of history.' *The New York Times* reported that several archaeologists, environmentalists and opposition politicians boycotted the event, among them Yigael Yadin who had led the team that discovered most of the remains in 1960.[78] To the beat of solemn martial music and firing of guns, a coffin containing the bone fragments, draped with the flag of Israel, was borne upon the shoulders of generals of the IDF to the grave site.[79] Israeli Prime Minister Begin spoke:

> Our glorious fathers, we have a message for you: We have returned to the place from whence we came. The People of Israel lives, and will live in its homeland in *Eretz Israel* for generations upon generations. Glorious fathers, we are back and we will not budge from here.[80]

A memorial of rocks had been erected upon a platform of concrete slabs and a marble plaque with an inscription in Hebrew was placed in front. In translation, the text reads:

> Here lie
> the bones of the warriors of
> Bar Kokhba who fought the Romans
> in the Judean Desert (132–135 CE),
> them and their families.
> The bones were collected in the
> Caves of Letters and the Caves of Horrors
> and buried in a ceremony. (11.5.1982).[81]

The dignitaries then flew back to Jerusalem to a second ceremony honouring the fallen of Bar Kokhba's war.[82]

Years later the plaque was vandalized and broken into pieces by someone with a sledgehammer. It was re-assembled in 2008. It was attacked a second time. Finally, a new inscription in Hebrew was set in a plinth, laid upon the same bed of concrete slabs. The mound was removed and its stones were used to surround the platform with a rough frame of rocks. The new, more strident text reads:

> Under this tombstone lie the bones of
> Bar Kokhba's warriors
> and their families
> who, at the foot of these cliffs, fought bravely
> for their beliefs and the freedom of their people (132–135 CE).
> With their deaths they marked the temporary end of Israel's
> independence.
> And in their will they commanded the rise of the State of Israel
> which grew once more out of the ashes and destruction
> after one thousand and eight hundred years (1948).
> May their souls be tied to the Knot of Life.
> This tombstone was erected a third time by the hands of the lovers
> of the land and its vistas
> after it was demolished by evil doers.
> *Hanukkah*, December 2012.[83]

The original plaque, sadly now reduced to a few fragments, lies at the bottom right-hand corner of the memorial. So far, the new slab has been left undisturbed. The bones entombed beneath have suffered enough indignity.

The exhibition in Tel Aviv had been a revelation to me. I thanked my host for generously giving me her time and said my farewell. Leaving the museum, I was struck by just how far fact and fantasy had parted ways. Bar Kokhba had been a hero and then become an anti-hero, not once but twice. Few real historical figures have two lives: the life they actually lived and the one people have invented for them. Here was one of these rare individuals. As a living man Shim'on Ben Kosiba had an impact on his world that fell short of his original vision, but as a legend he inspired later generations of people to try again and this time to fulfil it. In an ironic twist, today the tale of Bar Kokhba is little known outside Israel and now questioned within it. Israel has succeeded in becoming the Jewish homeland. Today nearly half of all the world's population of 14.7 million Jews lives in Israel.[84]

Our knowledge of the man popularly known as Bar Kokhba has come a very long way since Samuel Mayer wrote his historical novella, Abraham Goldfadn composed his opera and Levin Kipnis contrived his children's song. The twentieth century has produced top-notch scholarship: the publication of the texts of the letters recovered from the caves at Wadi Murabba'at and Nahal Hever (1961, 1989–2002); the exhaustive study of the rebels' coinage by Leo Mildenberg (1984); the dissection of the rabbinic tradition and Bar Kokhba by Richard G. Marks (1994) and Peter Schäfer (2003); the reviews of the causes of the war by Aharon Oppenheimer (2003); the reports of excavations of the hiding complexes by Amos Kloner and Boaz Zissu (1983–2016); the analysis of language in documents from Iudaea by Hannah Cotton (1999) and Michael Owen Wise (2015); and the surveys of the military aspects of the war by Werner Eck (1999) and Menachem Mor (2016) to name but a few. They have greatly contributed to our understanding of Shim'on the man and his times. Yet for all that he *still* remains enigmatic. The rabbis too are still split on the legacy of the 'Son of a Star' and of Akiba's support of him. Rabbi Binyamin Lau writes in *The Sages* (2011), 'the Bar Kokhba revolt turned out to be illusory', adding 'Bar Kokhba was not the Messiah, and redemption was not at hand.'[85]

My time in Israel had ended. As the engines roared and the aeroplane lifted off the runway of Ben Gurion Airport, my thoughts turned to when I would return. This small but exciting country always beckons one to come back to explore its myriad stories and mysteries. The past is always alive there. It is a place where a chance find dug up from the ground or discovered in a cave really *can* rewrite history. What new discoveries, I wondered, might yet be made that could yield more truths about the man who had defied Hadrian and challenged the might of Rome?

Epilogue

To search for the truth of the epic struggle between two strong-willed leaders over who would rule Judea is the reason I embarked on this remarkable journey. It proved to be a fascinating and all-consuming historical detective story. Facts were hard to come by, and the written accounts were not always what they seemed. Yet, by clearing away the fog of that ancient war and penetrating the mists of time, some of the truth has been exposed.

How then to sum up my findings?

Shim'on Ben Kosiba, a devout Jew from an obscure background, was intent on founding an independent nation for his people. Why, we can only speculate. The alleged ban on circumcision or on the study of *Torah* seem, on balance, unlikely causes. The building of Aelia Capitolina as a Roman colony over the ruins of the Jewish city, however, may have provided him with a national rallying cry. He was another in a long line of Jewish rebels with grievances against the Romans, but his campaign was among the best organized. The success of the Maccabees in ousting their Greek-speaking overlords some three centuries before may have inspired him. Like the Maccabbees before him, he chose the official title *nasi*. Remarkable is that his creation – Israel, which he led as its first and only president – endured for three and a half years against the onslaught of professional Roman troops. In doing so, and against the odds, he became one of the most successful rebel leaders in all of Roman history. He could be arrogant, a bully and a micro-manager directing his people in the smallest details. His plan was always a high-stakes gamble and he badly underestimated his Roman adversary. There was only so much a semi-professional army of farmers and townsfolk could do, no matter how resourceful. Ben Kosiba's goal of restoring Jerusalem to Jewish hands ultimately failed. Without the City of David, Israel would never be complete. Retreating, he died fighting for his dream at Betar, now the village of Battir and the place that still bears the name 'Ruin of the Jews'.

Where Ben Kosiba is the real historical man, Bar Kokhba 'Son of a Star' is the avatar, the figure of legend. The war was not just about who would control Judea, but arguably about who would control Judaism itself. There was a 'third man' in this story. Allegedly championed in life by Akiba Ben Yosef as the King Messiah, the warrior may have been an unwitting instrument in the radical sage's plan to promote the authority of the rabbis by waging a national holy war. In death, the warlord was bemoaned by other rabbis as the failed messiah and perceived as the subject of remorse. Ben Kosiba's name transmuted into 'Ben Koziba', the 'Son of a Lie' or 'Son of Deceit' as he is called in the Talmudic accounts. Nevertheless, Akiba succeeded in *his* mission: the power and influence of the rabbis did grow. The war also ensured that the split between Christians and Jews became permanent. That too may have been part of Akiba's plan. Yet he underestimated the new upstart sect. The Christians always reviled the man they called 'Barchochebas' or 'Chochebas' and portrayed him as a fraud, patently a false messiah. Meeting in secret at first, people flocked to hear the story of the 'Son of God' and their numbers grew steadily. They also blamed the Jews for crucifying *their* messiah. Years of persecution and pain would follow.

The nineteenth and twentieth centuries were times of rising nationalism and unremitting anti-Semitism. Driven by a swelling desire for a new Jewish homeland, Jews in the diaspora championed this failed rebel, forgave him his errors and recast him as a muscular hero and a figure of hope. Zionists wrote novels, plays, performed operas, made artworks and competed in sports in his assumed name. They even co-opted a holy day and repurposed it to make celebration of Bar Kokhba's achievement an annual fixture. In the popular imagination the warlord was recast as a lion-taming, big cat-riding superhero.

The aspiration for a homeland was fully realized in 1948 with the founding of the State of Israel. When the new nation celebrated its thirteenth anniversary, Ben-Gurion, the country's first prime minister, invoked the name of his predecessor, Bar Kokhba. By chance, letters were later found in the refuge caves and his real name was finally discovered. The letters are now read by new generations in Israel, raised on the children's tale, curious to know the true story. Yet Ben Kosiba remains enigmatic. There are no busts or paintings of him. Even the surviving letters were more likely written by scribes on his behalf, rather than dictated by the man himself. We know more about some of the people who followed him than of the leader himself.

What of his adversary? P. Aelius Hadrianus was a successful product of the Roman political and military system. Related to the popular soldier emperor Trajan, it was soon apparent that Hadrian would assume ultimate power. When his time came, he embodied many of the qualities of the ideal ruler. Modelling himself on Caesar Augustus, Hadrian travelled the world, shared the bounties of empire with his subjects, encouraged the best in arts and architecture, disciplined the army and stabilized the apparatus of government, allowing the Empire to function largely unchanged for another 150 years. He was generous with his benefactions to the communities he visited and they generally responded gratefully. Yet he could be arrogant and cruel. While there is reason to doubt the truth of his alleged bans on circumcision and on the study of *Torah*, he should have known that his plans for rebuilding Jerusalem as a *colonia* would be offensive to many Jews. Perhaps his obsession with building simply blinded him to local sensitivities. What the Flavian emperors had done for Caesarea, he was intent on doing for Jerusalem but on a grander scale. He carried on regardless. His vision for Aelia Capitolina was fully realized, but at the cost of a drawn-out war. Unlike Trajan, he avoided wars of choice and did not lead from the front in wars of necessity. Faced with a revolt in Province Iudaea, he delegated execution of the counterinsurgency to his deputies. Like Augustus, Hadrian chose good generals to fight his wars for him. He had greater resources than the rebels and the stubborn determination to achieve final victory. Of course Hadrian won.

Three years later Hadrian died an unhappy man from chronic disease or a heart attack. By then he was a leader despised by many of his own people. Reluctantly the Senate consented to his deification. In death his image would be seen everywhere. There are an estimated 150 portrait busts in museums and galleries around the world today, making him one of the most represented figures from antiquity. He too has been reinvented through the ages as an enlightened renaissance man and, in recent times, as a gay icon. Even the cult of Antinous he founded has been re-established. Talmudic accounts generally present Hadrian as a tyrant who realized too late how impressive a man was his nemesis. Yet he also remains enigmatic. He is best known today for the wall in northern Britain which bears his name, but largely unknown for the extraordinary Pantheon he designed in Rome which does not.

In their respective societies, both men were considered outsiders. Ben Kosiba, a country man from the South who spoke Aramaic and colloquial Hebrew, was unsophisticated, yet a champion of the book hand in which religious texts were written. Hadrian, a man with deep ties to the Iberian Peninsula and a strong regional accent – which he strove to overcome – was unconventional and a lover of all things Greek. In some ways they were alike: both men were confident military leaders, uncompromising in their dealings, intent on winning at all costs, communicating constantly with their people, sweating the 'small stuff' and behaving as autocrats. The two men's names are forever bound in a tragic story of a war that caused heartache on both sides and had far-reaching consequences neither man could have envisaged.

Ben Kosiba's Israel was a daring and short-lived experiment in the second century, but the Bar Kokhba story helped establish the State of Israel in the twentieth. Where Rome crushed the upstart nation, the modern successor still exists, despite numerous attempts by many enemies to destroy it. In that country memories are long and old grievances are not easily forgotten. Faulkner's observation that 'the past is never dead, it's not even past' seems particularly apposite to Israel.[1] When Hadrian's name is mentioned it is often accompanied by the curse, 'May his bones be ground to dust.' Ironically, most Israelis still do not recognize the name Shim'on Ben Kosiba, but everyone knows legendary Bar Kokhba and how he rode a lion from the song they were taught as children and continue to sing each year at *Lag B'Omer* (fig. 46).

Figure 46. On the night of *Lag B'Omer* a bonfire rages in Israel. Around it families will sing the song of Bar Kokhba and the lion and how he was a hero.

Places to Visit

Shim'on Ben Kosiba's Israel and the theatre of the Bar Kokhba War encompassed what are now parts of modern Israel and the West Bank territory of the Palestinian Authority. There are several archaeological sites and museum collections well worth visiting. Some of them are listed here.

ISRAEL

Adullam
Website:https://www.kkl-jnf.org/tourism-and-recreation/forests-and-parks/adulam-france-park.aspx
Adulam-France Park is situated in the heart of the Judean Plain below the Hebron Hills. The conserved ruins of three villages can be visited. Adullam is difficult to reach but the visitor is rewarded with a commanding view of the surrounding countryside. Horbat Burgin and Horbat 'Etri each have well-preserved buildings and hiding complexes, some of which date to the Bar Kokhba War period.

Caesarea
Website: https://www.parks.org.il/en/reserve-park/caesarea-national-park
Colonia Prima Flavia Augusta Caesarea is now a world-class archaeological site in the care of the Israel Nature and Parks Authority. On view are paved streets, residential and commercial buildings, the circus (or hippodrome) and the theatre, as well as the harbour and the *praetorium*.

A preserved section of aqueduct upon stone arches stands 1 kilometre to the north of the *colonia* along the sandy beach. Upon the hill above is a villa with a large mosaic floor.

Ein Gedi

Website: https://www.parks.org.il/en/new/en-gedi-ancient-synagogue
On the western shore of the Dead Sea are the remains of the commercial community's synagogue with its lovely mosaic floor. The site is managed by the Israel Nature and Parks Authority.

Caves occur naturally in the local geology, examples of which can be seen in the cliffs at the Ein Gedi Nature Reserve encompassing the river valleys of the Nahal David and Nahal Arugot. About 5 kilometres (3 mi.) south-west of Ein Gedi on the north side of the adjacent valley of Nahal Hever are the entrances to the so-called 'Cave of Letters'.

Further up the valley on the other side is the 'Cave of Horrors', so-named on account of the several skulls and skeletons discovered there. Above it is a monument and inscription placed over the grave where the remains were re-buried in 1982.

The small Roman siege fort, whose garrison watched for people trying to escape from the 'Cave of Letters', is located nearby. A low wall of loose stones encloses a roughly square-shape space with footings of internal structures visible, including traces of stoves and other elements of military camp life.

The caves are strictly inaccessible to visitors, but tours that take visitors to the top of the canyons for panoramic views can be booked with private guides.

Herodium

Website: https://www.parks.org.il/en/reserve-park/herodium-park
Built by Herod the Great, it was occupied by men loyal to Ben Kosiba – including the rebel leader himself – in the early years of the war. Remains of a workshop dating the period were found in the upper courtyard. Cut deep into the hillside are tunnels dug by troops during the First Jewish War and extended by Ben Kosiba's men. The free site guide is available to download online: https://static.parks.org.il/wp-content/uploads/2018/06/herodiun-eng-for-internet.pdf

Jerusalem

There are several places associated with Hadrian and the Bar Kokhba War which the visitor to Israel must see in the city:

Roman Square at Damascus Gate

Evidence of Hadrian's *Colonia* Aelia Capitolina is still preserved in the modern street plan of Jerusalem. The city's northern gate (now known as the Damascus Gate) has a well-preserved arched portal on the left side of the gate about 5 metres (16ft) below modern street level. The holes for its door hinges and recesses for the beams, used to bolt the wooden door, can also be seen. An area of excavated paved piazza from Aelia Capitolina is on view directly below the Damascus Gate. An exhibit explains the history of the gate using maps, photographs and illustrations.

Ecce Homo Arch

Hadrian's triumphal arch straddles the eastern end of the Via Dolorosa, while one of the smaller flanking arches is preserved inside the adjacent Ecce Homo Church.

Davidson Centre

The Jerusalem Archaeological Park and Temple Mount Excavations, near the Dung Gate, displays and explains some of the findings from the site through artefacts, interpretative videos and models. It has a large collection of bricks and tiles made at the workshops of *Legio* X *Fretensis* – now located under Jerusalem's International Convention Centre (*Binyane Ha-Umma*) – with the distinctive legionary logo of a boar and ship.

Israel Museum

Website: http://www.imj.org.il/en

The museum has a collection of Bar Kokhba War relics. It includes surviving letters of Ben Kosiba, the documents of Babatha, keys, baskets, Jewish religious artefacts and coins overstruck by the revolutionary administration, as well as arrows and other weapons recovered from various caves near Ein Gedi. The remains of the bronze bust and torso of the Emperor Hadrian, which likely came from a temporary camp of *Legio* VI *Ferrata* at Tel Shalem, is the centrepiece of the Roman gallery. Adjacent cases display fragments of Roman arms and armour of the period, including a complete legionary helmet, a visored cavalry helmet, fused chain mail, a *gladius* and a *spatha*. Examples of bricks and tiles made by *Legio* X *Fretensis* are also on display. The museum has fragments of the Roman inscription from the supposed triumphal arch at Tel Shalem, and one piece of the inscription of *Legio* X from the Damascus Gate in Jerusalem.

Knesset Menorah

Website: https://knesset.gov.il/birthday/eng/KnessetBuilding2_eng.htm Benno Elkan's giant bronze *menorah* – standing at the edge of Gan Havradim (Rose Garden) opposite the Knesset building – shows Shim'on Ben Kosiba on an inner branch (opposite King David). The stylized figure is depicted in his moment of death.

Studium Biblicum Franciscanum

The archaeological museum at the Lion's Gate of the old city has the other fragment of the inscription of *Legio* X *Fretensis* from the Damascus Gate in Jerusalem.

Meron

The tomb of Rabbi Bar Yohai (Rashbi) is at Meron, located in Upper Galilee near Safed. It is the site of annual public commemoration of *Lag B'Omer*.

Sanhedrin Trail

https://www.youtube.com/watch?v=IF6sAk6tqmo
https://shvila.co.il/index.html#home/index
In 2017, the IAA laid a path through the Galilee tracing the route taken by the sages when they moved from Yavne to Tiberias. Established to mark Israel's 70th anniversary, the 70km (43.5 mi.)-long trail has 70 stops with markers each bearing a saying of a sage or rabbi.

The trail begins at the ancient village at Usha. After 135 CE, the rabbis moved from Yavne to Usha, not once but twice. There, several of the pupils of Rabbi Akiba resided – including Rabbi Shim'on Bar Yohai – and wrote the so-called 'Usha Enactment'. Major archaeological excavations have uncovered buildings, including ones with oil and wine production facilities, and each with *mikwa*. The trail progresses from Usha to Shefar'am, to Bet She'arim, to Zippori, and terminates at Tiberias where Rabbi Akiba is buried.

Tiberias

The tomb of Rabbi Akiba is at Tiberias, located on the mountainside behind the Kiryat Moshe neighbourhood, overlooking the town and the Sea of Galilee.

WEST BANK (PALESTINIAN AUTHORITY)

Battir

It is generally believed that Khirbet el-Yahud beside the modern village of Battir (or Bittir) is the most likely site of Betar where Ben Kosiba made his last stand. Remains of the defensive circuit wall, buttresses and towers can be seen in places.

The adjacent ancient irrigation system and terraces are on the UNESCO World Heritage List (https://whc.unesco.org/en/list/1492/).

Glossary

Language:	*A* = Arabic *G* = Greek *H* = Hebrew *L* = Latin
Ab	*H*: Eleventh month of the Jewish civil calendar, coinciding with parts of July and August.
Adventus	*L*: 'Arrival', used in the context of an official visit by the emperor to a province.
Aes	*L*: 'Copper', a coin worth one half *dupondius* (*asses* pl.).
Ala	*L*: 'Wing', legionary cavalry on wings of battle formation (*alae* pl.).
Am ha'aretz	*H*: 'The people of the land'.
Amphora	*L*: Pottery jar in which olive oil, fish sauce, wine and other products were carried and stacked in the holds of ships, warehouses and shops (*amphorae* pl.).
Aquila	*L*: 'Eagle', the eagle standard of a legion.
Aquilifer	*L*: Standard-bearer carrying the *aquila*.
Arava	*H*: Willow (*aravot* pl.).
As	*L*: 'Copper', Roman coin worth half one *dupondius* (*aes, asses* pl.).
Auctoritas	*L*: Influence from having prestige, personal authority.
Augustus	'Revered One', honorific title originally voted to Imp. Caesar *Divi filius* (Octavianus) in 27 BCE and adopted by all subsequent emperors.
Aureus	*L*: 'Gold', highest denomination gold coin worth 25 *denarii* (*aurei* pl.).
Auxilia	*L*: 'Helpers', support troops of allied or non-Roman citizens.
Ballista	*L*: Artillery weapon throwing bolts or stones.

Beit Din	*H:* 'House of Judgement', Jewish court.
Beit HaMikdash	*H:* 'Sanctified House', the Temple in Jerusalem.
Beit Knesset	*H:* 'House of Gathering', synagogue.
Beit Midrash	*H:* 'House of Interpretation', study group, synagogue (*batei midrash* pl.).
Biryonim	*H:* 'Thugs', extremist Zealots.
Brit	*H:* 'Covenant'.
Brit bein HaBetarim	*H:* Covenant agreed between *Yahweh* and Patriarch Abraham.
Brit Milah	*H:* Covenant of circumcision (also called *bris*).
Campus Martius	'Field of Mars', a large park and recreation ground in north-west Rome.
Capitolinus	*L:* Hill in Rome on which was built the Temple of Iuppiter Optimus Maximus.
Cardo	*L:* The main north-south road that ran through the city, the *Cardo Maximus* intersected the *Decumanus Maximus*.
Catapulta	*L:* Artillery weapon throwing bolts.
Centuria	*L:* 'Century', unit of eight *contubernia*, eighty men; sixty centuries formed a *legio*.
Centurio	*L:* 'Centurion', officer in charge of a *centuria*.
Clementia	*L:* 'Clemency', the Roman virtue of showing mercy.
Cohors	*L:* 'Cohort', unit of six centuries or twelve in a First Cohort (*cohortes* pl.).
Cohors Praetoria	*L:* 'Praetorian Cohort', Praetorian Guard (*Cohortes Praetoriae* pl.).
Colonia	*L:* 'Colony', city founded for retired *legionaries* (*veterani*) (*coloniae* pl.).
Concilium	*L:* Advisory committee of the senior commanding officer formed of his immediate reports.
Consulis	*L:* One of the two highest magistrates of the *res publica*, elected annually.
Curia Iulia	*L:* Senate House.
Cursus honorum	*L:* 'Race of honour', the career ladder leading to the consulship.

Decumanus	*L*: The east-west-orientated road in a Roman city; the *Decumanus Maximus* crossed the perpendicular *Cardo Maximus*.
Denarius	*L*: Silver coin, worth four *sestertii* (*denarii* pl.).
Drachma	*G*: Silver coin worth approximately the same as a *denarius* (*drachmai* pl.).
Dupondius	*L*: Bronze coin, worth two *asses* or one half a *sestertius* (*dupondii* pl.).
Elul	*H*: Twelfth month of the Jewish civil calendar, coinciding with parts of August and September.
Equites	*L*: 'Knights', the middle or business class of Roman society.
Etrog	*H*: Citron (*etrogim* pl.).
Evocatus	*L*: 'Summoned one', reservist, an honorably-discharged *miles gregarius* available for recall on the orders of a consul or military commander (*evocati* pl.).
Fiscus Iudaicus	*L*: 'Jewish Treasury', the punitive tax levied on the Jews after 70 CE.
Forum Romanum	*L*: Roman Forum in central Rome.
Gibbor	*H*: Strong and mighty man (*gibborim* pl.).
Gladius	*L*: Short stabbing and thrusting weapon used by legionaries (*gladii* pl.).
Hadas	*H*: Myrtle (*hadassim* pl.).
Halakhah	*H*: 'Law', body of Jewish religious laws derived from the written and oral *Torah*.
Hanukkah	*H*: 'Dedication', Festival of Lights.
Hasta	*L*: Javelin used by Roman *auxilia* and cavalry.
Ianus	*L*: 'Arch', portal or triumphal arch.
Impedimenta	*L*: Baggage train.
Imperator	*L*: 'Commander', a title shouted by troops to a victorious leader after a victory.
Imperium	*L*: Legal power vested in an elected Roman magistrate.
Iyyar	*H*: Eighth month of the Jewish civil calendar, coinciding with parts of April and May.
Kashrut	*H*: Dietary mandates on eating kosher food.

Kohanim Gedolim	*H*: High Priest of the Temple in Jerusalem.
Legatus Augusti Pro Praetore	*L*: Governor of one of the provinces of Caesar (propraetorian provinces) 'delegated' the imperium by Augustus.
Legatus Legionis	*L*: Commander of a *legio* 'delegated' the *imperium* by Augustus.
Legio	*L*: Unit of ten *cohortes*, approximately 5,600–6,000 men (*legiones* pl.).
Lorica hamata	*L*: Body armour made of chain or ring mail.
Lorica segmentata	*L*: Body armour made of articulated metal plates (a non-Roman term coined in the sixteenth century).
Lorica squamata	*L*: Body armour made of scales attached to a backing of cloth or leather.
Lulav	*H*: Closed frond of a date palm tree (*lulavim* pl.).
Magen	*H*: Shield.
Mahaneh	*H*: 'Camp', base of Jewish rebel militia.
Midrash	*H*: 'Textual interpretation' or 'investigation', the compendium of rabbinic commentaries of the *Tanakh*.
Mishnah	*H*: 'Study by repetition', the collection of 'Oral Law' and rabbinic traditions that supplements, complements, clarifies and systematizes the commandments of the *Torah* into six divisions: agriculture, festivals, family life, civil law, sacrificial and dietary laws, and purity.
Mitzvah	*H*: 'Commandment' (*mitzvot* pl.).
Munera	*L*: Roman blood games held for political and entertainment purposes.
Municipium	*L*: Chartered provincial Roman city (*municipia* pl.).
Nahal	*A*: Brook.
Nasi Y'Israel	*H*: President or prince of Israel.
Officium	*L*: 'Service', the staff – office – responsible for record-keeping.
Onager	*L*: 'Wild ass', an artillery weapon throwing stones.
Ornamenta	*L*: Ceremonial trappings of a lower-grade triumph (*ovatio*).

Palatinus	*L*: Hill in Rome, location of homes originally of the Roman elite.
Parnas	*H*: Civil administrator of Jewish rebel-held town (*parnasim* pl.).
Pesakh	*H*: 'Passover', a major eight-day festival celebrated in the early spring to commemorate the emancipation of the Israelites from slavery in Egypt.
Pilum	*L*: Roman javelin used by legionaries (*pila* pl.).
Praedia	*L*: Booty captured from a defeated enemy in war.
Praefectus	*L*: 'Prefect', senior officer or magistrate.
Praetor	*L*: Senior magistrate responsible for administering law, the *ludi* and *feriae*.
Praetorianus	*L*: Soldier in the Praetorian Cohorts (*praetoriani* pl.).
Praetorium	*L*: 'Praetor's building', house of the senior officer of a *legio*.
Primus Pilus	*L*: 'First javelin', the most senior centurion of a *legio*.
Princeps	*L*: 'The First One', the title adopted by Augustus to describe his leadership position.
Princeps Praetorii	*L*: Officer in charge of the army unit's *officium*.
Principia	*L*: 'Front line', headquarters building in a Roman fort.
Proconsulis	*L*: 'Former consul', governor of a senatorial province.
Propraetor	*L*: 'Former praetor', governor of an imperial province.
Prutah (Perutah)	*H*: Rebel coin made by overstamping a Roman *dupondius* or *sestertius* (*perutot* pl.).
Quaestor	*L*: Junior magistrate in charge of law courts and public financial accounting.
Rabbi	*H*: 'My master', teacher of *Tanakh*.
Res Publica	*L*: 'Public Thing', the commonwealth of the Roman state.
Restitutor	*L*: 'Restorer'.
Rosh HaMahanaya	*H*: 'Head of Camp', commander of Jewish rebel militia.
Rosh Hashanah	*H*: Jewish New Year.

Rostra	*L*: Tribunal, speaker's platform in *Forum Romanum*.
Scutum	*L*: Roman shield (*scuta* pl.).
Sel'a	*H*: Rebel coin made by overstamping a Roman *tetradrachma*; also known as *shekel*.
Semis	*L*: Roman coin worth half one *as*.
Senatus Consultum	*L*: Decree of the Senate.
Sestertius	*L*: Brass coin, equal in value to one-quarter *denarius* (*sestertii* pl.).
Shavuot	*H*: Originally a harvest festival (held fifty days after the second day of *Pesach*), it now also commemorates the giving of the *Torah* by God to the Jews at Mount Sinai.
Shekalim	*H*: Temple tax.
Shekel	*H*: Rebel coin made by overstamping a Roman *tetradrachma* (*shekelim* pl.); also known as *sel'a*.
Shevat	*H*: Fifth month of the Jewish civil calendar, coinciding with parts of January and February.
Signum	*L*: Unit standard (*signa* pl.).
Suffectus	*L*: A consul replacing another who had resigned during his term in office.
Sukkot	*H*: 'Feast of Tabernacles', a major festival held in the autumn (beginning on the 15th day of *Tishri*) to commemorate the sheltering of the Israelites in the wilderness.
Talmud	*H*: 'Study', the book of 613 commandments given by *Yahweh* to the Jews.
Tanakh	*H*: A word comprising the first Hebrew letter of each of the three traditional subdivisions of the authoritative Hebrew and Aramaic texts: *Torah* ('Teaching'), *Nevi'im* ('Prophets') and *Ketuvim* ('Writings').
Tetradrachma	*G*: High denomination coin worth four *drachmai*.
Tifilin	*H*: Phylacteries, a set of two small black leather boxes containing scrolls of parchment inscribed with verses from the *Torah*; a Jewish man is

required to place one box on his head and tie the other one on his arm.

Tishri　　H: First month of the Jewish civil calendar, coinciding with parts of September and October.

Torah　　H: Jewish 'Written Law', also known as the Five Books of Moses (*Pentateuch*) or Hebrew Bible (*Tanakh*), comprising the first five books of the Old Testament.

Tosefta　　'Additions', the texts omitted or noted from *Mishnah*.

Tribunus　　L: Tribune: *tribunus plebis*, a representative of the people elected annually; *tribunus laticlavius*, the second-in-command of a *legio* was accompanied by five junior *tribuni angusticlavii*.

Triumphator　　L: The military commander awarded an *ovatio* or *pompa triumphalis*.

Tropaeum　　L: 'Trophy' made of captured weapons (*tropaea* pl.).

Veteranus　　L: 'Veteran', honourably discharged soldier having served his full term (*veterani* pl.).

Vexillatio　　L: Detachment (*vexillationes* pl.).

Vexillum　　L: Flag standard of a *vexillarius*.

Via Praetoria　　L: Crossroad in a Roman camp leading to *principia*.

Via Principalis　　L: Main street of a Roman camp.

Via Sacra　　L: 'Sacred Way', the main road running through the *Forum Romanum*.

Virtus　　'Manliness', Roman virtue of courage.

Wadi　　A: Brook.

Yahweh　　H: The creator god of the Jews.

Yehudim　　H: 'Jews'.

Yom Kippur　　H: 'Day of Atonement', a high holiday falling ten days after the Jewish New Year (*Rosh HaShanah*) on the 10th of *Tishri*.

Zuz　　H: Rebel coin made by overstamping a Roman *denarius* or *drachma* (*zuzim* pl.).

Place Names

Ancient:	Modern:
Adraa	Draa (Syria)
Antiocheia (on the Orontes)	Antakya (Turkey)
Antiocheia (on the Chrysorhoas)	Jersah (Jordan)
Antipatris	Rosh ha-Ayyin (Israel)
Apollonia	Arsuf (Israel)
Ascalon	Ashkelon (Israel)
Azotus	Ashdod (Israel)
Betar	Battir, Bittir, Khirbet el-Yahud (Palestine); alternatively, et-Tira (Palestine) or Qalansawe (Israel)
Bethel	Bethel (Israel)
Bostra	Bosra, Busra (Syria)
Caesarea Philippi	Now an archaeological site within Hermon Stream Nature Reserve (Israel)
Caparcotna	Roman camp near Tel Megiddo or Kefar Othnai (Israel); alternative name for Legio
Colonia Aelia Capitolina	Jerusalem (after 130 CE)
Colonia Prima Flavia Caesarea	Caesarea (Israel)
Damascus	Damascus (Syria)
Deva	Chester (United Kingdom)
Diocaesarea	Zippori (Israel)
Dora	Dor (Israel)
Eboracum	York (United Kingdom)
Ein Gedi	Ein Gedi, 'En Gedi (Israel)
Eleutheropolis	Beit Guvrin (Israel)
Emmaus	Uncertain: perhaps Kiryat Anavim or Beit Mizzeh

Esebus	Heshbon (Jordan)
Flavia Neapolis	Nablus (Palestine)
Gadara	Umm Qais (Jordan)
Gaza	Gaza City (Gaza Strip)
Gell	Aulus Gellius, *Noctes Atticae*
Gerasa	Jersah (Jordan)
Gischala	Gush Halav, Jish (Israel)
Hebron	Hebron (Palestine)
Herodium	Hilltop fortress in the Herodion National Park (Palestine)
Hierichous	Jericho (Palestine)
Hierosolyma	Yerushalayim, Jerusalem (before 130 CE)
Hippos	Now the archaeological park of Hippos-Sussita (Israel)
Iamnia	Yabneh, Yibna, Yavne (Israel)
Ioppe	Yafe (Israel)
Legio	Roman camp near Tel Megiddo or Kefar Othnai (Israel); alternative name for Caparcotna
Livias	Tall el-Hammam (Jordan)?
Londinium	London (United Kingdom)
Lydda	Lod (Israel)
Mamre	Ramet el-Khalil (Palestine)
Pella	Pella (Jordan)
Philadelphia	Amman (Jordan)
Ptolemais	Acre, Akko (Israel)
Scythopolis	Beth Shean (Israel)
Sebaste	Sebastia, Nablus (Palestine)
Sepphoris	Zippori (Israel)
Tekoa	Tuqu' (Palestine)
Tiberias	Tiberias, Tveria (Israel)
Tyrus	Tyre (Lebanon)

Notes

Abbreviations used in Notes:

AE	*Année Épigraphique*
AGRW	*Associations in the Greco-Roman World*
Ammian.	Ammianus Marcellinus, *Res Gestae*
Aur. Vict., *De Caes*	Aurelius Victor, *De Caesaribus*
BM	British Museum
BMC	*British Museum Catalogue*
BMCRE	*Coins of the Roman Empire in the British Museum*
Caes., *Bell. Gall.*	Caesar, *Bellum Gallicum*
Catull.	Catullus
CIL	*Corpus Inscriptionum Latinarum*
CIIP	*Corpus Inscriptionum Iudaeae/Palaestinae*
Cohen	*Description historique des monnaies frappées sous l'Empire Romain*
Dio	Cassius Dio, *Historia Romana*
Epiph., *Mens.*	Epiphanius, *De Mensuris et Ponderibus*
Euseb., *Chron.*	Eusebius, *Chronicon*
Euseb., *Eccl.*	Eusebius, *Historia Ecclesiastica*
Gell.	Aulus Gellius, *Noctes Atticae*
HA, Had.	*Historia Augusta, Vita Hadriani*
Hendin	*Ancient Jewish Coins*
IAA	Israel Antiquities Authority
IG	*Inscriptiones Graecae*
IGR	*Inscriptiones Graecae ad Res Romanas Pertinentes*
ILS	*Inscriptiones Latinae Selectae*
IM	Israel Museum
IRCyr	*Inscriptions of Roman Cyrenaica*
Jos., *Ant. Iud.*	Josephus, *Antiquitates Iudaicae*
Jos., *Ap.*	Josephus, *In Apionem*
Jos., *Bell. Iud.*	Josephus, *Bellum Iudaicum*
Mur.	Papyrus Wadi Murabba'at in *Discoveries in the Judaean Desert: Les Grottes de Murabba'at*
P. Oxy.	Papyrus Oxyrhynchus in *The Oxyrhynchus Papyri*
P. Yadin	Papyrus Yadin in *The Documents from the Bar-Kokhba Period in the Cave of Letters*
Paus.	Pausanias, *Hellados Periegesis*
Plaut., *Mil.*	Plautus, *Miles Gloriosus*
Pliny, *Epist.*	Pliny the Younger, *Epistulae*
Pliny, *NH*	Pliny the Elder, *Naturalis Historia*
RIB	*Roman Inscriptions of Britain*

RIC	*Roman Imperial Coinage*
RPC	*Roman Provincial Coins*
Tac., *Agricola*	Tacitus, *Agricola*
Tac., *Ann.*	Tacitus, *Annales*
Talm. B.	*Talmud* Bavli (Babylonian Talmud)
Talm. Y.	*Talmud* Yerushalmi (Jerusalem Talmud)
Tert., *Apol.*	Tertullian, *Apologeticum*
Ver., *Aen.*	Vergil, *Aeneid*

Chapter One: 'An Explorer of Everything Interesting'

1. Art historians call this style the *Rollockenfrisur*, characterized by nine curls, which evenly frame the face of the subject and roll onto themselves in a movement to the left side. It is one of six sculptural types attributed to the surviving corpus of portraits of Hadrian conceived by Max Wegner, a German specialist on Roman portraiture. A seventh 'type' was subsequently added.
2. The 'Marble bust of the Emperor Hadrian shown naked' (BM 1805,0703.94) is 79cm tall. It was purchased for the British Museum in 1805 from Barwell Browne in March 1795 for £105. He had acquired it from Villa Montalto, Rome, which belonged to Pope Sixtus the Fifth.
3. For an overview of the British Museum exhibition see Opper (2008).
4. This is Hadrian's formal name as it usually appears on inscriptions. Hurlet (2015), 182.
5. Powell (2018), 193–194.
6. *HA, Had.* 11.3. On Suetonius' role as *Ab Epistulis* to Hadrian, see Lindsay (1994).
7. After his dismissal, and now with time on his hands, Suetonius wrote the *De Vitis Caesarum, Lives of the Caesars.*
8. For brief surveys of *HA*, see Bruce (1981), and Golan (1988). Daniels (2013) argues persuasively that the book is satirical.
9. Rohrbacher, 2003, 146 cites the work of Hermann Dessau who demonstrated that the *HA* was composed by a single author.
10. Bruce (1981), 552.
11. Burian (2004).
12. E.g. *HA, Had.* 7.2 and 16.1. The translator of the Loeb 1921 edition remarks: 'It seems to have been written toward the close of his life, and, to judge from scanty citations from it, its purpose was to contradict current statements about himself which he considered derogatory to his reputation and to present him in a favourable light to posterity.'
13. For a discussion of *De Caesaribus* and its sources see Bird (1981).
14. Mordechai (1986) 15: 'The passages 12–14 of Book 69 of Xiphilin's 11th century epitome of Dio's *Roman History* are the only Roman sources dealing at some length with the uprising of Bar Kokhba against Hadrian.'
15. Mordechaai (1986), 19 citing Fergus Millar's 1964 review of Dio, and 22–23 citing P. Schlatter's observation (1897).
16. *HA, Had.* 1: 'the ninth day before the Kalends of February in the seventh consulship of Vespasian and the fifth of Titus.'
17. *HA, Had.* 1.1 explicitly says his birthplace was Rome. On the question of his birth city as Rome see Birley (1997), 10 and Opper (2008), 36.
18. Dio, 69.3.1.
19. Trajan was the son of Hadrian's maternal great-uncle. There is a fine nude bust of him in the Wolfson Gallery too, viz. BM 1805,0703.93.
20. For a comprehensive biography of Trajan, see Bennett (1997).

21. Or their suffects.
22. *HA, Had.* 2.2 confirmed by *IG* II² 3286: *trib(uno) leg(ionis) II Adiutricis P(iae) F(idelis).*
23. Dio, 68.4.1–2.
24. *HA, Had.* 2.3. *Legio* V is listed among his other offices in an inscription set up in his honour at Athens in 112 /113 CE, viz.*CIL* III.550 (Attica) = Dessau, *Inscr. Sel.* 308 = *IG* II² 3286: *trib(uno)... item legionis V Macedonicae.*
25. *HA, Had.* 2.5 confirmed by *IG* II² 3286: *trib(uno)... item leg(ionis) XXII Primageniae p(iae) f(idelis).*
26. *HA, Had.* 3.1.
27. Dio, 68.8.1–15.5. For a critical survey of evidence for the Dacian Wars see Wheeler, (2010). Dacia corresponds to the present-day countries of Romania and Moldova, and parts of Bulgaria, Serbia, Hungary, Poland, Slovakia and the Ukraine.
28. *HA, Had.* 3.1.
29. *HA, Had.* 3.1.
30. *HA, Had.* 3.2.
31. *HA, Had.* 3.4.
32. *HA, Had.* 3.8.
33. *HA, Had.* 3.6 confirmed by *IG* II² 3286: *praetori eodemque tempore leg(ato) leg(ionis) I Minerviae p(iae) f(idelis) bello Dacico.*
34. Dio, 69.14.3–5.
35. *HA, Had.* 3.7.
36. *HA, Had.* 3.9 confirmed by *IG* II² 3286: *leg(ato) pro pr(aetore) Imp(eratoris) Nervae Traiani Caesaris Aug(usti) Germanici Dacici Pannoniae inferiori.*
37. *HA, Had.* 3.9.
38. *HA, Had.* 3.10, and Dio 69.1.2.
39. *IG* II² 3286.
40. Dio, 68.33.1 and 69.1.2, and *HA, Had.* 4.6.
41. Dio, 68.17.1.
42. Dio, 68.18.2.
43. Dio, 68.23.1.
44. *HA, Had.* 5.2. For the background and context see Horbury (2014), 164–190, and Lau (2011), 283.
45. Dio, 68.32.2. For commentary on the events and sources, see Horbury (2014), 246–252.
46. Dio, 68.32.1, and Horbury (2014), 191–203.
47. Dio, 68.32.2.
48. Dio, 68.32.2. For commentary on the events and sources, see Horbury (2014), 203–246.
49. Appian, *Roman History* Book 24 on the Arabian War in Viereck, Roos & Gabba (1962), fr. 19.1.
50. For commentary on the events and sources, see Horbury (2014), 252–256.
51. Dio, 68.32.3; Bennett (1997), 200, and Schürer (1973), 518.
52. *AE* 1929, 167. For commentary on the events and sources, see Horbury (2014), 257–264.
53. *Midrash*, Genesis *Rabbah* 64.10 on *Genesis* 26:28–29, and *Semahot* 8:15. The various traditions are discussed in Horbury (2014), 264–269.
54. Dio, 68.32.1.
55. 68.33.2–3, and Birley (1997), 75: he argues that while poisoning was suspected, oedema or a stroke is the more likely cause.

56. *HA, Had.* 4.6. See Bitner (2012) on *P.Oxy* 55.3781.
57. *HA, Had.* 4.8–10; *cf.* Dio, 69.1.2–4. For a discussion, see Brassloft (1914). Fuelling speculation about a conspiracy, an inscription (*CIL* VI.1884 in the Vatican Museums) states that on 12 August 117 CE Trajan's freedman and personal servant, 28-year-old M. Ulpius Phaedimus, died in Selinus in Cilicia just a few days after his master and within just a single day of Hadrian receiving the news of Trajan's death.
58. They are listed as Palma, Celsus, Nigrinus and Lusius: Dio, 69.2.5; and *HA, Had.* 5.5–6. Dio, 69.9.3 states that Hadrian 'always attributed their execution to the designs of Attianus'.
59. *HA, Had.* 5.7. *Praefectus Urbi*, Baebius Macer, was one of the friends and correspondents of the younger Pliny; see Pliny, *Epist.* 3.5. Apparently his execution was recommended on the advice of Attianus, *HA, Had.* 5.5. M'. Laberius Maximus likely held a command in the First Dacian War and was consul for the second time in 103 CE.
60. C. Calpurnius Crassus Frugi had conspired against Nerva and was banished to Tarentum. Later brought to trial on the charge of conspiring against Trajan, he was condemned: see Dio, 68.3.2 and 68.16.2.
61. *HA, Had.* 5.7; *cf.* Dio 69.7.3. Augustus set the precedent of doubling the pay of the praetorian cohorts in 27 BCE, as reported by Dio, 53.11.5.
62. *HA, Had.* 5.8; *cf.* Dio 68.32.4–5.
63. Dio, 69.7.3, and *HA, Had.* 5.8 and 6.6.
64. *HA, Had.* 5.8. Attianus was his former guardian (*tutor*): see Dio, 69.1.2, and *HA, Had.* 4.2.
65. Dio, 69.7.3, and *HA, Had.* 5.9.
66. *HA, Had.* 5.1–4. The *Pax Romana* is more correctly the *Pax Augusta*: see Powell (2018), 171 and 212–214.
67. The policy was originally established by Augustus after a career-long policy of expansion, 27 BCE–14 CE recorded in Tac., *Ann.* 1.11, which effectively set the Empire's borders at the Rhine, Danube, Euphrates and Sahara Desert. Claudius added Britannia in 43 CE, Trajan added Dacia in 101 CE, Armenia, Babylonia and Mesopotamia in 115–16 CE.
68. Dio, 69.9.1; and *HA, Had.* 5.2.
69. Dio, 69.9.1.
70. *HA, Had.* 10.1–13.7, and Aur. Vict., *De Caes.* 14.4. On Aurelius Victor, see Bird (1978) and Starr (1956).
71. 'MBWA' was the management style of senior executives at the Hewlett-Packard Company in the 1970s.
72. Modern historians seem unable to agree on the exact itineraries of the two grand tours, but for the most comprehensive surveys see Birley (1997), 113–278, and Birley (2003).
73. For Augustus' travels see the Chronology in Powell (2018).
74. Dio, 69.9.2–6; and Aur. Vict., *De Caes.* 14.5.
75. For the breakdown of the number, see Hassall (2000).
76. Dio, 69.9.1.
77. The system of milecastles and turrets continued along the Cumbria coast as far as Risehow, south of Maryport, to watch over the Irish Sea.
78. *HA, Had.* 11.2. The wall runs 73 miles or 117.5 km from end to end.
79. There are numerous books about Hadrian's Wall. Among the best studies about its history is Dobson and Breeze (2000), while for walkers there is Burton (2007) and the essential *Explorer OL43 Hadrian's Wall Map* by Ordnance Survey (2015).
80. *HA, Had.* 10.3; *cf.* Dio, 69.5.2 and 69.9.2–6.

81. A series of coins commemorates the army (*exercitus*) of Britannia, Dacia, Mauretania, Raetia and Syria.
82. Opper (2008), 68–72. For a survey of known statues of Hadrian in military panoply, see Karanastasi (2012/2013).
83. Powell (2018), 218.
84. *HA, Had.* 10.2–5, 10.6 and 21.9.
85. Reconstructed text in Speidel (2006), quoted in: 'Hadrian and his Soldiers. The Lambaesis Inscription' in *Core of the Legions. The Roman Imperial Centuria = Ancient Warfare Special*, 2010. *Cf.* Dio, 69.9.2.
86. Dio, 69.14.3.
87. For his surviving letters and speeches, see Alexander (1938) and Lewis (1991).
88. *HA, Had.* 20.9–10.
89. Dio, 69.11.1, and Aur. Vict. *De Caes.* 14.3.
90. *HA, Had.* 20.11.
91. *HA, Had.* 20.8.
92. *HA, Had.* 17.6–7.
93. *HA, Had.* 26.1.
94. Tert, *Apol.* 5.
95. *HA, Had.* 2.2, 14.8 and 26.2.
96. *HA, Had.* 2.2, 14.8 16.1–6, and Aur. Vict. *De Caes.* 14.2.
97. *HA, Had.* 16.10 and 26.4.
98. *HA, Had.* 19.2–8.
99. Opper (2008), 100.
100. *HA, Had.* 19.2 and 19.10. On buildings he repaired he inscribed the original builder's name rather than his own; this seems to be a practice dating back to Augustus (Suet., *Aug.* 31.5 and Dio, 56.40.5) and Tiberius (Dio, 57.10.2.). See Boatwright (2013) and Jones (2013).
101. *HA, Had.* 19.9.
102. Boatwright (2000), 15 and 206.
103. For examples see Paus., 1.5.5. For a discussion of Hadrian's benefactions, see Boatwright (2000), 207–209.
104. *HA, Had.* 1.5.
105. Ver., *Aen*, 2.49, spoken by the Trojan priest Laocoön.
106. *HA, Had.* 26.1.
107. On Hadrian and his beard, see Oldstone-Moore (2015), 52–56.
108. On Hadrian's love of Greek archaism, see Den Boer (1955), 128.
109. Birley (1997), 13.
110. For a discussion of Hadrian's palatial villa complex in Tivoli, see MacDonald & Pinto (1995).
111. *HA, Had.* 26.5.
112. The 'Marble bust of the emperor Hadrian wearing military dress' in the British Museum (BM 1805,0703.95) comes from Hadrian's Villa. Thorsten Opper relished telling me that he had the pleasant task of leading a team under the auspices of the British Museum in an ongoing programme of archival research and fieldwork in the Pantanello at the villa, which has produced many important finds. See a lecture entitled 'Sculptures from Hadrian's Villa during the age of the Grand Tour' given by Thorsten Opper to the Hellenic and Roman Society on 28 June 2017, https://www.youtube.com/watch?v=qoeRqfBsGQk (accessed 30 July 2020).
113. *HA, Had.* 14.8.
114. Dio, 69.2.6².
115. *HA, Had.* 15.3, 15.5–6, 15.10, 16.8–10, 18.1, 17.1, 17.12 and 20.1.

116. *HA, Had.* 15.12–13. Favorinus was a well-known teacher of rhetoric (*rhetor*) and a native of Arelate (Arles) in Gallia Narbonenis. He was a friend of Plutarch and of Aulus Gellius, whose *Noctes Atticae* are full of allusions to him.

117. *HA, Had.* 15.4, 15.8 and 23.3–7.

118. The 'Marble portrait head from a statue of Antinous (as Dionysus?) wearing a wreath of ivy' (BM 1805,0703.97) stands 81cm tall. Like many ancient artefacts, it has a curious history. The British Museum website records: 'The head is first mentioned in a bill from Jenkins dated 12 July 1773 (TY 8/74/9). Jenkins comments that it is "to be received from the Duke of Dorset". In Townley's later documents there is no mention of the Duke, and the head is reported to have been found in 1770 in grounds known as the Tenuta della Tedesca, near the Villa Pamphili, re-used in post-classical times with fragments of the statue to which the head belonged in a wall that ran under the road to Palo from the gate of San Pancrazio. (The first Townley inventory; 1786 Transcript, fo. 18; "L" catalogue; Notes on the disposition of marbles in CT's house, fo. 21v.)' It was acquired for the museum in 1805 for £105.

119. For the edition of the novel with reflections by the author, see Yourcenar (1992). For commentaries on the novel, see Houston (1961) and Taylor (1988).

120. Dio, 69.11.2. Bithynia was a minor province in Northern Anatolia, which hugged the coast of the Black Sea and the Propontis. His hometown (modern Balo) was located inland and named after the Emperor Claudius. Strabo, 12.4.7 mentions it was celebrated for its pastures and cheese.

121. *AGRW* 310 = *CIL*, XIV.2112 = *ILS* 7212. The inscription states '*Die natalis Antinoi V K[alendas] Dec[embres].*' It was celebrated in Lanuvium by a *collegium* (association) dedicated to Antinous and the goddess Diana. The year of his birth is not known for certain, but 110 CE is likely. It is usually assumed that he met Hadrian when the emperor was touring the provinces and on his return from Ancyra to the Danube in 123 CE, but the evidence is thin.

122. However, many busts were carved after his death and may be idealized representations copied from an archetype approved by Hadrian himself. See Burns (2008). In *Les 120 Journées de Sodome ou l'école du libertinage* (*The 120 Days of Sodom*), the Marquis de Sade created a character named Antinous based on the Bithynian boy, describing him as having the 'most voluptuous arse'.

123. Dio, 69.1.2. See Bird (1982), 45.

124. Aur. Vic., *De Caes.* 14.8.

125. *HA, Had.* 11.7.

126. The admission by a historian caused a stir in the media. Arifa Akbar writes: 'He was also the first leader of Rome to make it clear that he was gay' and 'it is the singular life-story of the gay emperor that is likely to capture the interest of most visitors' in 'Hadrian the gay emperor', the *Independent*, 11 January 2008 (https://www.independent.co.uk/news/uk/this-britain/hadrian-the-gay-emperor-769442.html accessed 30 July 2020). Mary Beard writes, 'where Nero's relationships with men have to be seen as part of the corruption of his reign, Hadrian has been turned into a troubled gay' in 'A Very Modern Emperor', the *Guardian*, 18 July 2008 (https://www.theguardian.com/books/2008/jul/19/history accessed 30 July 2020). Nowadays Hadrian is often included among lists of historical gay icons such as in Parkinson (2013), 54–55. Some institutions, like the Ashmolean in Oxford, express caution and continue to use the term 'boy-favourite' as in its 2018–19 exhibition *Antinous: Boy Made God*; see Smith, Gigante, Lenaghan & Melfi (2018).

127. *HA, Had.* 2.7.

128. For a full-length study of the relationship, see Lambert (1984).

129. *Pathicus*, the 'bottom' or passive partner in anal sex, (Catull, 16.2; Juv. 2.99). *Pedico*, 'bugger'. *Exoletus*, the 'top' or active partner. *Cinaedus*, a male prostitute (Plaut., *Mil.* 668). *Catamitus*, a boy prostitute or lover. *Glabrarius*, lover of smooth-skinned boys (Mart. 4.28.7). These words derive from Greek or Etruscan. For their use see Adams (1990), 2, 123, 133, 190 and 228.

130. Dio, 69.11.2, and Origen, *Contra Celsum* 3.36–38 both describe Antinous as *paidika*, a word that has connotations of sexual submission and specifically slavery. Intergenerational relationships had been the cultural norm in Athens, Sparta and Thebes in the fifth century BCE. The older partner was not to be ridiculed as long as he was the active partner or 'top' (*erastes*), not the passive partner or 'bottom' (*eromenos*). The perfect *erastes* would be a mentor or teacher, while the *eromenos* would receive this training and offer sexual gratification in return. The ideal man/boy association was portrayed in the legend of Zeus and Ganymede (see Holmen (2010)). Antonius Svbia believes that Hadrian's relationship with the young man was sexual as well as emotional; there is no good reason to assume it was not.

131. Aur. Vict., *De Caes.* 14.7.

Chapter Two: 'Iudaea Recaptured'

1. De Lange (2003), 1–8. See Israel Ministry of Foreign Affairs' website: https://mfa.gov.il/mfa/aboutisrael/spotlight/pages/about%20the%20jewish%20religion.aspx (accessed 30 July 2020).

2. The word God, which may not be uttered by orthodox believers, is written as four consonants in Hebrew – יהוה – (known by the Greek term *tetragrommatron*); for the same reason English translations of Hebrew texts often use the form 'G*d' or 'G-d'.

3. On the deep, emotional significance of *Shabbat* to Jews, see Wouk (1974), 35–45.

4. Schwartz (1997), 3.

5. Schwartz (1997), 5 lists as examples the Book of Esther, Ecclesiastes and Daniel.

6. https://www.imj.org.il/en/content/welcome-museum (accessed 30 July 2020).

7. Schwartz (1997), 6.

8. Schwartz (1997), 7.

9. IAA reference: 1996–125, 1993–3162. The ninth-century BCE inscription, written in Aramaic, commemorates the military victories of Hazael, king of Aram-Damascus, in which the regent boasts that he 'killed [Ahaz]iahu son of [Jehoram kin]g of the House of David'. See https://www.imj.org.il/en/collections/371407 (accessed 30 July 2020). The text actually contradicts the account in 2 Kings 8–13.

10. Asia, Europe and Africa.

11. 2 Kings 17.

12. Kings 17:6.

13. Talm. B., *Ta'anit* 29a; Josephus, *Apion* 1.21. Nevins (2006), 24 and Schiffman (2003a), 31 both note that 2 Kings 25:8 states that the Temple burned on the 7th of *Av*, but the parallel in Jeremiah 52:12–13 dates the burning to the 10th of *Ab*.

14. Schwartz (1997), 5.

15. Ezra 6:13–18. Schwartz (1997), 15.

16. IAA reference: 1980–1495, 1980–1496. The lower part of the inscription has been identified as a version of Numbers 6:24–26. See https://www.imj.org.il/en/collections/198069 (accessed 30 July 2020).

17. VanderKam (2012), 71.

18. Leviticus 23 and Numbers 28–29.

19. Lau (2011), 131.

20. The precise location of the altar is still disputed among scholars.

21. 1 Chronicles 24:7–18; Jos., *Bell. Iud.* 6.420.

22. VanderKam (2012), 71–72.
23. Psalms 113–118; Mishnah, *Pesakh* 5:7.
23. Schwartz (1997), 17–19.
24. Heliodorus was a deputy of Seleucus IV Philopator c. 187–175 BCE. See https://www.imj.org.il/en/exhibitions/heliodorus-stele (accessed 30 July 2020).
25. Bowersock (1980) doubts the report about the statue of Zeus.
26. 1 Maccabees 2:6–28. For a discussion of the background and history of the Maccabean Revolt, see Schwartz (1997), 20–40.
27. Grainger (2012), 46–47.
28. VanderKam (2012), 77–78.
29. For coins of John Hyrcanus I, see Jacobson (2013).
30. Grainger (2012), 143–145.
31. Schwartz (1997), 33–36.
32. Jos., *Ant. Iud.* 14.4.71–73.
33. Schwartz (1997), 37 and 43–44.
34. Powell (2015), 170–177.
35. VanderKam (2012), 71.
36. Schwartz (1997), 45–47.
37. Exodus 30:13; Mark 11:15. The coins were actually *tetradrachmai* from Tyre. See Mandell (1984), 223–225.
38. Mishnah, *Talmud* 7:3; Psalms 98:6. The practice is mentioned in Jos., *Bell. Iud.* 4.12.12.
39. Something of its ancient magnificence can be judged from viewing a 1:50 scale reconstruction model located near the Shrine of the Book on the museum campus. The Model of Jerusalem in the second Temple period, measuring some 1,000 m², used to be displayed in the Holy Land Hotel grounds in Jerusalem's Bayit Vegan neighbourhood, but was sawn into 100 parts, moved to and reassembled at the Israel Museum in 2006.
40. Schwartz (1997), 48–49.
41. Sarcophagus: IM accession number K39628, K39627. See https://www.imj.org.il/en/collections/548675. For a virtual exhibition about Herod the Great, see https://museum.imj.org.il/exhibitions/2013/herod/en (accessed 30 July 2020).
42. Eck (2017), 93–94.
43. *AE* 1963 104; IAA 1961–529. The limestone block was found re-used in the staircase of the Roman theatre of Caesarea Maritima and was likely originally set into a temple built in the city in honour of Emperor Tiberius. The inscription reads: '[Dis Augusti]s Tiberieum | [...Ponti]us Pilatus | [...Praef]ectus Iud[ea]e | [...fecit d] e[dicavit]'. See https://www.imj.org.il/en/collections/395572 (accessed 30 July 2020). The post is often confused with *procurator*, an official charged with collecting taxes. On the *Tiberieum*, see Holum, Hohlfelder, Bull & Raban (1988), 110–111.
44. Schwartz (1997), 49–50.
45. Jos., *Ant. Iud.* 18.1.2–5; Josephus, *Jewish War* 2.119–166. Schwartz (1997), 41.
46. Jos., *Ant. Iud.* 17.42, and Holtz (2017), 27–28.
47. Jos., *Ant. Iud.* 8.1.2–6, and Josephus, *Jewish War* 7, 268–270.
48. For a discussion of differences in material culture, see Berlin (2005).
49. Jos., *Ant. Iud.* 18.33–35; John 18:28; and Matthew 26:56–67.
50. Schwartz (1997), 50–51.
51. Jos., *Bell. Iud.* 2.14.4–5.
52. Jos., *Bell. Iud.* 2.14.4.
53. Leviticus 14 refers to practices regarding cleansing as a precaution against skin diseases.

54. Jos., *Bell. Iud.* 2.17.2.
55. Jos., *Bell. Iud.* 2.295; *cf.* Jos., *Ant. Iud.* 18.1.2–6.
56. For detailed studies of First Jewish War rebel coinage, see the several excellent papers in Jacobson & Kokkinos (2012). Zion is the synonym for Jerusalem in the Hebrew Bible named after the hill in Jerusalem on which the Temple was built.
57. Jos., *Bell. Iud.* 3.4.2.
58. Sheppard (2013), 24–28.
59. Jos., *Bell. Iud.* 3.387–399.
60. Jos., *Bell. Iud.* 7.26.
61. Talm. B., Gittin 55a-b.
62. Jos. *Bell. Iud.* 6.250, 267–270 states that the Second Temple was set on fire on the 10th of *Ab*.
63. Jos., *Bell. Iud.* 7.275–407.
64. Magness (2019), 181–184.
65. Jos., *Bell. Iud.* 6.9.3.
66. Schwartz (2006), 23.
67. Eck (2017), 94 citing *CIL* III.12117, *CIL* VI.41113, *CIL* X.6321=*AE* 1980.202, and *AE* 2003.811=*AE* 2008.610.
68. Avi-Yonah (1973), 213; Eck (2017), 96–99; Schürer (1973), 518.
69. On the Roman army in Palestine, see Chancey, M. (2005), 43–70.
70. Jerusalem or Sebaste, Palestine, *AE* 1984.915; *AE* 1985.832: *Leg(ionis) X Fre(tensis) | Coh(ors) IIX.*
71. Jerusalem, *AE* 1939.157; *AE* 1984.912: *Ti(berius) Cl(audius) Ti(beri) f(ilius) Pop(lilia) Fatalis | (domo) Roma Ↄ leg(ionis) II Aug(ustae), Leg(ionis) XX | Vic(tricis), Leg(ionis) II Aug(ustae), Leg(ionis) XI C(laudiae) p(iae) f(idelis), | Leg(ionis) XIV G(eminae) M(artiae) V(ictricis), leg(ionis) XII Ful(minatae), | Leg(ionis) X Fr(etensis), III hast(atus) vix(it) an(nos) | XLII, mil(itavit) ann(os) XXIII. Cl(audia) | Ionice lib(erta) et heres ob me- | rita eius. O(ssa) t(ibi) b(ene) q(uiescant). T(erra) t(ibi) l(evis) s(it). |* 'Ti. Claudius Fatalis, son of Tiberius, of the tribe Poplilia, born in Rome. He was centurion in *Legio II Augusta*, in *Legio XX Victrix*, in *Legio II Augusta*, in *Legio XI Claudia* (the pious and trustworthy), in *Legio XIV Gemina Martia Victrix*, in *Legio XII Fulminata*, and in *Legio X Fretensis*, where he had the rank of a *tertius hastatus*. He lived for forty-two years and served in the army for twenty-three years. Claudia Ionice, his freedwoman and heiress, erected this tomb on account of his merits: 'May your bones rest quietly, may the earth be light upon you.'
72. IM accession number: 71.91.343. Weinberg (1979), 85.
73. IM accession number: 71.91.342. Weinberg (1979), 82–83.
74. IM accession number: 71.91.341. Weinberg (1979), 83–85.
75. Zollschan (2019) argues: 'The *aureus* of Vespasian with the legend *Iudaea recepta* on the reverse illustrates Roman formalities for the conclusion of wars. … *Iudaea recepta* indicates surrender, and the *aureus* with the legend *Iudaea recepta* thus commemorates the Roman acceptance of the unconditional surrender of the Jewish rebels in Jerusalem.' Gambash, Gitler & Cotton (2013). See https://www.imj.org.il/en/exhibitions/unique-coin-recaptured-judea (accessed 30 July 2020).
76. Elkins (2006), 212–213.
77. Mandell (1984), 230.
78. Goodman (2005), 176, and Mandell (1984), 226 and 232.
79. Shaye (2020), 39–41. Judaism attracted converts: see Lau (2011), 13–17 and 300–301.
80. Suet., *Domit.* 12.1–2.
81. Essenes may have fled from Qumran to Masada: Magness (2019), 164.

82. Sand (2012), 121.
83. Talm. Y., *Berakhot* 32b.
84. The synagogues are Kadavumbagam synagogue Cochin, Southern India, 1539–44; Vittorio Veneto synagogue, Italy, 1700; Horb synagogue, Horb am Main, Germany, 1735; Tzedek ve-Shalom Synagogue, 1736, Paramaribo, Suriname. https://www.imj.org.il/en/wings/jewish-art-and-life/synagogue-route (accessed 30 July 2020).
85. De Lange (2003), 36–38.
86. Gruen (2012), 99–101.
87. Holtz (2017), 30–33.
88. Jos., *Ap.* 1.8.
89. Jos., *Ap.* 1.8.
90. Jos., *Ap.* 1.8. de Lange (2003), 52–64.
91. See Schäfer (2020); Lau (2011), 296–298.
92. Schwartz (1997), 15–17.
93. Linder (2006), 133, and Seeman & Marshak (2012), 62.
94. Linder (2006), 134–136.
95. Gruber (1999), 29–30.
96. Lapin (2006), 208 and 225, and Seeman & Marshak (2012), 63.
97. Lau (2011), 4.
98. Seeman & Marshak (2012), 63.
99. Talm. B., *Gittin* 56a-b. On the 'meeting with a king' *topos*, see Novenson (2009), 565–570.
100. Holtz (2017), 84–85. By permitting the foundation of the study group, the story suggests that Vespasian was not personally anti-Judaism, but rather just anti-rebel.
101. Lau (2011), 4, and Schäfer (2003b), 1.
102. Balfour (2012), 91.
103. Before 200 CE rabbis rarely sat as judges: Holtz (2017), 34.
104. Gruber (1999), 95. Holtz (2017), 27 citing Tractate *Avot*. Goldenberg (2006), 199.
105. Lau (2011), 48.
106. Jos., *Bell. Iud.* 4.3.9. Holtz (2017), 85–86, and Seeman & Marshak (2012), 62.
107. Lau (2013), 78–79.
108. Dio, 68.1.2.
109. *RIC* II 52, reverse. Hendin (2010), 458 argues that the Romans accorded themselves sole authority to raise and collect taxes within the Empire and thus 'the idea that this coin represents a Roman apology, or a Roman acknowledgment of its own callous behavior, must be abandoned.'
110. On the application of the *Fiscus Iudaicus*, see Heemstra (2010a), 13–20 and 33, citing references to Christians as 'Not-Jews', e.g. being 'put outside the synagogue' (John 9:22, 12:42 and 16:2). For a discussion of the meaning of the legend of the coin of Nerva, see Goodman (2005), 176 and Heemstra (2010b).
111. Talm. B., *Sanhedrin* 88b. *Torot* is the plural of *Torah*.
112. Talm. B., *Eruvin* 13b; Talm. Y., *Berakhot* 1:4; Lau (2013), 84–85.
113. Lau (2011), 131–132.
114. Lau (2011), 134 and 138–139.
115. Holtz (2017), 19–20.
116. Lau (2011), 191–197.
117. Lau (2011), 193 citing *Avot deRabbi Natan*, recension A, chapter 6; and Holtz (2017), 55–62 citing *Avot deRabbi Natan*, recension B, chapter 12, and Talm. B., *Ketubot* 62b-63a and *Nedarim* 50a.
118. Holtz (2017), 65 citing Talm. B., *Nedarim* 50a.
119. Holtz (2017), 83.

120. Gruber (1999), 101.
121. Gruber (1999), 58–59, 65.
122. Gruber (1999), 51–52, 83.
123. Gruber (1999), 27, 69, 98 and 106–107.
124. Gruber (1999), 83.
125. Gruber (1999), 111 citing Talm. B., *Baba Mezia* 59b and 192.
126. Gruber (1999), 97 and 99.
127. Gruber (1999), 121–125.
128. Holtz (2017), 92–98 citing Talm. B., *Ta'anit* 25b, and Talm. Y., *Pesahim* 'Passover' 6:3, and Song of Songs *Rabbah* 1:20.
129. Holtz (2017), 43 citing Talm. B., *Pesahim* 'Passover' 49b, and 98–99 citing Talm. B., *Berakhot* 31a, and Sifre Deuteronomy, chapter 1, Proverbs 9:8.
130. Talm. B., *Makkot* 24a-24b. Lau (2011), 207 citing Tosefta, *Berakhot* 4:15 and 299, citing *Avot* de-Rabbi Natan, recension A, chapter 16.
131. Holtz (2017), 180–181.
132. Talm. B., *Sanhedrin* 86a. On Mishnah, see Goldenberg (2006), 200 and 202, and Lapin (2006), 214–217.
133. The evidence is slight: Holtz (2017), 15.
134. Lau (2011), 189. Holtz (2017), 32, 34–35 and 104, citing Talm. B., tractate *Sanhedrin* ('Law Court' 32b).
135. Lapin (2006), 221.
136. Holtz (2017), 31 and Lapin (2006), 206.
137. Gruber (1999), 131, 135–137, and Seeman & Marshak (2012), 63.

Chapter Three: 'At Jerusalem He Founded a City'

1. Rankov & Hook (1994), 12–14.
2. The temple had been started in around 520 BCE but abandoned after ten years; various attempts were made to finish the work, but they were also aborted. Hadrian found the semi-finished building on his visit to the city in 124 CE and arranged for its completion 638 years after its conception. The steps and sixteen Corinthian columns still survive. For a survey of works undertaken by Hadrian in Athens, see Laboygianni-Georgakarakou and Papi (2018).
3. Ὀλύμπιος: *HA, Had.* 13.6; Dio, 69.16.1; Paus. 1.3.2 and 1.5.5.
4. Dio, 69.11.1. Birley (2007), 215 and Lambert (1984), 48. The rites, ceremonies and beliefs were kept secret through antiquity and still remain unclear to this day. It likely involved some kind of dramatic revelation celebrating the eternal cycle of life, death and the afterlife, embodied in the story of the annual rebirth of Persephone. Antonius Svbia had suggested to me in Hollywood that this powerful, shared experience may have connected the man and boy at a spiritual level.
5. *HA, Had.* 13.6–9. The base of *Legio* XII *Fulminata* was at Melitene, located near the upper Euphrates River. Hadrian would likely have travelled there from Antiocheia. His visit to the army camp was commemorated on coins with the inscription *Exercitus Cappadocicus* (Cohen, II2 153, No. 553).
6. The date is carved on an inscription cited by Baker (2012), 160–161.
7. *HA, Had.* 13.10.
8. To the foreign dignitaries Hadrian met 'he gave huge gifts, but none greater than to the king of the Hiberi, for to him he gave an elephant and a band of fifty men, in addition to magnificent presents. And having himself received huge gifts from Pharasmanes, including some cloaks embroidered with gold, he sent into the arena three hundred condemned criminals dressed in gold-embroidered cloaks for

the purpose of ridiculing the gifts of the king' (*HA, Had.* 17.11–12 and 21.13). Hadrian likely did not meet the Parthian king in person (Dolezal (2017)). The Hiberi inhabited part of the district of what is now Trans-Caucasia. On this trip, apparently Pharasmanes 'had haughtily scorned his invitation' to meet with Hadrian (*HA, Had.* 13.9).

9. For a survey of the ancient civilizations situated between Rome and the Middle East, see Fowlkes-Childes and Seymore (2019).
10. Browning (1979), 27.
11. Isaac (1990), 355 citing *IGR* III 1054.
12. Bergstein (2016), and Terrill (2017).
13. For examples see Stinespring (1939), Bowersock (1983), 110–111 and Baker (2012), 160–161.
14. Baker (2014), 162 citing Epiphanius.
15. Boatwright (2000), 24 and 99.
16. M. Antonius, M. Agrippa, Germanicus Caesar and Trajan were among the high-profile Romans staying in Antioch on the Orontes. Hadrian commissioned many fine public buildings while there.
17. Bryce (2014), 238.
18. Cohen, II2 108 f., Nos. 20-23.
19. *IGR.* III 1347.
20. Stinespring (1939), 361–363, and Baker (2012), 161–162. Confusingly the city was also known by the name Antiocheia on the Chrysorhoas.
21. The triumphal arch comprised three gateways and architectural ornaments and featured a panel, measuring 1.03 m in height and 7.14 m in width. The inscription it bore, carved in Greek characters, is 12–13cm tall. For a discussion of the monument, see Scheck (1997) and Nassar (2014).
22. Baker (2014), 162 citing Epiphanius.
23. Stinespring (1939), 365.
24. *Sestertius* struck in Rome, 136–138 CE (*GBC* 1604a).
25. Bronze coins minted at the city confirm the official title *COL[ONIA] I[PRIMA] FL[AVIA] AVG[VSTA] CAESA[I]EN[SIS]* on the reverse. See Holum, Hohlfelder, Bull & Raban (1988), 122–124 and fig. 81 on 124 and fig. 99 on 143. Eck (2012b), 234 notes the difficulty of dating when the *colonia* was founded; the earliest-known coin dates to 5 April 71 CE.
26. Ulpian, *Digests* 50.15.1; Bieberstein (2007), 136; Boatwright (2000), 199.
27. Hadrian's own definition of a *colonia* is preserved in Gell. 16.13.8–9. For a discussion see Boatwright (2000), 200.
28. For example, the assaults upon *colonia* Sirmium (Mitrovica) during the Batonian Revolt of 6–9 CE (Vell. Pat. 2.110.6) and *colonia* Camulodunum (Colchester) during the revolt led by Boudicca in 60/61 CE (Dio, 57.1.1; Tac., *Ann.* 14.31–32.): however, taken by surprise, the Roman defenders were overwhelmed in both situations.
29. For a discussion of what is known about Caesarea, see Levine (1975) and Holum, Hohlfelder, Bull & Raban (1988).
30. Holum, Hohlfelder, Bull & Raban (1988), 90–105.
31. Explorations by marine archaeologists have revealed that the moles were constructed using wooden forms, which were filled with rubble and concrete and then sunk one on top of each other. Gambash (2013b) argues that the harbour was a prestige project, overengineered for the local function it performed.
32. Holum, Hohlfelder, Bull & Raban (1988), 135–137.
33. Levine (1975), 9 citing several modern sources. For city maps see Holum, Hohlfelder, Bull & Raban (1988), 83 and 130.

34. Holum, Hohlfelder, Bull & Raban (1988), 78–79 and 127–129.
35. Holum, Hohlfelder, Bull & Raban (1988), 129–133.
36. Holum, Hohlfelder, Bull & Raban (1988), 85–86.
37. Holum, Hohlfelder, Bull & Raban (1988), 83–85.
38. On the so-called 'Promontory Palace' see Holum, Hohlfelder, Bull & Raban (1988), 86.
39. Eck (2003), 155, n.11: *[Imp(eratori) Caes(ari) divi Traiani Parth(ici) f(ilio), divi Nervae nep(oti) Traiano Hadriano] Aug(usto) pont(ifici) ma[x(imo) tr(ibunicia) pot(estate) XVI(?) co(n)s(uli) III, p(atri) p(atriae)] b(eneficiarii) Tinei Rufi [Leg(ati) Aug(usti) pr(o) pr(aetore) –] [–].* For a discussion see Eck (2001), 57; Eck (2011a); Eck (2014), 26; Cotton & Eck (2001), 215ff and 235. On the *officium consularis*, see Rankov (1999).
40. For a discussion see Applebaum (1989), and Schürer (1973), 518–519. In Jerome's Latin version of Eusebius' *Chronikon* – the *Chronicle* – under the 227th Olympiad Tineius Rufus is called 'Tinnio Rufo'.
41. For a discussion of the garrison of Province Iudaea under Hadrian see Keppie (1973).
42. For a discussion of the camp of *Legio* X in Jerusalem see Geva (1984). Scholars dispute whether the entire legion or just a cohort or two was encamped within the walls of Jerusalem. Trajan's father had been its *legatus legionis* before the end of 70 CE during the First Jewish War; see Isaac & Roll (1976).
43. On the governor's staff see Dise Jr (1997), and Eck (2017), 102–104.
44. On the road network in Iudaea see Avi-Yonah (1950–51), Applebaum & Neusner (1989), 98–103, Tepper (2004), and Tepper (2011).
45. Sepphoris was renamed Diocaesarea around the time of Hadrian's visit.
46. Dorsey (1987) and Di Segni (2003).
47. Shinan (2006), 679.
48. Horbury (2014), 348–349.
49. Avi-Yonah (1950–51), 57.
50. Avi Yonah (1950–51), 56–60.
51. Epiphanius was an early Christian writer and later a saint. For the debate on the dating of the trip, see Baker (2014), 162 and Di Segni (2014), 445–448.
52. Epiph., *Mens.* 54c; he uses the names of the provinces as he knew them in the third century.
53. For a discussion of what is known about Jerusalem, see Galor & Bloedhorn (2013), 113–126.
54. The stone is called *meleke* from the Arabic word meaning 'kingly' or 'royal', implying that it is the preferred 'stone of kings'.
55. See Cline (2004), map 14, 132.
56. See the press release of the Israeli Missions Around the World, 21 October 2014: https://embassies.gov.il/MFA/IsraelExperience/history/Pages/Inscription-dedicated-to-Emperor-Hadrian-uncovered-in-Jerusalem-21-Oct-2014.aspx (accessed 30 July 2020).
57. Mevorah, Kreinin & Opper (2015), 22–23: *Imp(erarori) Caes[ari di]v[I Traiani] | Parthic(i) [f(ilio) divi Nerv]ae nep(oti) | Traiano [Hadri]ano August(o) | pont(ifici) ma[xim(o)] trib(unicia) pot(estate) XIIII | [co(n)n(uli)] III P(atri) P(atriae) | L[eg(io) X F]reten[sis].* The word *[Antoninia]na(e)* was added clumsily at the end of the text at a later date.
58. Jos., *Bell. Iud.*, 7.1.1.
59. Epiph., *Mens.* 54c.
60. Cline (2004), 130.

61. Jos., *Bell. Iud.* 7.1.1: 'Now as soon as the army had no more people to slay, or to plunder, because there remained none to be the objects of their fury (for they would not have spared any, had there remained any other work to be done), Caesar gave orders that they should now demolish the entire city and temple, but should leave as many of the towers standing as were of the greatest eminency – that is, Phasaelos, and Hippikos, and Mariamne – and so much of the wall as enclosed the city on the west side. This wall was spared, in order to afford a camp for such as were to lie in garrison, as were the towers also spared in order to demonstrate to posterity what kind of city it was, and how well fortified, which the Roman valour had subdued.'

62. Zissu & Eshel (2016), 388–389.

63. Dio, 69.12.1. For a reappraisal, see Gichon (1986).

64. For the case for a visit to Jerusalem in September 117 CE, see Capponi (2010). Di Segni (2014) examines statement in Epiph., *Mens.* [Syriac Version] 54c and debates the argument of Baker (2012) for 130 CE. Gray (1923), 254–255 cites Papyrus No. 189 of the Rylands collection (published 1914), apparently mentioning a campaign being undertaken in Iudaea in the month of *Choiak* (December) of year '13 of Hadrian' (128 CE) involving troops drafted in from Egypt.

65. Boatwright (2000), 197: 'we should assume that the colony was begun before 132, but completed only after the war', a view supported by excavations reported by Weksler-Bdolah (2014), 56. The rescue excavations were undertaken 2005–2010. See also Kindler (2000) and Arnould-Béhar (2005).

66. Weksler-Bdolah *et al* (2012), 47.

67. On coins showing the ploughing ceremony, see Boatwright (2000), 199–200 and Mildenberg (1984), 99–100 citing Meshorer (1967), 96.

68. Eck (2014), 28.

69. For a discussion of the location of the Capitol in Aelia Capitolina, see Murphy-O'Connor (1994). Weksler-Bdolah (2015) argues that the archaeological finds indicate the great importance of the Mount in the layout of the new Roman *colonia*; moreover, 'this supports the interpretation that the new temple raised by Hadrian to Jupiter and reported by Cassius Dio stood on the Temple Mount and not elsewhere in the city' (from the Abstract in English).

70. Dio, 69.12.1; *cf.* Euseb., *Eccl.*, 39.6.3.

71. Bronze coins minted at the city confirm the title '*COL[ONIA] AEL[IA] KAPIT[OLINA] COND[ITA]* on the reverse; see Boatwright (2000), 199 and fig. 18 on 200.

72. Eck (2012a), 234–235.

73. Zissu & Eshel (2016), 388.

74. Midrash Tanhuma, *Bereshit* 10:7.

75. Epiph., *Mens.* [Syriac Version] 54c. For a discussion, see Di Seigni (2014).

76. Di Segni (2014).

77. Epiph., *Mens.* For a discussion of whether the man named in the text was L. Statius Aquila, suffect consul of 116 CE, see Baker (2012), 165.

78. Galor & Bloedhorn (2013), 117–120.

79. Galor & Bloedhorn (2013), 234–235.

80. Galor & Bloedhorn (2013), 117–120.

81. For discussions on the architecture and planning of Aelia Capitolina, see Arnould (1998), Arnould-Béhar (2005), and Bieberstein (2007).

82. Geva and Behat (1998), 225–227.

83. The Arabic names for Damascus Gate are Bab al-Nasr, which means 'Gate of Victory', and Bab al-Amud, which means 'Gate of the Column'. The column is

shown on the Masaba Map, a mosaic made in the Byzantine period that shows a bird's-eye view of Aelia Capitolina at that time.

84. Galor & Bloedhorn (2013), 117–118.
85. For plans of Jerusalem and Aelia Capitolina, see Cline (2004), map 14 on 133 and Eliav (2003), map 2 on 277.
86. For a discussion of evidence for the lost circus of Aelia Capitolina, see Patrich (2002).
87. Paus., 1.5.
88. The enclosed area, 45.7 m x 61.0 m (150ft x 200ft), was one of three markets, Acco and Gaza being the other two. For a discussion of the annual market, see Bacher (1909).
89. Jos., *Bell. Iud.* 4.553, and Jos. *Ant. Iud.* 1.196; Richardson (1996), 60–61 citing Genesis 13:18, 14:13 and 18:1.
90. Holum, Hohlfelder, Bull & Raban (1988), 125–127 and Levine (1975), 21–22.
91. Filiu (2014), 9–11.
92. Filiu (2014), 11.
93. Boatwright (2000), 99 and 101, n. 84; and Eck (2014), 21.
94. Dio, 69.11.1, and Baker (2012), 161.
95. The poem is preserved on papyrus from Oxyrhynchus, *P. Oxy.* 8.1085. For a discussion of the document, see Trevor Thompson (2013).
96. Iulia Balbilla, one of the entourage, inscribed four verses into the sculpture to commemorate their visit. For the full poem – with another dedicated to Sabina – see the translation by E.L. Bowie quoted in Brian Fagan (2006), 14.
97. Dio, 69.11.2, and *HA, Had.* 14.5. Whether Antinous was murdered or committed suicide is still debated.
98. *HA, Had.* 14.5.
99. Bell (1940), 133–136 and Boatwright (2000), 172.
100. Dio, 69.11.2; *HA, Had.* 14.5.
101. On the Antinous cult see Evers (2013), and Smith, Gigante, Lenaghan & Melfi (2018), 11–28; the authors note in fig. 11 that some eighty-eight busts have been found, with find sites concentrated in Italy, Greece, North Africa, Spain, Egypt, Asia and Syria, although about half of them have no provenance.

Chapter Four: 'Son of a Star'
1. The attack is reported in Gross (2016).
2. The Meir Amit Intelligence and Terrorism Information Centre report: http://www.terrorism-info.org.il/en/article/21019 (accessed 30 July 2020).
3. Appian, *Syrian Wars*, 50.
4. Cassius Dio, 69.12.1–2.
5. For a discussion of Hadrian's actions in the Temple Mount, see Eliav (1997).
6. Lau (2011), 328.
7. Talm. Y., *Ta'anit* 4:4 [69b] cited by Lau (2011), 328.
8. *Midrash*, Genesis *Rabbah* 64.10 in *Genesis* 26:28–29.
9. Interviewing Milena Melfi, Assistant Curator of the Cast Gallery at the Ashmolean Museum, for this book she told me that the cult of Antinous was short-lived: 'It slowly disappeared after Hadrian's death. We don't have temples. There's some mention in the sources of temples, but archaeologically there's no evidence. But we don't really know. That's the problem with the archaeology of Antinous.' For a discussion, see Powell (2019).
10. Joannes Chrysostom, *Orationes* III. *Adversus Judaeos*.

11. *Chron. Alex.* in the year 118 CE; Nicephorus Xanthopulos, *Hist. Eccl.* 3.24; George Cedrenus, *Corpus Script. Byz.* 12.249.
12. *Epistle of Barnabus* 16.3–4.
13. Boatwright (2000), 201 states that the Temple Mount 'was desolate until the sixth century'.
14. *HA, Had.* 14.2.
15. Lau (2011), 300 citing Talm. B., *Rosh HaShana* 19a. Gruber (1999), 16, n.2 citing Isaac & Oppenheimer (1985), 38.
16. Genesis 17:9–14, and de Lange (2003), 9.
17. Schwartz (2006), 34; Smallwood (1959), 334.
18. Hodges (2001).
19. Eshel (2006), 107–108 citing third-century CE jurist Modestinus in Justinian's *Digest*, 48.8.11.1 and *Epistle of Barnabus*; Geiger (1976); Holtz (2017), 163; Lau (2007), 323–327; Mildenberg (1984), 106–109; Oppenheimer (2003); Rabello (1995); Smallwood (1959) and Smallwood (1961).
20. Holtz (2017), 163; Lau (2013), 300 citing Talm. B., *Rosh Hashana* 19a.
21. Lau (2011), 300 citing Talm. B., *Rosh Hashana* 19a.
22. Schwartz (2006), 25. Zissu (2017).
23. Applebaum (1987), 10ff; see a critique of his interpretation in Mor (2016), 81–82.
24. Talm. B., *Sefaria Shabbat* 33b.
25. Jagersma (1986), 149.
26. Schwartz (2006), 23 and figure 1.1.
27. Chancey (2005), 43–70 argues 'that because Galilee did not receive a long-term garrison until c. 120 CE, contact with Roman soldiers in Galilee would have been uncommon in Jesus' lifetime, the story of his famous exchange with a centurion at Capernaum [in Matthew 8:5–13] notwithstanding.'
28. Talm. B., *Gittin* 57a. The story is problematic in historical terms and may just be folklore: Yassif (2009), 134.
29. Grainger (2012), 12–13.
30. Schäfer, (2003b), 9 citing *Nahal Hever* 50. On the name Simon/Shimeon/Shim'on, see Fitzmeyer (1963); and Gruber (1999), 21.
31. Names are written disemvowelled since in Hebrew only consonants are given.
32. *Mur* 43 is the only known document signed by Shim'on, *Nasi* of Israel. See Eschel (2006), 109–110, and Wise (2015), 244 and 369.
33. Schwartz (2006), 35.
34. Talm. B., *Gittin* 57a.
35. Perhaps Kirbet Kosiba, a village or town located north-west of Hebron, Palestine.
36. *Seder 'Olam Raba* 30; *Sotah* 9:14. Lau (2011), 281–283, and Seeman & Marshak (2012), 65.
37. Harkabi (1983), 43.
38. Euseb., *Eccl.* 4.6.2.
39. *Midrash*, Lamentations *Eikha Rabbah* 2:2.4.
40. Talm. Y., *Ta'anit* 4:5 [68d].
41. *Mur* 43–45.
42. Yadin (1971), 132. Alexander (1984), 590, n.38 compares Ben Kosiba's followers to the way early Christians addressed each other, and n.39 citing examples in Aramaic (Hev 1 and 10), Hebrew (*Mur* 42, 43, 44, 46 and 48, Cave 5/6 Hev 12), and Greek (5/6 Hev 3 and 6).
43. *P. Hever* 30; Yadin (1971), 132.
44. *P. Yadin* 42 is dated 1 *Iyyar* in Year 1 presumed to be May 133 CE, discussed in Eshel (2003), 101, noting the 'Fall 131 [Tishri]' as 'the beginning of the year during which

the Bar Kokhba Revolt broke' and the 'beginning of Summer 132' for the 'outbreak of the revolt'. See the summary in Horbury (2014), 285.

45. E.g. *P. Yadin* 42, 45, 46 and 47, XHev/Se 7, 8, 13 and 49, and *Mur* 24 cited by Eschel (2003), 97. Some translators spell the title *nasy* or *nsy*.
46. For a discussion of the history and politics of using 'Land of Israel', see Sand (2012), 22–30.
47. Sand (2012), 87.
48. E.g. 2 Chronicles 34:7.
49. Sand (2012), 102–103.
50. Sand (2012), 28.
51. Talm. Y., *Ta'anit* 'Fast Days' 4:8, 68d.
52. Numbers 24:17. 'Sheth' would be interpreted as Rome per Schäfer (2003a), 16.
53. Mildenberg (1980), 313–314.
54. Gruber (1999), 21.
55. Weiss (2014), 105.
56. Marcus (1989).
57. Segal (1986), 16.
58. Schiffman (2006), 1059; Schiffman (2012), 430; Holz (2017), 153.
59. Isaiah 14:1–2.
60. 1 Enoch 85–90, and Psalms of Solomon 17:21–32.
61. Isaiah 11:1–4.
62. The prophets Isaiah, Jeremiah, Ezekiel, Amos, Joel and Hosea all refer to the messianic era. For a discussion see Waxman (1987), 175–176 and Schiffman (2006), 1060–1062.
63. E.g. 4 Ezra 6:55, 7:6 and 8:1.
64. Goldenberg (2006), 20 citing Ulla, Talm. B., *Sanhedrin* 98a.
65. Reinhartz (1989), 172–177 provides a useful summary of scholarly opinion.
66. Curran (2005), 92, and Marcus (1989). O'Neill (2000), 39 notes that the sole exception is Jesus in Mark 14:62.
67. Talm. Y., *Ta'anit* 'Fast Days' 4:8, 68d.
68. Evans (1997), 194–196; Novenson (2009), 556; Schäfer (2003a), 4–5.
69. Schiffman (2006), 1063. Schäfer (2003a), 17. A firm historical association between the two men cannot be established today beyond a doubt as authentic, yet the venerable rabbi is now forever associated with the warlord. (Holtz (2017), 149. Some argue that Akiba actually had nothing to do with Ben Kosiba in his lifetime and that the connection between commander and rabbi is a storyline imposed at a much later date. The argument is fully discussed in Novenson (2009), and Schäfer (2003b), 2–7.
70. Maimonides, *Mishneh Torah*, The Laws of Kings 11:3.
71. In biblical texts the arms-bearer carried the large shield and perhaps other weapons for a king (1 Samuel 31:4), commander-in-chief (2 Samuel 23:37), captain (1 Samuel 14:7), or champion (1 Samuel 17:7).
72. His name appears on coins; see Mildenberg (1984), 64–65.
73. For a review see Meir (2016), 49e/98 [Hebrew]; Mor (2016), 429–439; Mildenberg (1949); Schäfer (2003b), 6–7.
74. Schäfer (2003), 19–20. Ezekiel 33:1–48:35 describes how the Jewish exile will come to an end, a new Jerusalem and new Temple will be built, and the Israelites will gather together.
75. Schäfer (2003b), 15–20.
76. E.g. Ezekiel 37:24. See Evans (1997), 201–202.
77. Holtz (2017), 151.

78. Evans (1997), 199.
79. Gruber (1999), 172–174. It differs from a *Milhemet Reshut*, which is a war of choice that required approval of the Sanhedrin, defined in Talm. Y., *Sotah* 8:10 (23a).
80. 1 Maccabees 14:36.
81. Harkabi (1983), 70–72 notes that, as the war continued it became more symmetrical in character, fought with irregular Jewish units that engaged in pitched battles with the Greeks, even fighting frontal assaults. For the practice of Maccabean warfare in the 'War of the Sons of Light and the Sons of Darkness', see Avi-Yonah (1952).
82. 1 Maccabees 14:41.
83. For an analysis of the patterns in the response of the Imperial Roman state to local resistance see Gambash (2015). For Arminius see Powell & Dennis (2014), 28–40, and Powell (2018), 152–157.
84. Mor (2016), 10–11.

Chapter Five: 'For The Redemption of Israel'

1. *Mur.* 24 from Wadi Murabba'at. See also references in *Mur.* 43 and 44. In favour of the interpretation that Ben Kosiba's headquarters were at Herodium, see Milik (1961) and Wise (2015), 249. Laperrousaz (1964a) and (1964b) argues for occupation between 132–133 CE, but not beyond autumn 134 CE. Yadin (1961) and (1971), 182–183 rejects the notion outright.
2. For a survey of Herodium, see Segal (1973).
3. Jos., *Bell. Iud.* 7.6.1.
4. Jos., *Bell. Iud.* 1.31.10; *cf.* Antiquities 14.323–325.
5. Porat, Kalman, Chachy & Zissu (2017).
6. For a discussion of Herod's burial place, see Rozenberg & Mevorah (2013).
7. Netzer & Arzi (1985), Netzer (1988) and Netzer, Kalman, Porat & Chachy (2011).
8. Stiebel (2003), 220.
9. Porat, Kalman, Chachy & Zissu (2017), 340–343.
10. E.g. from *Mur.* 42. For a discussion of letters mentioning Yeshua Ben Galgula, see Wise (2015), 106–107.
11. Talm. Y., *Ta'anit* 4:5 [68d].
12. *Mishna, Sota* 8:5.
13. *Sifrei Devarim* 197.
14. Grainger (2012), 12–13 and 16.
15. Zissu (2017), 19.
16. Wise (2015), 249.
17. Yadin (1971), 66–85.
18. The scale measures 2.5cm (1in) by 1.5cm (0.5in).
19. For a discussion of finds at the Teomin Cave, see Zissu, Porat, Langford & Frumkin (2011).
20. Eshel (1989); Porat, Eshel & Frumkin (2007), 45, pl. 7:3.
21. The fragment of wood measures 8cm (3in) by 3cm (1.25in).
22. For a discussion on slings, see Skov (2013).
23. 1 Samuel 17:48–49. For a discussion of slingers and Hebrew terminology, see Deem (1978).
24. On bandits (*listim*) in Iudaea, see Curran (2005), 93, and Isaac (1984).
25. Stiebel (2003), 216–217 and 220.
26. Herodium: Stiebel (2003), 216–217 and 220, figs. 15, 16, 17, 18, 19 and 20. Har Yishai Caves: Porat, Eshel & Frumkin (2007), figs. 10 and 11.
27. Stiebel (2003), 220.

28. For a discussion on arrowheads from Ḥorvat 'Eqed', see Gichon & Vitale (1991).
29. For a discussion on artefacts from the 'Caves of the Spear', see Porat, Eshel & Frumkin (2009).
30. Zissu, Porat, Langford & Frumkin (2011), 269 and fig. 11B.
31. Yadin (1971), 151–155.
32. On the equipment supply chain see MacCullen (1960), Crone (2007), 69–70 and Mairs (2012). An example of requisitioning is when Germanicus Caesar looked to the provincials in the three Gauls and Italy for cash and goods in kind to replace losses of horses and equipment during his campaign in Germania of 16 CE in Tac., *Ann.* 1.71. Also see Adams (1995), 121–122 citing *P. Lond. II.* 482, where, in 130 CE in far-off Britannia, Serenus, a *procurator*, issued a receipt to 'hay contractors' (*conductores faenarii*) on behalf of members of his cavalry unit (*turma*), having paid for the freight charge himself.
33. On *Legio* X roof tiles, see Arubas & Goldfus (2006) and Arubas & Goldfus (2019).
34. Cassius Dio, 69.12.2.
35. Zissu, Porat, Langford & Frumkin (2011), 269 and fig. 11A.
36. Cassius Dio, 69.12.2.
37. Dio, 69.14.2.
38. Dio, 69.12.2.
39. The first year of the conflict is confirmed as 132 CE in Euseb, *Chron.* under the entry for 'Hadrian's Year 16'. See Eshel (2003), 102–103 based on a reading of *P. Yadin* 42.
40. 1 Maccabees 2:27 NABRE.
41. Cf. Pliny, *NH* 5.14. Jericho had been devastated during the First Jewish war, see Mowry (1952). The location of Kiryat Arabaya is not known; see Yadin (1971), 130.
42. Eshel (2006), 111.
43. On weights and measures see Deutsch (2000–2002) and Deutsch (2001).
44. Examples of weights are discussed in Deutsch (2001), Deutsch (2000–2002) and Zissu & Ganor (2006).
45. IAA Inventory Number 1987.1541, *CIIP*, CIX, 3426 [Horbat Alim].
46. Mor (2016), 80–81.
47. *Mur.* 24. For a discussion of the document, see Wise (2015), 118–121.
48. Schäfer (2003b), 10–12.
49. Euseb., *Chron.* 'Hadrian's Year 16'.
50. Hendin (2012), 140–141.
51. Zissu & Eshel (2013), 31.
52. Two *zuzim* equalled the half-*shekel* Temple tax required of every adult male Israelite per Exodus 30:13. There were 1,500 *sela'im* in a *talent*.
53. Barkay (2012), 25.
54. Exodus 20:4–6 NIV; *cf.* Deuteronomy 4:16–18.
55. Four Species: Leviticus 23:40. On symbols, see Hendin (2012), 133–139.
56. Evans (1997), 202; Schäfer (2003), 20.
57. Hendin (2012), 131–132.
58. Hendin (2012), 131–132; Mildenberg (1980), 328–331; Mildenberg (1984), 70; Zissu & Abadi (2014).
59. Schäfer (2003b), 20, and Owen (2015), 256–257.
60. Yadin (1971), 181.
61. Wise (2015), 243–244.
62. Ben Kosiba is believed to have dictated three extant letters to a scribe, viz. *Mur.* 43, 44 and 45. See Wise (2015), 230–231.
63. Yadin (1971), 181.
64. Wise (2015), 257–272.

65. *P.Yadin* 42.
66. 1 Maccabees 13:41–42 NRSV: 'In the one hundred seventieth year the yoke of the Gentiles was removed from Israel, and the people began to write in their documents and contracts: "In the first year of Simon the great high priest and commander and leader of the Jews."'
67. Kanael (1971), 1; Eshel (1995); Mor (2016), 257. The messaging is reproduced in correspondence; e.g. *Mur.* 22.
68. Mildenberg (1984), 69.
69. Hendin (2012), 130–131.
70. Hendin (2012), 138; Sporty (1983).
71. Mor (2016), 257.
72. For a discussion of the evidence for whether or not the rebels took Aelia Capitolina, see Eschel (2007), who concludes that 'Ben Kosiba never captured the city. Jerusalem remained under Roman control through the entire revolt' (from the Abstract in English). A fourth coin, a *perutah* of 'Year Two', was found in the William Davidson Archaeological Park next to the Western Wall in May 2020. According to *The Times of Israel* dated 11 May 2020, 'Israeli Antiquities Authority archaeologists Moran Hagbi and Dr. Joe Uziel speculated the coins may have been brought to Jerusalem by Roman legionaries who helped crush the revolt and saved them as souvenirs, noting Bar Kochba's forces were never able to penetrate the city's ancient borders': https://www.timesofisrael.com/year-2-of-freedom-ancient-coin-from-bar-kochba-revolt-found-near-temple-mount/ (accessed 30 July 2020).
73. Mor (2016), 273 and 287–288.
74. Mor (2016), 255–256 and 280–281.
75. For a discussion of territorial reach of the Bar Kokhba Revolt, see surveys in Mor (1991), (2003), 107–132 and (2016), 147–288.
76. Barag (1980), map on 33; Tsafrir & Zissu (2002); Zissu, Eshel, Langford & Frumkin (2010); Zissu & Eshel (2013); Zissu & Kloner (2019).
77. For a discussion of Galilee, see Crown (1991); Geiger (2016); Mor (2003), 170–171 and 155–159; Jensen (2014); Shivtiel (2017). Coins have been found at the Elqana Cave in Western Samaria: see Zissu, Langford, Raviv, Davidovich, Porat & Frumkin (2014) and Zissu, Langford, Porat & Frumkin (2016).
78. Dio, 69.12.3.
79. Kloner & Zissu (2016), 51e/69; Shivtiel & Frumkin (2014); Zissu & Kloner (2014), fig. 7 on 102, and 120.
80. Kloner & Zissu (2016), 27e–28e/62–65 [Hebrew].
81. Genesis 38:12 and 38:20; Joshua 12:7 and 12:15.
82. 2 Maccabees 12:38.
83. Zissu & Ganor (2009), 91, and Klein, Zissu, Goldenberg & Ganor (2015).
84. Zissu & Ganor (2009), and Zissu, Ganor & Neugeborn (2010).
85. Talm. B., *Megillah* 27a teaches that building a *mikwa* takes precedence even over a synagogue. The *mikwa* must contain enough water to cover the entire body of an average-sized man according to Talm. B., *Eruvin* 4b.
86. Zissu & Kloner (2014), 115 report that rebel coins been discovered in hideout XIII at Horbat 'Etri (a half *shekel* from the Third Year of the Bar Kokhba War), Susya (a *shekel* from the Second Year) and Khirbet Zeita (a hoard of 755 *perutot* from the Second and Third Years).
87. Safrai (1994), 238.
88. Zissu & Ganor (2009), 97, note that a pottery sherd was found in cistern XII with Hebrew for 'dried figs' written on the outside. See also Zissu, Ganor & Neugeborn (2010).

89. For a discussion of the Horbat 'Etri complex and environs, see Zissu, Ganor & Neugeborn (2010).
90. For example, hideouts I, VI, XII and XIII at Horbat 'Etri.
91. Notably hideouts II, III and XV at Horbat 'Etri.
92. Zissu & Ganor (2009), 95.
93. Hideout XXXIV.
94. Dio, 69.12.3.
95. For a discussion of the Horbat Burgin complex and environs, see Zissu, Porat, Langford & Frumkin (2011), and Zissu, Ganor, Klein & Klein (2013).
96. Meaning 'Oasis of Peace', it is, as its website declares, 'a village of Palestinian and Jewish citizens of Israel dedicated to building justice, peace and equality in the country and the region': https://wasns.org (accessed 30 July 2020).

Chapter Six: 'Do Not Help or Hinder Us!'

1. Dio, 69.13.1.
2. Rankov (1999), 27–29 notes the importance of *beneficiarii* in gathering and relaying field intelligence between the governor and his army.
3. Dio, 69.13.1.
4. Ulpian, *Digest* 1.18.13.pr.
5. For a discussion of controlling civil unrest, see Kelly (2007). From a military perspective, the Romans interpreted rebellion (*seditio*) as a breach of treaty they regarded as an injury (*iniuria*) to the Roman people. In their eyes, such wrongdoing had to be met with revenge (*ultio*). See Powell (2018), 182–183.
6. Powell (2018).
7. Tac., *Ann.* 1.9.
8. For a discussion of the statue, see Gergel (1991), 231–232. On the discovery, see Smith (1975).
9. Gergel (1991), 249.
10. Gambash (2009 and 2015); Powell (2018), 89 and 190.
11. *HA, Had.* 21.8.
12. Fronto, *Correspondence* 2.
13. *HA, Had.* 14.2, and Jarrett (1976).
14. For discussion on the evidence of the burning of Londinium, see Perring (2017).
15. For a discussion of civil unrest in Britannia, see Frere (2000).
16. Birley (2000), 202.
17. Alternatively, *Bellum Iudaeorum*. The phrasing occurs on *CIL*, III.7334 = *ILS* 2080, *CIL*, VI.40524 and *CIL*, VIII.8934 = *ILS* 400. Writing in Greek, Cassius Dio, 69.12.1 similarly refers to the conflict as 'war', πόλεμος, while Euseb., *Eccl.* 4.6.1 refers to the event as a 'Jewish revolt', Ἰουδαίων ἀποστασίας. Compare to the revolt in Cyrene, Cyrenaica (Libya) of 115/116 CE where it is referred to on inscriptions as *Tumultum Iudaicum*, e.g. *IRCyr* 2020 C.21, *IRCyr* C. 281 and 292; my thanks to Dr Caroline Barron, Birbeck, University of London for the references.
18. Dio, 69.13.2.
19. A *vexillatio* could be as small as a single *centuria* (80 men), or whole *cohortes* comprising six centuries (480 men), or multiples thereof; each marched under a flag (*vexillum*) to identify the legion from which it came.
20. Determining the positions of individual units in Province Iudaea has challenged scholars for years; e.g. Keppie (1973), Powell (2017), and Zeichmann (2018).
21. Dio, 55.23.2–24.4 provides a list of units and their locations at the time he wrote his *Roman History*.
22. Mor (2016), 290–293, and Geva (1984). For the case for its legionary base at Bet Guvrin/Eleutheropolis, see Zissu & Ecker (2014).

23. Mor (2016), 294, Kennedy (1980), Lifshitz (1960) and Tully (1998). An inscription marking work completed by a unit of *Legio* VI now in the Hecht Museum, Haifa reads: '*Vexilla | tio Leg[ionisI] VI Ferr[ata]* | 'Detachment of *Legio* VI *Ferrata*'.

24. Partially excavated in 2015, the camp at Caparcotna/Legio was c. 300 m x c. 500 m (c. 984ft x c. 1,640ft), large enough for two legions or the legion plus auxiliaries. On the camp, see M'Elderry (1908), Ritterling (1903), Tepper (2004), Tepper (2007), Tepper (2017), Tepper, David & Adams (2015), Tzori (1971) and Zissu & Ecker (2014).

25. Horbury (2014), 349 citing Menachem Mor. For a discussion of the Samaritans, see Mor (2016), 363–384; on 382 he states that the late Samaritan texts make no mention of the Bar Kokhba War.

26. Mor (2016), 294–295.

27. Dabrowa (1998), 92–94. Marcellus left *Legio* IIII *Scythica* at Zeugma and XVI *Flavia Firma* at Samosata (Mor (2016), 307; and Schürer (1973), 518 and 549 n.151 citing *IGR* III 174–175.

28. Mor (2016), 296–298, Isaac & Roll (1979), Rea (1980), Ritterling (1903), Roll (1982), Speidel (1986) and Urloiou (2010).

29. *CIL* VI.2080. Bowersock (1971), 232; Mor (2016), 298–302; Strobel (1988).

30. 119 CE. *CIL*, XI.5213.

31. *CIL*, III.39.

32. Eck (1999), 84–86; and Bowersock (2003), 178 raise the possibility that the Jews in Arabia took advantage of the rebellion in Iudaea and *did* rise up. If so, Nepos then authorized a massacre of Jews. The evidence, however, is inconclusive.

33. Mor (2016), 302–303.

34. Mor (2016), 303–304.

35. Mor (2016), 303–304.

36. Mor (2016), 303–306.

37. *CIL*, VIII.6706 = *ILS* 1965 (Castellum Tidditanorum): '*Legato imp[eratoris] Hadriani in expeditio Iudaica*.'

38. Maxfield (1981), 147–148. Syme (1988), 166 argues 'that is decisive. The Emperor himself took the field.' If so, the question arises why he is not mentioned by Dio, 69.13.2 or other Roman extant sources. Rabbinic sources place him in Judea.

39. *CIL*, VI.3505: '*Sextus Attius Senecio praefectus alae i flaviae Gaetulorum, tribunus legionis X Geminae, emissusa divi Hadriano in expeditione Judaica ad vexillationes deducendus in …*'

40. *Leg.* VIIII: Birley (2016), 61–62; Campbell (2011). *Leg.* XXII: Schwartz (1989). Mor (1986) convincingly demolishes the cases for *Legiones* VIIII *Hispana* and XXII *Deiotariana* being destroyed during the Bar Kokhba War, and restates so in Mor (2016), 308.

41. Dio, 55.24.45: 'there were also allied forces of infantry, cavalry, and sailors, whatever their numbers may have been (for I cannot state the exact figures).'

42. Powell (2018), Appendix 3.4.

43. Holder (2003), 114–115.

44. Mor (2016), 311–316 citing *CIL* XVI.87, which was reportedly discovered at Aphek on the Golan Heights above Lake Tiberias; it is now in the Musée de Louvre (Inventory Number BR4088).

45. The initialization 'C R.' stands for *Civium Romanorum* (the 'E.' for *Equitata*).

46. Mor (2016), 314–316.

47. Birley (2016), 69; Mor (2016), 319–323. The initialization 'M' stands for *milliaria* or 'thousand-strong', the 'Eq.' for *Equitata*.

48. Speidel (1979), discussing the Rockefeller Museum – formerly the Palestine Archaeological Museum (PAM) – Inventory Number IDAM 37.277. On Thracian cohorts see Jarrett (1969). See also Holder (2003), 114–115 and Yadin (1971), 49, arguing the cohort was at Ein Gedi in 124 CE and may have been temporarily based up at Camp A and B at Nahal Hever in 135–136 CE.

49. Both Mor (2016), 210–212 and Eck (2003), 163–164 discuss various interpretations based on a reading of the inscription *CIL*, VIII.8934 = *ILS* 1400. See also Garrett (1963), 212 and 220.

50. Mor (2003), 114.

51. The phrasing *expeditio Iudaica* appears on *AE* 1904, 9 (Aequum); *CIL*, VI.3503; *CIL* VIII.6706 = *ILS* 1965; and *CIL*, XI.5212 = *ILS* 1058.

52. See Ch.1, n.75.

53. Euseb., *Eccl.* 4.6.1.

54. The maxim is a paraphrase of the insight articulated by Feldmarschall Helmuth Karl Bernhard Graf von Moltke in *On Strategy* | *Über Strategie* (1871): 'No plan of operations extends with any certainty beyond the first contact with the main hostile force. | *Kein Operationsplan reicht mit einiger Sicherheit über das erste Zusammentreffen mit der feindlichen Hauptmacht hinaus.*'

55. Talm. Y., *Ta'anit* 4:5 [68d]; *cf.* Midrash, Lamentations *Eikha Rabbah* 2.2.4.

56. Psalm 60:9–12 NIV.

57. Lau (2011), 343; and Marks (1994), 30–31 and 33–34. See Chapter 4, note 28 concerning Bar Daroma at Tur Malka.

58. *Midrash*, Lamentations *Eikha Rabbah* 2.2.4. Lau (2011), 341 notes that Kefar Haruba may lie between Lod and Sha'alavim or near Susita. For a discussion see Mor (2016), 98–102. The historical Hadrian was not actually in Iudaea *during* the war. His role in the story is simply to heroize two unnamed men who placed their complete trust in their god and were fighting for the freedom of Israel. The citation refers to Deuteronomy 32.30.

59. Kanael (1971), 1; Eshel (1995); Mor (2016), 257. Letters show a corresponding year number date format, though still using the 'For The Redemption of Israel' terminology, e.g. *XHev/Se* 49, *Mur.* 24b.

60. Mildenberg (1980), 315.

61. Mildenberg (1984), 64–65.

62. Porat, Eschel & Frumkin (2007), 42–43. A single *denarius* with the engraved emblem of *Leg.* VI was found among a hoard of sixty silver and bronze coins in a cave at Khirbet Wadi Hamam, which may or may not be connected to the Bar Kokhba War; see Leibner (2009b) and Mor (2016), 169.

63. Jacobson (2013), 31–34.

64. 1 Maccabees 13. Grainger (2012), 36 and 68 disputes that any Maccabean took a fortified place by siege as they lacked siege equipment.

65. 1 Maccabees 13:51 NRSV.

66. Examples: Palm frond – Mildenberg (1984), nos. 14, 17, 42, 50, 55, *et al*; harp: Mildenberg (1984), nos. 9, 11, 12, 13, 15, 27 *et al.*

67. Dio, 69.13.2.

68. *P. Yadin* 52.

69. Talm. B., *Yevamot* 61b; and Aggadic Midrash, Genesis *Rabbah* 62b.

70. An *omer* is a sheaf of barley, and this festival is held at the time of the barley harvest in April or May in accordance with Leviticus 23:15–16.

71. For an explanation see Holtz (2017), 154–156. The message of the story is that the students did not have *kavod* (honour or respect) for one another.

72. E.g. Luke 1:32, 35; John 1:49; Matthew 16:15–16. For a discussion on Christian messianism, see Marcus (1989); and Schiffman (2012), 393–397.
73. E.g. Matthew 6:33, Mark 1:14–15, and Luke 4:43.
74. Matthew 6:10 NIV.
75. Jerome, *Apology for Himself Against the Books of Rufinus* 3.31.
76. Euseb., *Eccl.* 4.8.4.
77. Euseb. *Chron.*, 'Hadrian's Year 17'.
78. Orosius, *Against the Pagans* 7.13.
79. Gruber (1999), 184–185.
80. Evans (1997), 193.
81. *Mur.* 24b.
82. Tiberius: Luke 3:1. Hadrian: Euseb., *Chron.*
83. *P. Yadin* 43.
84. Evans (1997), 200.
85. Milik (1961); Lewis, Yadin & Greenfield (1989); Yadin, Greenfield, Yardeni & Levine (2002); and Yadin (1971), 159–167.
86. *Mur.* 42. For a discussion, see Wise (2015), 233–236.
87. *P. Yadin* 42–47. For a discussion on witnessing of documents, see Schiffman (2003b).
88. *P. Yadin* 42. See Wise (2015), 156.
89. For a discussion of the so-called 'Babatha Archive', see Wise (2015), 148–149, 154–155 and 189–192, and Lewis (1994).
90. Broshi (1992), Ilan (1993), Cotton (1993) and (1999); and Oudshoorn (2007).
91. *P. Yadin* 12.
92. *P. Yadin* 14.
93. *P. Yadin* 15.
94. *P. Yadin* 21 and 22. Katzoff (2007).
95. *P. Yadin* 17. It was not an insignificant sum of money; a Roman legionary's annual salary was 225 *denarii*.
96. *P. Yadin* 26.
97. Dio, 69.14.3.
98. Dio, 69.13.2; and Schürer (1973), 519.
99. *Leg.* XX: – Disertus – *CIL*, XI.5960; Felix – *CIL*, XI.3108 = *RIB* 1814. *Coh.* I *Hispanorum M. Eq.*: Cornelianus – *CIL*, VII.371 = *RIB* 814; Mor (2016), 314–315, 323 and 325; Jarrett (1994), 61. *Coh.* III *Bracaugustanorum*: *CIL* XVI, 69; Mor (2016), 314–315 and 325; Jarrett (1994), 57. *Coh.* IV *Lingonum*: *CIL* XVI, 69; Mor (2016), 315 and 325; Jarrett (1994), 62.
100. Maxfield (1981), 194–196.
101. *CIL*, XI.5960: *C(aio) Ligustinio C(ai) f(ilio) Clu(stumina) Diserto > (centurioni) leg(ionis) XX V(aleriae) V(ictricis), 7 (centurioni) leg(ionis) IIII Scyth(icae), item > (centurioni) leg(ionis) XX V(aleriae) V(ictricis) evocato Aug(usti), benef(iciario) praef(ecti) praet(orio) Eutyches lib(ertus) patrono optimo ob merita cuius dedicatione decurionib(us) et plebei crus[tu]lum et mulsum dedit.* For a discussion see Birley (2016), 67; and Maxfield (1981), 195 citing Birley (1965), 29–30, n.7.
102. See Dio, 55.24.8: 'the *Evocati* ... Augustus began to make a practice of employing from the time when he called again into service against [Marcus] Antonius the troops who had served with his father [Julius Caesar], and he maintained them afterwards; they constitute even now a special corps, and carry rods, like the centurions.'
103. *IGLS* 13.1.9188, discussed in Tacoma, Ivleva & Breeze (2016).
104. Birley (2016), 78.

105. *CIL*, VII.371 = *RIB* 814: *Iovi Aug(usto) M(arcus) Censorius M(arci) fil(ius) Voltinia [C]ornelianus > (centurio) leg(ionis) [X Fr]etensis prae[fec]tus coh(ortis) I Hisp(anorum) ex provincia Narbone[n(si)] domo Nemauso [V.]S.L.M.*
106. Birley (2016), 65.
107. Jarrett (1994), 61.
108. For a discussion of the relationship of Rufus to Severus, see Applebaum (1989).
109. Birley (2016), 62.
110. Cooley & Salway (2012), 223.
111. E.g. Talm. B., *Gittin* 57a-b, and Midrash, Lamentations *Eikha Rabbah* 2.2.4. See Mildenberg (1984), 98.
112. Powell (2018), 184–185.
113. Euseb., *Church Eccl.* 4.6.3.
114. Dio, 69.13.3.
115. For a discussion of the complex at Horbat Zalit, see Alon (1986).
116. On the latest finds from Horbat Zalit, see Fabian, Golan & Goldfus (2015).
117. On excavations at Horbat 'Etri, see Zissu & Ganor (2009).
118. On excavations at Horbat Burgin see Zissu, Ganor, Klein & Klein (2013).
119. *Midrash*, Lamentations *Eikha Rabbah* 1. Emmaus is surmised to have been located in the west of Judea, Kefar Lakatia in the north-east, and Beit El in the north. The location of Emmaus (perhaps a Greek version of the Hebrew word *hammah*, or 'hot spring'), referred to in Luke 24:13–35 as 'about seven miles from Jerusalem', is not known with certainty and has been linked to the Byzantine town of Emmaus Nicopolis, located in the Ayalon Valley near the modern-day Latrun junction, the modern-day village of Motza, between Kiriath Yearim and Jerusalem, and recently with Kiryat Yearim.
120. Kanael (1971), 1; Eshel (1995); Mor (2016), 257. Letters still show a year number date format, though still using the 'For The Redemption of Israel' terminology, e.g. *Mur.* 25; *P. Yadin* 44, 45, 46 and 47; *XHev/Se* 7, 8, 8a and 13; Sedir 2.
121. *P. Yadin* 57. See Yadin (1971), 128–129. The requirement fulfils Leviticus 23:40.
122. See Yadin (1971), 128–129; Havim (1993), 112–113, and Wise (2015), 248–249.
123. *P. Yadin* 52. See Yadin (1971), 130; and Wise (2015), 245–246 and 249–250.
124. Havim (1993), 114–122. Millar (1993), 373 suggests the writer means he did not know how to write Hebrew, rather than Aramaic in calligraphic book hand.
125. *P. Hever* 30. See Wise (2015), 268.
126. *P. Yadin* 53. This letter, found in the 'Cave of Letters', is one in a cache of fifteen belonging to Yehonathan Bar Be'ayan, the co-commander at Ein Gedi: nine are written in Aramaic (*P. Yadin* 50, 53–58, 62–63), four in Hebrew (*P. Yadin* 49, 51, 60–61) and two in Greek (*P. Yadin* 52, 59). For a discussion see Wise (2015), 159.
127. *P. Yadin* 49. Translation in Yadin (1971), 133.
128. *P. Yadin* 49. Translation in Yadin (1971), 139 and Helyer (2002), 435.
129. *P. Yadin* 55.
130. *P. Yadin* 56. Birley (1997), 271 notes that this is the only direct reference to the Romans in all the extant correspondence.
131. Wise (2015), 219. The correspondent had a choice of writing the message in two columns or across the entire width of the 'tablet'. It was then folded to protect the contents inside. A string was wrapped around the outside, held in place via V-shaped notches cut into the ends of the tablet, and the ends of the string would then be tied and optionally sealed. The address of the recipient was written on the outside. For examples from Vindolanda, see Bowman (1994), plate V, VI, VII and VIII.
132. *P. Yadin* 54, column I. Translation in Mevorah, Kreinin & Opper (2015), 25.

133. *P. Yadin* 54, column II. Translation in Mevorah, Kreinin & Opper (2015), 25.
134. *P. Yadin* 50.
135. Evans (1997), 202.
136. Evans (1997), 201.
137. *P. Yadin* 44. Yadin (1971), 176–177.

Chapter Seven: 'A Fence Consisting of the Slain'
1. For a discussion of the archaeological evidence, see Porat, Kalman, Chachy & Zissu (2017), 342 and fig. 11, and 346–347.
2. *Midrash*, Lamentations *Eikha Rabbah* 2.2.4; *cf.* Talm. Y., *Ta'anit* 4:5 [24a].
3. On the spelling of the name and its etymology, see Carroll (1923–24), 78–80.
4. Euseb., *Eccl.* 4.6.3. The '18th year' corresponds to 10 August 134 CE–9 August 135 CE.
5. Carroll (1923–24), 79 mentions several locations. Applebaum (1987) argues for et-Tira. Zissu (2008), 187 notes that there is support for Horbat Tura (or Khurbet Sammunieh by its Arabic name), lying some 7.5 km (4.1 mi.) to the west of Battir. The ancient site is not to be confused with the modern Israeli town of Beitar Illit which is also located nearby.
6. The explorers to Battir include E. Robinson (1852), V. Guérin (1868), C. Clermont-Ganneau (1874) and E. Zickermann (1906).
7. Yadin (1971), 192–193.
8. The 'mountains of Bether' are mentioned in Canticles (Song of Solomon) 2:17. The valley was inscribed in the UNESCO World Heritage List in June 2014: https://whc.unesco.org/en/list/1492 (accessed 30 July 2020).
9. Clermont-Ganneau (1899), 470.
10. Talm. Y., *Ta'anit* 4:8 [69a]; *Midrash*, Lamentations *Eikha Rabah* 2:2 no. 4; *cf. Midrash* Haggadah to Deuteronomy 28:52.
11. Ussishkin (1993), 95.
12. For examples, see Hirschfeld (1998).
13. On a possible *mutatio* or road station at Betar see Neef (1981).
14. Talm. B., *Gittin* 58a.
15. Talm. B., *Gittin* 57a.
16. Ussishkin (1993), 95.
17. For the paper on his excavations, see Carroll (1923–24).
18. Carroll (1923–24), 94 referring to bastions B4–B5, the blocked-up G1 and open G2.
19. Carroll (1923–24), 78 and 85.
20. Carroll (1923–24), 97.
21. Ussishkin (1993), 95.
22. Ussishkin (1993), 78–82.
23. Ussishkin (1993), 84 and 94.
24. Euseb., *Eccl.* 4.6.3.
25. Ussishkin (1993), 93–94.
26. Ussishkin (1993), 91–92.
27. Ussishkin (1993), 84.
28. Ussishkin (1993), 92–93.
29. *Midrash*, Lamentations *Eikha Rabbah* 2.2.4.
30. *Midrash*, Lamentations *Eikha Rabbah* 2.2.4. The last line of *Zechariah* 11:17 NIV reads: 'May his arm be completely withered, his right eye totally blinded!'
31. Camps: Yadin (1971), 193 states the larger measures 400 m x 200 m (1,312ft x 656ft), the smaller 200 m x 120 m (656ft x 394ft); Kennedy & Riley (1990), 103

states Camp 'A' measures c. 380 m x c. 218 m (c. 1,240ft x c. 710ft) vs. Camp 'B' c. 198 m x 133 m (c. 645ft x 435ft) covers 2.63 ha (6.5 acres). On the logistics of the Roman army and the role of the *praefectus castrorum*, see Roth (1999), 272–273 and 279–328.

32. Kennedy & Riley (1990), 103, see fig. 50.
33. Kennedy & Riley (1990), 103 and 99 citing several scholars who estimated '7,500 Roman men, almost entirely infantry' were at the siege of Masada.
34. *Midrash*, Lamentations *Eikha Rabbah* 2.2.4.
35. Euseb., *Eccl.* 4.6.3.
36. Caes., *Bell. Gall.* 7.69, 7.72–73.
37. Jos., *Bell. Iud.* 7.8.3–5.
38. *Midrash*, Lamentations *Eikha Rabbah* 2.2.4.
39. Ussishkin (1993), 68.
40. Ussishkin (1993), 66 citing Alt (1927), 11–16.
41. Clermont-Ganneau (1899), 464.
42. Clermont-Ganneau (1899), 464–465.
43. Clermont-Ganneau (1899), 465.
44. Clermont-Ganneau (1899), 465.
45. Clermont-Ganneau (1899), 465–466.
46. Euseb., *Eccl.* 4.6.
47. While a full member of the Ermine Street Guard re-enactment and research society I often fired the reconstructed Roman artillery weapons to demonstrate their capabilities to the public. An iron-tipped bolt fired from the *catapulta* can penetrate a plywood board placed 30.5 m (100ft) away. A stone – or an orange or cabbage as a safe substitute – can be thrown by either a *ballista* or *onager* over 91.4 m (300ft).
48. Bennett (1997), 100; on 199 he notes that Trajan took Seleucia and Ctesiphon during the Parthian War in 116 without a fight.
49. Apollodorus' *Poliorcetica* Introduction is discussed by Mor (2016) 154–155, citing Blyth (1992) and other scholars.
50. *Midrash*, Lamentations *Eikha Rabbah* 2.2.4.
51. *Tosefta*, *Yevamot* 14:15.
52. Ussishkin (1993), 95.
53. Talm. B., *Gittin* 57a.
54. Talm. B., *Gittin* 57a-b. Forty *se'ah* weigh approximately 217.5kg (700lb). Four *mil* are approximately 4.0 km (2.5 mi.).
55. Talm. B., *Gittin* 57a-b. The parable of the tractate concludes: 'Their sins immediately caused them to be slain. Their heads were brought to Hadrian, who asked: "Who killed them?" A Cuthean replied: "I slew him." And the emperor ordered him to fetch their bodies. He went and found a snake encircling their necks. So Hadrian, when told of this, exclaimed: "If their God had not slain them, who could have overcome them?" And there was applied to him the verse: *Except their rock* [Kefar] *had given them over.*'
56. It echoes the alleged meeting between Vespasian and Rabbi Ben Zakkai in Jerusalem.
57. *Mishnah*, *Ta'anit* (4:6). Perhaps 4 August 135 CE. See Schulman (1858).
58. *Midrash*, Lamentations *Eikha Rabbah* 2.2.4.
59. Talm. B., *Gittin* 57a.
60. Talm. B., *Gittin* 57a.
61. Talm. B., *Gittin* 57b.

Chapter Eight: 'They Were Sitting in a Cave'

1. Joshua 15:2.
2. For a discussion of the town of Ein Gedi, see Hadas (2006) and Wise (2015), 180–183.
3. For a discussion on housing at Ein Gedi, see Cotton (1996) and Wise (2015), 182–183.
4. *P. Yadin* 19. The word '*beit midrash*' is partly restored.
5. For a discussion on the Roman army in Ein Gedi, see Hadas (1993), 47; Holder (2003), 114–115; and Isaac (1990), 137, 174 and 430. Cotton (1996), 197 and 199 notes that the Romans left between the time *P. Yadin* 11 (6 May 124 CE) and *P. Yadin* 19 (16 April 128 CE) were written.
6. Pliny, *NH* 5.17 comments on the fertility of the soil and groves of palm trees being second only to Jerusalem. On *balsamum*, see *NH* 12.54.
7. For a discussion of fish remains found at Win Gedi, see Lernau (2005).
8. Pliny, *NH* 13.9.
9. For a discussion on the perfume produced at Ein Gedi, see Porath & Porath (2005), 237 and Iluz, Hoffman, Gilboa-Garber & Amar (2010).
10. Pliny, *NH* 12.54.
11. Wise (2015), 181 citing the Aramaic inscription in the mosaic floor of the Byzantine-era synagogue referring to 'secret of the village'.
12. For a discussion on the trade, see Manolaraki (2015), and Wise (2015), 181.
13. *P. Yadin* 50.
14. Hadas (1993), 47–49 and fig. 1.
15. *P. Yadin* 12. See Yadin (1961), 47.
16. Hadas, Liphschitz & Bonani (2005), 301–304.
17. Pliny, *NH* 2.106 and 35.178. Nissenbaum, Aizenstat & Golderg (1984).
18. For a discussion of boats used on the Dead Sea, see Oron, Galili, Hadas & Klein (2015), 65.
19. Scientists estimate that at the present rate of decline it will disappear by 2050. Sue Surkes writes in an article entitled 'Sinking Israel-Jordan relations leave Dead Sea, a natural wonder, low and dry' in *The Times of Israel* dated 7 November 2019: 'Israel's Regional Development Ministry reports that since 1976, the Dead Sea's surface area has almost halved and its elevation has dropped more than 40 metres (130 feet) – from 390 metres (1,280 feet) below sea level to minus 434 metres (minus 1,425 feet) today.': https://www.timesofisrael.com/sinking-israel-jordan-relations-leave-dead-sea-a-natural-wonder-low-and-dry (accessed 30 July 2020).
20. The correspondence refers to a 'Fourth Year': e.g. *Mur* 30.
21. Eusebius, *In Isaiam Prophetam* 2:15.
22. Porath & Porath (2009), 239.
23. For a discussion of hiding complexes, see Zissu & Kloner (2014), fig. 7 on 102, Zissu & Kloner (2014), and Shivtiel & Frumkin (2014).
24. Caves were also used in the Galilee as refuges: see Shivte'el (2019). Contra Shivte'el on their use in the Bar Kokhba War see Mor (2016), 165–168.
25. For an analysis of sediments in the 'Cave of the Letters', see Frumkin (2001).
26. For a review of documents found, see Feldman (2019).
27. Porat, Kalman, Chachy & Zissu (2017), 347. See also the Leon Levy Dead Sea Scrolls Digital Library: https://www.deadseascrolls.org.il/home (accessed 30 July 2020).
28. For a discussion of the 'Cave of the Spear' see Porat, Eshel & Frumkin (2009), 39–41.
29. Porat, Eshel & Frumkin (2009), 33 and fig. 9:13; the spearhead was found in Cave 84b.

30. For a discussion of the 'Har Yishai Cave, see Porat, Eshel & Frumkin (2007), 35–44.
31. For a discussion of the Sabar Cave, see Porat, Eshel & Frumkin (2007), 44–51.
32. For a discussion of the 'Cave of the Rope', see Klein and Porat (2016).
33. For a discussion of the 'Cave of the Vulture', see Yadin (1961).
34. Called 'Cave 32', it is located at the top of a high vertical cliff in the northern bank of Nahal Ze'elim Valley near Masada. It is also known as the 'Cave of Skulls' because seven human skulls were found there in 1960. See Booth & Eglash (2016).
35. Aharoni (1962), 186–188.
36. For a discussion of Cave B, see Klein, Davidovich, Ganor & Sukenik (2019).
37. Yadin (1961), 50 and plate 22; Yadin (1971), 120–121; Wise (2015), 202.
38. Yadin (1971), 113–114, photograph on 112; Wise (2015), 301–302.
39. For photographs see Yadin (1961), plates 18–21 and Yadin (1971), 67–68, 70–72, 74–77, 80–83, 91–119, 195–196, 198–200 and 202–210.
40. Yadin (1961), 197–200.
41. For a discussion of the 'Cave of Horrors' see Aharoni (1962).
42. Aharoni (1962), plates 25–34.
43. Aharoni (1962), 186.
44. Yadin (1971), 49.
45. *P. Yadin* 11 refers; Holder (2003), 114–115. Cotton (1996), 197 and 199 notes that the Romans left between the time *P. Yadin* 11 (6 May 124 CE) and *P. Yadin* 19 (16 April 128 CE) was written.
46. *Midrash*, Lamentations *Eikha Rabbah* i 45. For a discussion of catastrophes in Jewish literature, see Cohen (1982).
47. For an analysis of the bones, see Aharoni (1962).
48. For an analysis of the bones, see Nathan (1961).
49. For photographs, see Yadin (1971), 62–64.
50. Wise (2015), 204–205.
51. For a discussion of later use of the caves, see Aharoni (1962) and Pearson (1998), 198.
52. Yadin (1971), 49.
53. Dio, 69.15.1.

Chapter Nine: 'He Liberated Syria Palaestina from the Enemy'
1. Euseb., *Eccl.* 4.6.1.
2. Powell (2018), 171 citing Augustus, *Res Gestae* 13.
3. Tac., *Agricola* 30.
4. Lau (2011), 283 citing *Seder Olam Raba* 30.
5. Dio, 69.13.2–3.
6. Dio, 69.14.1–2.
7. *Midrash*, Lamentations *Eikha Rabbah* 2:2.4.
8. *Midrash*, Exodus *Rabbah* 30.12 [on 21:1].
9. Dio, 69.14.3.
10. Fronto, *Correspondence* 2.
11. Manning (1980), 113–114 and 120.
12. Jos., *Ant. Iud.* 17.288 and 295 records that after the revolt of the summer of 4 BCE Varus rounded up the culprits and, though he let many go, he crucified 2,000.
13. See Powell (2018), 183. Having defeated the rebellious Salassi in 25 BCE, A. Terentius Varro sold some 36,000 prisoners of war into slavery; Nero Claudius Drusus had used the same approach against the Raeti in 15 BCE, and his brother Ti. Caesar had employed it after a revolt in Illyricum in 12 BCE.

14. Watson (1987), 8 citing Justinian, *Institutes* 1.3.3. Hadrian made changes to the laws on the treatment of slaves, per *HA, Had.* 18.7–8: 'He forbade masters to kill their slaves, and ordered that any who deserved it should be sentenced by the courts. He forbade anyone to sell a slave or a maid-servant to a procurer or trainer of gladiators without giving a reason therefore.'

15. Lau (2011), 382. Mor (2016), 472 notes that no Jewish sources make direct reference to this activity, only the Christian.

16. Jerome, *Commentaria in Jeremaiam* 31; Jerome, *Commentaria in Zechariam* 9:2.

17. Lau (2011), 383. For a discussion of Hadrian's anti-Jewish decrees, see Herr (1968).

18. Euseb., *Eccl.* 4.6.3–4; *cf.* Orosius, *Against the Pagans* 7.13: 'The emperor gave orders that no Jew should be permitted to enter Jerusalem and that only Christians should be permitted to occupy the city.' For commentary see Mor (2016), 473–474.

19. Euseb., *Chron.* 'Hadrian Year 20' (136 CE).

20. Boatwright (2000), 202, and Horbury (2014), 408.

21. *CIL*, XVI.87: The trooper is named Caius, son of Lucius, who originated from Nicaea in Bithynia. He had served in *Cohors* II *Ulpia Galatarum*.

22. For a discussion of *Legio* VI *Ferrata*, see Cotton (2000).

23. Mor (2016), 472.

24. Maxfield (1981), 55–66 and 194–197.

25. *CIL*, XI.6339. Mor (2003), 121. See Maxfield (1981), 76–79 for a discussion of the *corona muralis* and 79–80 for the *corona vallaris*.

26. *CIL*, XIV.3610 = *ILS* 1071.

27. Priscus: *CIL*, VI.1523 = *ILS* 1092 – *[M(arco) Stati]o M(arci) f(ilio) Cl(audia) Prisco [L]icinio Italico, leg(ato) Augustorum pr(o) pr(aetore) prov(inciae) Cappadociae, leg(ato) Aug[g.=Augustorum duorum)] pr(o) pr(aetore) prov(inciae) Brittanniae, leg(ato) Aug[g.=Augustorum duorum)] pr(o) pr(aetore) prov(inciae) Moesiae super(ioris), curato[ri] alvei Tiberis et cl[o]acarum urbis, c[o(n)s(uli)], leg(ato) Aug(usti) prov(inciae) Daciae, leg(ato) leg(ionis) XIII G(eminae) p(iae) f(idelis), leg(ato) leg(ionis) [X] IIII Gem(inae) Martiae Victricis, sacerdoti Titiali [Fl]aviali, pr(aetori) inter cives et peregrinos, tr(ibuno) pl(ebis), quaes[t(ori)], proc(uratori) Aug(usti) XX (Vicesimae) hereditatium prov(inciarum) Narbone(n)s(is) et Aquita[n(iae), p]r(aefecto) eq(uitum) alae I pr(aetoriae) c(ivium) R(omanorum), tr(ibuno) mil(itum) leg(ionis) I Adiutr(icis) p(iae) f(idelis) et ;eg(ionis) X [G(eminae)] p(iae)[f(idelis) e]t leg(ionis) IIII [sic: a mistake for III] Gallicae, praef(ecto) coh(ortis) IIII Lingonum, vexillo mi[l(itari) d] onato a divo Hadriano in expeditione Iudaic[a], Q(uintus) Cassius Domitius Palumbus.* Dexter: *CIL*, VIII.8934 = *ILS* 1400 – *Sex(to) Cornelio Sex(ti) filio Ar(nensi tribu) Dextro proc(uratori) Asiae, iuridico Alexandriae, proc(uratori) Neaspoleos et mausolea, praef(ecto) classis Syr(iacae), donis miltarib(us) donato a divo Hadriano on bellum Iudaicum hasta pura et vexillo, praef(ecto) alae I Aug(ustae) Gem(ellae) colonorum, trib(uno) leg(ionis) VIII Aug(ustae), praef(ecto) coh(ortis) V Raetorum, praef(ecto) fabrum III, patrono coloniae, P. Blaesius Felix (centurio) leg(ionis) II Traian(ae) fort(is), adfini piisimo, ob merita.* For a discussion of *dona* see Maxfield (1981) – *vexillum*: 82–84; – *hasta*: 84–86.

28. *CIL*, III.7334 = *ILS* 2080; Offord (1898), 62. See Maxfield (1981), 82–84 for a discussion of the *corona aurea*.

29. *AE* 1937, 101.

30. *CIL*, XI.3108.

31. *CIL*, XI.3733 = *ILS* 2083. On Constans see Mor (2003), 120–121 and Maxfield (1981), 211–212.

32. For a report on the archaeological research at the site, see Kloner (1988).

33. *CIL*, VIII.6706 = *ILS* 1965 (Castellum Tidditanorum) – *Q(uinto) Lollio M(arci) f(il)(io) Quir(ina) Urbico, co(n)s(uli) leg(ato) Aug(usti) provinc(iae) Germ(aniae) inferioris, fetiali, legato Imp(eratoris) Hadriani in expedition(e) Iudaica qua donatus est hasta pura corona aurea, leg(ato) leg(ionis) X Geminae, praet(ori) candidat(o) Caes(aris), trib(uno) pleb(is), candidat(o) Caes(aris), leg(ato) proco(n)s(ulis) Asiae, quaest(oris) urbis, trib(uno) laticlavio leg(ionis) XXII Primigeniae, IIIIviro viarum curand(arum) patrono d(ecreto) d(ecurionum) p(ecunia) p(ublica).* For a discussion, see Eck (2003), 166–170.
34. Marcellus: *AE* 1934, 231 – *C(aius) Quinctius C(ai) f(ilius) Vel(ina tribu), Certus Poblicius Marcellus co(n)s(ul), augur, legat(us) divi Hadrian(i) provinc(iarum) Syriae et German(iae) Superior(is), ornament(is) triumphalibus.* Nepos: *CIL*, XI.5212 = *ILS* 1058 – *T. Haterio Nepoti Atinati Probo Publicio Mateniano co(n)s(uli), pontif(ici), triumphalib(us) [ornamentis honoration –].* Severus: *AE* 1904, 9 (Aequum) – *Cn(aeo) Iul(io) S[evero] co(n)su(uli), le[g]ato) Aug(usti)] pr(o) pr(aetore) pr[ovic(iae)] Syriae Pa[laestinae], triunf[alibus [sic: a mistake for triumphalibus] ornamen]tis [honoratio –];* and *CIL*, III.2830 – *Huic [senatus a]uctore [imp(eratore) Trai]ano Hadrian[o Au] g(usto) ornamenta triu[mph]alia decrevit ob res in [Iu]daea [sic] prospere ge[st]as.*
35. Dio, 54.33.5.
36. The triumph was held on 26 May 17 CE. See Powell (2013), 120–122.
37. Marcellus in Aquileia; Nepos in Fuligniae; Severus in Burnum and Aequum; Urbicus in Castellum Tidditanorum.
38. Eck (2003), 169.
39. Mor (2016), 170.
40. Maxfield (1981), 241.
41. Mor (2003), 121; Eck (2003), 160, n.31.
42. Augustus had received twenty-one acclamations: see Powell (2018), 193–194 and Table 7.
43. *CIL*, VI.974 = 40524. See Eck (2003), 162–163.
44. For a discussion see Fuchs (2014), and Eck (2003b), 162. The restored text reads: *[S(enatus) P(opulus)que] R(omanus) [Imp(eratori) Caes(ari) divi Traiani] Parthici f(ilio) [divi Nervae nep(oti) Traiano Ha]driano Aug(usto), [pont(ifici) max(imo), trib(unicia) potest(ate) XX(?), imp(eratori)] II, co(n)s(uli) III, p(atri) p(atriae), [quod summon pugnandi a]dore misso [exercitu suo superatis imperat]oribus max[imis Syriam Palaestinam ab ho]ste liberavit.*
45. Horbury (2014), 280.
46. The first restoration of the text by Eck (2001) reads: *Imp(eratori) Cae[s(ari) divi T]ra [iani Par] | th[i]ci f(ilio) d[ivi Nervae Nep(oti) Tr]aiano [Hadriano Aug |(usto)] pon[t]if(i) m[ax(imo), Trib(unicia pot(estate) XX(?), imp(eratori) I]I, co(n)s(uli) [III, p(atri) p(atriae) S(enatus) P(opulus)Q(ue) R(omanus)?].* The alternative restoration of the text by Eck (2001) reads: *Imp(eratori) Cae[s(ari) divi T]ra [iani Par] | th[i]ci f(ilio) d[ivi Nervae Nep(oti) Tr]aiano [Hadriano Aug | (usto)] pon[t]if(i) m[ax(imo), Trib(unicia potest(ate) XIII]I(?), imp(eratori) I]I, co(n)s(uli) [III, p(atri) p(atriae) Leg(ionis) X Fret(ensis)?].* See Bowersock (2003), 171–176 and fig. 7, 8; Eck (2005); and Eck & Foerster (1999).
47. Bowersock (2003), 175 critiquing Eck (1999), and Eck (2001).
48. Bowersock (2003), 174.
49. Eck (2003), 170.
50. *Senatus Consultum de Honoribus Germanici Decernendis (Tabula Siarensis)*, Fragment 1 in Powell (2013), 220–221.
51. Boatwright (2000), 202.
52. Galor & Bloedhorn (2013), 120–122.

53. The words reportedly uttered by Pontius Pilatus of Jesus of Nazareth (c. 33 CE) in John 19:5. It translates as 'Behold! The man.'
54. Eliav (2003), 243–245 and 277, map 2.
55. For the dimensions of the arch in Gerash see Ch. 3, n.21. The Arch of Constantine is the largest-known Roman triumphal arch, with overall dimensions of 21.0 m high x 25.9 m wide x 7.4 m deep (68.9ft x 84.9ft x 24.3ft). It has three bays, the central one being 11.5 m high x 6.5 m wide (37.7ft x 21.3ft); the laterals each measure 7.4 m x 3.4 m (24.3ft x 11.2ft).
56. Gimbash (2009), 66.
57. *Aureus*, gold, Rome mint, struck 136 CE; Hadrian, bareheaded bust right, slight drapery, with rejuvenated features, *HADRIANVS AVG COS III P P*; reverse: *IOVI VICTORI*, Jupiter, naked to waist, seated left on throne, holding Victoriola on his extended right hand and a vertical sceptre in left. *RIC* II.3 2209, *BMCRE* 658, *cf.* Biaggi 616–7, Mazzini 863.
58. *Aureus*, gold Rome mint, 136 CE; *HADRIANVS AVG COS III P P*, bareheaded and draped bust right; reverse: *VICTOR IA AVG*, Victory, naked to waist, advancing right, head left, holding up wreath in right hand and palm frond in left. *RIC* II.3 2238, Calicó 1393 var., *BMCRE* 764 var., Biaggi 763 var., Mazzini 1453 var. *Denarius*, silver, Rome mint, struck 134–138 CE; *HADRIANVS AVG COS III P P*, laureate head of Hadrian to right; reverse: *VICTORIA AVG* Nemesis-Victory standing to right, drawing out fold of her dress with her right hand and holding branch with her left; *BMC* 761. Cohen 1455, *RIC* 282, *RIC²* 2239.
59. Eshel, Zissu & Barkay (2010) report that bronze rebel coins have been found in the former Roman provinces of Britannia (Londinium), Dacia (Ilişua, Pojejena and Ulpia Traiana Sarmizegetusa) and Pannonia (Brigetio, Carnuntum and Vindobona).
60. Dio, 69.23.2; and *HA, Had.* 25.7.
61. Dio, 69.20.1.
62. Dio, 69.22.1–3 and *HA, Had.* 24.12–13.
63. *HA, Had.* 25.6.
64. *HA, Had.* 25.9.
65. Translation in D. Johnson (1876). For a discussion see Barb (1950) and Barnes (1968). In his last days, Hadrian may also have written an autobiography of which *P. Fay* 19 might be a part: see Bollansée (1994).
66. The 6th day before the Ides of July. Dio, 69.23.1; *HA, Had.* 25.11.
67. Petrakis (1980) writes: 'This diagnosis [that Hadrian died from congestive heart failure resulting from hypertension and coronary atherosclerosis] is supported by the identification of bilateral diagonal ear creases on sculptures of several busts of Hadrian as well as literary evidence of behaviour pattern A.'
68. The circular, conical Mausoleum of Augustus measured 90 m (295ft) in diameter and rose to 42 m (137ft) in height. The conical Mausoleum of Hadrian rose to 50 m (164ft) in height at the top of its central tower, set within a square compound measuring 115 m (377ft) on each side.
69. *HA, Had.* 25.7.
70. Dio, 69.23.2 and *HA, Had.* 24.1 and 27.2–3. See text of OIM E8349, *P.Fay* 19 in Bollansée (1994).
71. *HA, Ant. Pius* 8 and *HA, Verus* 3.
72. Jerome, *On Matthew* 24:15.

Chapter Ten: 'Son of a Lie'

1. Translation by Ovadia Abed.
2. *Tosefta, Berakhot* 2:13. Lau (2011), 357.

3. Holtz (2017), 166 notes that the story appears in a *Midrash* on Proverbs dating to the ninth century CE and in this telling Akiba is already dead and was taken to Caesarea for burial.
4. Lau (2011), 357.
5. Lau (2011), 358.
6. Lau (2011), 359.
7. Lau (2011), 357–361.
8. It is a punishment cited in 1 Kings 12:11. Jesus of Nazareth was scourged with such a whip prior to his crucifixion per Matthew 27:26.
9. One of two daily prayers specified in the *Torah* (Deuteronomy 6:4), beginning 'Hear, O Israel, the Lord is our God.'
10. Talm. Y., *Berakhot* 9:5; *cf.* Talm. B., *Berakhot* 61b.
11. For a discussion of the differences in the accounts and meaning of the scenes, see Holtz (2017), 167–172.
12. For a discussion of Akiba's alleged support of Ben Kosiba, see Novenson (2009).
13. Novenson (2009), 572; and Gruber (1999), 75.
14. Novenson (2009), 564–565 and 570–571.
15. See Chapter 6, n.55.
16. Exodus 23:2; *Mishnah Rosh Hashanah* 2.8.9.
17. Gruber (1999), 193.
18. Schürer (1973), 552.
19. The other nine were Rabbi Yishmael Ben Elisha, Kohen Gadol, Rabban Shim'on Ben Gamliel, Rabbi Chanina Ben Teradyon, Rabbi Chutzpit Hameturageman, Rabbi Elazar Ben Shamua and Rabbi Chanina Ben Chachinai. Rabbi Yeshayvav the Scribe, Rabbi Yehuda Ben Dama and Rabbi Yehuda Ben Bava.
20. Scholars now agree that it was composed in Spain, likely by the thirteenth-century Castilian kabbalist Rabbi Moshe de Leon and multiple other authors. This book forms the basis of mystical Judaism known as *kabbalah*.
21. Zerubavel (2003), 283.
22. On the centres of Jewish learning, see Jensen (2014). Akiba's students began their work at Usha: see Mantel (1957).
23. For a discussion of the early history of the *Halakah* see Lauterbach (1915). The *Gemara* were in Caesarea and Tiberias, Sura, Pumbedita and later Baghdad.
24. Segal (1986), 174.
25. Schäfer (2003b), 2; and Horbury (2014), 422.
26. Marks (1994), 13–56.
27. *Kazab* means 'falsehood' in Aramaic and 'lie' in Hebrew. Weiss (2014), 105.
28. Hammer (1985), 41.
29. Hammer (1985), 53.
30. Evans (1997), 202, n.66.
31. Horbury (2014), 425.
32. Tert., *Apol.* 21.1. For a discussion of *licita religio*, see Hasselhof & Strothmann (2016).
33. A statue was erected and dedicated to Antoninus Pius in Jerusalem (*CIIP* 2, 718). The rectangular block of stone had been inserted upside-down, high up in the southern wall of the Ummayad Palace on the Temple Mount. It was first published in 1843.
34. Horbury (2014), 423 citing Jerome, *In Daniel* on 11:34–35.
35. Ammian., 23.1.2.
36. Ammian., 23.1.3.
37. Mor (2016), 484.
38. Visotzky (2016); Seder, 98–99 and 104; Homeric style of study, 100–104; Midrash, 90–98; mosaics, 49–50 and 190–200.

39. Mor (2016), 484.
40. Zissu & Ganor (2009), 103–104; and Seelentag (2017), 200–202.
41. Zissu, Ganor, Klein & Klein (2013), 34–35, 39 and 50.
42. Zissu (1999), 95–96.
43. The text portion of the mosaic was removed and is now displayed at Jerusalem's Schottenstein Campus.
44. A scroll from the Book of Leviticus and a bronze seven-branched *menorah* were found during excavations of the site.
45. For a discussion of Jewish soldiers in the Roman army, see Oppenheimer (2005b) and Schoenfield (2006).
46. For a discussion of the wall paintings of the Dura-Europos synagogue, see Weisman (2012).
47. Schoenfield (2006), 124. The Edict specifically approved Nicene Christianity; other Christian sects were deemed heretical and lost their legal status, and their properties were confiscated by the Roman state.
48. Callincum: Ambrose, *Epistles* 40, 41.27. Ban: Schoenfield (2006), 124.
49. Limor (1997), 94–95; and Schoenfield (2006), 124–125.
50. Augustine of Hippo, *City of God* 18.46.
51. For a discussion of the legal position of Jewry, see Brewer (2005).
52. Segal (1986), 174. In Galatians 3:28 St Paul argues the only way to equality is through Christ.
53. For a discussion of Jews in Christian lands, see Limor (1997).
54. Limor (1997), 99.
55. Limor (1997), 87–90.
56. Limor (1997), 105.
57. For a discussion of Jews in Muslim lands, see Gerber (1997).
58. For a discussion of *dhimmi* law, see Shah (1998).
59. Gerber (1997), 156–158.
60. Lehmann & Magid (2010), 1; Sorkin (1997), 232.
61. Gubbay (2000), 59.
62. Kurtz (2019) argues that between 1820 and 1880 'ancient Jewish history did not provide a compelling model for the dominant (Protestant) German scholars of the age, which then prompted the decline of antique Judaism as a field of interest.' Moreover, 'the perceived national and political failures of ancient Jews – alongside the ethnic or religious ones discerned by others – thus made antique Judaism an unattractive object of study in this period' (from the Abstract).
63. Marks (1994), 57–97.
64. Marks (1994), 99–134.
65. Marks (1994), 135–183.

Chapter Eleven: 'He Was a Hero'

1. For a discussion of the evolution of the King Arthur legend, see Wood (1981), 37–60.
2. For the full text of the story, see Mayer (1840).
3. Mayer (1840), 142–144 is the first time the lion appears in the Bar Kokhba legend. See also Turel (2016), 11e, 13 [Hebrew].
4. For a discussion of Goldfadn's work, see Wolitz (2002).
5. The New York edition has seventeen pieces, while the London edition has eighteen.
6. Turel (2016), 11e, 14–15 [Hebrew].
7. Sorkin (1997), 234–235; and Wolitz (2002), 53–54.
8. Dorf, 5.

9. Dorf, 14.
10. Dorf, 14.
11. For a critical survey of Szyk's work, see Luckert (2002).
12. Sorkin (1997), 232.
13. Penslar (1997), 315–318. *Alliyah* is Hebrew for 'ascent'.
14. Penslar (1997), 309–313.
15. Penslar (1997), 313; and Tuchman (2014), 242–266. Though often called the 'Uganda Scheme', the proposed area was in what is now Kenya.
16. The enlarged nose and pointed hat were typical tropes, e.g. Limor (1997), 99 and 118.
17. Presner (2007), 1.
18. For a discussion of sporting clubs, see Brenner & Reuveni (2006).
19. Turel (2016), 12e/18 [Hebrew], and 16 fig. 4. The guiding principle of Bar Kokhba groups was heroism or strength (*Hagibor*), while for the rival Makkabi it was power (*Hakoach*).
20. Presner (2007), 73.
21. Turel (2016), 13e, 20–21 [Hebrew].
22. Founded in 1938, the Museum of Art at Ein-Harod was one of the first art museums to be founded in Israel.
23. Penslar (1997), 303–322.
24. The original letter is in the collection of the British Library, London.
25. Eban (1972), 30. For a discussion of the Jewish Legion, see Watts (2004).
26. Penslar (1997), 322–326.
27. Turel (2016), 12e, 20 [Hebrew].
28. Penslar (1997), 339–343. The Betar group was founded in Lithuania in 1923.
29. Zerubavel (2003), 283.
30. Hear the song at: https://kkl-jnf-education.kulam.org/a/34333 (accessed 30 July 2020). For a discussion on the song, see Zerubavel (1995), 105–107. Zerubavel (2003), 297, n.46 claims that 'the hero's encounter with the lion first appeared in a serialized novel' by Levner, but it is wrong as that honour goes to Samuel Mayer. On Bar Kokhba in Israeli popular culture, see Weiss (2014) and Weiss (2017).
31. Zerubavel (2003), 297.
32. Being Jewish, the Nazi German government did not permit her to participate in the 1936 Summer Olympic Games.
33. *Bar Kochba Berlin* was the largest club with a total of 1,300 members, but clubs with more than 200 members existed in Breslau, Hannover, Kassel and Frankfurt (Main).
34. Yad Vashem, *Jews and Sport Before the Holocaust: A Visual Retrospective*. https://www.yadvashem.org/yv/en/exhibitions/sport/index.asp# (accessed 30 July 2020).
35. For a discussion of the Jewish sports movement in Nazi Germany, see Wahlig (2015).
36. Other minorities who were victims of the Nazi death camps included communists, gypsies, disabled and gay men. Lili Henoch and her mother were deported from the Riga Ghetto and machine-gunned to death by an *Einsatzgruppe* mobile killing unit in September 1942.
37. Penslar (1997), 343.
38. Naor (2016), 81e–95e/152–177 [Hebrew].
39. Naor (2016), 95e/169 [Hebrew] citing the review of A. Uriel.
40. Wasserstein (1997), 357.
41. On 29 November 1947, the United Nations General Assembly adopted the Partition Plan for Palestine published as 'A/RES/181(II)'.
42. Rowland (1985), 252 and 256–257.
43. Cline (2004), 269–270.

44. Wasserstein (1997), 357. Cline (2004), 272–273 notes that the 14th was a Friday and in order to comply with *Shabbat*, Ben Gurion read the Declaration over the radio at 16:00 hours local time and announced that it came into force at 24:00 hours.
45. Wasserstein (1997), 358.
46. Cline (2004), 267–284.
47. For a discussion of the *menorah* project, see Towndrow (1949).
48. For a discussion of the funding of the *menorah* project, see Arbel & Ben Hanan (1972).
49. Zerubavel (2003), 284, n.11.
50. Zerubavel (2003), 284, n.12.
51. Zerubavel (2003), 285.
52. For examples, see Turel (2016), 40–45, 117–122, 133 and 156–157.
53. Stamps were issued featuring different coins in 3, 5, 10, 30, 40, 60, 85, 95, 100 and 125 *Israeli Pound* denominations. On the history of hyper-inflation in Israel, see Bahar (2016).
54. According to the explanatory leaflet printed by Israel Coins and Medals Co. Ltd, the large medal of 115g of silver was 'not for sale', but a limited edition of 5,000 were made of 30g of silver and 20,000 were made of 120g of bronze.
55. Turel (2016), 40–41. First day of issue was 21 August 1961.
56. The image appears modelled on a Syrian archer (*Sagittarius*) of the type seen on Trajan's Column in scenes LXX.1–10, CVIII.28, 30–1 and CXV.2, 4–5.
57. First day of issue was 17 December 2008. The *New Israeli Shekel* (NIS) replaced the old currency on 1 January 1986 and replaced the hyper-inflated old *shekel* at the ratio of 1000:1.
58. The featured letter is *Mur* 43. See Ch. 5, n.62.
59. Quoted in Turel (2016), 15e/24 [Hebrew]. For the Eichmann trial, see Shapira (2004b).
60. Quoted from the dust jacket of the Random House first American edition.
61. Quoted from the dust jacket of the Random House first American edition.
62. Quoted from the dust jacket of the Random House first American edition.
63. For a discussion of propagating the Bar Kokhba legend in Israeli education, see Grossman (2016).
64. Zerubavel (2003), 295.
65. Grossman (2016), 150–151.
66. Harkabi (1983), 36.
67. Harkabi quoted in Friedman (1982).
68. Harkabi (1983), 65.
69. Harkabi (1983), 79–84.
70. Wasserstein (1997), 368–369.
71. Zerubavel (2003), 291–292.
72. Eldad (1971), 69–70, 84–87 and 106–107.
73. Turel (2016), 16e/24 [Hebrew].
74. The event is described in *The New York Times* report by Friedman (1982).
75. Turel (2016), 15e/24 [Hebrew].
76. Zerubavel (2003), 292–293.
77. The event is described in *The New York Times* report by Shipler (1982).
78. There was bad feeling between the two men. The year before, while Deputy Prime Minister, Yadin had told Prime Minister Begin, 'You have lost control of the defence establishment.' He retired from politics in 1981.
79. Elon (1996), 179.
80. Quoted in Shipler (1982).
81. Quoted in Singer (2015).

82. Elon (1996), 179.
83. Translated by Asia Arutyunov. She notes that the expression 'May their souls be tied to the Knot of Life' is a common saying in Hebrew, equivalent to 'Rest in Peace' in English: *Tehi nishmatam tsrura be'tsror ha'khaim* (or in its shortened form *Tantseva*, .ה.ב.צ.נ.ת.)
84. Malz (2018). Some 70 per cent of the other half of the Jewish population lives in the USA.
85. Lau (2011), 364.

Epilogue
1. William Cuthbert Faulkner, 'Requiem for a Nun' (1951), Act 1, Scene 3.

Bibliography

Ancient References and Sources:

Jewish:
Avot de-Rabbi Natan
Maimonides, *Mishneh Torah*, The Laws of Kings
Midrash:
    Exodus *Rabbah*
    Genesis *Rabbah*
    Lamentations *Eikha Rabbah*
    Tanhuma, *Bereshit*
    Mishnah, Talmud
    Sifre, *Devarim*
Talmud Bavli (Babylonian Talmud):
    Baba Mezia
    Eruvin
    Gittin
    Ketubot
    Nedarim
    Pesahim
    Rosh Hashana
    Sanhedrin
    Sefaria Shabbat
    Yevamot
Talmud Yerushalmi (Jerusalem Talmud):
    Berakhot
    Sotah
Tosefta, Berakhot

Roman:

Aelius Spartianus	*Historia Augusta, Vita Hadriani* (Augustan History, Hadrian)
Ambrose of Milan	*Epistulae* (Letters)
Ammianus Marcellinus	*Res Gestae* (History of Rome)
Apollodorus	*Poliorcetica* (Manuals on Siege Warfare)
Appian	*Romaika-Historia Romana* (Syrian Wars)
Augustine of Hippo	*De Civitate Dei Contra Paganos* (City of God)
Aurelius Victor	*Epitome De Caesaribus* (Summary of the Caesars)
Barnabus	*Barnaba Epistoli* (Epistle of Barnabus)
Cassiodorus	*Chronika* (Chronicles)
Cassius Dio	*Romaike Historia-Historia Romana* (Roman History)
Epiphanius of Salamis	*To Peri Metron kai Stathmion – De Mensuris et Ponderibus* (On Measures and Weights)

Eusebius of Caesarea	*Commentarius in Isaiam Prophetam* (Commentary on Isaiah the Prophet)
Eusebius of Caesarea	*Ekkistiastike Historia-Historia Ecclesiastica* (Church History)
Eusebius of Caesarea	*Pantodape Historia-Chronicon* (Chronicle)
Eutropius	*Breviarium Historiae Romanae* (Summary of Roman History)
Fronto	*Epistulae* (Correspondence)
Jerome	*Apologia Adversus Libros Rufini* (Apology for Himself Against the Books of Rufinus)
Joannes Chrysostom	*Orationes* III. *Adversus Judaeos* (Orations 3. Against the Jews)
John Malalas	*Chronographia* (Chronology)
Josephus	*Pero Archaiostitos Ioudaion Logos-In Apionem* (Against Apion)
Josephus	*Ioudaiki archaiologia-Antiquitates Iudaicae* (Jewish Antiquities)
Josephus	*Historia Ioudaikou Polemou Pros Romaious Biblia-Bellum Iudaicum* (Jewish War)
Justinian	*Digesta* (Digest)
Justinian	*Institutiones* (Institutes)
Orosius	*Historiarum Adversum Paganos* (History Against the Pagans)
Pausanias	*Hellados Periegesis* (Description of Greece)
Tertullian	*Apologeticum* (Apology)
Xiphilinus	*Epitome* (Epitome of Roman History)

Modern References and Sources:

Abramovich, A. (2011), *Building and Construction Activities of the Legions in Roman Palestine 1st-4th Centuries CE*, Ph.D. Thesis, University of Haifa, Dept. of Archaeology, Haifa. [Hebrew].

Abu-'Uqsa, Hanaa (2016), *Kefar 'Otnay and Legio: Remains from the Roman and Early Byzantine Periods. Final Report 2016*, The Israel Antiquities Authority. [Hebrew with English synopsis]: http://www.hadashot-esi.org.il/report_detail_eng.aspx?id= 24904&mag_id=124 (accessed 30 July 2020).

Adams, Colin E. P. (1995), 'Supplying the Roman Army: "Q. Petr." 245', *Zeitschrift für Papyrologie und Epigraphik*, Bd. 109 (1995), 119–124.

Adams, J.N. (1990), *The Latin Sexual Vocabulary*, Baltimore: Johns Hopkins University Press.

Adams, J.N. (1982), *The Latin Sexual Vocabulary*, London: Gerald Duckworth.

Adams, Matthew J., David, Jonathan & Tepper, Yotam (2014) 'Legio. Excavations at the Camp of the Roman Sixth Legion in Israel', *Biblical Archaeology Review* 39 (May): https://www.biblicalarchaeology.org/daily/biblical-sites-places/biblical-archaeology-sites/legio/ (accessed 30 July 2020).

Almagor, Eran & Maurice, Lisa (2017), *The Reception of Ancient Virtues and Vices in Modern Popular Culture, Beauty, Bravery, Blood and Glory* (Metaforms: Studies in the Reception of Classical Antiquity), Leiden: Brill Publishers.

Alexander, Paul J. (1938), 'Letters and Speeches of the Emperor Hadrian', *Harvard Studies in Classical Philology* 49, 141–177.

Alexander, P. S. (1984), 'Epistolary Literature' in: Stone, Michael (ed.) (1984), *Jewish Writings of the Second Temple Period: Apocrypha, Pseudepigrapha, Qumran Sectarian Writings, Philo, Josephus* (The Literature of the Jewish People in the Period of the Second Temple and the Talmud, Book 2), Minneapolis: Fortress Press, 579–596.

Alon, D. (1986), 'Horbat Zalit (es-Salantah)', *Hadashot Arkheologiyot: Excavations and Surveys in Israel* 88, 30–32. [Hebrew].

Alt, A. (1927), 'Das Institut im Jahr 1926', *Palästinajahrbuch* 23, 5–51.

Ameling, Walter, Cotton, Hannah M., Eck, Werner, *et al* (eds.) (2018), *Corpus Inscriptionum Iudaea/Palaestinae Volume IV*: Iudaea/Idumaea. Part 2: 3325–3978. Berlin: De Gruyter.

Amit, David (1992), 'Hebron – 'En Gedi, Survey of Ancient Road', *Eretz-Israel: Archaeological, Historical and Geographical Studies*, 345–362.

Applebaum, Shimon (1976), *Prolegomena to the Study of the Second Jewish Revolt (AD 132–135)*, Oxford: Oxford University Press.

Applebaum, Shimon (1987), 'Betthar and the Roman Road System', *Zeitschrift des Deutschen Palästina-Vereins* (1953–) 103, 137–140.

Applebaum, Shimon (1989), 'Tineius Rufus and Julius Severus', in: Applebaum, Shimon *Judaea in Hellenistic and Roman Times. Historical and Archaeological Essays*, Leiden: Brill Academic Publishers, 118–123.

Applebaum, Shimon & Neusner, Jacob (eds.) (1989), *Judaea in Hellenistic and Roman Times: Historical and Archaeological Essays* (Studies in Judaism in Late Antiquity 40) , Leiden: Brill Academic Publishers.

Arbel, Naftali & Ben Hanan, Michael (1972), *High Lights of Jewish History as Told By the Knesset Menorah*, Israel Biblos Publishing House.

Arnould, Caroline (1998), 'Remarques Sur La Place Et La Fonction De La Porte De Damas (Porte Romaine) Dans La Cité D'Aelia Capitolina', *Zeitschrift Des Deutschen Palästina-Vereins (1953–)* 114.2, 179–183.

Arnould-Béhar, Caroline (2005), 'L'espace urbain d'Aelia Capitolina (Jérusalem): rupture ou continuité?', *Histoire urbaine* 13(2), 85.

Arubas, B., & Goldfus, H. (2006), *Excavations on the Site of the Jerusalem International Convention Centre (Binyanei Ha-Uma): The Pottery and Other Small Finds* (Journal of Roman Archaeology Supplementary Series No. 60), Portsmouth, Rhode Island.

Arubas, B., & Goldfus, H. (2019), 'The *Legio X Fretensis* Kilnworks at the Jerusalem International Convention Center', in Hillel, Geva (ed.), *Ancient Jerusalem Revealed: Excavations 1998–2018*, Israel Exploration Society, Jerusalem: Old City Press, 184–194.

Ascough, Richard S., Harland, Philip A., & Kloppenborg, John S. (2012), *Associations in the Greco-Roman World: A Sourcebook*, Waco: Baylor University Press.

Avigad, Nahman (1984), *Discovering Jerusalem*, Hoboken: Wiley-Blackwell Press.

Avi-Yonah, Michael (1950–51), 'The Development of the Roman Road System in Palestine', *Israel Exploration Journal* 1.1, 54–60.

Avi-Yonah, Michael (1952), 'The 'War of the Sons of Light and the Sons of Darkness' and Maccabean Warfare', *Israel Exploration Journal* 2.1, 1–5.

Avi-Yonah, Michael (1970–71), 'The Caesarea Porphyry Statue Found in Caesarea', *Israel Exploration Journal* 20, 203–208.

Avi-Yonah, Michael (1973), 'When Did Judea Become a Consular Province?', *Israel Exploration Journal* 23.4, 209–213.

Bacher, A. (1909), 'Der Jahrmarkt an der Terebinthe bei Hebron. Nachtrag zu S. 148', *Zeitschrift für die Alttestamentliche Wissenschaft* 29.3, 221.

Bahar, Dany (2016), 'How Shimon Peres saved the Israeli economy', *Brookings*, (30 September): https://www.brookings.edu/blog/markaz/2016/09/30/how-shimon-peres-saved-the-israeli-economy/ (accessed 30 July 2020).

Baker, Renan (2012), 'Epiphanius, "On Weights and Measures" §14: Hadrian's Journey to the East and the Rebuilding of Jerusalem', *Zeitschrift für Papyrologie und Epigraphik* 182, 157–167.

Balberg, Mira (2012), 'The Emperor's Daughter's New Skin: Bodily Otherness and Self-Identity in the Dialogues of Rabbi Yehoshua ben Hanania and the Emperor's

Daughter', *Jewish Studies Quarterly* 19.3, Rabbis and Others in Conversation II, 181–206.

Balfour, Alan (2012), *Solomon's Temple: Myth, Conflict, and Faith*, Chichester: Wiley-Blackwell.

Barag, Dan P. (1980), 'A Note on the Geographical Distribution of Bar Kokhba Coins', *Israel Numismatic Journal* 4, 30–33.

Barb, A.A. (1950), 'Animula Vagula Blandula… Notes on Jingles, Nursery-Rhymes and Charms with an Excursus on Noththe's Sisters', *Folklore, 61*(1), 15–30.

Barkay, Rachel (2012), 'Roman Influence on Jewish Coins' in: Jacobson, David M. & Kokkinos, Nikos (eds.) (2012), *Judaea and Rome in Coins, 65 BCE-135 CE*, London: Spink & Son, 19–26.

Barnes, Timothy D. (1967), 'Hadrian and Lucius Verus', *The Journal of Roman Studies* 57.1/2, 65–79.

Barnes, Timothy D. (1968), 'Hadrian's Farewell to Life', *The Classical Quarterly, New Series* 18.2 (Nov.), 384–386.

Bazzana, Giovanni Battista (2010), 'The Bar Kokhba Revolt and Hadrian's religious policy', in: Rizzi, Marco (ed.), *Hadrian and the Christians. Millennium-Studien = Millennium studies* Bd. 30, Berlin/ New York: De Gruyter, 85–109.

Bell, H. I. (1940), 'Antinoopolis: A Hadrianic Foundation in Egypt', *The Journal of Roman Studies* 30, 133–147.

Ben-Shalom, Israel (1993), *The School of Shammai and the Zealots' Struggle against Rome*, Jerusalem: Yad Izhak Ben-Zvi. [Hebrew].

Ben-Yehoshua, Shimshon & Rozen, Baruch (2009), 'The Secret of Ein-Gedi', *Cathedra: For the History of Eretz Israel and Its Yishuv* 132, 70–100. [Hebrew].

Ben-Zeev, Miriam Pucci (2000), 'L. Tettius Crescens' *expeditio Iudaeae*', *Zeitschrift für Papyrologie und Epigraphik* 133, 256–258.

Bennett, Julian (1984), 'Hadrian and the Title 'Pater Patriae'', *Britannia* 15, 234–235.

Bennett, Julian (1997), *Trajan, Optimus Princeps. A Life and Times*, Bloomington: Indiana University Press.

Benoit, P. (1971), 'L'Antonia D'Hérode Le Grand Et Le Forum Oriental D'Aelia Capitolina', *The Harvard Theological Review* 64.2/3, 135–167. [French].

Benoit, P., Milik, J.T., & De Vaux, R. (1961), *Discoveries in the Judaean Desert, Volume 2: Les Grottes de Murabba'at*, Oxford: The Clarendon Press.

Bentwich, Norman (1933), 'The Graeco-Roman View of Jews and Judaism in the Second Century', *The Jewish Quarterly Review* 23.4 (April), 337–348.

Belayche, Nicole (1997), 'Du Mont du Temple au Golgotha: le Capitole de la colonie d'Aelia Capitolina', *Revue de l'histoire des religions* 214.4 (October-December), 387–413. [French with English synoposis].

Bergler, Siegfried (1998) 'Jesus, Bar Kochba und das messianische Laubhüttenfest', *Journal for the Study of Judaism in the Persian, Hellenistic, and Roman Period* 29.2, 143–191.

Bergstein, Mary (2016), 'Palmyra and Palmyra: Look On These Stones, Ye Mighty, And Despair', *Arion: A Journal of Humanities and the Classics* 24.2, 13–38.

Berlin, Andrea (2005), 'Jewish Life Before the Revolt: The Archaeological Evidence', *Journal for the Study of Judaism* 36.4, 417–470.

Bieberstein, Klaus (2007), 'Aelia Capitolina' in: Kafafi, Zeidan & Schick, Robert (eds.), *Jerusalem Before Islam* (British Archaeological Reports International Series 1699), Oxford: BAR Publishing, 134–168.

Bird, H. W. (1978), 'S. Aurelius Victor: Some Fourth Century Issues', *The Classical Journal* 73.3, 223–237.

Bird, H. W. (1981), 'The Sources of the *De Caesaribus*', *The Classical Quarterly* 31.2, 457–463.

Bird, H. W. (1982), 'Aurelius Victor on Women and Sexual Morality', *The Classical Journal* 78.1, 44–48.

Birley, Anthony R. (1977), *The Roman Emperor Hadrian: A New Biography*, Haltwhistle: Barcombe Publications.

Birley, Anthony R. (1997), *Hadrian: The Restless Emperor. (Roman Imperial Biographies)*, London: Routledge.

Birley, Anthony R. (2003), 'Hadrian's Travels', in: de Blois, L. *et al* (eds.), *The Representation and Perception of Roman Imperial Power*. Proceedings of the Third Workshop of the International Network Impact of Empire (Roman Empire c. 200 B.C.-A.D. 476), Rome, March 20–23, 2002, Amsterdam, 425–441.

Birley, Anthony R. (2016), '*Viri militares* moving from west to east in two crisis years (AD 133 and 162)' in: Lo Cascio, E. & Tacoma, L.E., with Groen-Valkinga, M.J. (eds), *The Impact of Mobility and Migration in the Roman Empire*, Impact of Empire 12, Brill: Leiden, 55–79.

Birley, Eric (1965), 'Promotions and Transfers in the Roman Army. II The Centurionate', *Carnuntum Jahrbuch* 1963/4, 21–33.

Bishop, Michael C. (1999), 'The Newstead *lorica segmentata*', *Journal of Roman Military Equipment Studies* 10, 27–43.

Bitner, Brad (2012), 'How to Celebrate Hadrian's Accession (P. Oxy. 3781)' in: Llewelyn, S.R. and Harrison, J.R., *New Documents Illustrating Early Christianity* Vol. 10, Eerdmans, 76–86.

Blyth, P.H. (1992), 'Apollodorus of Damascus and the *Poliorcetica*', *Greek, Roman, and Byzantine Studies* 33, 127–158.

Boatwright, Mary Taliaferro (1987), *Hadrian and The City of Rome*, Princeton: Princeton University Press.

Boatwright, Mary Taliaferro (2000), *Hadrian and the Cities of the Roman Empire*, Princeton: Princeton University Press.

Boatwright, Mary Taliaferro (2013), 'Hadrian and the Agrippa Inscription on the Pantheon' in: Opper, Thorsten (ed.) (2013), *Hadrian: Art, Politics and Economy*, Research Publication 175, London: The British Museum, 19–30.

Bollansée, Jan (1994), '"P. Fay." 19, Hadrian's Memoirs, and Imperial Epistolary Autobiography', *Ancient Society* 25, 279–302.

Booth, William & Eglash, Ruth (2016), 'Israeli archaeologists rush to dig at Cave of Skulls before looters take everything', *Washington Post*, 8 June: https://www.washingtonpost.com/world/middle_east/israeli-archaeologists-rush-to-dig-at-cave-of-skulls-before-looters-take-everything/2016/06/08/7f0e0e6a-281c-11e6-8329-6104954928d2_story.html (accessed 30 July 2020).

Boswell, John (1994), *Same Sex Unions in Premodern Europe*, New York: Villard Books.

Bowersock, Glenn W. (1970), 'The Annexation and Initial Garrison of Arabia', *Zeitschrift für Papyrologie und Epigraphik* 5, 37–47.

Bowersock, Glenn W. (1971), 'A Report on Arabia Provincia', *The Journal of Roman Studies, 61*, 219–242.

Bowersock, Glenn W. (1980), 'A Roman Perspective on the Bar Kokhba War' in: Green, William S. (ed.), *Approaches to Ancient Judaism* Vol. 2, Scholars' Press.

Bowersock, Glenn W. (1982), 'Review of A. Spijkerman, *The Coins of the Decapolis and Provincia Arabia*, Jerusalem 1978', *Journal of Roman Studies* 72, 197–198.

Bowersock, Glenn W. (1983), *Roman Arabia*, Cambridge, Mass.: Harvard University Press.

Bowersock, Glenn W. (2003), 'The Tel Shalem Arch and P. Nahal Heer/Seiyal 8' in: Schäfer, P. (ed.), *The Bar Kokhba War Reconsidered: New Perspectives on the Second Jewish Revolt Against Rome*, Tübingen: Mohr Siebeck, 171–180.

Bowman, Alan K., (1994), *Life and Letters on the Roman Frontier*, London: British Museum Press.

Brassloff, Stephan (1914), 'Die Rechtsfrage Bei Der Adoption Hadrians', *Hermes* 49.4, 590–601. [German].

Brenk, Frederick E. (2011), '"Hierosolyma". The Greek Name of Jerusalem', *Glotta* 87, 1–22.

Brennan, T.C. (1998), 'The Poets Julia Balbilla and Damo at the Colossus of Memnon', *The Classical World* 91.4 (Mar. - Apr.), 215–234.

Brenner, Michael & Reuveni, Gideon (eds.) (2006), *Emanzipation durch Muskelkraft: Juden und Sport in Europa (Judische Religion, Geschichte und Kultur (JRGK))*, Göttingen: Vandenhoeck & Ruprecht.

Brewer, Catherine (2005), 'The Status of the Jews in Roman Legislation: The Reign of Justinian 527–565 CE', *European Judaism: A Journal for the New Europe* 38.2, 127–139.

Broshi, Magen (1992), 'Agriculture and Economy in Roman Palestine: Seven Notes on the Babatha Archive', *Israel Exploration Journal* 42.3/4, 230–240.

Broshi, Magen (2005), 'Ladanum at 'En Gedi?', *Israel Exploration Journal* 55.1, 94–96.

Broshi, Magen & Qimron, Elisha (1986), 'A House Sale Deed from Kefar Baru from the Time of Bar Kokhba', *Israel Exploration Journal* 36.3/4, 201–214.

Browning, Iain (1979), *Palmyra*, London: Chatto and Windus.

Bruce, Lorne D., (1981) 'A Reappraisal of Roman Libraries in the "Scriptores Historiae Augusta"' *The Journal of Library History* (1974–1987), 16.4 (Fall), 551–573.

Bruun, Christer (1992), 'The Spurious "Expeditio Ivdaeae" under Trajan', *Zeitschrift für Papyrologie und Epigraphik* 93, 99–106.

Bryce, Trevor (2014), *Ancient Syria: A Three Thousand Year History*, Oxford: Oxford University Press.

Büchler, A. (1903), 'Die Schauplätze des bar-Kochbakrieges und die auf Diesen Bezogenen Jüdischen Nachrichten', *The Jewish Quarterly Review* 16.1 (Oct.), 143–205.

Burian, Jan (2004), 'Hadrianův Dopis a Jeho Funkce v Historii Auguste', *Listy Filologické / Folia Philologica* 127.3/4, 205–213. [Czech].

Burns, Bryan E. (2008), 'Sculpting Antinous', *Helios* 35.2, 121–142.

Burton, Anthony (2007), *Hadrian's Wall Path: National Trail Guide*, London: Aurum Press.

Campbell, Duncan B. (2011), 'The Fate of the Ninth: The Curious Disappearance of *Legio VIII Hispana*', *Ancient Warfare* IV-5, 48–53: https://www.karwansaraypublishers.com/schrijfsels/wp-content/uploads/Ancient-Warfare/fateoftheninth.pdf (accessed 30 July 2020).

Capponi, Livia (2010), 'Hadrian in Jerusalem and Alexandria in 117', *Athenaeum* 98/2, 489–502.

Carroll, W.D. (1923–1924), 'Bittîr and Its Archaeological Remains', *The Annual of the American Schools of Oriental Research* 5, 77–103.

Chancey, M. (2005), *Greco-Roman Culture and the Galilee of Jesus* (Society for New Testament Studies Monograph Series), Cambridge: Cambridge University Press.

Champlin, Edward (1976), 'Hadrian's Heir', *Zeitschrift für Papyrologie und Epigraphik* 21, 79–89.

Chowen, Richard H. (1954), 'Traveling Companions of Hadrian', *The Classical Journal* 50.3 (Dec.), 122–124.

Chowen, Richard H. (1970), 'The Problem of Hadrian's Visits to North Africa', *The Classical Journal* 65.7 (Apr.), 323–324.

Clermont-Ganneau, Charles (1899), *Archaeological Researches in Palestine during the Years 1873–1874*, Volume 1, Palestine Exploration Fund, London.

Cline, Eric H. (2004), *Jerusalem Besieged: From Ancient Canaan to Modern Israel*, Ann Arbor: University of Michigan Press.

Cohen, Jeremy (ed.) (1991), *Essential Papers on Judaism and Christianity in Conflict: From Late Antiquity to the Reformation*, New York: New York University Press.

Cohen, Shaye J. D. (1982), 'The Destruction: From Scripture to Midrash', *Prooftexts* 2.1, 18–39.

Cohen, Shaye J. D. (2014), *From the Maccabees to the Mishnah*, Third ed., Louisville, Kentucky: Westminster John Knox Press.

Cohen, Shaye J. D. (2020), '"Those Who Say They Are Jews and Are Not": How Do You Know a Jew in Antiquity When You See One?' in: Cohen, Shaye J. D. & Frerichs, Ernest S. (eds.), *Diasporas in Antiquity*, Providence, RI: Brown Judaic Studies, 1–45.

Collins, John J. & Harlow, Daniel C. (eds.) (2012), *Early Judaism: A Comprehensive Overview*, Grand Rapids, Michigan: Wm. B. Eerdmans Publishing.

Cooley, Alison E. & Salway, Benet (2012), 'Roman Inscriptions 2006–2010', *Journal of Roman Studies* 102, 172–286.

Cornfled, Gaalyahu (1962), *Daniel to Paul Jews in Conflict with Graeco-Roman Civilization: Historical and Religious Background to the Hasmoneans, Dead Sea Scrolls, the New Testament World, Early Christianity, and the Bar-Kochba War*, New York: MacMillan Co.

Cotton, Hannah M. (1993), 'The Guardianship of Jesus, Son of Babatha: Roman and Local Law in the Province of Arabia', *Journal of Roman Studies* 83, 94–108.

Cotton, Hannah M. (1996), 'Courtyard(s) in Ein-Gedi: P.Yadin 11, 19 and 20 of the Babatha Archive', *Zeitschrift Für Papyrologie Und Epigraphik* 112, 197–201.

Cotton, Hannah M. (1999), 'The Languages of the Legal and Administrative Documents from the Judaean Desert', *Zeitschrift für Papyrologie und Epigraphik* 125, 219–231.

Cotton, Hannah M. (2000), 'The Legio VI Ferrata' in: Le Bohec, Yann & Wolff, Catherine (eds.) (2000), *Les légions de Rome sous le Haut-Empire - actes du congrès de Lyon, 17–19 septembre 1998*, Lyons: CEROR, 351–360.

Cotton, Hannah M. & Eck, Werner (1997), 'Ein Staatsmonopol und seine Folgen: Plinius, *Naturalis Historia* 12, 123 und der Preis für Balsam', *Rheinisches Museum für Philologie*. Neue Folge 140.2, 153–161. [German].

Cotton, Hannah M. & Eck, W. (2001), 'Governors and their Personnel on Latin Inscriptions from Caesarea Maritima', *Proceedings of the Israel Academy of Sciences and Humanities* 7 215–238.

Cotton, Hannah M. & Eck, Werner (2002), 'P. Murabba 'at 114 und die Anwesenheit römischer Truppen in den Höhlen des Wadi Murabba 'at nach dem Bar Kochba Aufstand', *Zeitschrift für Papyrologie und Epigraphik* 138, 173–183.

Cotton, Hannah M. & Eck, Werner (2006), 'Governors and their Personnel on Latin Inscriptions from Caesarea Maritima', *Cathedra* 122, 31–52. [Hebrew].

Cotton, Hannah M., & Eck, Werner (2009), 'An Imperial Arch in the Colonia Aelia Capitolina: A Fragment of a Latin Inscription in the Islamic Museum of the Haram as-Sharif', in: Geiger, J. *et al* (eds.), *Israel's Land. Papers Presented to Israel Shatzman on his Jubilee*, Jerusalem, 97–118.

Cowan, Ross (2013), *Roman Legionary, AD 69–161* (Warrior 166), Oxford: Osprey Publishing.

Crone, Patricia (2007), 'Quraysh and the Roman Army: Making Sense of the Meccan Leather Trade', *Bulletin of the School of Oriental and African Studies*, University of London 70.1, 63–88.

Crown, Alan D. (1991), 'Redating the Schism between the Judaeans and the Samaritans', *The Jewish Quarterly Review* 82.1/2 (Jul. - Oct.), 17–50.

Curran, John (2005), 'The Long Hesitation': Some Reflections on the Romans in Judaea', *Greece & Rome* 52.1, 70–98.

D'Amato, Raffaele & Sumner, Graham (2009), *Arms and Armour of the Imperial Roman Soldier: From Marius to Commodus, 112 BC-AD 192*, Barnsley: Frontline.

Dabrowa, E. (1998), *The Governors of Roman Syria from Augustus to Septimius Severus*, Bonn, Habelt.

Daniels, Shawn Gaius (2013), *Satire in the Historia Augusta, Dissertation*, University of Florida: http://ufdcimages.uflib.ufl.edu/UF/E0/04/59/15/00001/DANIELS_S.pdf (accessed 30 July 2020).

Davies, Gwyn (2011), 'Under Siege: The Roman Field Works at Masada', *Bulletin of the American Schools of Oriental Research* 362 (May), 65–83.

Davies, Roy W. (1968), 'Fronto, Hadrian and the Roman Army', *Latomus* 27.1 (Janvier-Mars), 75–95.

Davies, Roy W. (1977), *Cohors I Hispanorum and the Garrisons of Maryport*, read at Temple Sowerby, July 8th, 1977.

De Lange, Nicholas (1997), *The Illustrated History of the Jewish People*, New York: Harcourt Brace.

De Lange, Nicholas (2003), Judaism, Oxford: Oxford University Press. (Second edition).

De Souza, P. (2008), '*Parta victoriis pax*: Roman emperors as peacemakers', in: De Souza, P. & France, J. (eds.), *War and Peace in Ancient and Medieval History*, Cambridge: Cambridge University Press, 76–106.

Deem, Ariella (1978), "'...and the Stone Sank into His Forehead". A Note on 1 Samuel XVII 49', *Vetus Testamentum* 28.3 (July), 349–351.

Den Boer, W. (1955), 'Religion and Literature in Hadrian's Policy', *Mnemosyne* 8.2, 123–144.

Deutsch, Robert (2000–2), 'A Lead Weight of Hadrian: The Prototype for the Bar Kokhba Weights', *Israel Numismatic Journal* 14, 125–128.

Deutsch, Robert (2001), 'A Lead Weight of Shimon Bar Kokhba', *Israel Exploration Journal* 51.1, 96–98

Di Segni, Leah A. (1994), 'New Toponym in Southern Samaria', *Liber Annuus* 44: 579–584.

Di Segni, Leah (2003), 'The Hadrianic Inscription from Southern Samaria', *Liber Annuus* 53, 335–340.

Di Segni, Leah (2014), 'Epiphanius and the date of foundation of Aelia Capitolina', *Liber Annuus* 64, 441–451.

Di Segni, Leah & Arubas, Benjamin Y. (2009), 'An Old-New Inscription from Beth Shean', in: Di Segni, L., Hirschfeld, Y., Patrich, J. & Talgam, R. (eds.) (2009), *Man Near a Roman Arch: Studies Presented to Prof. Yoram Tsafrir*, Jerusalem, 115–124.

Di Segni, Leah & Weksler-Bdolah, Shlomit (2012), 'Three Military Bread Stamps from the Western Wall Plaza Excavations, Jerusalem', *'Atiqot* 70, 21–31.

Dimont, Max I. (2004). *Jews, God and History*, New York: Signet Classics (2 edition).

Dise Jr, Robert L. (1997), 'Trajan, the Antonines, and the Governor's Staff', *Zeitschrift für Papyrologie und Epigraphik*, Bd. 116, 273–283

Dobson, Brian & Breeze, David (2000), *Hadrian's Wall* (Fourth Edition), London: Penguin Books.

Doležal, Stanislav (2017), 'Did Hadrian Ever Meet a Parthian King?', *Acta Universitatis Carolinae Philologica* 2, 111–125.

Dorf, E. (Undated), *Oriental Theatre Libretto: Bar Kochba Or The Last Hour of Zion*, New York.

Dorsey. D. (1991), *The Roads and Highways of Ancient Israel,* Baltimore: Johns Hopkins University Press.

Eban, Abba (1972), *My Country: The Story of Modern Israel,* London: Weidenfeld and Nicolson.

Eck, Werner (1999), 'The bar Kokhba Revolt: The Roman Point of View', *The Journal of Roman Studies* 89, 76–89.

Eck, Werner (2001), 'Ein Spiegel der Macht. Lateinische Inschriften römischer Zeit in Iudaea/Syria Palestina', *Zeitschrift des Deutschen Palästina-Vereins* 117, 46–63.

Eck, W. (2003a), 'The Language of Power: Latin in the Inscriptions of Iudaea/Syria Palestina', in: Schiffman, L.H. (ed.), *Semitic Papyrology in Context: A Climate of Creativity. Papers from a New York University conference marking the retirement of Baruch A. Levine,* Leiden: Brill, 123–144.

Eck, Werner (2003b), 'Hadrian, the Bar Kokhba Revolt, and the Epigraphic Transmission' in: Schäfer, P. (ed.), *Bar Kokhba Reconsidered: New Perspectives on the Second Jewish Revolt Against Rome,* Tübingen: Mohr Siebeck, 153–170.

Eck, Werner (2005), 'Ehret den Kaiser. Bögen und Tore als Ehrenmonumente in der Provinz Iudaea', in: Perani, M. (ed.), *The Words of a Wise Man's Mouth are Gracious (Qoh 10, 12). Festschrift for G. Stemberger on the Occasion of his 65th Birthday,* Berlin, 153–165. [German].

Eck, Werner (2007), *Rom Herausfordern: Bar Kochba im Kampf Gegen das Imperium Romanum. Das Bild des Bar Kochba – Aufstandes im Spigel der Neuen Epigraphischen Uberlieferung,* Roma.

Eck, Werner (2010), 'Zu alten und neuen Inschriften aus Caesarea Maritima Vorarbeiten für den 2. Band des CIIP', *Zeitschrift für Papyrologie und Epigraphik* 174, 169–184. [German].

Eck, Werner (2011a), 'Latin Dedication to Hadrian by the *Beneficarii* of the Governor Tineius Rufus', *Corpus Inscriptionum Iudaeae/Palaestinae* Vol. II: 1121–2160, ad no.1276.

Eck, Werner (2011b), 'Lucius Flavius Silva, Burger von Urbs Salvia und Eroberer von Masada (zu Picus 26, 2006, 45 ff.)', *Picus* 31, 45–53. [German].

Eck, Werner (2012a), 'Der Bar Kochba-Aufstand der Jahre 132–136 und seine Folgen für die Provinz Judaea/Syria Palaestina' in: Urso, G. (ed.), *Iudaea Socia – Iudaea Capta,* Atti del convegno internazionale Cividale del Friuli, 22–24 settembre 2011, Pisa, 249–265. [German].

Eck, Werner (2012b), 'Caesarea Maritima – eine römische Stadt?' in: *Zwischen Antike und Moderne: Festschrift für Jürgen Malitz zum 65. Geburtstag dargebracht von Kollegen, Freunden, Schülern und Weggefährten,* Speyer: Kartoffeldruck-Verlag Kai Brodersen, 233–244. [German].

Eck, Werner (2014), '"Praesentia Caesaris" in der Provinz Judäa/Syria Palästina', *Scripta Classica Israelica* 33, 17–32. [German].

Eck, Werner (2016), 'Herrschaft, Widerstand, Kooperation: Rom und das Judentum in Judaea/Palestina vor dem 4. Jh. n. Chr.' in: Baltrusch, Ernst & Puschner, Uwe (eds.), (2016), *Jüdische Lebenswelten. Von der Antike bis zur Gegenwart,* Frankfurt am Main: Peter Lang GmbH, 31–52. [German].

Eck, Werner (2017), 'Position and Authority of the Provincial Provincial Legate and the Financial Procurator in Judaea, 70–136 AD' in: Schwartz, Joshua J & Tomson, Peter J (eds.), *Jews and Christians in the First and Second Centuries: The Interbellum 70–132 CE,* (Compendia Rerum Iudaicarum Ad Novum Testamentum), Leiden: Brill 2017, 93–105.

Eck, Werner & Foerster, G. (1999), 'Ein Triumphbogen für Hadrian im Tal von Beth Shean bei Tel Shalem', *Journal of Roman Archaeology* 12, 294–313. [German].

Eck, Werner, & Pangerl, Andreas (2006), "Die Konstitution Für Die Classis Misenensis Aus Dem Jahr 160 Und Der Krieg Gegen Bar Kochba Unter Hadrian", *Zeitschrift Für Papyrologie Und Epigraphik* 155, 239–252. [German].

Eck, Werner, Holder, Paul & Pangerl, Andreas (2010), 'A Diploma for the Army of Britain in 132 and Hadrian's Return to Rome from the East', *Zeitschrift für Papyrologie und Epigraphik* 174, 189–200.

Eck, Werner, Tepper, Yotam (2001), 'A Dedication to Silvanus near the Camp of the Legio VI Ferrata near Lajjun', *Scripta Classica Israelica* 20, 85–88.

Eck, Werner & Pangerl, Andreas (2007), 'Eine Konstitution für die Hilfstruppen von Syria Palaestina vom 6. Februar 158 n. Chr.', *Zeitschrift für Papyrologie und Epigraphik* 159, 283–290. [German].

Eckhardt, Benedikt (ed.) (2011), *Jewish Identity and Politics between the Maccabees and Bar Kokhba. Supplements to the Journal for the Study of Judaism*, Volume 155, Leiden: Brill.

Edelman, Marsha Bryan (2003), *Discovering Jewish Music*, Philadelphia: The Jewish Publication Society.

Ehrman, Bart D. (2014), *How Jesus Became God: The Exaltation of a Jewish Preacher from Galilee*, New York: HarperOne.

Ehrman, Bart D. (2020), *Heaven and Hell: A History of the Afterlife*, New York: Simon & Schuster.

Eldad, Israel (1971), *The Jewish Revolution: Jewish Statehood*, New York: Gefen Publishing House.

Eliav, Yaron Z. (1997), 'Hadrian's Actions in the Jerusalem Temple Mount According to Cassius Dio and Xiphilini Manus', *Jewish Studies Quarterly* 4.2, 125–144.

Elkins, Nathan T. (2006), 'The Flavian Colosseum Sestertii: Currency or Largess?' *The Numismatic Chronicle (1966–)* 166, 211–221.

Elon, Amos (1996), *Jerusalem: City of Mirrors*, London: Flamingo.

Eshel, Hanan (1987), 'A Coin of Bar Kokhba from a Cave in Wadi el-Mackuck', *Israel Numismatic Journal* 9, 51–52.

Eshel, Hanan (1989), 'Nailed sandals in the Jewish sources in light of the finds of the refuge caves' in: Eshel, H. and Amit, D. (eds), *Refuge Caves of the Bar Kokhba Revolt*, Tel-Aviv, 225–231. [Hebrew].

Eshel, Hanan (1995), 'The Policy of Minting Coins during the Bar Kokhba in Light of the Findings from the Judaean Desert, *Judaea and Samaria Research* 5, 173–182. [Hebrew].

Eshel, Hanan (2003), 'The Dates Used During the Bar Kokhba Revolt', in: Schäfer, Peter (ed.) (2003), *Bar Kokhba War Reconsidered: New Perspectives on the Second Jewish Revolt Against Rome*, Texts and Studies in Ancient Judaism 100, Tübingen: Mohr Siebeck, 93–105.

Eshel, Hanan (2006), 'The Bar Kochba Revolt, 132–135' in: Katz, Steven T. (ed.), *The Cambridge History of Judaism*, IV. *The Late Roman Period*, Cambridge: Cambridge University Press, 105–127.

Eschel, Hanan (2007), '"Bethar was captured and the city was plowed": Jerusalem, Aelia Capitolina and the Bar Kokhba Revolt', *Eretz-Israel: Archaeological, Historical and Geographical Studies*, Teddy Kollek Volume, 21–28. [Hebrew].

Eshel, Hanan & Amit, David (1991), 'A Tetradrachm of Bar Kokhba from a Cave in Nahal Hever', *Israel Numismatic Journal* 11, 33–35.

Eshel, Hanan (1998), 'The History of Research and Survey of the Finds of the Refuge Cave' in: Eshel, H. and Amit, D. (eds.), *The Bar-Kokhba Refuge Caves*, 60–61. [Hebrew].

Eshel, Hanan & Zissu, Boaz (1999), 'Roman Coins from the 'Cave of the Sandal' West of Jericho', *Israel Numismatic Journal* 13, 70–77.

Eshel, Hanan, Zissu, Boaz & Barkay, Gabriel (2010), 'Sixteen Bar Kokhba Coins from Roman Sites in Europe' in: Barag, D. & Zissu, B. (eds.) *Studies in Honour of Arnold Spaer* [*Israel Numismatic Journal* 17], 91–97.

Eshel, Hanan & Zissu, Boaz (2015), *The Bar Kokhba Revolt – An Archaeological Perspective*, Jerusalem: Yad Ben Zvi. [Hebrew].

Evans, Craig A. (1997), *Jesus and His Contemporaries: Comparative Studies* (Arbeiten Zur Geschichte Des Antiken Judentums Und Des Urchristentums, 25), Leiden: Brill.

Evers, Cécile (2013), 'Images of a Divine Youth: The Brussels Antinous and its Workshop' in: Opper, Thorsten (ed.) (2013), *Hadrian: Art, Politics and Economy*, Research Publication 175, London: The British Museum, 89–99.

Fabian, Peter, Golan, Karni, & Goldfus, Haim (2015), 'Horbat Zalit 2011', *Hadashot Arkheologiyot: Excavations and Surveys in Israel* 127.

Fagan, Brian (2006), *From Stonehenge to Samarkand: An Anthology of Archaeological Travel Writing*, Oxford: Oxford University Press.

Farhi, Yoav (2016), 'Gaza Coins as Flans for Bar Kokhba Overstrikes', *Israel Numismatic Journal* 19, 56–62.

Feldman, Ariel (2019), 'An Overlooked Psalm Addressing Zion from Wadi Murabba'at', *Journal of Biblical Literature* 138.2, 365–376.

Feldman, Louis (1996), *Studies in Hellenistic Judaism* (Arbeiten Zur Geschichte Des Antiken Judentums Und Des Urchristentums, Bd. 30), Leiden: Brill.

Filiu, Jean-Pierre (2014), *Gaza: A History*, Oxford: Oxford University Press.

Fisher, Moshe (2011), 'Rome and Judaea during the First Century CE: A strange *modus vivendi*' in: Moosbauer, G. & Wiegels, R. (eds) *Römische Okkupations- und Grenzpolitik im frühen Principat Beiträge zum Kongress*, Fines imperii – imperium sine fine?' *in Osnabrück vom 14. bis 18. September 2009, Osnabrücker Forschungenzu Altertum und Antike-Rezeption* 14, Diepholz, 143–156.

Fishman-Duker, Rivkah, and Rivkah Duker-Fishman (2008), 'Perspectives: 'Jerusalem: Capital of the Jews': The Jewish Identity of Jerusalem in Greek and Roman Sources', *Jewish Political Studies Review* 20.3/4, 119–140.

Fitzmyer, Joseph A. (2008), *A Guide to the Dead Sea Scrolls and Related Literature*, Grand Rapids, Mich.: Eerdmans.

Foerster, G. (1977), 'Galilee on the Eve of the Bar-Kokhba Revolt – The Archeological Evidence', *Cathedra* 4, 77–80. [Hebrew].

Foerster, G. (1980), 'A Cuirassed Statue of Hadrian', *Israel Museum Notes* 16, 107–110.

Foerster, G. (1985), 'A Cuirassed Bronze Statue of Hadrian', *Atiqot* (English Version) 17, 139–157.

Foerster, G., Arubas, B., Mevorach, David (2008), 'The Bronze Statue of the Emperor, the Hadrian Arch and the Legion Camp. Returning to Tel Shalem'. [Hebrew]: http://www.antiquities.org.il/article_heb.aspx?sec_id=17&sub_subj_id=493&id=1364 (accessed 30 July 2020).

Fowlkes-Childs, Blair & Seymour, Michael (2019), *The World between Empires: Art and Identity in the Ancient Middle East*, New York: Metropolitan Museum of Art.

Fox, Tatiana Eileen (2014), *The Cult of Antinous and the Response of the Greek East to Hadrian's Creation of a God*, Dissertation, Ohio University: https://etd.ohiolink.edu/!etd.send_file?accession=ouashonors1399414457&disposition=inline (accessed 30 July 2020).

Fredriksen, Paula (2018), *When Christians Were Jews: The First Generation*, New Haven: Yale University Press.

Frere, Sheppard S. (2000), 'M. Maenius Agrippa, the 'Expeditio Britannica' and Maryport', *Britannia* 31, 23–28.

Freund, Richard A. & Arav, Rami, 'Return to the Cave of Letters: What Still Lies Buried?', *Biblical Archaeology Review* 27:1 (January/February 2001): https://members. bib-arch.org/biblical-archaeology-review/27/1/3 (accessed 30 July 2020).

Friedman, Jane (1982), 'For Israelis, Bar Kochba Isn't Ancient History', *New York Times*, 31 January, https://www.nytimes.com/1982/01/31/weekinreview/for-israelis-bar-kochba-isnt-ancient-history.html

Frumkin, Amos (2001), 'The Cave of the Letters Sediments—Indication of An Early Phase of the Dead Sea Depression?', *The Journal of Geology* 109.1, 79–90.

Fuchs, Michaela (2014), 'Ein Ehrenbogen Für Hadrian in Rom: Würdigung Eines Vielseitigen Kaisers Am Ende Seines Lebens', *Bullettino Della Commissione Archeologica Comunale Di Roma* 115, 125–148. [German].

Fuks, Alexander (1953), 'The Jewish Revolt in Egypt (A. D. 115–117) in the light of the papyri', *Aegyptus* 33.1, Raccolta di Scritti in Onore di Girolamo Vitelli IV (January-June), 131–158.

Gager, John G. (1983), *The Origins of Anti-Semitism: Attitudes toward Judaism in Pagan and Christian Antiquity*, New York: Oxford University Press.

Galor, Katherina & Bloedhorn, Hanswulf (2013), *The Archaeology of Jerusalem*, New Haven: Yale University Press.

Gambash, Gil (2009), 'Official Roman Responses to Indigenous Resistance Movements: Aspects of Commemoration' in: Cotton, Hannah M., Geiger, J. & Stiebel, Guy (eds.), *Israel's Land: Collected Papers*, Tel Aviv/ Jerusalem: Open University, 53–76.

Gambash, Gil (2013a), 'Foreign Enemies of the Empire: The Great Jewish Revolt and the Roman Perception of the Jews,' *Scripta Classica Israelica* 32, 173–194.

Gambash, G. (2013b), 'Caesarea Maritima and the Grand Strategy of the Roman Empire', *Skyllis* 13.1, 53–58.

Gambash, Gil (2015), *Rome and Provincial Resistance (Routledge Monographs in Classical Studies 21)*, New York: Routledge.

Gambash, Gil, Gitler, Haim, & Cotton, Hannah M. (2013), 'Iudaea Recepta', *Israel Numismatic Research* 8, 89–104.

Garrett, Michael G. (1963), 'The African Contribution to the Imperial Equestrian Service', *Historia: Zeitschrift Für Alte Geschichte* 12.2, 209–226.

Geiger, Gregor (2008), 'Mur 174: A Hebrew I. O. U. Document from Wadi Murabba'at', *Studium Biblicum Franciscanum. Liber Annuus* 58, 313–326.

Geiger, Joseph (1976), 'The Ban on Circumcision and the Bar-Kokhba Revolt', *Zion* 41, 139–147. [Hebrew].

Geiger, Joseph (2016), 'The Bar-Kokhba Revolt: The Greek Point of View', *Historia* 65.4 (October), 497–519 (23).

Gergel, Richard A. (1991), 'The Tel Shalem Hadrian Reconsidered', *American Journal of Archaeology* 95.2 (April), 231–251.

Geva, Hillel (1984), 'The Camp of the Tenth Legion in Jerusalem: An Archaeological Reconsideration', *Israel Exploration Journal* 34.4, 239–254.

Geva, Hillel & Dan Bahat (1998), 'Architectural and Chronological Aspects of the Ancient Damascus Gate Area', *Israel Exploration Journal* 48.3/4, 223–235.

Gichon, Mordechai (1986), 'New Insight into the Bar Kokhba War and a Reappraisal of Dio Cassius 69.12–13', *The Jewish Quarterly Review* 77.1 (July), 15–43.

Gichon, Mordechai & Vitale, Michaela (1991), 'Arrow-Heads from Ḥorvat 'Eqed', *Israel Exploration Journal* 41.4, 242–257.

Gilad, Elon, (2016), 'Judaism and Homosexuality: A Brief History', *Haaretz* (2 June): https://www.haaretz.com/jewish/features/.premium-1.722822 (accessed 30 July 2020).

Golan, David (1986), 'Hadrian's Decision to supplant "Jerusalem" by "Aelia Capitolina"', *Historia: Zeitschrift für Alte Geschichte* 35.2 (2nd Qtr.), 226–239.

Goldenberg, Robert (2006), 'The Destruction of the Jerusalem Temple: Its Meaning and Its Consequences' in: Katz, Steven T. (2006) (ed.), *The Cambridge History of Judaism, Volume 4: The Late Roman-Rabbic Period*, Cambridge: Cambridge University Press, 191–205.

Goodman, Martin (2004), 'Trajan and the Origins of Roman Hostility to the Jews', *Past & Present* 182 (Feb.), 3–29.

Goodman, Martin, (2005), 'The *Fiscus Iudaicus* and Gentile Attitudes to Judaism in Flavian Rome' in: Edmondson, J., Mason, S. & Rives, J. (eds.), *Flavius Josephus and Flavian Rome*, Oxford: Oxford University Press, 167–177.

Goodman, Martin (2007), *Rome and Jerusalem: The Clash of Ancient Civilizations*, New York: Alfred A. Knopf.

Goodman, Martin (2018), *A History of Judaism: From Its Origins to the Present*, Princeton: Princeton University Press.

Gordis, Daniel (2016), *Israel: A Concise History of a Nation Reborn*, New York: HarperCollins.

Gould, S. (1933), 'Inscriptions. I. The Triumphal Arch' in: *The Excavations at Dura-Europos conducted by Yale University and the French Academy of Inscriptions and Letters*, Vol. IV, New Haven, 56–65.

Gould, S. (1936), 'Supplementary Inscriptions. I. An Addition to the Inscriptions of the Arch of Trajan' in: *The Excavations at Dura-Europos conducted by Yale University and the French Academy of Inscriptions and Letters*, Vol. VI, New Haven, 480–482.

Grainger, John D. (2012), *The Wars of the Maccabees*, Barnsley: Pen and Sword Books.

Grant, Michael (1994), *The Imperial Roman Army*, Barnes and Noble (reprint).

Grant, Michael (1995), *The Jews in the Roman World*, Barnes and Noble (reprint).

Gray, William D. (1923), 'The Founding of Aelia Capitolina and the Chronology of the Jewish War under Hadrian', *The American Journal of Semitic Languages and Literatures* 39.4 (July), 248–256.

Grayzel, Solomon (1968), 'The Jews and Roman Law', *The Jewish Quarterly Review* 59.2, 93–117.

Greenfield, Jonas C. (1986), 'Découvertes épigraphiques récentes au service de l'histoire de retour de l'exil à Bar-Kokhba', in: Laperrousaz, E.-M. (ed.) *Archéologie, art et histoire de la Palestine: Colloque du centenaire de la section des sciences religieuses, Ecole Pratique des Hautes Etudes, septembre.* Paris: Cerf, 41–53. [French].

Gregorovius, Ferdinand (1898), *Emperor Hadrian: A Picture of the Graeco-Roman World In His Time*, New York: The Macmillan Co.

Gross, Judah Ari (2016), 'The gunmen ordered dessert, then opened fire', *The Times of Israel*, 8 June, 11:46 pm: https://www.timesofisrael.com/the-gunmen-ordered-dessert-then-opened-fire/ (accessed 30 July 2020).

Grossman, Haim (2016), '"Long Ago In Israel Lived a Man Named Bar Kokhba": Hero and Heroism of Lag Boamer in the Culture of Israeli Children' in: Turel, Sara (ed.) (2016), *Bar Kokhba: Historical Memory and the Myth of Heroism*, Tel Aviv: Eretz Israel Museum, 54e-80e/106-151 [Hebrew].

Gruber, Daniel (1999), *Rabbi Akiba's Messiah: The Origins of Rabinic Authority*, Hanover: Elijah Publishing.

Gruen, Erich S. (2010), *Disapora: Jews Amidst Greeks and Romans*, Cambridge, Massachusetts: Harvard University Press.

Gruen, Erich S. (2012), 'Judaism in the Disapora', in: Collins, John J. & Harlow, Daniel C. (eds.) (2012), *Early Judaism: A Comprehensive Overview*, Grand Rapids, Michigan: Wm. B. Eerdmans Publishing, 95–120.

Grüll, Tibor (2005), 'Fragment of a Monumental Roman Inscription at the Islamic Museum of the Haram as-Sharif (Temple Mount), Jerusalem', *American Schools of Oriental Research Newsletter* 55, 16–17.

Grüll, Tibor (2006), 'A fragment of a monumental Roman inscription at the Islamic Museum of the Haram ash-Sharif, Jerusalem,' *Israel Exploration Journal* 56, 183–200.

Gubbay, Lucien (2000), 'The Rise, Decline and Attempted Regeneration of the Jews of the Ottoman Empire', *European Judaism: A Journal for the New Europe* 33.1, 59–69.

Guttmann, Alexander (1942), 'Akiba, "Rescuer of the Torah"', *Hebrew Union College Annual* 17, 395–421.

Hadas, Gideon (1993), 'Where was the Harbour of 'En-Gedi Situated?', *Israel Exploration Journal* 43.1, 45–49.

Hadas, Israel Gideon, Liphschitz, Nili & Bonani, Georges (2005), 'Two Ancient Wooden Anchors from Ein Gedi, on the Dead Sea', *International Journal of Nautical Archaeology* 34.2 (October), 299–307.

Hadas, Gideon (2006), "En Gedi', *Hadashot Arkheologiyot: Excavations and Surveys in Israel, 118.*

Haley, Evan (2005), 'Hadrian as Romulus or the Self-Representation of a Roman Emperor', *Latomus* 64.4 (Oct.-Dec.), 969–980.

Hammer, Reuven (1985), 'A Rabbinic Response to the Post Bar Kochba Era: The Sifre to Ha-Azinu', *Proceedings of the American Academy for Jewish Research 52*, 37–53.

Har-el, Menashe (1978), 'The Route of Salt, Sugar and Balsam Caravans in the Judaean Desert', *GeoJournal* 2.6, Geography in Israel, 549–556.

Harel, M. (1967), 'Israelite and Roman Roads in the Judean Desert', *Israel Exploration Journal* 17.1, 18–26.

Harkabi, Yehoshafat (1983), *The Bar Kokhba Syndrome: Risk and Realism in International Politics*, Chappaqua, New York: Russel Books.

Hassall, M.W.C. (2000), 'The Army' in: Bowman, A.K., Garnsey, P. & Rathbone, D. (eds.), *The Cambridge Ancient History, Volume 11: The High Empire, A.D. 70–192* (2nd ed.); Cambridge: Cambridge University Press, 320–43.

Hasselhof, G.K. & Strothmann, M. (2016), *Religio Licita?: Rom Und Die Juden* (Studia Judaica 84), Berlin: Walter de Gruyter. [German].

Heemstra, Marius (2010a), *The* Fiscus Judaicus *and the Parting of the Ways*, Tübingen: Mohr Siebeck.

Heemstra, Marius (2010b), 'The Interpretation and Wider Context of Nerva's *Fiscus Judaicus* Sestertius" in: Jacobson, David M. & Kokkinos, Nikos (eds.) (2012), *Judaea and Rome in Coins, 65 BCE-135 CE*, London: Spink & Son, 187–201.

Heichelheim, F. M. (1943), 'New Light on the End of Bar Kokba's War', *The Jewish Quarterly Review, New Series* 34.1 (July), 61–63.

Helyer, Larry R. (2002), *Exploring Jewish Literature of the Second Temple Period: A Guide for New Testament Students* (Christian Classics Bible Studies), Downers Grove, Ill., InterVarsity Press Academic.

Hekker, M. (1961), 'The Roman Road of Legio-Sepphoris', *Yediot* 25, 175–186. [Hebrew].

Hendin, David (2012), 'Jewish Coinage of the Two Wars, Aims and Meaning' in: Jacobson, David M. & Kokkinos, Nikos (eds.) (2012), *Judaea and Rome in Coins, 65 BCE-135 CE*, London: Spink & Son, 123–144.

Hendin, David (2014), 'On the Identity of Eleazar the Priest', *Israel Numismatic Journal* 18, 155–167.

Hendin, David & Kreindler, Herbert (2010), *Guide to Biblical Coins*, New York: Amphora Books, (Fifth edition).

Herr, Moshe D. (1968), 'The Decrees of Destruction and Sanctification of God's Name in the Time of Hadrian', *Holy Wars and Martyrology*, 73–91. [Hebrew].

Herr, Moshe D. (1972), 'Persecution and Martyrdom in Hadrian's Days', *Scripta Hierosolymitana* 23, 85–125.

Herr, Moshe D. (1977), 'The Participation of the Galilee in the War of Qitos, and in the Bar Kosba Revolt', *Cathedra* 4, 67–73. [Hebrew].

Hill, G.F. (1914), *A Catalogue of the Greek Coins in the British Museum: Palestine*, London.

Hodges, Frederick Mansfield (2001), 'The Ideal Prepuce in Ancient Greece and Rome: Male Genital Aesthetics and Their Relation to *Lipodermos*, Circumcision, Foreskin Restoration, and the *Kynodesme*', *Bulletin of the History of Medicine* 75.3 (Fall), 375–405.

Holder, Paul (2003), 'Auxiliary Deployment in the Reign of Hadrian', *Bulletin of the Institute of Classical Studies*. Supplement 81, Documenting the Roman Army: Essays in Honour of Margaret Roxan, 101–145.

Holmen, Nicole (2010), 'Examining Greek Pederastic Relationships', *Inquiries Journal/Student Pulse* 2(02): http://www.inquiriesjournal.com/articles/175/examining-greek-pederastic-relationships (accessed 30 July 2020)

Holum, Kenneth G. (1992), 'Hadrian and Caesarea, An Episode in the Romanization of Palestine', *Ancient World* 23, 51–61.

Holum, Kenneth G., Hohlfelder, Robert L., Bull, Robert J., & Raban, Avner (1988), *King Herod's Dream: Caesarea on the Sea*, New York: W.W. Norton and Company.

Holz, Barry W. (2017), Rabbi Akiva: Sage of the Talmud (Jewish Lives), New Haven: Yale University Press.

Horbury, William (2014), *Jewish War under Trajan and Hadrian*, Cambridge: Cambridge University Press.

Houston, John (1961), '*The Memoirs of Hadrian* by Marguerite Yourcenar', *Yale French Studies* 27, 140–141.

Howard, G. & Shelton, J.C. (1973), 'The Bar-Kokhba Letters and Palestinian Greek', *Israel Exploration Journal* 23.2, 101–102.

Hirschfeld, Yizhar (1998), 'Early Roman Manor Houses in Judea and the Site of Khirbet Qumran', *Journal of Near Eastern Studies* 57.3 (July), 161–189.

Hufer, Holger (2013), *Der Bar Kochba-Aufstand (132–135/36 n. Chr.): Ursachen, Verlauf und Folgen unter Einbeziehung aktueller wissenschaftlicher Erkenntnisse*, München: Grin Verlag. [German].

Hufer, Holger (2014), *Die Erhebung der Juden unter Bar Kochba: Der heroische Kampf des jüdischen Volkes gegen die römische Besatzung im 2. Jhd. n. Chr*, Diplomica. [German].

Hurlet, Frédéric (2015), 'The Roman Emperor and the Imperial Family' in: Bruun, C. & Edmondson, J. (eds.) (2015), *Oxford Handbook of Roman Epigraphy*, Oxford: Oxford University Press, 178–201.

Hurwit, Jeffrey M. (2007), 'The Problem with Dexileos: Heroic and Other Nudities in Greek Art', *American Journal of Archaeology* Vol. 111.1 (January), 35–60.

Ilan, Tal (1993), 'Premarital Cohabitation in Ancient Judea: The Evidence of the Babatha Archive and the Mishnah (Ketubbot 1.4)'. *The Harvard Theological Review* 86.3, 247–264.

Iluz, David, Hoffman, Miri, Gilboa-Garber, Nechama & Amar, Zohar, (2010), 'Medicinal properties of *Commiphora gileadensis*', *African Journal of Pharmacy and Pharmacology* 4, 516–520.

Irshai, Oded (1997) 'The Making of the Diaspora' in: De Lange, Nicholas (ed.), *The Illustrated History of the Jewish People*, New York: Harcourt Brace and Company, 53–85.

Irshai, Oded (2011), 'Confronting a Christian Empire: Jewish Life and Culture in the World of Early Byzantium', in: Bonfil, Robert; Irshai, Oded; Stroumsa, Guy G.; Talgam, Rina (eds.), *Jews in Byzantium: Dialectics of Minority and Majority Cultures*, Leiden: Brill, 15 - 64.

Isaac, Benjamin H. (1978), 'Milestones in Judaea, from Vespasian to Constantine', *Palestine Exploration Quarterly* 110, 47–60.

Isaac, Benjamin H. (1984), 'Bandits in Judaea and Arabia', *Harvard Studies in Classical Philology* 88, 171–203.

Isaac, Benjamin H. (1990), *The Limits of Empire: The Roman Army in the East*, Oxford: Clarendon Press. (Revised edition, 1992).

Isaac, Benjamin H. & Oppenheimer, Aharon (1985), 'The Revolt of Bar Kochba: Ideology and Modern Scholarship', *Journal of Jewish Studies* 36, 33–60.

Isaac, Benjamin, and Roll, Israel (1976), 'A Milestone of A.D. 69 from Judaea: The Elder Trajan and Vespasian', *The Journal of Roman Studies* 66, 15–19.

Isaac, Benjamin H. & Roll, Israel (1979a), 'Judaea in the Early Years of Hadrian's Reign', *Latomus* 38, 54–66.

Isaac, Benjamin H. & Roll, Israel (1979b), 'Legio II Traiana in Judaea', *Zeitschrift für Papyrologie und Epigraphik* 33, 149–156.

Isaac, Benjamin H. & Roll, Israel (1982a), 'Legio II Traiana in Judaea: A Reply', *Zeitschrift für Papyrologie und Epigraphik* 47, 131–132.

Isaac, Benjamin H. & Roll, Israel (1982b), *Roman Roads in Judaea I: The Legio-Scythopolis Road*. BAR International Series 141, Oxford.

Isaac, Benjamin H. & Roll, Israel (2004), 'Judaea in the Early Years of Hadrian's Reign', *Nofim* 13–14, 41–54. [Hebrew].

Israel, Gerard & Lebar, Jacques (1973), *When Jerusalem Burned*, London: Vallentine Mitchell and Co..

Jacobson, David M. (2013), 'Military Symbols on the Coins of John Hyrcanus I', *Strata: Bulletin of the Anglo-Israel Archaeological Society* 31, 25–38.

Jacobson, David M. & Kokkinos, Nikos (eds.) (2012), *Judaea and Rome in Coins, 65 BCE-135 CE*, London: Spink & Son.

Jagersma, Henk (1986), *A History of Israel from Alexander the Great to Bar Kochba*, Minneapolis: Fortress Press.

Jarrett, Michael G. (1969), 'Thracian Units in the Roman Army', *Israel Exploration Journal* 19.4, 215–224.

Jarrett, Michael G. (1976), 'An Unnecessary War', *Britannia* 7, 145–151.

Jarrett, Michael G. (1994), 'Non-Legionary Troops in Roman Britain: Part One, the Units', *Britannia* 25, 35–77.

Jensen, Morten Hørning (2014), 'The Political History in Galilee from the First Century BCE to the end of the Second Century CE' in: Fiensy, David A. & Strange, James Riley, *Galilee in the Late Second Temple and Mishnaic Periods: Life, Culture and Society*, Volume 1, Minneapolis: Fortress Press, 51–77.

Johnson, D. (1876), *Translation, Literal and Free, of the Dying Hadrian's Address to His Soul*, Bath.

Johnson, John de Monins, Martin, Victor & Hunt, Arthur S. (eds.) (1915), *Catalogue of the Greek papyri in the John Rylands Library, Manchester. Vol. II. Documents of the Ptolemaic and Roman Periods (Nos. 62–456)*, Manchester: The University Press.

Jones, Christopher P. (2007), 'Three New Letters of the Emperor Hadrian', *Zeitschrift für Papyrologie und Epigraphik* 16, 145–156.

Jones, Mark Wilson (2013), Who Built the Pantheon? Agrippa, Apollodorus, Hadrian and Trajan' In: Opper, Thorsten (ed.) (2013), *Hadrian: Art, Politics and Economy*, Research Publication 175, London: The British Museum, 31–49.

Kadman, Leo (1959), 'When Was Aelia Capitolina Named 'Commodiana' and by Whom?', *Israel Exploration Journal* 9.2, 137–140.

Kanael, B. (1971), 'Notes on the Dates Used During The Bar Kokhba Revolt', *Israel Exploration Journal* 21.1, 39–46.

Karanastasi, Pavlina, (2012/2013), 'Hadrian im Panzer. Kaiserstatuen zwischen Realpolitik und Philhellenismus', *Jahrbuch des deutschen archäologischen Instituts* 127/128, 323 – 391.

Katz, Steven T. (2006) (ed.), *The Cambridge History of Judaism, Volume 4: The Late Roman-Rabbic Period*, Cambridge: Cambridge University Press.

Katzoff, Ranon (2007), "'P. Yadin" 21 and Rabbinic Law on Widows' Rights', *The Jewish Quarterly Review* 97.4 (Fall), 545–575.

Kelly, Benjamin (2007), 'Riot Control and Imperial Ideology in the Roman Empire', *Phoenix* 61.1/2, 150–76.

Kennedy, David L. (1980), 'Legio VI Ferrata: The Annexation and Early Garrison of Arabia', *Harvard Studies in Classical Philology* 84, 283–309.

Kennedy, David L. (1983), 'Milliary Cohorts: The Evidence of Josephus, BJ, III.4.2(67) and of Epigraphy', *Zeitschrift für Papyrologie und Epigraphik*, Bd. 50, 253–263

Kennedy, David L., & Riley, Derrick (1990), *Rome's Desert Frontier from the Air*, Austin: University of Texas Press.

Kenyon, Kathleen M. (1974), *Digging Up Jerusalem*, London: Ernest Benn Limited.

Keppie, Lawrence J. F. (1973), 'The Legionary Garrison of Judaea under Hadrian', *Latomus* 32. 4, 1973, 859–864.

Kindler, Arie (2000), 'Was Aelia Capitolina Founded before or after the Outbreak of the Bar Kokhba War? A Numismatic Evidence', *Israel Numismatic Journal* 14, 176–79.

Kirshner B. (1946), 'A Mint of Bar-Kochba?', *BJPES* 12, 153–160 [Hebrew; English summary, XI].

Kislev, M.E. (1992), 'Vegetal food of Bar Kokhba rebels at Abi'or Cave near Jericho', *Review of Palaeobotany and Palynology* 73 1–4 (30 September), 153–160.

Klein, Eitan, Davidovich, Uri, Ganor, Amir & Sukenik, Naama (2019), 'Naḥal Ḥever: Final Report', *Hadashot Arkheologiyot: Excavations and Surveys in Israel*, vol. 131.

Klein, Eitan, Zissu, Boaz, Goldenberg, Gideon & Ganor, Amir (2015), 'New Studies on the Hideouts Complexes in the Judean Foothills', in: Stiebel, G.D., Peleg-Barkat, O., Ben-Ami, D. & Gadot, Y. (eds.), *New Studies in the Archaeology of Jerusalem and its Region, Collected Papers, Vol. IX*, Jerusalem, 235–255. [Hebrew].

Klein, Eitan & Porat, Roi (2016), 'Nahal 'Arugot: Final Report', *Hadashot Arkheologiyot: Excavations and Surveys in Israel*, vol. 128.

Kloner, Amos (1983), 'Underground Hiding Complexes from the Bar Kokhba War in the Judean Shephelah', *The Biblical Archaeologist* 46.4 (December), 210–221.

Kloner, Amos (1988), 'The Roman Amphitheatre at Beth Guvrin Preliminary Report', *Israel Exploration Journal* 38, No. 1/2, 15–24.

Kloner, Amos & Zissu Boaz (2009), 'Underground Hiding Complexes in Israel and the Bar Kokhba Revolt', *Opera Ipogea* 1, 9–28

Kloner, Amos, & Zissu, Boaz (2014), 'The Geographical Distribution of Hiding Complexes and Refuge Caves during the Bar Kokhba Revolt – Some New Insights' in: Tavger, A., Amar, Z., & Billig, M., (eds.), *Highland's Depth, Ephraim Range and Binyamin Research Studies* 4, Ariel-Talmon, 57–68. [Hebrew].

Kloner, Amos, & Zissu, Boaz (2016), 'The Bar Kokhba War: Archaeological Aspects and Updates' in: Turel, Sara (ed.) (2016), *Bar Kokhba: Historical Memory and the Myth of Heroism*, Tel Aviv: Eretz Israel Museum, 18e-42e/46-87 [Hebrew].

Kramer, J. (1993), 'Die Wiener Liste von Soldaten der III. und XXII. Legion (P. Vindob. L2)', *Zeitschrift für Papyrologie und Epigraphik* 97, 147–158. [German].

Krauss, Samuel (1950), 'The Armies of Bar-Kkhva', in Saul Lieberman (ed.), *Alexander Marx Jubilee Volume* (New York: Jewish Theological Seminary), 391–392 [Hebrew].

Kurtz, Paul Michael (2019), 'How Nineteenth-century German Classicists Wrote the Jews Out of Ancient History', *History and Theory* 58 (2), 210–232.

Laboygianni-Georgakarakou Maria & Emanuele, Papi (2018), *Hadrianus. Hadrian, Athens and the Gymnasia*, Athens: National Archaeological Museum. (Catalogue of the exhibition 'Hadrian and Athens. Conversing with an Ideal World' on display at the National Archaeological Museum, Athens, 27th November 2017 - 29th November 2019.)

Lambert, Royston (1984), *Beloved and God: The Story of Hadrian and Antinous*, London: Weidenfeld and Nicholson.

Laperrousaz, E. M. (1964a), 'L'Hérodium, quartier général de Bar Kokhba?', *Syria* 41.3/4, 182–183.

Laperrousaz, E. M. (1964b), 'L'Hérodium, quartier général de Bar Kokhba?', *Syria* 41.3/4, 347–358.

Lapin, Havim (1993), 'Palm Fronds and Citrons: Notes on Two Letters from Bar Kosiba's Administration', *Hebrew Union College Annual* 64, 111–135.

Lapin, Havim (2006), 'The Origins and Development of the Rabbinic Movement in the Land of Israel' in: Katz, Steven T. (2006) (ed.), *The Cambridge History of Judaism, Volume 4: The Late Roman-Rabbic Period*, Cambridge: Cambridge University Press, 206–229.

Lau, Benyamin (2011), *The Sages, Vol. II: From Yavne to the Bar Kokhba Revolt*, Koren Publishers Jerusalem. Second Printing.

Lauterbach, Jacob Z. (1915), 'Midrash and Mishnah. A Study in the Early History of the Halakah', *The Jewish Quarterly Review*, New Series 6.2 (Oct.), 303–323.

Lehmann, Matthias B & Magid, Shaul (2010), 'Introduction: Jewish Life and Letters in the Ottoman Empire', *Jewish Studies Quarterly* 17.1, 1–3.

Leibner, Uzi (2009a), *Settlement and History in Hellenistic Roman and Byzantine Galilee: An Archeological Survey of the Eastern Galilee*, Tübingen: Mohr Siebeck.

Leibner, Uzi (2009b), 'Kh. Wadi Hamam: A Village and a Synagogue from the Roman Period in Galilee', *Qadmoniot* 139: 32–40 [Hebrew].

Leibner, Uzi (2011), 'Excavations at Khirbet Wadi Hamam (Lower Galilee): The Synagogue and the Settlement', *Journal of Roman Archaeology* 23, 225–226.

Lehmann, Clayton Miles & Holum, Kenneth G. (1999), *The Joint Expedition to Caesarea Maritima: Excavation Reports. The Greek and Latin Inscriptions of Caesarea Maritima*, Volume 5, Boston: American School of Oriental Research.

Lendering, Jona (2014), *Israël verdeeld: hoe uit een klein koninkrijk twee wereldreligies ontstonden*, Amsterdam: Athenaeum-Polak & Van Gennep. [Dutch].

Lernau, Omri & גדי מעין דגים עצמות). 2005'. / (ע, לרנאו / Fish Remains from 'En Gedi', *'Atiqot 49*, 49–56.

Levine, Lee I. (1975), 'Roman Caesarea: An Archaeological-Topographical Study', *Qedem* 2, 1–56.

Lewis, Napthali (1991), 'Hadriani Sententiae', *Greek, Roman and Byzantine Studies* 32.3 (Autumn), 267–280.

Lewis, Naphtali, Yadin, Yigael & Greenfield, Jonas C. (eds.) (1989), *The Documents from the Bar Kokhba Period in the Cave of Letters, Vol. 1, Greek Papyri, Aramaic and Nabatean Signatures and Subscriptions, JDS 2*. Jerusalem: Israel Exploration Society, The Hebrew University of Jerusalem, and the Shrine of the Book.

Lifshitz, Baruch (1960), 'Sur la date du transfert de la *legio* VI *Ferrata* en Palestine', *Latomus* 19.1 (January-March), 109–111. [French].

Limor, Ora (1997), 'A Rejected People' in: De Lange, Nicholas (1997), *The Illustrated History of the Jewish People*, New York: Harcourt Brace, 87–140.

Linder, Amnon (2006), 'The Legal Status of the Jews', in: Katz, Steven T. (2006) (ed.), *The Cambridge History of Judaism, Volume 4: The Late Roman-Rabbic Period*, Cambridge: Cambridge University Press, 128–173.

Lindsay, Hugh (1994), 'Suetonius as 'Ab Epistulis' to Hadrian and the Early History of the Imperial Correspondence', *Historia: Zeitschrift Für Alte Geschichte* 43.4, 454–468.

Luckert, Steven (2002), *The Art and Politics of Arthur Szyk*, Washington: U.S. Holocaust Memorial Museum.

Ma'ani, Sultan Abdullah, Al-Maani, Abd alrzaq, & Al-Nasarat, Mohammed (2014), 'Jerusalem in Classical Ages: A Critical Review', *University of the Aegean 2014: Mediterranean Archaeology & Archaeometry* 14.2, 139–154.

MacCullen, Ramsey (1960), 'Inscriptions on Armor and the Supply of Arms in the Roman Empire', *American Journal of Archaeology* 64.1 (Jan.), 23–40.

MacDonald, William L. & Pinto, John A. (1995), *Hadrian's Villa and its Legacy*, New Haven: Yale University Press.

Magness, Jodi (2011), 'Aelia Capitolina: A review of some current debates about Hadrianic Jerusalem', in: Galor, K. & Avni, G. (eds.), *Unearthing Jerusalem; 150 Years of Archaeological Research in the Holy City*, Winona Lake, Indiana, 313–324.

Magness, Jodi (2012), *The Archaeology of the Holy Land: From the Destruction of Solomon's Temple to the Muslim Conquest*, Cambridge: Cambridge University Press.

Magness, Jodi (2019), *Masada: From Jewish Revolt to Modern Myth*, Princeton: Princeton University Press.

Mairs, Rachel (2012), "Interpreting' at Vindolanda: Commercial and Linguistic Mediation in the Roman Army', *Britannia* 43, 17–28.

Maltz, Judy (2018), 'World Jewish Population on Eve of New Year – 14.7 Million', *Haaretz* (9 September): https://www.haaretz.com/jewish/.premium-world-jewish-population-on-eve-of-new-year-14-7-million-1.6464812 (accessed 30 July 2020).

Manolaraki, Eleni (2015), '*Hebraei Liquores*: The Balsam of Judaea in Pliny's *Natural History*', *American Journal of Philology* 136.4 (Whole Number 544), Winter, 633–667.

Mandell, Sara (1984), 'Who Paid the Temple Tax When the Jews Were under Roman Rule?', *The Harvard Theological Review* 77.2, 223–232.

Manning, Roger B. (1980), 'The Origins of the Doctrine of Sedition', *Albion: A Quarterly Journal Concerned with British Studies* 12.2, 99–121.

Mantel, Hugo (1957), 'The Removals of the Sanhedrin from Yabneh to Usha', *Proceedings of the American Academy for Jewish Research* 26, 65–81.

Mantel, Hugo (1968a), 'The Causes of the Bar Kokba Revolt', *The Jewish Quarterly Review* 58.3 (Jan.), 224–242.

Mantel, Hugo (1968b), 'The Causes of the Bar Kokba Revolt (Continued)', *The Jewish Quarterly Review* 58.4 (Apr.), 274–296.

Marcus, Joel (1989), 'Mark 14:61: "Are You the Messiah-Son-of-God?"', *Novum Testamentum* 31.2 (Apr.), 125–141.

Marks, Richard G. (2005), *The Image of Bar Kokhba in Traditional Jewish Literature: False Messiah and National Hero* (Hermeneutics: Studies in the History of Religions), University Park: Penn State University Press.

Masalha, Nur (2018), *Palestine: A Four Thousand Year History*, London: Zed Books.

Mattingly, Harold (1936), *Coins of Roman Empire in the British Museum, Vol. 3: Nerva to Hadrian*, London: The British Museum.

Mattingly, Harold & Sydenhman, Edward A. (1926), *Roman Imperial Coinage, Vol. 2: Vespasian to Hadrian*, London: Spink & Son.

Maxfield, Valerie (1981), *The Military Decorations of the Roman Army*, London: Batsford.

Mayer, Samuel (1840), 'Simon Barcocheba, Der Messias-Knig' in: *Israelitischer Musenalmanach* 1, Dinkelsbühl, 90–216. [Yiddish].

Mazar, Eliat (2011), *The Temple Mount Excavations in Jerusalem 1968–1978 Directed by Benjamin Mazar. Final Reports Vol. IV: The Tenth Legion in Aelia Capitolina*, Qedem 52, 111–348.

McGlynn, Sean (1998), *Robin Hood: A True Legend*, Sharpe Books.

Meckler, Michael (1966), 'The Beginning of the "Historia Augusta"', *Historia: Zeitschrift für Alte Geschichte* 45.3 (3rd Qtr.), 364–375.

Meir, Cecilia (2016), 'The Bar Kokhba Coinage' in: Turel, Sara (ed.) (2016), *Bar Kokhba: Historical Memory and the Myth of Heroism*, Tel Aviv: Eretz Israel Museum, 43e-53e/88-105 [Hebrew].

M'Elderry, R. Knox (1908), 'The Second Legionary Camp in Palestine', *The Classical Quarterly* 2.2 (Apr.), 110–113.

Merrill, Elmer Truesdell (1919), 'The Expulsion of Jews from Rome under Tiberius', *Classical Philology*, Vol. 14, No. 4 (October), 365–372.

Meshorer, Y. (1989), *The Coinage of Aelia Capitolina*, Jerusalem. [Hebrew].

Mevorah, David, Kreinin, Rachel Caine & Opper, Thorsten (2015), *Hadrian: An Emperor Cast in Bronze*, Jerusalem: The Israel Museum.

Mildenberg, Leo (1949), 'The Eleazar Coins of the Bar Kochba Rebellion', *Historia Judaica* 11.1 (April), 77–108.

Mildenberg, Leo (1980), 'Bar Kokhba Coins and Documents', *Harvard Studies in Classical Philology* 84, 311–335.

Mildenberg, Leo (1984), *The Coinage of the Bar Kokba War, Typos VI*, Sauerländer.

Milik, J. T. (1961), 'Textes Hebreux et Arameens' in: Benoit, P., Milik, J.T. & De Vaux, R. (eds.), *Discoveries in the Judaean Desert II: Les Grottes de Murrabba'at*, Oxford: Oxford University Press, 67–205. [French].

Millar, Fergus (1993), The Roman Near East, 31 BC-AD 337, Cambridge, Mass.: Harvard University Press.

Mnookin, Robert H. (2018), *The Jewish American Paradox: Embracing Choice in a Changing World*, New York: PublicAffairs.

Montefiori, Simon Sebag (2011), *Jerusalem: The Autobiography*, New York: Vintage Books.

Mor, Menachem (1986), 'Two Legions: The Same Fate? (The Disappearance of the Legions IX *Hispana* and XXII *Deiotariana*)', *Zeitschrift für Papyrologie und Epigraphik* 62, 267–278.

Mor, Menahem (1991), *The Bar-Kokhba Revolt, Its Extent and Effect*, Jerusalem: Yad Ben Zvi, The Israel Exploration Society. [Hebrew].

Mor, Menachem (2003), 'The Geographical Scope of the Bar Kokhba Revolt', in: Schäfer, P. (ed.), *The Bar Kokhba War Reconsidered: New Perspectives on the Second Jewish Revolt Against Rome*, Tübingen: Mohr Siebeck, 107–131.

Mor, Menachem (2012), 'Are There Any New Factors Concerning the Bar-Kokhba Revolt?', *Studia Antiqua et Archaeologica* 18, 161–193.

Mor, Menachem (2013), 'What Does Tel Shalem Have To Do With The Bar Kokhba Revolt?', *Scripta Judaica Cracoviensa* 11, 79–96.

Mor, Menachem (2016), *The Second Jewish Revolt: The Bar Kokhba War 132–136 CE.* (Brill Reference Library of Judaism), Leiden: Brill.

Morley, Neville (2010), *The Roman Empire: Roots of Imperialism*, London: Pluto Press.

Mowry, Lucetta (1952), 'Settlements in the Jericho Valley during the Roman Period (63 B.C. - A.D. 134)', *The Biblical Archaeologist* 15.2, 26–42.

Münter, Friedrich (1821), *Der jüdische Krieg unter den Kaisern Trajan und Hadrian*, Altona-Leipzig: J.F. Hemmerich. [German].

Murphy-O'Connor, Jerome (1994), 'The Location of the Capitol in Aelia Capitolina', *Revue Biblique (1946–)*, 101.3, 407–415.

Nassar, Mohammad (2014), 'Hadrian's Arches from Roman Period, Jordan: A Comparative Study', *Mediterranean Archaeology and Archaeometry* 14.1, 247–259: http://maajournal.com/Issues/2014/Vol14-1/Full20.pdf (accessed 30 July 2020).

Noar, Mordechai, (2016), 'Bar Kokhba or Bar Kosiva? The Controversy Over the Play *Bar Kokhba* That Premiered at the *Ohel* Theatre in 1945' in: Turel, Sara (ed.) (2016), *Bar Kokhba: Historical Memory and the Myth of Heroism*, Tel Aviv: Eretz Israel Museum, 81e-95e/152-177 [Hebrew].

Nathan, H. (1961), 'The Skeletons of the Naḥal Mishmar Caves', *Israel Exploration Journal* 11.1/2, The Expedition to the Judaean Desert 1960, 65–69.

Neef, Heinz-Dieter (1981), 'Die Mutatio Betthar: Eine Römische Straßenstation Zwischen Caesarea Und Antipatris', *Zeitschrift Des Deutschen Palästina-Vereins (1953–)* 97.1, 74–80. [German].

Netzer, Ehud (1988), 'Jewish Rebels Dig Strategic Tunnel System', *Biblical Archaeology Review* 14.4 (July/August): https://www.baslibrary.org/biblical-archaeology-review/14/4/2 (accessed 30 July 2020).

Netzer, Ehud & Arzi, S. (1985), 'Herodium Tunnels', *Qadmoniot* 18, 33–38. [Hebrew].

Netzer E., Kalman Y., Porat R., & Chachy R. (2011), 'Herodium During the Two Revolts' in: A. Tavger, A., Amar, Z. & Billig, M. (eds.), *In the Highland's Depth* I, 59–68. [Hebrew].

Nevins, Arthur J. (2006), 'When was Solomon's Temple Burned Down? Reassessing the Evidence', *Journal for the Study of the Old Testament* 31.1, 3–25.

Nissenbaum, Arie, Serban, A., Amiran, R. & Ilan, O. (1984), 'Dead Sea Asphalt from the Excavations in Tel Arad and Small Tel Malhata', *Paléorient* 10.1, 157–161.

Noreña, Carlos F. (2007), 'Hadrian's Chastity', *Phoenix* 61.3/4 (Fall-Winter), 296–317.

Novenson, Matthew V. (2009), 'Why Does R. Akiba Acclaim Bar Kokhba as Messiah?', *Journal for the Study of Judaism in the Persian, Hellenistic, and Roman Period* 40.4/5, 551–572.

Offord, Joseph (1898), 'Roman Inscriptions Relating to Hadrian's Jewish War', *Proceedings of the Society of Biblical Archaeology* 20 (February), 59–69.

Olami, J. & Ringel, J. (1975), 'New Inscriptions of the Tenth Legion Fretensis from the High Level Aqueduct of Caesarea', *Israel Exploration Journal* 25.2/3, 148–150.

O'Donnell, James (2015), *Pagans: The End of Traditional Religion and the Rise of Christianity*, New York: Ecco.

O'Neil, J.C. (2000), 'The Mocking of Bar Kokhba and of Jesus', *Journal for the Study of Judaism in the Persian, Hellenistic, and Roman Period* 31.1, 39–41.

Oldstone-Moore, Christopher (2015), *Of Beards and Men: The Revealing History of Facial Hair*, Chicago: University of Chicago Press.

Oppenheimer, Aharon (1977), 'The Jewish Community in Galilee during the Period of Yavneh and the Bar Kokhba Revolt', *Cathedra* 4, 53–66, 82–83. [Hebrew].

Oppenheimer, Aharon (2003), 'The Ban of Circumcision as a Cause of the Revolt: A Reconsideration' in: Schäfer, Peter (ed.), *Bar Kokhba War Reconsidered: New Perspectives on the Second Jewish Revolt Against Rome*, Texts and Studies in Ancient Judaism 100, Tübingen: Mohr Siebeck, 55–70.

Oppenheimer, Aharon (2005a), 'Urbanisation and City Territories in Roman Palestine' in: Oppenheimer, Aharon, *Between Rome and Babylon. Studies in Jewish Leadership and Society*, Tübingen: Mohr Siebeck, 30–46.

Oppenheimer, Aharon (2005b), 'Jewish Conscripts in the Roman Army?' in: Oppenheimer, Aharon, *Between Rome and Babylon. Studies in Jewish Leadership and Society*, Tübingen: Mohr Siebeck, 183–194.

Oppenheimer, Aharon (2005c), 'Die jüdische Bewohnerschaft Galiläas zur Zeit von Jawne und während des Bar-Kochba-Aufstands', in: Oppenheimer, Aharon, *Between Rome and Babylon. Studies in Jewish Leadership and Society*, Tübingen: Mohr Siebeck, 225–242.

Oppenheimer, Aharon (2005d), 'Betar als Zentrum vor dem Bar-Kochba-Aufstands', in: Oppenheimer, Aharon, *Between Rome and Babylon. Studies in Jewish Leadership and Society*, Tübingen: Mohr Siebeck, 303–319.

Oppenheimer, Aharon & Isaac, Benjamin (2005), 'The Revolt of Bar Kokhba' in: *Between Rome and Babylon: Studies in Jewish Leadership and Society* (Texts and Studies in Ancient Judaism), Tübingen: Mohr Siebeck, 197–224.

Oppenheimer, Aharon & Oppenheimer, Nili (eds.) (2005), *Between Rome and Babylon: Studies in Jewish Leadership and Society* (Texts and Studies in Ancient Judaism), Tübingen: Mohr Siebeck.

אהרן, אופנהיימר, & Oppenheimer, Ahron (2009), 'Developments in the Study of the Bar Kokhva Revolt During the Sixty Years of the State of Israel, *Zion*, 2009, 65–94. [Hebrew].

Opper, Thorsten (2008), *The Emperor Hadrian: Empire and Conflict*, London: The British Museum.

Opper, Thorsten (ed.) (2013), *Hadrian: Art, Politics and Economy*, Research Publication 175, London: The British Museum.

Oron, A., Galili, E., Hadas, G., & Klein, M. (2015), 'Early Maritime Activity on the Dead Sea: Bitumen Harvesting and the Possible Use of Reed Watercraft', *Journal of Maritime Archaeology* 10(1), 65–88.

Oudshoorn, Jacobine G. (2007), *The Relationship between Roman and Local Law in the Babatha and Salome Komaise Archives* (Studies on the Texts of the Desert of Judah), Leiden: Brill.

Parkinson, Richard B. (2013), *A Little Gay History: Desire and Diversity Across the World*, London: The British Museum Press.

Patrich, Joseph (2002), 'On the Lost Circus of Aelia Capitolina', *Scripta Classica Israelica* 21, 173–188.

Pearson, Brook W. R. (1998), 'Dry Bones in the Judean Desert: The Messiah of Ephraim, Ezekiel 37, and the Post-Revolutionary Followers of Bar Kokhba', *Journal for the Study of Judaism in the Persian, Hellenistic, and Roman Period* 29.2, 192–201.

Peleg, Y. (1989), 'Caesarea's Water Supply System' in: Amit, D., Hirschfeld, Y. & Patrich, J. (eds.), *The Aqueducts of Ancient Palestine. Research Collection*, Jerusalem, 115–122. [Hebrew].

Peleg, Y. (1990), 'The Storage Lake of the Low Level Aqueduct to Caesarea', *Cathedra* 56, 19–32. [Hebrew].

Peleg, Y. (2002), 'The Dams of Caesarea's Low Level Aqueduct' in: Amit, D., Patrich, J., & Hirschfeld, Y. (eds.), *The Aqueducts of Israel*, Portsmouth, RI, 141–148.

Penslar, Derek J. (1997), '"To Be a Free Nation"' in: De Lange, Nicholas (1997), *The Illustrated History of the Jewish People*, New York: Harcourt Brace, 303–354.

Perring, Dominic (2017), 'London's Hadrianic War?', *Britannia* 48, 37–76: https://doi.org/10.1017/S0068113X17000113 (accessed 30 July 2020).

Perowne, Stewart H. (1986), *Hadrian*, Croom Helm (reprint).

Petrakis Nicholas L. (1980), 'Diagonal earlobe creases, type A behavior and the death of Emperor Hadrian', *The Western Journal of Medicine* 132.1, 87–91.

Pincus, Jessie A., DeSmet, Timothy S., Tepper, Yotam, & Adams, Matthew J. (2013), 'Ground Penetrating Radar and Electromagnetic Archaeogeophysical Investigations at the Roman Legionary Camp at Legio, Israel', *Archaeological Prospection* 20, 175–188.

Pollard, N. (2001), *Soldiers, Cities and Civilians in Roman Syria*, Ann Arbor: University of Michigan Press.

Porat, Roi, Eschel, Hanan & Frumkin, Amos (2007), 'Finds from the Bar Kokhba Revolt from Two Caves at En Gedi', *Palestine Exploration Quarterly*, 139.1, 35–53.

Porat, Roi, Eshel, Hanan & Frumkin, Amos (2009), 'The 'Caves of the Spear': Refuge Caves from the Bar-Kokhba Revolt North of 'En-Gedi', *Israel Exploration Journal* 59.1, 21–46.

Porat, Roi, Kalman, Ya'akov, Chachy, Rachel & Zissu, Boaz (2017), 'Underground Herodium: Guerrilla Warfare during the Bar Kokhba War (132–136 CE) under Herod's Royal Palace Fortress', in: Parise, Mario *et al* (eds), *Cappadocia-Hypogea 2017: Proceedings of International Congress of Speleology in Artificial Caves, Cappadocia, Turkey, March 06/10–2017*, Ege Yayinlari: Istanbul, 337–348.

Porath, Yosef, & Porath, Josef (2005), 'Survey of Ancient Agricultural Systems at the 'En Gedi Oasis', *'Atiqot*, vol. 50, 237–239.

Powell, Lindsay (1987), 'Bar Kokhba: The Roman Army in the Second Jewish Revolt AD 132–5', *Exercitus* (Bulletin of The Ermine Street Guard) 2.3 (Summer), 40–45.

Powell, Lindsay (2013), *Germanicus: The Magnificent Life and Mysterious Death of Rome's Most Popular General*, Barnsley: Pen and Sword Books.

Powell, Lindsay (2015), *Marcus Agrippa: Right-Hand Man of Caesar Augustus*, Barnsley: Pen and Sword Books.

Powell, Lindsay (2018), *Augustus at War: The Struggle for the* Pax Augusta, Barnsley: Pen and Sword Books.

Powell, Lindsay (2019), '*Ave, vive, Antinoe!* The Boy Made God Revived', *Ancient History* 20, 54–57.

Powell, Lindsay & Dennis, Peter (2014), *Roman Soldier Versus Germanic Warrior, 1st Century AD* (Combat 6), Oxford: Osprey Publishing.

Powell, Lindsay & Dennis, Peter (2017), *The Bar Kokhba War AD 132–136: The Last Jewish Revolt Against Imperial Rome* (Campaign 310), Oxford: Osprey Publishing.

Presner, Todd Samuel (2007), *Muscular Judaism: The Jewish Body and the Politics of Regeneration* (Routledge Jewish Studies Series), Abingdon: Routlege.

Qimron, E. (1994–1995), 'The Use of ב שיש – "Which Is in ..." - An Aramaism in the Bar Kokha Documents', *Leš* 58/4, 313–315.

Quint, Alyssa (2000), 'Abraham Goldfadn's Play *Bar Kokhba*', *Hulyot: Journal of Yiddish Research* 6, 79–90. [Hebrew].

Rabello, A.M. (1995), 'The Ban on Circumcision as a Cause of Bar Kokhba's Rebellion', *Israel Law Review* 29, 176–214.

Rankov, Boris & Hook, Richard (1994), *The Praetorian Guard*, (Elite Series 50), London: Osprey Publishing.

Rankov, Boris (1999), 'The governor's men: the *officium consularis* in provincial administration', in: Goldsworthy, Adrian & Haynes, Ian (eds), *The Roman Army as a Community*. JRA Supplementary Series, 15–34.

Raviv, Dvir, (2016), 'Khirbet Kelafa – A Jewish settlement from the Second Temple period and the Bar-Kokhba Revolt in the Northern Hebron Mountains', *Journal for the Study of Archaeology and History of the highland's region* 6, 51–66.

Raviv, Dvir, Har-Even, B., & Tavger, A. (2016), 'Khirbet el-Qutt – A Fortified Jewish Village in Southern Samaria from the Second Temple Period and the Bar Kokhba Revolt', *Judea and Samaria Research Studies* 25, Ariel, 17–35.

Rea, J. R. (1980), 'The Legio II Traiana in Judaea?', *Zeitschrift für Papyrologie und Epigraphik* 38, 220–221.

Rénan, Ernest (1878), 'The Emperor Hadrian and Christianity', *The North American Review* 127.265 (Nov. - Dec.), 492–508.

Reinhartz, Adele (1989), 'Rabbinic Perceptions of Simeon bar Kosiba', *Journal for the Study of Judaism in the Persian, Hellenistic, and Roman Period* 20.2, 171–194.

Richardson, Peter (1996), *Herod: King of the Jews and Friend of the Romans* (Routledge Ancient Biographies), Columbia: University of South Carolina Press.

Ritterling, E. (1903), 'Caparcotna = Leğğûn in Galilaea', *Rheinisches Museum für Philologie, Neue Folge* 58, 633–635.

Rohrbacher, David (2003), 'The Sources of the *Historia Augusta* Re-examined', *Histos* 7, 146–180.

Roll, Israel (1976), 'The Roman Road Network in Eretz-Israel', *Qadmoniot* 9, 38–50. [Hebrew].

Roll, Israel (1996), 'Roman Roads to Caesarea Maritima', in: A. Raban, K.G. Holum (eds.), *Caesarea Maritima: A Retrospective after Two Millennia*, Leiden: Brill.

Roll, Israel (1999), 'The Roads in Roman-Byzantine Palaestina and Arabia', in: Alliata, E. & Piccirillo, M. (eds.), *The Madaba Map Centenary, 1897–1997: Traveling through the Byzantine Umayyad Period. Proceedings of the International Conference held in Amman, 7–9 April 1997*, Jerusalem, 109–113.

Roll, Israel (2011), 'Roman Roads to Caesarea Maritima', in: Ayalon, E. & Izdarechet, A. (eds.), *Caesarea Treasures: Summaries and Research on Caesarea and its Vicinity Submitted in honor of Josef Porath, Vol. 1*, Jerusalem: 239–256. [Hebrew].

Roll, Israel & Ayalon, Eitan (1986), 'Roads in Western Samaria', *Palestine Exploration Quarterly* 118, 113–134.

Roll, Israel & Ayalon, Eitan (1986/87), 'Main Highways in the Sharon in the Roman and Byzantine Archaeological Periods', *Israel – Am ve-Aretz* 4/22, 156–157.

Rosenblum, J. D. (2010), "Why Do You Refuse to Eat Pork?" Jews, Food, and Identity in Roman Palestine', *The Jewish Quarterly Review* 100.1, 95–110.

Rowland, Robert C. (1985), *The Rhetoric of Menachem Begin: The Myth of Redemption Through Return*, Lanham: University Press Of America.

Roth, Jonathan P. (1999), *The Logistics of the Roman Army at War (265 B.C.-A.D. 235)*, Leiden: Brill.

Rozenberg, Silvia & Mevorah, David (2013), *Herod the Great: the King's Final Journey*, Jerusalem: The Israel Museum.

Russell, Frank (2016), 'Roman Counterinsurgency Policy and Practice in Judaea', in: Howe, Timothy & Lee L. Brice (eds.). *Brill's Companion to Insurgency and Terrorism in the Ancient Mediterranean*, Brill's Companions in Classical Studies: Warfare in the Ancient Mediterranean World, Leiden: Brill, 248–281.

Safrai, Ze'ev (1994), *The Economy of Roman Palestine*, London: Routledge.

Sagiv, Nachum & Zissu, Boaz (2006), 'A Note on a Bar Kokhba Coin from Tel Goded in the Judean Shephelah', *Israel Numismatic Journal* 15, 87–89.

Sand, Schlomo (2012), *The Invention of Israel: From Holyland to Homeland*, Verso.

Sanders, E. P. (1973), 'R. Akiba's View of Suffering', *The Jewish Quarterly Review* 63.4 (Apr.), 332–351.

Sartre, Maurice (2005), *The Middle East Under Rome*, Cambridge, Mass.: Belknap Press.

Schäfer, Peter (1998), *Judeophobia: Attitudes toward the Jews in the Ancient World*, Cambridge, Massachusetts: Harvard University Press.

Schäfer, Peter (ed.) (2003a), *Bar Kokhba War Reconsidered: New Perspectives on the Second Jewish Revolt Against Rome*, Texts and Studies in Ancient Judaism 100, Tübingen: Mohr Siebeck.

Schäfer, Peter (ed.) (2003b), 'Bar Kokhba and the Rabbis' in: Schäfer, Peter (ed.), *Bar Kokhba War Reconsidered: New Perspectives on the Second Jewish Revolt Against Rome*, Texts and Studies in Ancient Judaism 100, Tübingen: Mohr Siebeck, 1–22.

Schäfer, Peter (2020), *Two Gods in Heaven: Jewish Concepts of God in Antiquity*, Princeton: Princeton University Press.

Schama, Simon M. (2013), *The Story of the Jews: Finding the Words (1000 BCE – 1492)* (Story of the Jews Vol. 1), London: The Bodley Head.

Scheck, Franz Rainer (1997), *Jordanien. Völker und Kulturen zwischen Jordan und Rotem Meer*, Köln: DuMont Kunstreiseführer. [German].

Schiffman, Lawrence H. (2003a), 'Jerusalem: Twice Destroyed, Twice Rebuilt', *The Classical World* 97.1 (Autumn), 31–40.

Schiffman, Lawrence H. (2003b), 'Witness and Signatures in the Hebrew and Aramaic Documents from the Bar Kokhba Caves' in: Schiffman, L.H. (ed.), *Semitic Papyrology in Context: A Climate of Creativity. Papers from a New York University conference marking the retirement of Baruch A. Levine*, Culture and History of the Ancient Near East 14, Leiden and Boston: Brill, 165–186.

Schiffman, Lawrence H. (2006), 'Messianism and Apocalypticism in Rabbinic Texts' in: Katz, Steven T. (2006) (ed.), *The Cambridge History of Judaism, Volume 4: The Late Roman-Rabbic Period*, Cambridge: Cambridge University Press, 1053–1072.

Schiffman, Lawrence H. (2012), 'Early Judaism and Rabbinic Judaism' in: Collins, John J. & Harlow, Daniel C. (eds.) (2012), *Early Judaism: A Comprehensive Overview*, Grand Rapids, Michigan: Wm. B. Eerdmans Publishing, 420–434.

Schlatter, Adolf (1897), *Die Tage Trajans und Hadrians*, Gütersloh: C. Bertelsmann.

Schoenfeld, Andrew J. (2006), 'Sons of Israel in Caesar's Service: Jewish Soldiers in the Roman Military', *Shofar: An Interdisciplinary Journal of Jewish Studies* 24.3 (Spring), 115–126.

Schulman, Kalman (1858), *Harisot Betar: sipur `al dever gevurat Bar Kokhva ve-hurban Betar bi-yad Adriyanus kesar Roma*, Vilna: Joseph Reuben b. Menaḥem Romm. [Hebrew].

Schürer, Emil, (1973), *The History of the Jewish People in the Age of Jesus Christ, Volume 1* (revised edition – Millar, Fergus & Vermes, Geza (eds.)), London: Bloomsbury.

Schwartz, Jacques (1989), 'Où a passé la legio XXII Deiotariana?', *Zeitschrift Für Papyrologie Und Epigraphik* 76, 101–102.

Schwartz, Seth (1997), 'Beginnings' in: De Lange, Nicholas (ed.) (1997), *The Illustrated History of the Jewish People*, New York: Harcourt Brace, 3–52.

Schwartz, Seth (2006), 'Political, Social and Economic Life in the Land of Israel 66–c. 235' in: Katz, Steven T. (2006) (ed.), *The Cambridge History of Judaism, Volume 4: The Late Roman-Rabbic Period*, Cambridge: Cambridge University Press, 23–52.

Seelentag, Gunnar (2017), 'Die Dynamik von Herrschaftsdarstellung und Triumphideologie im ausgehenden 1. und frühen 2. Jh.' in: Goldbeck, Fabian & Wienand, Johannes (eds.), *Der römische Triumph in Prinzipat und Spätantike*, Berlin: De Gruyter, 177–214.

Seeman, Chris & Marshak, Adam Kolman (2012), 'Jewish History from Alexander to Hadrian' in: Collins, John J. & Harlow, Daniel C. (eds.) (2012), *Early Judaism: A Comprehensive Overview*, Grand Rapids, Michigan: Wm. B. Eerdmans Publishing, 30–69.

Segal, Aaron, (1973), 'Herodium', *Israel Exploration Journal* 23.1, 27–29.

Segal, Alan F. (1986), *Rebecca's Children: Judaism and Christianity in the Roman World*, Cambridge, Mass.: Harvard University Press.

Shah, Nasim Hasan (1988), 'The concept of Al-Dhimmah and the rights and duties of Dhimmis in an Islamic state', *Institute of Muslim Minority Affairs. Journal*, 9:2, 217–222.

Shapira, Anita (1997), 'Ben-Gurion and the Bible: The Forging of an Historical Narrative?', *Middle Eastern Studies* 33.4 (October), 645–674.

Shapira, Anita (2004a), 'The Bible and Israeli Identity', *AJS Review* 28.1, 11–41.

Shapira, Anita (2004b), 'The Eichmann Trial: Changing Perspectives', *Journal of Israeli History* 23:1, 18–39.

Sheppard, Si (2013), *The Jewish Revolt, AD 66–74* (Campaign 252), Oxford: Osprey Publishing.

Shimony, Carmela, Yucha, Rivka & Werker, Ella (1992), 'Ancient Anchor Ropes from the Dead Sea', *'Atiqot* 21, 58–62.

Sidebottom, Harry (2003), 'The Army in Syria', *The Classical Review* 53.2 (Oct.), 431–433.

Simkins, Michael & Embledon, Ronald (1979), *The Roman Army from Hadrian to Constantine* (Men-at-Arms Series, 93), Oxford: Osprey Publishing.

Sherk, Robert (1971), 'Specialization in the Provinces of Germany', *Historia: Zeitschrift Für Alte Geschichte* 20.1, 110–121.

Shinan, Avigdor (2006), 'The Late Midrashic, Paytanic, and Targumic Literature' in: Katz, Steven T. (2006) (ed.), *The Cambridge History of Judaism, Volume 4: The Late Roman-Rabbic Period*, Cambridge: Cambridge University Press, 678–698.

Shipler, David K. (1982), 'Israel Buries Remains of Ancient Warriors', *The New York Times*, (12 May), A2: https://www.nytimes.com/1982/05/12/world/israel-buries-bones-of-ancient-warriors.html (accessed 30 July 2020).

Shivti'el, Yinon (2017), 'Hiding Complexes in the Galilee, Israel: Artificial Refuge Caves in the Early Roman Period' in: Parise, Mario, Galeazzi, Carla, Bixio, Roberto & Yamac, Ali (eds.) *Hypogea 2017 - Proceedings of International Congress of Speleology in Artificial Cavities - Cappadocia, March 6/8, 2017*, 85–94.

Shivti'el, Yinon (2019), *Cliff Shelters and Hiding Complexes: The Jewish Defense Methods in Galilee During the Roman Period, The Speleological and Archaeological Evidence* (Novum Testamentum et Orbis Antiquus. Series Archaeologica - Band 006), Vandenhoeck & Ruprecht Verlage.

Shivtiel, Yinon & Frumkin, Amos (2014), The use of caves as security measures in the Early Roman Period in the Galilee: Cliff Settlements and Shelter Caves', *Caderno de Geografia* 24.41, 77–85: http://www.redalyc.org/html/3332/333229407006/

Singer, Saul Jay (2015), 'The Burial of the 'Bar Kochba Bones', (12 February), *Jewish Press*: https://www.jewishpress.com/sections/features/features-on-jewish-world/the-burial-of-the-bar-kochba-bones/2015/02/12/ (accessed 30 July 2020).

Sijpesteijn, P. J. (1984), 'A Note on P. Murabba'at 29', *Israel Exploration Journal* 34.1, 49–50.

Skov, Eric T. (2013), 'Experimentation in Sling Weaponry: Effectiveness of and Archaeological Implications for a World-Wide Primitive Technology', University of Nebraska-Lincoln: http://digitalcommons.unl.edu/cgi/viewcontent.cgi?article=1032&context=anthrotheses (accessed 30 July 2020).

Smallwood, E. Mary (1956), 'Some notes on the Jews under Tiberius', *Latomus* T. 15, Fasc. 3 (July-September), 314–329.

Smallwood, E. Mary (1959), 'The Legislation of Hadrian and Antoninus Pius against Circumcision', *Latomus* 18, 334–347.

Smallwood, E. Mary (1961), 'The Legislation of Hadrian and Antoninus Pius against Circumcision: Addendum', *Latomus* 20, 93–96.

Smallwood, E. Mary (1962), 'Atticus, Legate of Judaea under Trajan', *The Journal of Roman Studies* 52, Parts 1 and 2, 131–133.

Smallwood, E. Mary (1981), *The Jews Under Roman Rule from Pompey to Diocletian.* (Studies in Judaism in Late Antiquity Book 20), Leiden: Brill.

Smith, R.R.R, Gigante, Frederica, Lenaghan, Julia & Melfi, Milena (2018), *Antinous: boy made god*, Oxford: Ashmolean Museum.

Smith, Terence (1975), 'Statue of Hadrian Is Found in Israel By a N. Y. Broker', *The New York Times* (5 August), front page: https://www.nytimes.com/1975/08/05/

archives/statue-of-hadrian-is-found-in-israel-by-a-ny-broker-new-york-broker.html (accessed 30 July 2020).

Speidel, Michael P. (2006), *Emperor Hadrian's Speeches to the African Army – A New Text*, (Romisch-Germanisches Zentralmuseum, Forschungsinstitut für Vor- und Frühgeschichte. Monographien des Romisch-Germanischen Zentralmuseums 65), Mainz: Verlag des Romisch-Germanischen Zentralmuseums Mainz.

Spijkerman, Augustus, & Piccirillo, Michele (1978), *The Coins of the Decapolis and Provincia Arabia* (Studii Biblici Franciscani Collectio Maior 25), Jerusalem: Franciscan Printing Press.

Sporty, Lawrence D. (1983), 'Identifying the Curving Line on the Bar-Kokhba Temple Coin', *The Biblical Archaeologist* 46.2 (Spring), 121–123.

Starr, Chester G. Starr (1956), 'Aurelius Victor: Historian of Empire', *The American Historical Review* 61.3, 574–586.

Stebnicka, Krystyna (2015), 'Identity of the Diaspora. Jews in Asia Minor in the Imperial Period', *Journal of Juristic Papyrology*, Supplement 26, Warsaw.

Steinitz, Yuval (1991), 'The Bar-Kokhba Revolt: A Proposition for New Perspective: War or Guerilla?', *Zemanim* 33, 62–71 [Hebrew].

Stiebel, Guy D. (2003), 'The *Militaria* from Herodium' in: Bottini, G.C., di Spegni, L., & Chrupcala, L.D. (eds.), *One Land – Many Cultures. Archaeological Studies in Honour of S. Loffreda*, Studium Biblicum Franciscanum Collectio Maior 41, Jerusalem: Franciscan Printing Press, 99–108.

Stiebel, Guy D. (2004), 'Military Equipment from the Period of the Second Revolt in the Judaean Desert Caves', *Judea and Samaria Research Studies* 13, 117–134. [Hebrew].

Stiebel, Guy D. (2014), 'Military Equipment' in: Syon, Danny (ed.) *Gamla III: The Shmarya Gutmann Excavations 1976–1989. Finds and Studies. Part 1*, Israel Antiquities Authority Report 56, 57–108.

Stinespring, William F. (1939), 'Hadrian in Palestine, 129/130 A. D.', *Journal of the American Oriental Society* 59.3 (Sep.), 360–365.

Stone, Michael (ed.) (1984), *Jewish Writings of the Second Temple Period: Apocrypha, Pseudepigrapha, Qumran Sectarian Writings, Philo, Josephus* (The Literature of the Jewish People in the Period of the Second Temple and the Talmud, Book 2), Minneapolis: Fortress Press.

Strack, Hermann Leberecht & Stemberger, Günter (1996), *Introduction to the Talmud and Midrash*, Minneapolis: Fortress Press (Second Ed.).

Strobel, Karl (1988), 'Zu Fragen der frühen Geschichte der römischen Provinz Arabia und zu einigen Problemen der Legionsdislokation im Osten des Imperium Romanum zu Beginn des 2. Jh.N.Chr.', *Zeitschrift Für Papyrologie Und Epigraphik* 71, 251–280.

Syme, Roland (1985), 'Curtailed Tenures of Consular Legates', *Zeitschrift Für Papyrologie Und Epigraphik* 59, 265–279.

Syme, Roland (1988), 'Journeys of Hadrian', *Zeitschrift für Papyrologie und Epigraphik* 73, 159–170.

Tacoma, Laurens E., Ivleva, Tatiana, & Breeze, David J. (2016), 'Lost Along the Way: A Centurion "Domo Britannia" in Bostra', *Britannia* 47, 31–42.

Taylor, Joan E. (2012), *The Essenes, the Scrolls, and the Dead Sea*, Oxford: Oxford University Press.

Taylor, John (1988). 'Waiting for Hadrian', *The Georgia Review* 42.1, 147–151.

Tepper, Yotam (2004), 'Roman Roads in the 'Airon Pass': Paving Remains from Caesarea to the Sixth Legion camp in Legio', in: Bar Gal, Y., Kliot, N. & Peld, A. (eds.), *Researches in the Land of Israel*, Aviel Ron's Book, Haifa, 47–82. [Hebrew].

Tepper, Yotam (2007), 'The Roman legionary camp at Legio, Israel: Results of an archaeological survey and observations on the Roman military presence at the site', in: Lewin, A.S. & Pellegrini, P. (eds.), *The Late Roman Army in the Near East from Diocletian to the Arab Conquest. Proceedings of a Colloquium Held at Potenza, Acerenza and Matera, Italy (May 2005)*, Oxford, 57–71.

Tepper, Yotam (2011), '19 Miles from… Roman road from Legio to Caesarea via Ramat Menasche', in: Ayalon, E., & Izdarechet, A. (eds.), *Caesarea Treasures: Summaries and Research on Caesarea and its Vicinity Submitted in honor of Josef Porath, vol. 1*, Jerusalem, 257–274. [Hebrew].

Tepper, Yotam (2017), 'Roof Tiles and Bricks Bearing Roman Legionary Stamps from Legio', *'Atiqot* 89, 123–124.

Tepper, Yotam, David, Jonathan & Adams, Matthew J. (2015), 'The Legionary Base of the Roman Sixth Ferrata Legion at Legio, Israel', *Popular Archaeology Magazine* 18, (Spring): http://popular-archaeology.com/issue/spring-2015/article/the-legionary-base-of-the-roman-sixth-ferrata-legion-at-legio-israel (accessed 30 July 2020).

Terrill, W. Andrew (2017), *Antiquities Destruction and Illicit Sales as Sources of ISIS Funding and Propaganda*, Strategic Studies Institute, Carlisle, Penn.: US Army War College.

Thompson, David L. (1981), 'The Lost City of Antinoos', *Archaeology*, vol. 34, no. 1, 44–50.

Thompson, Trevor (2013), 'Antinoos, The New God: Origen on Miracle and Belief in Third-Century Egypt' in: Tobias Nicklas & Janet E. Spittler (eds.), Credible, Incredible: The Miraculous in the Ancient Mediterranean, Tübingen: Mohr Siebeck, 160–161.

Thomsen. P. (1917), 'Die römischen Meilensteine der Provinzen Syria, Arabia und Palaestina', *Zeitschrift des Deutschen Palästina-Vereins* 40, 1–103.

Tommasini, Anthony, 'Review: Rufus Wainwright's 'Hadrian' Is a Step Forward, but Still Frustrating', *The New York Times*, 3 November 2018.

Towndrow, Kenneth Romney (1949), 'Project for a Great Menorah I., The Sculptor Benno Elkan' in: *The Menorah Journal* 37.2, (Spring).

Tsafrir, Yoram & Zissu, Boaz (2002), 'A Hiding Complex of the Second Temple Period and the Time of the Bar-Kokhba Revolt at 'Ain-'Arrub in the Hebron Hills', *Journal of Archaeology* Supplementary Series 49 The Roman and Byzantine Near East Vol. 3, 7–36.

Tracy, S. (1998), 'An Imperial Inscription from Petra', in: M. Joukowsky (ed.), *Petra Great Temple, Volume I, Brown University Excavations 1993–1997*, Providence: Brown University Petra Exploration Fund, 370–375.

Tracy, S. (1999), 'The dedicatory inscription to Trajan at the 'metropolis' of Petra', in: Humphery, J.H. (ed.), *The Roman and Byzantine Near East, vol. II: Some Recent Archaeological Research*, Portsmouth, RI, 51–58.

Tropper, Arm (2016), *Rewriting Ancient Jewish History: The History of the Jews in Roman Times and the New Historical Method* (Routledge Studies in Ancient History), London: Routledge.

Tuchman, Barbara (2014), *Bible and Sword: England and Palestine from the Bronze Age to Balfour*, New York: Random House Trade Paperback.

Tully, Geoffrey D. (1998), 'The στρατάρχης of "Legio" VI Ferrata and the Employment of Camp Prefects as Vexillation Commanders', *Zeitschrift Für Papyrologie Und Epigraphik* 120, 226–232.

Turel, Sara (2016), 'Bar Kokhba: Construction of a Myth' in: Turel, Sara (ed.) (2016), *Bar Kokhba: Historical Memory and the Myth of Heroism*, Tel Aviv: Eretz Israel Museum, 8e–17e/10-45 [Hebrew].

Tzori, N. (1971), 'An Inscription of the *Legio* VI *Ferrata* from the Northern Jordan Valley', *Israel Exploration Journal* 21, 53–54.

Urloiu, Radu (2010), 'Legio II Traiana fortis and Judaea under Hadrian's reign', *Cogito* II.4, 110–127: http://cogito.ucdc.ro/n4e/LEGIO-II-TRAIANA-FORTIS-AND-JUDAEA-UNDER-HADRIAN-REIGN.pdf (accessed 30 July 2020).

Ussishkin, David (1993), 'Archaeological Soundings at Betar, Bar-Kochba's Last Stronghold', *Tel Aviv* 20, 66–97.

VanderKam, James C. (2012), 'Judaism in the Land of Israel' in: Collins, John J. & Harlow, Daniel C. (eds.) (2012), *Early Judaism: A Comprehensive Overview*, Grand Rapids, Michigan: Wm. B. Eerdmans Publishing, 70–94.

Viereck, Paul, Roos, Anton Gerard, & Gabba, Emilio (1962), *Appiani. Historia Romana.: Vol. I. Prooemium Iberica Annibaica Libyca Illyrica Syriaca Mithridatica Frgmenta* (Bibliotheca scriptorum Graecorum et Romanorum Teubneriana) (German Edition), Braunschweig: Vieweg+Teubner Verlag.

Vishnia, Rachel Feig (2002), 'The Shadow Army: The Lixae and the Roman Legions', *Zeitschrift für Papyrologie und Epigraphik* Bd. 139, 265–272.

Visotzky, Burton L. (2016), *Aphrodite and the Rabbis: How the Jews Adapted Roman Culture to Create Judaism as We Know it*, New York: St Martin's Press.

Vout, Caroline (2005), "Antinous, Archaeology and History", *The Journal of Roman Studies* 95, 80–96.

Vrchlichého, Jaroslava (1897), *Bar-Kochba*, V Praze: J.R. Vilímek.

Wahlig, Henry (2015), *Sport im Abseits: Die Geschichte der jüdischen Sportbewegung im nationalsozialistischen Deutschland*, Göttingen: Wallstein Verlag.

Wasserstein, Bernard (1997), 'The Age of Upheavals' in: De Lange, Nicholas (1997), *The Illustrated History of the Jewish People*, New York: Harcourt Brace, 355–397.

Watson, Alan (1987), *Roman Slave Law*, Baltimore: Johns Hopkins University Press.

Watts, Martin (2004), *The Jewish Legion and the First World War*, Basingstoke: Palgrave Macmillan.

Waxman, Chaim I. (1987), 'Messianism, Zionism, and the State of Israel', *Modern Judaism* 7.2 (May), 175–192.

Webber, Christopher (2001), *The Thracians 700 BC–AD 46* (Men-at-Arms 360), Oxford: Osprey Publishing.

Weinberg, Saul S. (1979), 'A Hoard of Roman Armor', *Antike Kunst* 22.2, 82–86.

Weiss, Haim (2014), "'There Was a Man in Israel – Bar-Kosibah Was His Name!'", *Jewish Studies Quarterly* 21.2, 99–115.

Weiss, Haim (2017), 'A Double-Edged Sword – The Power of Bar-Kosibah: From Rabbinic Literature to Popular Culture' in: Almagor, Eran & Maurice, Lisa (eds.), *The Reception of Ancient Virtues and Vices in Modern Popular Culture Beauty, Bravery, Blood and Glory*, Leiden: Brill, 341– 356.

Weisman, Stefanie (2012), 'Militarism in the Wall Paintings of the Dura-Europos Synagogue: A New Perspective on Jewish Life on the Roman Frontier', *Shofar* 30.3, 1–34.

Weksler-Bdolah, Shlomit (2014), 'The Foundation of Aelia Capitolina in Light of New Excavations along the Eastern Cardo', *Israel Exploration Journal* 64.1, 38–62.

Weksler Bdolah, Shlomit (2015), 'The Role of the Temple Mount in the Layout of Aelia Capitolina: The Capitolium after All', *Eretz-Israel: Archaeological, Historical and Geographical Studies*, 126–137. [Hebrew].

Weksler-Bdolah, Schlomit, Onn, A., Kisilevitz, S. & Ouahnouna, B. (2012), 'Layers of Ancient Jerusalem', *Biblical Archaeology Review* 38.1, 36–47, 69–71.

Welles, G.B. (1938), 'The Inscriptions' in: Kraeling, C.H. (ed.), *Gerasa, City of the Decapolis*, New Haven: Yale University Press.

Wheeler, Everett J. (2010), 'Rome's Dacian Wars: Domitian, Trajan, and Strategy on the Danube, Part I*', *The Journal of Military History* 74 (October), 1185–1227.

Williams, Craig A. (2010), *Roman Homosexuality*, New York: Oxford University Press.

Wise, Michael Owen (2015), *Language and Literacy in Roman Judaea: A Study of the Bar Kokhba Documents* (The Anchor Yale Bible Reference Library), Cambridge, Mass.: Yale University Press.

Wodak, Ruth (1989), 'Iudeus ex Machina', *Grazer Linguistische Studien*, 153–180.

Wolitz, Seth L. (2002), 'Forging a Hero for a Jewish Stage: Goldfadn's "Bar Kokhba"', *Shofar* 20.3 (Spring), 53–65.

Wood, Michael (1981), In Search of the Dark Ages, BBC Worldwide Limited.

Wouk, Herman (1974), *This is My God: The Jewish Way of Life*, New York: Pocket Books. (Revised edition).

Yadin, Yigael (1961), 'Was Bar-Kokhba's Headquaters in Herodium?', *Israel Exploration Journal* 11, 51.

Yadin, Yigael (1961), 'Expedition D', *Israel Exploration Journal* 11.1/2, The Expedition to the Judaean Desert 1960, 36–52.

Yadin, Yigael (1971), *Bar-Kokhba: The Rediscovery of the Legendary Hero of the Last Jewish Revolt Against Imperial Rome*, London: Random House.

Yadin, Yigael (1994), *Ancient Jerusalem Revealed,* Jerusalem: Israel Exploration Society.

Yadin, Yigael, Greenfield, Jonas C., Yardeni, A. & Levine, B.A. (2002), *The Documents of the Bar Kokhba Period in the Cave of Letters. Hebrew, Aramaic and Nabatean-Aramaic Papyri.* Judean Desert Studies. Jerusalem: Israel Exploration Society/Institute of Archaeology, Hebrew University/ Shrine of the Book, Jerusalem: Israel Museum.

Yassif, Eli, (2009), *The Hebrew Folktale: History, Genre, Meaning* (Folklore Studies in Translation), Bloomington: Indiana University Press. [Annotated edition].

Yavetz, Zvi (1998), 'Latin Authors on Jews and Dacians', *Historia: Zeitschrift für Alte Geschichte* 47.1 (1st Qtr.), 77–107.

Yeivin, Shmuel (1946), *The Bar-Kokhba War*, Jerusalem: Bialik Institute. [Hebrew].

Yourcenar, Margeurite (1992), *Memoirs of Hadrian and Reflections on the Composition of Memoirs of Hadrian*, New York: The Noonday Press.

Zahrnt, Michael (1988), 'Vermeintliche Kolonien des Kaisers Hadrian', *Zeitschrift für Papyrologie und Epigraphik* 71, 229–249.

Zeichmann, Christopher B. (2018), 'Military Forces in Judaea 6–130 ce: The *status quaestionis* and Relevance for New Testament Studies', *Currents in Biblical Research* 17(1), 86–120. https://journals.sagepub.com/doi/pdf/10.1177/1476993X18791425 (accessed 30 July 2020).

Zeitlin, Solomon (1952), 'Bar Kokba and Bar Kozeba', *The Jewish Quarterly Review* 43.1 (Jul.), 77–82.

Zeltser, Arkadi (2014), 'How the Jewish Intelligentsia Created the Jewishness of the Jewish Hero: The Soviet Yiddish Press' in: Murav, Harriet & Estraikh, Gennady (eds.), *Soviet Jews in World War II: Fighting, Witnessing, Remembering,* Academic Studies Press, Brighton, MA, 2014, 104–128.

Zerubavel, Yael (1995), *Recovered Roots: Collective Memory and the Making of Israeli National Tradition*, Chicago: University of Chicago Press.

Zerubavel, Yael (2003), 'Bar Kokhba's Image in Modern Israeli Culture' in: Schäfer, Peter (ed.), *Bar Kokhba War Reconsidered: New Perspectives on the Second Jewish Revolt Against Rome*, Texts and Studies in Ancient Judaism 100, Tübingen: Mohr Siebeck, 279–297.

Zissu, Boaz (2008), 'The Hellenistic Fortress at Horvat Tura and the Identification of Tur Shimon', *Israel Exploration Journal* 58.2, 171–194.

Zissu, Boaz (2017), 'Interbellum Judea 70–132 ce: An Archaeological Perspective' in: Schwartz, Joshua J. & Tomson, Peter J. (eds.), *Jews and Christians in the First and Second Centuries: The Interbellum 70–132 CE*, Compendia Rerum Iudaicarum ad Novum Testamentum 15, Leiden: Brill, 19–49.

Zissu, Boaz & Ganor, Amir (2009), 'Horvat 'Ethri – A Jewish Village from the Second Temple Period and the Bar Kokhba Revolt in the Judean Foothills', *Journal of Jewish Studies* LX, 90–136.

Zissu, Boaz, Ganor, Amir, & Neugeborn, Hagit (2010), 'Horbat 'Etri', *Hadashot Arkheologiyot: Excavations and Surveys in Israel* 122: http://www.hadashot-esi.org.il/report_detail_eng.aspx?id=1572&mag_id=117 (accessed 30 July 2020).

Zissu, Boaz & Abadi, Omri (2014), 'Paleo-Hebrew Script in Jerusalem and Judea from the Second Century BCE. Through the Second Century C.E.: A Reconsideration', *Journal for Semitics* 23/2i, 653–664.

Zissu, Boaz & Ecker, Avner (2014), 'A Roman Military Fort North of Bet Guvrin/Eleutheropolis?', *Zeitschrift für Papyrologie und Epigraphik* 188, 293–312.

Zissu, Boaz & Eshel, Hanan (2013), 'Coins and Hoards from the Time of the Bar Kokhba Revolt', *Hoards and Genizot as Chapters in History* [Hecht Museum Catalogue no. 33], Haifa, 31–39.

Zissu, Boaz & Eshel, Hanan (2016), 'Religious Aspects of the Bar Kokhba Revolt: The Founding of Aelia Capitolina on the Ruins of Jerusalem', in: Ulanowski, Krzysztof (ed.) *The Religious Aspects of War in the Ancient Near East, Greece, and Rome*, Ancient Warfare Series Volume 1, Series: Culture and History of the Ancient Near East, Volume: 84, Leiden: Brill Publishers, 387–405.

Zissu, Boaz, Eshel, Hanan, Langford, Boaz & Frumkin, Amos (2010), 'Coins from the Bar Kokhba Revolt Hidden in Me'arat Ha-Te'omim (Mŭghâret Umm et Tûeimîn), Western Jerusalem Hills', *Israeli Numismatic Journal* 17, 113–147.

Zissu, Boaz & Ganor, Amir (2004), 'Metal Utensils from the Time of the Bar Kokhba discovered in the Southern Judaean Foothills', *Babesch* (Bulletin Antieke Beschaving) 79, 111–121.

Zissu, Boaz & Ganor, Amir (2006), 'A Lead Weight of Bar Kokhba's Administration', *Israel Exploration Journal* 56.2, 178–182.

Zissu, Boaz & Ganor, Amir (2009), 'Horvat 'Ethri – a Jewish village from the Second Temple period and the Bar Kokhba Revolt in the Judean foothills', *Journal of Jewish Studies* 60.1 (Spring), 90–136.

Zissu, Boaz, Ganor, Amir, Klein, Eitan & Klein, Alon (2013), 'New Discoveries at Horvat Burgin in the Judaean Shephelah: Tombs, Hiding Complexes and Graffiti', *Palestine Exploration Quarterly* 145.1, 29–52.

Zissu, Boaz & Klein, Eitan (2011), 'A Rock-Cut Burial Cave from the Roman Period at Beit Nattif, Judaean Foothills', *Israel Exploration Journal* 61.2, 196–216.

Zissu, Boaz, Klein, Eitan, & Kloner, Amos (2014), 'Settlement Processes in the Territorium of Roman Jerusalem (Aelia Capitolina)', in: Alvarez, J.M, Nogales, T. and Roda, I. (eds.), *XVIII CIAC: Centre and Periphery in the Ancient World*, Merida, 219–223.

Zissu, Boaz & Kloner, Amos (2010), 'The Archaeology of the Second Jewish Revolt against Rome (The Bar Kokhba Revolt) – Some New Insights', *Bollettino di Archeologia On Line* I Volume speciale F / F8 / 4, 40–52.

Zissu, Boaz, & Kloner, Amos (2014), 'Rock-Cut Hiding Complexes from the Roman Period in Israel', *Der Erdstall, Beitraege zur Erforschung kuenstlicher Hoehlen* 40, 96–119.

Zissu, Boaz & Kloner, Amos (2015), 'Subterranean Complexes at Maresha and Additional Notes on the Judean Hiding Complexes' in: S.R. Wolff (ed.), *Villain or Visionary? Macalister and the Archaeology of Palestine* [PEF Annual XII], London, 96–111.

Zissu Boaz, & Kloner Amos (2019), 'Underground Explorations at Horvat Qasra, Southern Judean Foothills, Israel' in: A. Zhalov, V. Gyorev, P. Delchev (eds.). *Hypogea 2019: Proceedings of International Congress of Speleology in Artificial Cavities*, Dobrich, Bulgaria, May 20–23. 2019. Dobrich. 125–130.

Zissu, Boaz, Langford, Boaz, Raviv, Dvir, Davidovich, U., Porat, Roi & Frumkin, Amos (2014), 'Coins from the Elqana Cave in Western Samaria', *Israel Numismatic Journal* 18. 146–154.

Zissu, Boaz, Langford, Boaz, Porat, Roi & Frumkin, Amos (2016), 'Coins from the 'Abud Cave in Southwestern Samaria from the Time of the Jewish Revolts Against Rome', *The Israel Numismatic Journal* 19, 33–44.

Zissu, Boaz, Porat, Roi, Langford, Boaz, & Frumkin, Amos (2011), 'Archaeological Remains of the Bar Kokhba Revolt in the Te'omim Cave (Mŭghâret Umm et Tûeimîn), Western Jerusalem Hills', *Journal of Jewish Studies* 42.2 (Autumn), 262–283.

Zissu, Boaz, Tepper, Yotam & Amit, David (2006), 'Miqwao' ot at Kefar 'Othnai near Legio', *Israel Exploration Journal* 56, 57–66.

Zlotnik, Yehoshua (2006), 'The Question of the Conquest of Jerusalem by the Bar Kokhba Rebels', 1–21: https://numis.co.il/Question_Jerusalem.pdf (accessed 30 July 2020).

Zlotnik, Yehoshua (2008), 'Coin Finds and the Question of the Conquest of Jerusalem by the Bar Kokhba', *Israel Numismatic Research* 3, 137–146.

Zollschan, Linda T. (2019), 'The Conclusion of the First Jewish Revolt: Interpreting IVDAEA RECEPTA', *Israel Numismatic Research Journal* 14, 97–118.

Index

A Jewish person is listed under his or her given name, or under Rabbi where ordained. A Roman citizen is listed under his or her *nomen gentilicium*, or *cognomen* where it is not known. A military unit is listed under its respective designation *ala*, *classis*, *cohors* or *legio*. A military campaign is listed under the designation *bellum* or *tumultum* when there is a contemporary Roman title, or under 'battle' or 'siege' when there is not.